FREE
DIGITAL
BONUS
OFFER

($149 value)

Go to this website and enter this code:

www.winthepresentationgame.com/bonuses
8574392

_____

Or scan this code:

_____

Here are your digital bonuses:

- Video showing you how to eliminate fear and anxiety before you get up to speak

- Video showing you the tips and keys for delivering outstanding virtual presentations

WIN THE PRESENTATION GAME

52 POWER PLAYS to CAPTIVATE, ENERGIZE & ACTIVATE your AUDIENCE

Tom McCarthy WITH David Hutchison

Published in the United States by
Thomas McCarthy & Associates
P.O. Box 132
Rancho Santa Fe, California 92067

For more information, please visit www.TomMcCarthy.com.

Also by Tom McCarthy

Fire Up Your Presentations & Fire Up Your Results:
A Powerful System for Creating and
Delivering Outstanding Presentations

"The tips in this book changed my view of public speaking from stressful, to an opportunity to have some fun, entertain and educate and most importantly build credibility with an audience. Follow this time tested approach and I guarantee you will see the difference!"
— MARK MOFFETT, Systems Engineer Director, Cisco Systems

"Tom has been working with my sales teams for over 10 years and his methodology and tips are field proven. The results I've experienced first hand are improved confidence and composure while public speaking, an increase in energy and connection with the audience and greater executive presence. I highly recommend Tom and his approach to delivering *Win the Presentation Game!*"
— PAUL WERNER, Vice President, F5 Networks

"If you do presentations of any type, this book is a must. Just using one of it's 52 tips will transform your presentations and make you look like a rock star!"
— ALAN AKINA, CEO & Founder, 101 Financial

"This book captures a powerful system that should be in every sales toolkit. Packed with practical, easy-to apply tips Tom has shared years of best practices that will leave your audience inspired!"
— WENDY YEAGER, Vice President of Global Sales Enablement, Cornerstone OnDemand

"After my team's training with Tom and David, I got excellent feedback and the team wanted more. However, what really struck me was that I consistently heard the team using the techniques and applying them to our business. These techniques became engrained in our ongoing business culture."
— GREGG FIDDES, Senior Vice President Sales, Quickoffice (acquired by Google)

"While I was reading this book, I started revising my next presentation. My audience will want to thank you Tom!"
— TAMI NEWCOMBE, Vice President Sales, Cisco Systems

"Tom and David helped me focus not just on developing my skill set, but more importantly I learned how to have connected conversations that inspire my audiences to action."

—VERN CARLSON, Vice President, MetLife

"*Win the Presentation Game* is the best book written on designing and delivering presentations. Tom's system is powerful and it works! Every organization that has people giving presentations needs this book."

—GINO BLEFARI, CEO, Berkshire Hathaway Properties

"*Win the Presentation Game* is a must read for all aspiring executives. In his latest work, Tom McCarthy leverages his lifetime mastery of the subject to provide the reader with a compelling roadmap of how to build this capability for themselves. In short, an outstanding book which will change your approach to presentations forever!"

—RICHARD DAVIES, Vice President, Coco Cola Enterprises

"*Win the Presentation Game* will help executives and managers move their teams to action and will help salespeople shorten the sales cycle and close more sales. If you are an executive, a manager or salesperson, this book is a must-read!"

—BRIAN TRACY, Chairman and CEO, Brian Tracy Learning Systems

"Working with Tom and reading his book has helped me be better prepared for professional and personal growth! In a large company we all work extremely hard to build a stronger company and team. *Win the Presentation Game* gives us tools that help us accomplish our goals."

—DAWN MARONEY, Chief Sales and Marketing Officer, Alignment Healthcare

"Tom McCarthy is an outstanding presenter and coach and his *Win the Presentation Game* is an absolute must for anyone who wants to take their presentations to the highest level! Tom has an amazing ability to connect with any audience and take them on an emotional journey with him. This book will help you identify the true outcome you're looking for in any presentation and provide you with the strategy and tools to achieve that outcome."

—DAVID HEALY, CEO, Aetna Health Insurance Co. Europe

"Any leader or sales executive who wants to persuade and motivate their audience, leaving them excited to take action NOW, should read this book. Tom captures the essence of not only how to communicate with passion, but what drives a listener to take action."
—DAVID RUGGIERO, President of Global Commercial Operations, Thermo Fisher Scientific

"*Win the Presentation Game* provides a wealth of information about a crucial subject! Many of Tom's tips I had to learn "the hard way" by making mistakes. Now, thanks to this book, you can take advantage of Tom's years of learning in how to makes."
—GAY HENDRICKS, Ph.D., author of *The Big Leap*

"Giving presentations is a great way to expand your network and enhance your brand. In *Win the Presentation Game*, Tom makes it easy for you to master the strategies of the best presenters in the world. You'll learn what it takes to stand out from other presenters and how to captivate any audience and move them to action!"
—IVAN MISNER, Ph.D., Founder and Chairman of BNI

"*Win the Presentation Game* is a quick read, packed with powerful ideas that will make anyone who reads it more successful in getting their audience enthused and ready to take action. If you give presentations, read this book!"
—JACK CANFIELD, Coauthor of NY Times Bestsellers *Chicken Soup for the Soul*

"The ideas in *Win the Presentation Game* have forever changed how my executive team and me approach the art and science of collaborating and presenting both internally and externally to our organization!"
—WAHEED CHOUDRY, President & COO, Nexus

"Tom McCarthy's book *Win the Presentation Game* is not only a must read for anyone doing presentations but for anyone wanting to up their game in almost any area of life. Tom's book really gets to the nuts and bolts of what works in a methodical and powerful way. One read of this book will eliminate any guess work on how to get your point across and deliver persuasive presentations and make you a superstar."
—BRIAN JOHNSON, President & CEO, Enterprises

"Tom has successfully worked with my leadership teams for over 10 years and his approach has helped them become some of the very best at Cisco. Tom's approach has helped me make better connections with my audience, tell better stories and fine tune my executive presence. This is a must read for anyone that has to speak in front of a group!"

—JEFF SHARRITTS, Senior Vice President, Cisco Systems

"I have seen Tom in action as one of the most powerful speakers and presenters I've encountered, so I know his methods work. In this book he outlines the elements of a great presentation and lays them out in an easy to follow and easy to implement manner. His method is now the blueprint I follow for every presentation I make. Bottom line is that his formula works both for the presentation itself and you as a presenter."

—JEFF LAMP, Former NBA Player, Lakers

"*Win the Presentation Game* is filled with insightful tips that will help you maximize your potential as a presenter."

—TONY ROBBINS, bestselling author and legendary presenter

"Tom started working with my team 6 years ago and the improvements were immediately noticeable. His book provides a concrete approach to connecting with your audience and motivating them to action. Whether you are a frequent or infrequent presenter, this is a guidebook to success."

—DOUG GOOD, Senior Director of Systems Engineering, Cisco Systems

"Giving presentations is a skill that unfortunately only a few people ever master, but it doesn't have to be that way. In *Win the Presentation Game*, Tom has given you the shortcuts you need to become an outstanding presenter."

—JOHN GRAY, bestselling author of
Men Are From Mars, Women Are From Venus

"I can personally say I use Tom's techniques and methods for all of my most critical meetings and presentations. Tom has a unique ability to bring out the best in people and he's the best investment a leader can make to develop both yourself and your team."

—TODD MCLAUGHLIN, Senior VP, Hewlett Packard

"This book is filled with valuable, tried and tested techniques to make your presentations impactful, less stressful and more memorable. I've used Tom's techniques to improve my presentation skills in front of my team, in front of thousands and even for a recent TED Talk. Tom's *Win the Presentation Game* book is an essential business asset for any professional looking to improve your game."

—CHRIS WHITE, Senior VP, Cisco Systems

"I learned Tom's techniques he details in *Win the Presentation Game* over 10 years ago and I still use them for every presentation I give. They've enabled me to connect with and impact audiences ranging from a few people to several thousand. They've worked wonders for me and they will for you too!"

—MIKE ETTLING, President, HR Line of Busines, SAP

Tom and David have been top instructors in our college hire program for many years. Their approach to presentations is unique because it incorporates attitude and technique. The 52 Power Moves in this book give our sellers the tangible techniques to support the confident attitude we need them to have when presenting to customers.

—JEFF CRISTEE, VP, Sales Operations, Cisco Systems

"With this newest book, *Win the Presentation Game: 52 Power Moves to Captivate, Activate and Energize Your Audience*, Tom has written the perfect companion to his original *FIRE-UP System of Persuasive Presentations*. The powerful principles and practical tips Tom lays out can help everyone become a better communicator. Anyone who is serious about improving their public speaking and presentation skills should make Tom's books the anchors of their business library."

—TROY McQUAGGE, CEO, US Health Group

"I have known Tom for many years and I have engaged him to do multiple trainings for my teams. The results of his trainings have always been outstanding. In *Win the Presentation Game*, Tom takes his very best tips and techniques for being a superstar presenter and delivers them to you in bite sized, easy to use nuggets."

—TRACEY NEWELL, Executive VP, Worldwide Sales, Proofpoint

"Tom's new book, *Win the Presentation Game*, is a must read for all human beings who wish to tap into their greater potential. Tom challenges us to share of our individuality, and engage with empathy, to more effectively communicate and powerfully influence. Tom's inspiration is as much about presentations as it is about character and empowerment, and poignant for nervous 'beginners' as well as for sage 'experts.' "

—CHRISTINE TODD, President, Standish Mellon Asset Management

"Thank you Tom and David for publishing this remarkable book! You have given us a tool which will help us to win over our audiences every time we give presentation."

—ALI KHALID, CEO, Themaar International Investment

"Highly practical, easy-to-read, and easy-to-implement. *Win the Presentation Game* would be immediately useful for anyone needing to do a presentation, even the most skilled presenter."

—PETE BISSONETTE, President, Learning Strategies

"Just one tip Tom shared with me years ago not only changed my entire presentation style but my philosophy as well. I was also able to take that tip and incorporate it into many aspects of my business, hence growing my business. Tom is so generous in sharing his insights in this book, it would be a grave injustice not to take immediate action."

—MARYELLEN TRIBBY, best selling author of
Reinventing the Entrepreneur: Turning Your Dream Business into a Reality
and founder of WorkingMomsOnly.com

"Our company was going through significant regulatory headwinds and downward pressure on performance and we needed someone to help our leaders get us to the other side. We brought in Tom and David to help, and many of the techniques they teach in this book were key in getting our company to turn around the regulatory and performance issues in a record 7 month period."

—ROBERT FAHLMAN, Chairman and CEO, Arcadian Management Services

DEDICATION

We dedicate this book to all the students that have trusted us to help them become outstanding presenters. Many of them showed up a little apprehensive and unsure of what to expect, but little by little, as they increased their trust and totally immersed themselves in the training, they connected with their greatness. There is nothing more fulfilling than to see fellow human beings open up and communicate from the most powerful place in the universe—their hearts!

CONTENTS

INTRODUCTION

What have I gotten myself into?

The guy at the front of the conference room had just said two words that made my heart sink. "Group presentations." The other guys around the table just nodded; I wanted to get up and make a run for the door. I'd been so excited to land this job, as the very first salesperson for motivational speaker Tony Robbins' seminars. What I hadn't realized, until that moment, was that it would entail something that terrified me: getting up and speaking in front of groups of people.

I left a fantastic job making a lot of money for this? I asked myself, sinking down into my chair as one of the other sales reps got up to give a demo presentation. Just a few months earlier, I'd been secure in what I thought was my dream job—a successful stockbroker for a New York Stock Exchange firm. I loved my company, enjoyed working with my clients, and was having great success, but slowly I'd begun to have a nagging feeling that something else was out there for me. And then, one morning, I turned on a news show and saw an interview with a young man, only a year older than me, who had just written a new book called *Unlimited Power.* I was fascinated by what the author was saying: He believed that no matter what happens, you have the power to control how you feel and how you act. The key to success, in his opinion, was to harness this power on a consistent basis to shape your thoughts and actions in a way that allows you to accomplish your wildest dreams.

Now we're talking! I thought. The author's name was Tony Robbins. This was in the days before Amazon.com, so I drove to the bookstore and bought his book. When I got home, I devoured it, feasting on every concept. Living a life without limits was something that excited me, but I'd never known there were people out there teaching others how to do it. Now, I wanted to be part of it.

I lived on the East Coast, and Tony's next Unlimited Power seminar was only one week later in Los Angeles. It wasn't the most convenient situation, but there was no way I was going to miss it. The seminar was fantastic; right then and there I decided this was the business I had been looking for, a business where I could help people make massive shifts in how they feel and what they're able to accomplish. Fortunately, Tony's young company needed someone just like me: a salesperson that could help bring more people to his seminars. Which was how I found myself in that conference room in Dallas, Texas, hearing those two terrifying words.

Because I was also the *only* salesperson for Tony's company, he'd partnered with an outside marketing company to promote his new seminar—a reputable company with a great track record of promoting big seminars. Tony wanted me to work with them for a few weeks and learn all I could from the experts. The first thing I learned was that their sales process started with calling companies and setting up appointments to give group sales presentations— something I'd never done and never wanted to attempt.

Fortunately for me, I had no Plan B. I had to find a way to succeed in this new role of being a presenter. Failure was not an option. I stopped looking at the door, and paid attention to the demo presentation, which I was recording so I could learn it, word for word. The sales rep seemed so confident and relaxed; I couldn't imagine ever mastering this presentation and being able to deliver it like that.

"Tom, what's your target?" Suddenly everyone was looking at me, and the head of the marketing company was asking me to set a goal for the number of enrollments I could produce in the next four weeks leading up to the seminar. Honestly, I had no clue. I'd never done this before, so I asked him what kind of goals the other people on the team had set. "Somewhere in the range of 250 to 300 enrollments," he replied. Determined to make a good impression, I decided to set my goal at the higher number. "Okay, 300 enrollments!" In hindsight, it wasn't a smart move. I had zero experience, unlike the other seasoned sales reps. And they had already been promoting the seminar for four weeks, so they had a huge head start.

After I left the meeting and realized the commitment I'd made, I was paralyzed with fear. How was I going to pull this off? It was then and there that I made a critical decision. I decided that I would not allow any doubt or fear to enter into my mind as I pursued this goal. No matter what happened, I would continue to press forward with confidence and belief in my ability to accomplish what I'd set out to do.

Even with this invincible confidence and belief, my first week was a disaster. The few presentations I was able to set up ended with nobody enrolling in the seminar. From an enrollment standpoint, I was a big failure. This was where it got tough, because part of me saw the clock and my opportunities ticking away, yet I had committed myself to maintaining my confidence and belief no matter what happened. The head of the marketing company must have felt sorry for me when he saw my results, or lack thereof, because he offered me an opportunity to save face by reducing my goal. Trust me, I was tempted to take him up on it, but I stuck to my guns. Reducing my goal would have crushed my commitment to maintain my confidence and belief.

Every night I'd go to bed planting the thought in my head that I would find a way to master my presentation and achieve my goal. It didn't happen overnight, but I did start seeing some success. A few enrollments here, a few enrollments there...and with each presentation, no matter what the result, my confidence and belief was becoming more and more entrenched.

I'd like to be able to tell you that I achieved my goal, but I didn't. I was about twelve enrollments short. However, I did finish as the number one sales rep, outselling the more experienced guys by dozens of enrollments. The experience of having to give more than forty pressure-packed presentations in such a short time period was invaluable. I'd made many mistakes and learned from them, and I did a few things right and learned from them, too.

Since that time, twenty-five years ago, I've spoken on topics like leadership, communication, and peak performance in twenty-one countries to audiences as large as 18,000 people, and I've trained thousands of people all over the world how to be outstanding presenters. In this book, I've taken the most important lessons I've learned and put them into bite-sized pieces that you can easily digest. No matter what type of presentation you have to give, I want to make it easier for you to unleash your potential and master your ability to design and deliver amazing presentations!

At a funeral, the average person
would rather be *in the casket* than giving the eulogy.
—Jerry Seinfeld

Before I began working with them, many people I trained had a genuine fear of failing, looking foolish, clamming up, or forgetting what they were supposed to say. In the United States, the fear of public speaking tops the list of phobias, coming in ahead of spiders, snakes, heights, and even death. Why? Because speaking in front of a group of people sets off all kinds of alarms about acceptance and worthiness. We want people to think we're awesome, and we worry about rejection. We start believing we have to be "perfect," so we overthink it and try too hard. When we do this, we go into what I call "presentation mode," where we either shut down or shift into some unnatural, technique-y, scripted version of ourselves. This results in self-consciousness, disconnects us from the audience, and makes it nearly impossible to persuade anyone of anything.

If you've ever stood up there in front of a crowd—at a wedding, in a business meeting, or at a conference—and felt your palms go clammy and your throat dry up as you stammer out a few awkward sentences, don't worry. If you've ever turned down an opportunity to promote your business or support a friend because you just didn't think you could get up and make a speech, that's understandable. Chances are, no one has taught you how to play the game.

It's not surprising that you are not yet a great presenter—and it's not your fault. If you sat down to play Monopoly, with no more than the basic rules to follow, you'd expect to lose the first few games. Until you understand the nuance, the tactics, and the tricks, you're not likely to win. The same is true of giving presentations. There are rules and strategies that can help you become a winning presenter. Yet most of us get up there thinking we should be able to just do it, and worse still, we have all kinds of outdated and unhelpful concepts in our heads about how we're supposed to "win over" the audience.

Here's the good news: *giving an outstanding presentation doesn't have to be so hard!* In fact, I believe you have the potential to be a *superstar* presenter. From my own awkward beginnings, I've come a long way and in the process, I figured out how to play—and win—the presentation game. In this book, I'll share with you the best strategies I've learned.

My personal experience and my experience coaching thousands of others have taught me that there are three major roadblocks to becoming a superstar presenter. The first roadblock is viewing your presentation content primarily as *information*. Many presenters think of their presentation as a list of facts and figures, and if they forget even one item, their presentation won't be a success. So they create a lot of detailed, content-heavy slides—and end up reading the slides. Audiences hate that. After all, if it's all on the slide, why do they need you?

Plus, trying to deliver too much information chokes your confidence and natural enthusiasm for your topic. If you don't feel good about what you are planning to say, or if you don't think it will be helpful to your audience, then you are going to struggle when you get up to present it. How do you overcome this roadblock? Put simply, you need more story and less slide! Great presenters don't think of their content as merely information—they think of it as a story, with main characters, a problem, and a solution that will save the day.

The second roadblock is showing up to your presentation feeling like you're not going to succeed. The sad fact is that many presenters show up for their presentations afraid of making a mistake and being rejected. If you're doubting yourself, everyone else is going to doubt you, too. The most important thing is how you feel! Based on my experience delivering presentations and training presenters, how you feel is 80 percent of how well you do. When you start out feeling like you are going to win, unseen forces shift in your favor. You might not always get the result you're looking for, but you will most certainly outperform the less confident version of yourself.

The third roadblock is expecting your audience to show up energized and excited about your presentation. Our studies show that approximately 80 percent of audiences tune out during presentations they find boring within the first ten minutes (probably because the presenter is reading his slides and making them feel uncomfortable). So don't expect your audience to stay on the edge of their seats without your help—most of them don't want to be there in the first place! The key is to be caring and confident from within—and then transfer that energy to your audience.

That's why the chapters in this book are divided into three sections:

PART ONE: Create an Engaging Story— ideas for developing and delivering dynamic content that instantly hooks your audience. Everyone loves a great story!

PART TWO: Feel Like a Winner!— ways to get yourself feeling confident, energized, and ready to go in front of anyone. There's simply nothing more important than how you feel.

PART THREE: Energize Your Audience— strategies for getting and holding your audience's attention, staying connected, and moving people to action.

Each section has a series of brief tips for delivering knockout presentations. I call these "Power Plays," because they're more than just the rules of the game. They're like the strategies a great coach teaches his team to surprise and outscore their opponents. They're not based on what "most people" do to try to get better at public speaking. They're based on what the truly outstanding presenters—the superstar presenters—do, because my objective is for you to stand out, not just make it through. And they're short, because becoming a superstar presenter doesn't have to be so hard. By whittling it down to the essentials, I've worked to make it easy for you. When you practice what you learn here and adopt it as a natural extension of who you already are, then you'll be ready to speak anytime, anywhere, in front of anyone.

The fact that you're reading this book is no accident. Some part of you wants to master the ability to deliver a powerful message, and some part of you suspects you can do it. You're right! If your presentation performances haven't earned you superstar status in the past, that has no bearing on what you're capable of achieving in the future. Will it take some work to become great? Absolutely. But if you use these Power Plays and you put in deliberate practice, I promise you'll attain a skill level that will set you apart from all the average presenters that nobody wants to see or hear. No matter what kind of presentations you're asked to give—whether they're status reports, work-team briefings, sales pitches, design reviews, a talk at your school or place of worship, or anything else—you can feel confident about succeeding. Thousands of people just like you, who initially thought it was almost impossible for them to excel at this, have used these strategies to wow their audiences and win the presentation game. You can, too.

PART ONE:
Create an Engaging Story

Often, the first hang-up in presenting comes from not knowing what to say—or, more precisely, how to say it in a way that will interest other people. If you've been asked to speak, you probably already have a topic, something you know about or are excited to share. Now put yourself in the audience's shoes. Which would you rather hear: someone giving a presentation or someone telling a fascinating story?

The trick is figuring out how to put together your message in the form of an engaging *story*. Don't worry—you don't have to craft the next Great American Novel. I'm talking about "story" in the simplest possible terms: following a process or storyline that begins with a problem your audience can personally relate to (the conflict) and ends with your solution (the happy ending). Most people love a good story, whether it's a powerful metaphor or the tale of how a business solution can make a customer's life easier; what they don't like is you reading one long paragraph after another or even bullet points to them. Great stories don't require you to read from a script. They inspire you, so you can be much more natural in telling them. Plus, a story of any kind has a way of drawing in your audience, especially when you put your heart and soul into it.

This section reveals the best ways to take an ordinary presentation and turn it into a fascinating story: how to organize your ideas, the method for bringing your audience into the heart of your message, and strategies for applying these principles in multiple situations, including the long-form presentation, the impromptu speech, and the elevator pitch.

POWER PLAY #1
Begin at the End

Bestselling *7 Habits of Highly Successful People* author Stephen R. Covey famously counseled that successful people "begin with the end in mind," by which he meant that if you want to accomplish something great, it's best if you first figure out what that *something* is. Metaphors abound: know what you want to make *before* you start cooking. Create a set of plans *before* you build a house.

Yet when it comes to making presentations, most people do it backwards. They start by asking, *What am I going to say?* Honestly, that's the wrong question. Totally overwhelming! There are *millions* of things you could say when you don't yet know the end result of your presentation.

Think about the GPS system in your car or on your phone. What's the first thing it asks you to do? It asks you to input your destination. Then, once it knows where you want to go, it gives you the exact directions on how to get there. But it can only do that if it knows where you want to go. You will be most successful in figuring out what to say in your presentations by first figuring out what you want to accomplish with your presentation. The best presenters give presentations to accomplish a quantifiable result, not just to recite a bunch of details and information.

So before you even begin drafting the presentation content, always start by thinking about what result you want the presentation to achieve. Ask yourself, ***What is my outcome? What do I want people to do after they hear me speak?***

The best presentations drive action. Average speakers get people excited or a little bit interested. Outstanding speakers do that too, but they also get people moving. The ideal is for your audience to take action to improve their situation, get rid of a problem, or fulfill a want or need—using an idea or a solution you offer them.

Years ago, back in the days before PowerPoint, I watched a seasoned presenter talk for three hours completely without notes. He was an amazing communicator who moved people to action without having to look at or think about what he was going to say! When he was done, I asked him how he was able to do that and he told me, "I knew my outcome. Because I know what I want to happen, I'm able to focus on that, and what I need to say stays easily available to me in the moment."

Four guidelines for creating a powerful outcome statement:

1. Be *specific*. Zero in on the *action* you want your audience to take, and consider what they need to get out of it, too. Hint: know what your audience expects from your presentation, what result they would like you to achieve, and what problems they want to solve. If you're not sure, ask someone who represents them.

2. Be audience-centric. Average presenters focus on what they want to get out of the presentation, while outstanding presenters focus on what they can help the audience get out of the presentation. So instead of having an outcome like, "This customer bought my product," you're better off creating a win-win like, "This customer eliminated their problem and delivered a 20 percent return on investment by implementing our solution."

3. Be exciting. When writing your outcome statement, choose words that make you eager to

accomplish your objective. You must believe in it if
you want anyone else to believe in it, too.

4. Be certain. Write your outcome statement in
the past tense, and you'll act as if it has already
happened. You'll be more confident and better able
to create the future you desire.

For example, if you're meeting with clients to tell them about ideas
you've generated for their ad campaign, a good outcome statement
could be: *my client enhanced her brand and increased revenues by
10 percent by implementing our advertising concept.* It's specific,
action-oriented, short, positive, upbeat, and in the past tense.

So start there: for every presentation you give, **create a
written outcome statement using these guidelines.** You might be
wondering if this is really necessary for every single presentation,
even if it's brief. Yes, it is—absolutely! Establish and write
down your outcome for every single one and you'll go into your
presentations with a huge edge.

POWER PLAY #2
Focus on Your Audience's Problems, Not Yours

One of the worst mistakes you can make is to think that the presentation is all about you—an opportunity to talk about your ideas, your products, and your solutions—and never relate it to anything the audience already cares about. Instead, remember why your audience is there in the first place: they want or need something from you. The best thing they can hear is that you care about them, that you get them, that you understand their problems, and that you can discuss it in a way that's meaningful to them. For both you and the audience, the ultimate objective is to improve their situation somehow, to give them a way to get what they really want. That's one of the secrets to winning the presentation game: understanding that it's not a win-lose game; it's a win-win! When your audience wins, you win too.

Of course, this means *you need to find out* what they want and need, what gives them a headache or heartache, what makes them frustrated or angry, what they've been itching to learn or improve. So ask!

Key Questions for Pre-presentation Preparation
Long before you give the presentation, get answers to both the obvious and the more subtle questions:
- What problems do your audience want to solve?
- What are the obstacles keeping them from where they want to go? What do they believe is keeping them from getting this result so far?

• Where are they now in terms of this result?

• Are there things about the company, industry, or economic climate you need to know?

• Is there anything else unique about the group that would help you tailor your presentation to their needs?

If you've learned about your audience in advance, when you give your presentation you can **engage with them and help them find solutions to their problems**. This is the difference between self-centered presenters, whose primary objective is only to enrich themselves ("I need someone to buy my stuff!") and a presenter that an audience can trust to help them. Separate yourself from everyone else by making sure your presentations revolve around solving the audience's problems and the outcome is a win-win. By the way, one of the perks for you in presenting like this is that it feels really good. When you know that the reason you're talking is to help someone else, you worry less about how you look and sound, and instead lose yourself in serving the audience and creating solutions that improve other people's lives.

POWER PLAY #3
See the World Through Their Eyes

Let's say you're on a car lot looking to buy. A salesperson saunters up for a meet and greet, gauges your interest, and determines you're serious. It's actually going pretty well—no pressure yet, and he seems nice enough. When he asks what you have in mind, you say you're interested in a compact hybrid, because you're looking for the fuel economy of a smaller car.

But then he gets all animated: "Look at this baby! The color is fabulous. And check out these rims and premium wheels! The body of this car is verrrry sexy."

If you're the type of person who buys cars for their styling, great. But didn't you just say that your primary need is fuel economy? Wasn't he listening?

Classic misstep on his part. You told him what was important to you and then he talked about what he thought might impress you or what interested him. Don't do this to your audience! Instead, try to see the world through their eyes.

When you're preparing your presentation, **remember to focus on what's *important* to your audience, what *interests* them, what *inspires* them.** Figure out what anecdotes, examples, stories, and experiences will resonate most with them. And when you share your solution, don't do it in a cookie-cutter way, as if you're delivering sales patter. Every audience is unique. The key is customization. What works for one audience may not work for another. When I'm speaking to a technology company, for instance, I use different examples than when I'm talking to a financial company, even when I'm talking about the exact same topic. It takes a bit more work on your part, but your audience will love it.

POWER PLAY #4
F----- the Audience

At the beginning of any presentation, attendees are usually restless. They have no idea whether they're going to be bored or get anything out of it. They're distracted, too, and often will be fiddling with their phones or whispering to someone next to them. Seriously, unless they've paid to be there or you're famous, it's likely they don't care about you and your presentation, and they just want to get it over with.

Well, you know what? F----- them!

In this case, F stands for *focus,* and that's right, your job is to **focus the audience on you and your message**. You can't expect them to arrive already focused, because they have too many other things on their minds. So plan for this as you develop your content. Know that before you dive into the heart of your message, you need to get their attention. How do you know when your audience is focused? What I always ask myself is: are they responding to me? Not just one or two people, but the whole group. Responses can include answering a question, raising their hands, closing their laptops and looking at me, leaning forward in their seats to listen, or any other action that gets them more involved in the presentation. Getting your audience to be responsive at the beginning is critical to the success of your presentation. The audience's response or lack thereof can set the tone for the entire presentation. Lack of audience response is incredibly painful when you're presenting. So commit right now to making sure you get your audience responding from the get-go.

Ways to Draw In Your Audience

Here are some of the best strategies for getting your audience to start responding to you.

- *Start conversations before the presentation.*
  Show up early for every presentation and strike up friendly conversations with people in your audience beforehand. Instead of waiting in the shadows, walk right up to people, smile, shake their hands, and talk to them. Let them get to know you and get to know them. This gets them responding to you before you even start, and the energy carries over into the beginning of your presentation. Everyone pays more attention to friends than strangers.

- *Be introduced.* Supply your host with a catchy biography of 150 words at most. Include details that will be of particular interest to your audience, along with your credentials. Ask that the leader of the group introduce you if possible by using the three Ws: what you are going to be talking about, why it's important to the group, and who will be talking (a little bit about you). A good introduction helps focus the audience and creates a sense of importance about the presentation.

- *Ask a question.* At the beginning of your presentation, ask, "How many of you have...?" "What would you do if...?" "Is it true that...?" People's brains are hardwired to respond when someone asks a question—we just can't help thinking of an answer of some kind. The key, though, is that your question elicits a response: a raise of the hand, a nod, or a verbal response.

• *Have them introduce themselves.* This works best in smaller groups. Give them a format to follow that insures their introductions are brief. An example is: "Give your name, how long you've been with XYZ company, and what you're most interested in getting out of this presentation today." By having your audience introduce themselves, they're automatically engaged in your presentation.

• *Get them moving.* If it's appropriate, have your audience stand up, stretch, shake hands with other attendees, or even move to another part of the room. Any movement you get them to take increases their engagement.

• *Break the ice.* I'll often use an icebreaker to begin a presentation. It might be a fun game, a demonstration, or even an optical illusion PowerPoint slide. The key to an icebreaker is that it has to be interesting and unexpected.

• *Get them laughing.* If you can crack them up, do it! Even a bad joke that elicits groans is okay, as long as you're laughing with them.

• *Be silent.* Walk to where you'll be speaking and look at your audience. For a few seconds make friendly eye contact, and then take a relaxing breath before you begin.

• *Be sincere.* Begin with a warm greeting and a friendly smile. Don't say, "It's a privilege to be

here" unless you mean it. Be honest from the
start, and you'll grab their attention and begin to
build trust.

You may be wondering, *This all sounds good, but what do these
techniques have to do with creating an engaging story?* It's simple:
the best storytellers tailor their stories according to the moment-
by-moment feedback they receive from their audience. Interacting
with your audience both before and during your presentation
will also help you share your message in a much more personal
and engaging way—increasing the likelihood of achieving your
intended outcome.

POWER PLAY #5
Make Them Itch, Then Scratch

Did you know that tens of thousands of presentations are going on right now, all over the world, where the audiences aren't paying any attention to the presenters? Or that in one of our recent surveys, 63 percent of people said that presentations they attend end up being a total waste of their time? Or that in another one of our surveys, 95 percent said that most presentations they attend are boring?

Imagine a system you could easily learn, where you could engage 100 percent of your audience right from the beginning and keep them fully engaged throughout the whole presentation. Well, you don't have to imagine it. You're absorbing that system right now as you read this book and begin to apply what you're learning.

And *right there* in the two paragraphs you just read is one of the key strategies for grabbing your audience's attention: **pose three questions right off the bat that make people catch their breath, and then reveal something that makes them comfortable enough to exhale.**

Here's a recap of the steps:

1. Right at the beginning, pose three questions that hit on your audience's own fears or uncomfortable experiences.

2. Ask them to imagine a world where these problems disappear.

3. Tell them they don't have to imagine it, because you've already created it.

(I learned this tip from my friend Sam Horn. To learn more from Sam, check out her new book, *Do I Have Your Attention?*)

POWER PLAY #6
Give Them a Sexy Headline

When you look at a newspaper or magazine, what determines which articles you read? It's the headline. If the headline catches your attention, you'll check out the article, but if the headline doesn't appeal to you, you move right on. This is the same way your audience looks at you.

Your audiences make a decision at the very beginning of your presentation whether they want to go on a journey with you or not. What determines whether they want to go or not? The "headline" you give them. For instance, if you were talking about wireless network solutions, your title slide could say "Wireless Networks Solutions," but how many people would be foaming at the mouth for that headline? A better one might be "Connecting to Your Network Anytime, Anywhere, with Any Device."

Who determines whether the headline is sexy or not? Your audience. Does it promise them something *they* want? That's the key. You need to let them know up front that you aim to take them on a ride they are going to love. And isn't it more fun to begin your presentation this way—*after* you've focused your audience? It's "Today we're going to show you how you can connect with anyone on your network, anytime, anywhere, with any device!" versus "Today we're going to talk about wireless network solutions."

POWER PLAY #7
Bring the Pain

You've heard the cliché, "No pain, no gain," and it's especially true when it comes to presenting. Earlier, we established that the best presentations solve the audience's problem, but it's not enough for you to know there's a problem, nor is it enough for them to know there's a problem. They need to remember how that problem makes them feel when they're in the middle of it. When people engage with that pain, some great things happen:

> **1. They're motivated to make a change, to embrace a new solution.** The reality is that no one *likes* to change. We like to do what we've always done, but we'll make a change when our current situation becomes painful to some degree. We buy a house or a car, adopt a new piece of technology, relate differently with our family, stop a bad habit— you name it—when we realize that what we're doing now isn't working any more. It's become too limiting or too difficult, or we think it's uncool, or we've grown beyond it. We don't just wake up one morning and decide to upset the apple cart on a whim. There's always some level of pain driving a new decision.

> **2. They're in the mood to do something now.** Nothing ups the ante like discomfort. The greater the discomfort, the more urgent it becomes to fix the situation. Always keep this in mind when you're

attempting to persuade your audience to take action.
The danger in pressing people's hot buttons is that they may
resent it if you're clumsy. One graceful way to remind people of
their pain is to tell a story or use a case study about someone else
or another company that experienced the same situation that's
currently troubling members of this audience. Being one degree
removed, people are able to listen to data and observations that
would be hard to hear if it was about them, and then they begin
to identify with the characters in your story, to root for them,
and to look for the resolution. Another way is to ask questions,
but remember the advice attorneys are always given: don't ask a
question you don't already know the answer to. You should already
know your audience's pain, so ask questions that will get them
telling you about it. As they tell you about it, it will become more
and more real to them, and their feelings will intensify.

Know that you don't have to rush to divulge the solution.
You'll be solving the problem in good time, but in the moment,
just pay attention to how heightened their motivation and urgency
become. As an effective presenter, you'll allow that to reach its
peak, so that the audience is at its most receptive when you throw
the lifesaver.

POWER PLAY #8
Share Three Big Concepts in the Body of Your Presentation

You've got your audience focused, and you've introduced your topic with a sexy headline. Now you're ready to serve up the meat of your presentation. It's time for the key ideas or concepts you'll be imparting to your audience. How many of your concepts do you think people will actually remember after you leave? I guarantee you it's not twenty-three! If you do your job well, they'll remember at least one. If you're outstanding, they'll remember as many as three, but don't expect much more than that.

The temptation is to give them more, but that's founded on the misconception that telling them more results in them getting more. I've seen so many presentations with fifteen key ideas, and ten strategies, and five tips, and, and, and...but the reality is that most of it won't be retained. With this in mind, I recommend you structure your presentation around three main ideas or concepts. When I teach our two-day presentation training class, FIRE-UP Your Presentations, the entire two days are based on three key concepts. And you've probably already noticed that this book follows the same approach: it may have fifty-two specific Power Plays, but they're presented in the form of three key concepts. Having three key concepts doesn't limit us, though; it focuses us and makes the content more powerful. Within your one to three key concepts, you can include plenty of tips, anecdotes, and other supporting points, but be sure the biggest chunk of your message supports your one to three key concepts.

So the strategy I recommend and have been using for many

years is to focus on the top few. Ask yourself: ***What are the three most important concepts I need to share with this audience to achieve my desired outcome from this presentation?*** Then develop and enrich those key concepts into the body of your presentation.

POWER PLAY #9
Use Pictures Instead of Bullet Points

Whenever I ask people to tell me what qualities they associate with ineffective speakers, one that always comes up is slide presentations with too much information on them. Probably the worst are entire paragraphs, which the presenter then recites to the audience. Second worst are endless lists of bullet points.

To improve, you could adopt the 5 x 5 rule, which means you don't use any more than five bullet points per slide, and no more than five words per bullet point. But there's something even better than that, something Steve Jobs used that blew bullet points out of the water: he knew how to **captivate with *pictures* only.**

Consider having a headline of two or three words and a picture underneath. No bullet points. This is where you can get really creative, choosing photos and illustrations that communicate ideas and feelings and situations without the literal restrictions of text. At first, you might think this is scary—you're taking yet another step back from having a script to read. But working from pictures frees you up to tell the story instead of making a bunch of points. I love using pictures in my presentations. The pictures I use energize me, and they actually make me more conversational and comfortable. It's been said that a picture paints a thousand words, and that's especially true in a presentation. The pictures inspire me to get out of my head and speak from my heart, which is where the most powerful presentations come from.

The way I do it is to search Google for the type of picture I need. Then I get picky. I don't like the standard pictures everyone uses in PowerPoint presentations. I want pictures that inspire me and have real impact. I may have to use several keywords and wrestle around with two or three great pictures before I settle on the one that speaks to me. For instance, recently I was giving a presentation on leading winning teams, and one of my key ideas was that as a leader you have to "Surround Yourself with Winners." I had just read a book about the US Navy SEALs, one of the most elite military forces in the world. They put their people through incredibly intensive training to see who the real winners are, so I found a picture of the SEALs bonding together in freezing cold ocean water, and I used that as the picture on my slide. This led perfectly into my story about how the SEALs are incredibly selective, and they only allow the best of the best to become a SEAL.

It's true—finding the right pictures to support your ideas and entertain your audience may take a bit of time, but it will make your presentation up to 300 percent more powerful. And it will enable you to become a charismatic, conversational speaker, instead of the person who just reads slides.

POWER PLAY #10
Give Them Exactly What They Want

It's always exciting when you get to the part of the presentation where you tell your audience about the solution you have for them. The problem is that many presenters get so hung up on telling every single aspect of the solution, every benefit and feature, that they lose sight of what people are really seeking.

What do they actually want? **They want to know how your solution is going to take away the pain.** They want a happy ending to the story! If there are more features and benefits than that one, fine, but telling them about it all can be confusing.

The best strategy is to think about the audience's pain points and then focus your demonstration of the solution on showing exactly how it alleviates that pain and moves them to where they want to be. Anything more than that is usually unnecessary and ineffective.

POWER PLAY #11
Use the "Invisible Call to Action"

Years ago, I was taught that you had to deliver a powerful "close." You almost had to strong-arm people into doing what you wanted, and it didn't feel good to me. Getting people to do something they don't want to do isn't fun. Everybody feels uncomfortable...*Uh-oh. Here comes the catch*. They stop listening and start wishing they were somewhere else.

Today, I understand that **if you're truly helping people solve a problem, you don't have to force it.** There's no "catch." From the beginning, the presentation is a collaborative effort, starting with your understanding of what the audience really wants. You focus them on that, and they start responding to you. Every response they have brings them closer to taking the action you want them to take at the end, which will be a win-win—good for them and good for you. This is called the "invisible call to action," because instead of broadcasting "THIS IS THE PART WHERE I'M ASKING YOU TO DO SOMETHING YOU DON'T WANT TO DO," it's the process of leading people to do something they truly want to do.

It's been proven that when a person takes a series of small actions (agreements), they are more likely to take a bigger action or make a larger agreement with you. One study had researchers come into a neighborhood with a huge billboard, asking people to post it on their front lawns for thirty days. The billboard promoted something almost everybody supports: stop drunk driving. But most of the homeowners balked. So the researchers went back to ask if they could put a much smaller poster in people's front yards, and a majority of people in the neighborhood agreed. Thirty days later, the researchers came back to ask if they could now put the big billboards up, and what happened? About one-third of the homeowners agreed to do it! Their small commitment made it much easier to take on the larger one.

The keys to applying this technique are:

1. Believe that what you are offering your audience has tremendous value to them and that you're there to help them.

2. From the beginning to the end of your presentation, get agreement from your audience by asking questions like, "Does that makes sense?" and "Can you see how that would work for you?"

3. Be confident and relaxed to the end of your presentation, knowing that you're there to help, and your self-worth will not be decided by their acceptance or rejection of your offer.

POWER PLAY #12
End With an Action

In the final stage of your presentation, audiences should be led to take an action that improves their situation: to fulfill the outcome you established at the very beginning of the process (see Power Play #1). Sometimes, they'll do something right then (e.g., register, buy something, give you a purchase order), and sometimes you'll ask them to do something later (e.g., agree to a demonstration, set up the next meeting). But even when the action is to take place later, you should **ask people to make some kind of commitment.**

In our presentation training programs, we always ask people to write down what actions they're going to take with the information they've received, to make a few commitments to themselves that will improve their skills, and to share those with us. If you don't do this or something like it with your audience, all the great work you've done in your presentation can be rendered ineffective. The motivation they had during the presentation might go away. And you're stuck calling people back, possibly trying to convince them to move forward on your outcome over the phone, with more meetings and an ambiguous outcome, stringing out the process.

Presentations end in one of four ways. The best, obviously, is with audience members agreeing to take the action you've designed the presentation to persuade them to take. Or maybe they don't take that action immediately, but the presentation advances them closer to it, which isn't so bad, either. The third thing that could happen is that they say they have some interest, but they don't commit to anything. In this case, they aren't any closer to taking action than they were before you arrived. I call this a "continuation," and it's the worst of all possibilities, because the chance of them following through on anything is very low, but you usually end up spending many hours of wasted energy chasing after them. Even the fourth alternative, a firm NO, is better than having to follow up endlessly with someone who's trying to avoid you!

When you sense someone is trying to give you a "continuation" rather than make a decision, see if you can turn that into something else. Ask for some kind of commitment. Rather than leave with them saying they'll be back to you in a few months, get specific: "What month are you targeting?" If they say July, for example, you can schedule an appointment on the spot—ask for a specific day and time when you can get together again. Ask if they need any more information between now and then. In other words, ask enough questions so that they can put some skin in the game and that you're assured they agree, at least in principle, that moving forward is a step in the right direction.

POWER PLAY #13
FIRE-UP Your Audience!

Years ago I came up with a system for a persuasive presentation, something anyone could use, no matter what they're selling. After studying all the research and methods I could find on persuasive presenting, I arrived at this acronym: FIRE-UP. Each letter stands for a step you need to take with your customer to persuade them to take action. You've already learned about each of these steps, so you can use it as a quick mnemonic to remember what to do at every presentation.

After you *create your intended outcome with your audience in mind* (Power Plays #1, #2, and #3), use the following process to *create an engaging story* and FIRE-UP your audience:

F—Focus your audience on you (Power Plays #4 and #5). I—Inform your audience of the outcome (Power Play #6). R—Remind your audience of their pain (Power Play #7). E—Educate and empower your audience (Power Plays #8 and #9). U—Use your audience's unique pain to demonstrate your solution (Power Play #10). P—Propose a commitment. (Power Plays #11 and #12).

These steps are already in the perfect order to present to your audience, and you can apply them to any type of presentation. They're especially helpful when you're speaking for fifteen minutes or more, because they provide a powerful structure that leads straight to the conclusion you've chosen: an outcome that moves your audience members to take powerful action to solve their problems with your solution. Plus it's an easy way to remember all the Power Plays you just learned!

But what about those more impromptu situations where you might not have the chance to put this full process into practice?

Keep the following two Power Plays in your back pocket, and you'll always be ready to share your message at a moment's notice.

POWER PLAY #14
Flash Your Brilliance

You've heard of an "elevator pitch," a presentation that's over in a flash and designed for maximum impact, a super-streamlined message delivered with crystal clarity. As a master persuader, it's something you want to have at the ready. Imagine you found yourself riding in an elevator with the most influential decision-maker you could ever meet, and you have sixty seconds to spark interest in you, your product, or your company.

Do you know what you'd say in a situation like that?

To figure it out, try beginning with "You know how..." and then fill in the blank with the problem your typical customer experiences. Follow up with "What I do is..." and tell your listener how you and/or your solution help them solve it. For example, I might say, **"You know how** many people struggle with giving presentations? Because first, they don't know what to say. Second, they're afraid of standing in front of a group of people that might reject them. And third, they don't know how to deliver what they're going to say in a captivating and charismatic way. **Well, what I do is** give people a system that shows them how to structure a message that will motivate their customers to take action, then I show them how to increase their confidence, and finally I help them master delivering their presentations with a charisma that seals the deal and leaves a permanent impression."

It's a formula that works for any situation. Try it with yours!

POWER PLAY #15
Be Ready at a Moment's Notice

If you've ever been caught off guard and asked to "say a few words," you know how tough impromptu presentations can be. They pose a real challenge because being unprepared tends to get the adrenaline going: if you freak out even a little bit, your fight-or-flight response kicks in, your brain shuts down, and you have no idea what to say. Then you think: *I don't want to do this! How dare they ask me to do this off the cuff?!*

What to do? Take a breath and fill your body with confidence (you'll learn more about how to do that in the second section of this book). Then, **take a moment to focus, first on clarifying an outcome and then formulating at most three ideas you can share with your audience that will achieve that outcome.** Don't ever let yourself feel rushed. If you have to rise and speak immediately, buy yourself a little time by asking a question of the person who requested you speak: see if she will clarify the results she wants from having you talk. You can say something like, "I'm happy to get up and talk about this, but help me out. What specifically do you want me to focus on and accomplish?"

Even if you're already standing, take a few moments to make mental notes while she speaks, and jot down the two or three ideas you want to share. Again, don't overdo it. You don't need a list of ten or fifteen things, and you don't want to start rambling, so get clear on your outcome, stick to those three things, and you're golden.

PART ONE SUMMARY:
Create an Engaging Story

POWER PLAY #1: **Begin at the End**

Begin your preparation for every presentation with a written outcome statement that clarifies what action you want your audience to take at the end of your presentation; make it specific, audience-centric, exciting, and certain.

POWER PLAY #2: **Focus on Your Audience's Problems, Not Yours**

Identify your audience's needs and wants as specifically as possible, and focus your presentation on their problems, not yours.

POWER PLAY #3: **See the World Through Their Eyes**

Every audience is unique. Find out what is important to them, what interests them, and what inspires them. Adjust the focus of your presentation and the examples you use accordingly.

POWER PLAY #4: **F----- the Audience**

Accept that it is your responsibility to focus the audience and have a specific and flexible plan to get their attention.

POWER PLAY #5: **Make Them Itch, Then Scratch**

Ask your audience three questions that address their problems and then ask them to imagine a world where those problems disappear. Assure them that such a world exists and you are about to tell them about it.

POWER PLAY #6: Give Them a Sexy Headline

In the title of your presentation, promise to deliver something your audience already wants.

POWER PLAY #7: Bring the Pain

Tell stories and ask questions that help your audience feel the pain of the problems you are addressing so that they will embrace the new solution you are offering and be motivated to do something about it now.

POWER PLAY #8: Share Three Big Concepts in the Body of Your Presentation

To help your audience retain what you say, organize all your material around the three most important concepts you need to share with them to achieve the desired outcome of your presentation.

POWER PLAY #9: Use Pictures Instead of Bullet Points

Create slides with brief titles and captivating photos that allow you to tell a story and speak from your heart.

POWER PLAY #10: Give Them Exactly What They Want

Give your audience the happy ending they want by telling them exactly how your solution is going to take away their pain—everything else is a distraction.

POWER PLAY #11: Use the "Invisible Call to Action"

If you are truly helping your audience solve a problem, you won't need to strong-arm them at the end—just suggest a small next step that will likely lead to a larger commitment.

POWER PLAY #12: End with an Action

Your presentation should lead your audience to take the action you established in Power Play #1, and even if that action will be taken later, ask people to make some kind of commitment in the form of an appointment or immediate next step.

POWER PLAY #13: FIRE-UP Your Audience!

Focus your audience on you. Inform your audience of the outcome. Remind your audience of their pain. Educate and empower your audience. Use your audience's unique pain to demonstrate your solution. Propose a commitment.

POWER PLAY #14: Flash Your Brilliance

Prepare your "elevator pitch" with the following formula: "You know how (fill in the blank with a problem your typical customer experiences)? What I do is (fill in the blank with how your solution solves that problem)."

POWER PLAY #15: Be Ready at a Moment's Notice

If you are asked to give an impromptu presentation, take a moment to clarify the outcome you want and formulate three concepts you want to share to help your audience achieve that outcome.

PART TWO:
Feel Like a Winner!

When it's time to give your presentation, you can't do any more preparation. *There's no more time*. So whether you're fully prepared or not, at that point it really doesn't matter—you need to find a way to achieve your outcome. What does matter is how you feel: **If you feel like a winner, you'll tend to do an outstanding job and achieve your outcome, even if your preparation hasn't been perfect.** (Now, I'm not saying you shouldn't prepare. Preparation is critical, so make sure you do it. But what most people don't prepare to do is to feel good.) Imagine a presenter who's done everything to put together a great presentation, and who's gifted at communicating that message—but who's also stricken with anxiety. How's that presenter going to do? You already know the answer: not very well.

Feeling like a winner means you show up for your presentation confident in the knowledge that you are going to do an outstanding job. It may be hard to understand how you can feel confident that you are going to do an outstanding job *before* you even start your presentation, but that's what you have to do if you want to be outstanding.

In this section, you'll gain some special strategies and Power Plays to make sure you feel like a winner every time you give a presentation.

POWER PLAY #16
Feel Like You're On a Mission

Have you ever had to do a task and felt motivated and inspired to do whatever it took to succeed—as if you were on a *mission* to accomplish it? **If so, capture that feeling and bring it into every presentation, and you'll be unstoppable.**

Back in my mid-twenties, I was booked to do a presentation at a real-estate office in Los Angeles. I lived in San Diego, so my plan was to drive up to LA that morning, do the presentation, and head back home. I had just bought a BMW convertible, so I was looking forward to the drive. Everything was going great until I hit LA. I didn't know the city well, but the directions seemed to be taking me into the sketchiest part of town.

This can't be right, I thought. *How could I be booked to do a presentation in this part of the city?* Surely no one there could afford what I was selling, which was a one-day sales training seminar happening a month later. And then came the biggest shock: The real-estate office that I was speaking at was a decrepit old building with a barbed-wire fence surrounding it. Instead of pulling in, I drove by and circled back. I wanted to see it again to make sure my eyes weren't deceiving me. This was such a rough part of town I didn't want to even risk leaving my brand- new car in the parking lot while I was inside giving my presentation. I made a split-second decision. I wasn't going to do it. I was just going to drive back home and call to let them know I couldn't make it. I'd even send them some of our books for free to make up for it.

Of course, it felt wimpy to be driving away, but I rationalized it by saying that they weren't even the right customers for me. And then I pulled over to the side of the road and stopped the car. *What am I doing?* I thought. *Why have I chosen to be in the business I am in? Because I love helping people be more successful! And even if this group can't afford to go to our one-day seminar, I owe it to them to go in there and give them my very best! I can help them increase their belief in themselves and hopefully take their careers and their lives to another level!*

I had reconnected with my mission. I turned my car around and made a beeline back to the real-estate office, parked my car, and headed into the office building with my heart on fire. I don't remember what I said that day, but I do remember that it came straight from my heart. It wasn't about closing a sale; it was about helping a wonderful group of people who needed some hope and inspiration. It was one of the best feelings I've ever had, and the end result was that almost every person in the meeting found a way to come up with enough money to invest in our one-day sales training.

To set yourself on fire before your presentation, always remind yourself that you aren't there just to sell an idea or a product to your audience. You're there to add tremendous value to them, to help them make a change in their business or life that only *you* can help them make!

POWER PLAY #17
It All Starts With Connection

If you could pick just one emotion to have at your core as a presenter, what would it be? I've asked this question of thousands of people, and the most common answers are *confidence* and *passion*. While I agree that these are critical, I believe there's another emotion that, when combined with confidence and passion, takes you to a whole new level. It's the feeling of being *connected* with your audience. In my opinion, connection is the most powerful core emotion you can have in any communication.

Have you ever seen a presenter with tremendous passion but no connection with the audience? How did they come across? Crazy! Or have you ever seen a presenter who was supremely confident but lacked connection with the audience? How did they come across? Arrogant!

But **when you combine passion or confidence with connection, the result is magical.** Everybody feels better, both the presenter and the audience.

In the pages that follow, you'll be asked to choose how you want to feel. And while there are many incredibly powerful emotions, make sure you wrap your choices around the most powerful one, the emotion of feeling connected.

POWER PLAY #18
You Determine How You Feel

Right now, point to the person who determines how you feel. I hope you're not pointing to your spouse, your boss, or anyone other than yourself, because—of course!—*it's you*. You determine how you feel. But here's the rub: Is there someone in your life who's an expert at ticking you off? If you're like most people, the answer is yes. But how can this be? How can you be the one who determines how you feel, yet believe that someone else can make you angry? Doesn't it have to be one or the other? Hmm.

To be an outstanding presenter, you must be the one to decide how you feel! The reality is that most of the time, the audience members won't be that interested in making you feel good. As a matter of fact, some of them won't even want to be in the room. I've stood in front of hundreds of audiences where, when I first looked at them, all I could see were people with no energy who didn't even want to be there. Fortunately, I've trained myself to get excited about these kinds of audiences. And it did take some serious training. When I first started giving presentations, an audience with no energy would psych me out. I'd blame them for me not being at the top of my game. But I learned a long time ago that's a loser's game to play. **As a presenter, it's your job to make sure that you feel great and then deliver your presentation with an energy that changes how the audience feels!** Winners know that the only way to ever be able to change how someone else feels is by taking control of how you feel.

POWER PLAY #19
Feel Great For Every Presentation

Is it too much to ask you to feel great for *every* presentation? What if you didn't get enough sleep the night before? Or you have a headache? Or your cat was sick? Or...fill in the blank with whatever circumstances tend to get in the way of you being at the top of your game.

If you're going to be great, **you can't make any excuses.** Getting yourself to feel great takes work, but you can do it for every presentation. This is one of my absolute commandments for myself: **feel great every time!** Believe me, there have been plenty of times when I've traveled internationally and had to do a presentation without getting any sleep. It's not that I'm naturally feeling good at that point, but I *make* myself feel good (most of the rest of Part Two will give you precise strategies for doing just that). The bottom line is that any time you get up to speak without being in a powerful mental state, your ability to communicate suffers. And when your ability to communicate suffers, you're held back from getting the results you're truly capable of producing. Hold yourself to the highest standard, and do what it takes to feel great for *every* presentation!

POWER PLAY #20
Prepare Like an Athlete

What do professional athletes and entertainers do before they perform? That's right, they *warm up*.

Watch any athletic contest on TV, and you'll get a glimpse of the players getting ready for the competition. You'll see them stretching, jumping up and down, and even saying things to themselves or their teammates. What they're really doing is getting their minds and bodies focused on the task at hand. Just like you and me, they have lives off the playing field. They have spouses, children, and even bills to pay. In terms of preparing their minds, their warm-up routine helps them shut off all thoughts and concerns that don't contribute to high performance. There's no such thing as multitasking when you're in the middle of a game and you're playing to win.

You may not think you're like the people you watch on TV, but you have a lot in common with them. As a presenter, you have to perform under pressure, and the clock is always ticking. You may even have some people in your audiences who don't want you to succeed. And just like the people on TV, you certainly have lots of other things going on in your life that you could focus on. The average person has about 60,000 thoughts a day without even trying. The answer isn't to think more thoughts, but to choose to focus only on the thoughts that will help you perform well. In that way, you can think of your performance the same way the professional athlete does. You need to *know* you're going to win and *feel* you're going to win to give yourself the best chance of peak performance.

So before every presentation, **warm up your body and**

mind. Before I even show up for a presentation, I start with some stretching or yoga exercises. That stretching is a must! Any tension in the body will be interpreted by the mind as nervousness, which will end up triggering even more nervousness and tension. In addition to stretching, I also like to do dynamic movements with my body, such as jumping up and down, or going on a brisk walk.

I also prepare my mind to think the perfect thoughts and feel the perfect emotions. Rarely do I wake up in the perfect mindset to give a presentation. It takes work. For a big presentation, I start preparing my mind the day before. I'll visualize the presentation and see it going incredibly well. I'll start telling myself how well it went, even though I haven't even done the presentation yet. Visualizing success before it happens is a technique that athletes and performers have been using for years, and it's something you should be using, too.

POWER PLAY #21
Cancel Thoughts You Don't Want

Have you ever heard a song and then couldn't get it out of your head? No matter what you did, it was stuck there, playing over and over again in your mind. How annoying! Has the same thing ever happened with a thought? It's even more insidious.

There are great thoughts, which I call *optimal performance thoughts*, and then there are bad thoughts, which inhibit your presentation performance. These bad or negative thoughts literally block you from using your full potential when you're presenting. The challenge most people face is that they don't even notice when bad thoughts enter their minds, and if they do notice, they don't know how to stop them. If you find yourself in this situation, try a strategy I call *Cancel Thought*. Using this strategy, you can actually cancel thoughts you don't want to be thinking and replace them with thoughts that will drive your presentation performance to new levels. It may sound too good to be true, but with practice you can do it.

First, know that at any point in time, you can be thinking only one thought. That thought might last a microsecond, but there's only one thought at a time. So if you're thinking a negative thought, it has total control over you during the time you're thinking it. Conversely, if you're thinking a powerful thought, it also has total control over you. With *Cancel Thought,* the goal is to eliminate the bad thoughts as soon as you notice them and replace them with good thoughts. This is especially critical in the minutes and hours before you're scheduled to give your presentation. Here are the steps for the *Cancel Thought* strategy:

1. Notice whenever a negative or bad thought enters your mind.

2. Immediately say to yourself: *Cancel thought!*
Say it like you mean it; you can't be a wimp and expect it to do anything. You've got to be powerful here. Your mind has to know that you're serious! I like to imagine a big red X stamping out the thought when I say this. You can say it out loud or, if you are in a setting where saying it out loud is inappropriate, you can "shout" it forcefully in your head.

3. Replace the thought you just canceled with an empowering thought. In many cases, the replacement can be the exact opposite of the thought you just canceled. Here's an example. A thought goes through your head just as you're about to give a presentation: *I'm not ready.* As soon as you notice that thought, you immediately say to yourself, *Cancel thought!* You replace it with *I'm ready to go right now!* Here, too, you have to say it like you mean it. The effectiveness of this strategy depends on you laying down the law and letting your brain know that you won't allow crappy thoughts in your head. And whenever you do notice a poor thought, you'll immediately remove it and replace it with a powerful thought that raises your performance.

POWER PLAY #22
Interrupt Poor Mental Patterns

Sometimes when you're working on a computer, things start to go haywire. It can slow down or stop functioning altogether. When this happens, it's impossible to get any work done, because the machine just can't perform. What's the magical fix? Often, it's as simple as a reboot: everything that was hampering the computer's performance has been shut down, and you have a fresh start.

Did you know that you can reboot your own mental system when it's not performing? There are many ways to do this, such as stopping whatever you're doing and jumping up and down, or shouting out "Yes!" or just taking a deep, clearing breath. What all of them have in common is that you **make a radical physical or mental shift.**

Just observe children to see how powerful this is. Once, when I was outside watching my son play, he fell and bumped his knee. Like most two-year-olds with a fresh bruise and a scrape, he began to cry. I went and picked him up, giving him a hug, but he continued to cry. I could see that he wasn't hurt physically as much as he was hurt emotionally, so I decided to interrupt his emotional pattern. To do this, I quickly turned and pointed in the distance, shouting, "Look, a bird!" This startled him, and he quickly turned to look, sniffling, asking where I'd seen the bird. So I looked for it with him, and at that point the tears stopped altogether. He had totally forgotten about his knee. His pattern of pain, fear, and crying was completely interrupted.

I use this on myself, too, when I notice any thought or emotion that I don't want to have, especially before a presentation. No, I wouldn't stand in the middle of a room and start jumping up and down in front of an audience, but if I need to I'll leave the room and go around the corner, and, yes, start jumping up and down to interrupt my pattern. I don't let any thoughts or emotions exist in me that could hurt my performance, and neither should you.

POWER PLAY #23
Use Your Power Move

My friend Tony Robbins is regarded by many as one of the most dynamic speakers in the world. If you were to watch him backstage before he goes out to deliver a presentation, you would see him energizing himself by performing a series of dynamic gestures where he thrusts his right hand forward in a powerful punching motion while drawing his left hand backward and pounding it on his chest. All while exhaling an explosive out-breath. Tony calls this his "*Power Move*" and he uses it as a staple for getting himself ready to go out and consistently deliver the amazing presentations that have made him a legend.

If you've ever watched Tiger Woods sink a big putt, you've seen his version of a *power move* when he shakes his fist and yells, "Yes!"

So what's your *power move*? I challenge you to come up with one right now. Once you do, try it out. The key to a great *power move* is that you have to play full out when you do it. You have to be "all in"! If you put everything you've got into your *power move,* it will create a quick and dramatic change that leaves you feeling like the winner you are.

POWER PLAY #24
Breathe Your Tension Away

When the average person gets up to speak, a few things happen. His heart starts beating faster, his blood pressure rises, and he begins breathing more rapidly. What are these characteristics indicating? They are signs that the mind and body are sensing imminent danger and have switched into "fight or flight" mode. If this presenter proceeds to do the presentation while he is in "fight or flight" mode, how will it impact his performance? Obviously, it will inhibit him. It will be virtually impossible for him to perform at his best.

"Fight or flight" mode is great when you are responding to a real physical threat, like a tiger attacking you, but it can be disastrous when you are giving a presentation. This section is filled with numerous tips to prevent or get you out of "fight or flight" mode. One of the simplest is to take a *clearing breath*. When done right, a *clearing breath* can ease the mind, increase confidence, and lower the heart rate and blood pressure.

There are many ways to do a clearing breath, but I recommend using the "6-2-7" method. In the "6-2-7" method, you inhale through your nose for 6 seconds, hold the breath for 2 seconds, and then exhale through the nose or mouth for 7 seconds. One of the keys to an effective clearing breath is that the out-breath must be longer than the in-breath. A longer out-breath sends a signal to the brain that everything is ok and it can relax.

Take a minute to do four "6-2-7" clearing breaths right now and notice the impact it has on you. It's a simple tool to calm your nerves and leave you feeling ready for every presentation.

POWER PLAY #25
Change Your Identity

Imagine that two people who have been fifty pounds overweight for the past ten years decide to go on a diet. After six months of dieting, both succeed in losing fifty pounds. A year later, one of them has gained back the fifty pounds, plus another ten, while the second person maintained this new healthier weight for the rest of her life. What do you think the critical difference was between these two people?

Some might say willpower, but willpower can only take you so far and ultimately it can be toppled. In my experience, for a change to take hold long term, it must happen at the deepest level of who you are. The deepest level of who you are is your "*identity*." No matter how much you change in the short-term, long-term you will always revert back to your *identity*.

If a person loses weight, but inwardly she still has an *identity* of being a person who is overweight, eventually she will gain that weight back. To maintain a healthy weight long term, she must change her *identity*.

What's your *identity* as a presenter? We've had people over the years come into our trainings with *identities* like the following:

I don't like giving presentations.
I always get nervous when I get up to speak.

Needless to say, this *identity* will severely limit the any hope these people have of becoming outstanding presenters, no matter how much training they receive. It's only when they make a shift in their *identities* that their true potential becomes available. The way to shift your *identity* is to create an *identity statement* that consists of two parts. The first part indicates a strength you currently have or want to have. The second part of your *identity statement* addresses what you want to accomplish. My own *identity statement* for giving presentations is:

I love giving presentations!
I always find a way to connect with and influence
every audience I speak to!

To create your *identity statement*, answer the following questions:

1. What is the foremost strength you possess (or want to possess) as a presenter that proves you can achieve greatness?

2. What do you ultimately hope to accomplish as a presenter?

Once you've answered these questions, combine the answers into your own two-part *identity statement* and begin using it right away. It might feel foreign at first, but remember, we become what we think about. Give yourself some time and let your new *identity statement* help you become the presenter you were meant to be.

POWER PLAY #26
Think Your Very Best Thoughts

Most presenters limit what they think they're capable of doing. They base their evaluation of themselves on their past experiences—which is a dangerous practice, because it doesn't allow for growth. **The thoughts you had yesterday don't have to be the thoughts you have today.** All increases in performance are built on this concept.

For instance, what if a two-year-old maintained the thought that he needed to wear diapers for the rest of his life? If he continued to think this, he'd reach thirty years old and still be pooping in his pants! Not a pretty picture. To prevent this from happening, the two-year-old's parents work relentlessly with the child to help him latch on to a more empowering thought: *I'm a big boy and I can use the toilet to go to the bathroom.* Even if there are occasional accidents, the parents keep encouraging the child, helping him see who he's becoming so that he matures.

My experience in training presenters is that almost every person needs to work on coming up with more empowering thoughts, or *optimal performance thoughts,* which you read about earlier in this book. These are the thoughts that allow you to tap into and maximize your potential, and you can figure out what these thoughts might be for yourself—and construct them and remember them—by answering a simple question: *If I knew that my presentation went perfectly, what would I be thinking?*

You might have thoughts about your content. Or thoughts about yourself and your ability as a presenter. Or even thoughts about your audience or customer.

When I'm figuring out what thoughts to construct and

remember for myself, they often remind me of a specific technique that I want to implement. For instance, the thought *I created a series of connected conversations* reminds me to talk to only one person at a time when I'm giving my presentation (you'll learn more about connected conversations in a later chapter). Here are a few more of the thoughts I use to get myself ready to give a presentation:

- *I loved being with this audience!*
- *My presentation went incredibly well!*
- *They are like my friends and family!*
- *The perfect content flowed through me effortlessly!*
- *I used my whole voice and body to make what I said fascinating!*

Notice that these are in the past or present tense, even though I'm talking about the future. That's because I'm using my thoughts to influence the future. To be an outstanding presenter, you must have the courage to say something's true even though it hasn't happened yet! Now, you're saying this to yourself because you need to convince yourself that your presentation went well and was a huge success, so that you have a chance for that to actually happen. People often ask me if this is a magic bullet and if it works every time. The answer is no. It doesn't work every time. Having optimal performance thoughts that you focus on before your presentation doesn't guarantee success, but it dramatically increases the likelihood that you'll succeed. Besides, it just makes you feel better.

How many optimal performance thoughts do you need? As many as you want, but I recommend four. These four optimal performance thoughts should make you feel unstoppable and ready to go. Think big here. Don't hold yourself back. Choose thoughts that only a courageous person would dare to think—the thoughts of a person who was tapping into their unlimited potential. When I ask people in our training classes, "How many of you are outstanding presenters?" usually only one or two people will raise their hands. I'm sure some people are just being modest, but I want every single person raising his or her hand and adopting the thought that he or she is an outstanding presenter! If you can't think that thought and see yourself as an outstanding presenter, you're preventing yourself from being your best.

When John F. Kennedy said that we would land a man on the moon before the end of the 1960s, he was saying we were going to do what was literally impossible at that time. But because he had the courage to see it, think it, and express it as if it was already done, he rallied the scientists to make it happen. Once you come up with your optimal performance thoughts, it's important that you say them to yourself in such a way that your whole body feels that the thought is true. Just thinking it isn't enough. *You must feel the thought*. That's the only way your brain truly accepts it.

POWER PLAY #27
Feel Your Very Best Emotions

Have you ever given a presentation where absolutely everything went perfectly? You know what I'm talking about: you looked good, felt good, and even smelled good—and the right words flowed effortlessly out of your mouth. I bet you've had at least one of those. What about the opposite: have you ever given a presentation where nothing seemed to be working? Where the words seemed to stick in your throat, and it was hard for you to string your thoughts together? I bet you've had at least one of those, too.

If you're capable of giving a flawless presentation, yet also capable of giving a presentation you're much less proud of, what's the difference between the two? Why aren't you always on or always off? The difference resides not only in your thoughts (the subject of the previous few pages), but also your emotions. As I've shared earlier, **your feelings are a huge factor in your performance.** But most presenters either are clueless about how they feel or think they're incapable of changing how they feel.

Consider this: over the course of a day, you'll have more than four hundred instances where your emotions will come into play. And depending upon which emotions you choose to acknowledge and nurture, the results you produce can range from poor to spectacular. Your emotions not only dictate your performance, but they are also passed on to your audience. Your audience actually experiences and feels what you are feeling. This is why I mentioned earlier that connection is such a powerful emotion for presenters. When you feel connected to your audience, they also feel connected to you. The problem is that most people don't wake up feeling connected to an audience they don't even know yet. It's much more likely that they wake up feeling nervous or wary about this unknown audience they will be speaking to later in the day.

However, in my mental preparation, I not only choose my optimal performance thoughts, I also choose my optimal performance emotions: I choose how I'm going to feel, the same way I choose what I'm going to wear. It's that simple.

The key is understanding that you don't have to feel anything less than perfect if you don't want to. There have been plenty of times when I've woken up before a presentation feeling tired and not wanting to give the presentation, but I always change from that feeling into my optimal performance emotions before I get in front of an audience. Some examples of my optimal performance emotions are these:

- *I am caring and connected!*
- *I am energized and excited!*
- *I am confident and committed!*
- *I am prepared and ready!*
- *I am playful and fun!*

Your optimal performance emotions can be whatever you want them to be. The key is making sure that whatever you choose, they take you to your highest level of peak performance. One of the ways I figured out what works best for me was by paying attention to what emotions I felt whenever I was at my best giving a presentation. I captured these by writing them down and chose them as the emotions I get myself to feel every single time. I also learned a lot from presentations that haven't gone well. After those, I asked myself what emotions I was feeling that hurt my performance, or what emotion was missing that didn't allow me to be my best. Over the years, I've figured out my perfect "emotional recipe," and that's what I'm suggesting you do, too.

Notice a couple of things about the list above. First, each of them begins with *I am*. Those two words allow you to claim an emotion in a powerful way. Along with using your body language (which is addressed below), they can help you get in that emotional state immediately. I don't just want to feel good when I start to speak; I want to feel great before I even get up to speak.

The second thing you'll notice is an exclamation mark at the end of each optimal performance emotion. This reminds me to feel that emotion with every cell of my body! You can't just say, "I am energized and excited." You have to make sure you're feeling energized and excited. So how do you do that? The most powerful way to make sure that you're actually feeling your optimal performance emotions is to use your whole body to express the statement. Don't just say it; change your posture, change your breathing, make a gesture, or create a facial expression to solidify the feeling in your mind and body. Every emotion has a physical component. For instance, what's a telltale sign that someone is happy? A big smile! If you want to feel happy, but you're not smiling, you're going to have a hard time. I have figured out the perfect body language for every one of my optimal performance emotions. When I want to feel the emotion, I simply focus on that emotion, and then I get in the proper body language position. This allows me to instantaneously access and feel that emotion. It allows me to feel emotions like confidence even when there is uncertainty all around me.

I challenge you to pick your top three optimal performance emotions and start practicing being able to create them instantaneously. The more you practice, the easier it gets. You'll actually be forming new circuitry in your brain that will allow you to easily feel whatever emotion you want to feel.

POWER PLAY #28
Use Your Superchargers

What short phrase can you say to yourself to provide instant energy? Something like, "Let's go!" "Have fun!" "Play full out!" "Just do it!" "This is a blast!" "I love it!" These are just a few examples of what I call *superchargers*. What supercharger will work best for you? Honestly, I don't know, because the true test of a supercharger is what it does for *you*. A phrase that supercharges me might not do anything for you. It's important for you to pick a couple of superchargers that can give you that extra edge before you begin your presentation. I love using superchargers, because they're short but also incredibly powerful.

The key to having a successful supercharger is knowing that it's not only what you say, but how you say it, that determines the impact it has. **When you say your supercharger with high energy, it can enliven every cell of your body.** What's more, it can create a radical, instantaneous emotional shift for you that will take your presentation to new heights.

POWER PLAY #29
Get on the Friends and Family Plan

Several years ago, a telephone company promoted a calling plan that allowed you to talk to your closest friends and family for free. It was a great deal, and many people took advantage of it. Why? Not just because it's a money saver, but also because we love talking to these people! We're comfortable with them. We trust them and we love them. We get to be ourselves with them.

Who do we not like to talk to? *Strangers.* When you were young, I'm sure your mother told you, "Don't talk to strangers!" Good advice for a child, but not for a presenter. Many of your presentations will be given to people you don't know very well, but you don't have to feel that they are "strange" to you. In fact, if you feel like your audience is made up of strangers, it puts you at a huge disadvantage. It's hard to be yourself when you're uncomfortable with your audience.

So what can you do to give yourself an advantage? You can **get on the "friends and family plan" with every audience,** even (*and especially*) with the audiences that appear anything but friendly!

Consider this interesting study. Researchers showed two groups of men pictures of two different women. The first group saw a picture of someone who could easily have been a supermodel, while the second group saw a picture of someone who would be considered somewhat physically unattractive. Each man was instructed to call the lady he'd seen in the picture for a ten-minute phone conversation. The men in the first group were very excited to call this stunning woman they had seen. They looked forward to it, and they savored every minute of anticipation.

The conversations were recorded, and the researchers could hear the excitement in the men's voices. They could also hear excitement in the lady's voice. As much as the men were enjoying the conversation, she was enjoying it just as much. The second group of men wasn't so enthusiastic, though, as they imagined talking with a woman many would have considered physically unattractive. These men considered their upcoming phone call to be just a job they had to do. Their conversations were also recorded, and you could hear that they weren't into the call at all. You could hear that it was a struggle for the lady, too. Nobody was having a good time.

In both groups, the men's excitement level transmitted to the person they called, and it was reflected back to them. When the men were eager to talk, so was she. When the men were uninterested, so was she. But here's the twist: **both groups of men were calling the exact same woman!** You see, neither photograph the men had seen was accurate. The images had caused them to form a mental picture of her and how excited they should be to talk to her. This happens with all presenters, too. We create mental pictures of our audiences. We see them as either attractive and friendly, or unattractive and foreboding. Whichever picture you choose has a major impact on your performance.

Two of the biggest fears human beings have are being rejected and being deemed unworthy. As presenters, we are constantly asking ourselves, *Will they like me? Am I good enough?* When you think you have an audience of strangers that is going to judge you, it's hard to be at your best. You'll worry too much about it, and your performance will suffer.

But with friends and family, we don't have these worries. We know our friends and families like us, and we know we're good enough with them. So I suggest you play the mental game of thinking of everyone in your audience as a friend or family member. It doesn't mean you have to invite them over to your house for the holidays; you just have to treat them and feel about them the same way you would a great friend. This may take a leap of faith to do, but trust me, it's one of the most powerful techniques you can use. This technique changed my life as a presenter, and I know it will change yours, too!

POWER PLAY #30
It's Just a "Presensation"

Yes, you read that right—it's not a typo. *"Presensation"* is a word I made up to describe the combination of *presentation* and *conversation*.

Remember this: the worst thing you can do when you get up to speak is to go into what I call "presentation mode," where you sound and look nothing like the real you, but instead like some artificial version of you. You operate wholly out of your head, and nothing comes from your heart. While you might be able to verbalize your key points this way, they probably won't be very interesting to your audience.

Contrast that with the mode you're in when you're having an energizing conversation with a group of coworkers or friends. It's completely different: in conversation mode, you're not worrying about every word you say. You're totally focused on conveying a message to someone else. You're coming from your heart *and* your head. This is you at your best.

When you're in conversation mode while you're giving a presentation, you're at your very best again. This is you being *"presensational"!* A multitude of great things happen: Your ideas flow effortlessly; you sound like a real person and not a robot; your audience can feel your energy.

Start thinking of your presentations in this new way. It's not business as usual anymore. No more trying to get everything perfect. Instead, **engage in a wonderful conversation while you're presenting.** In other words, have a "presensation" with your audience.

POWER PLAY #31
Visualize Your Audience Below

Visualize an imaginary audience. Go on, close your eyes and get a mental picture of them right now. (Go on, do it!) Now, as you pictured them, where were they in relation to you? Were they on the same level as you? Or above you so that you were looking up at them? Or below you so that you were looking down?

Presenters who tend to be nervous typically imagine the audience above them. Believe it or not, when I ask these same people to re-imagine this scenario and change the orientation of the audience in their mind's eye, it changes the way they feel. **The ideal placement of your audience in a mental picture is below you.** Why? This tends to give your brain the feeling that *you're helping them* and that *you have something to share with them.* Conversely, when you see your audience above you, it's as if you're placing them on a pedestal, where they're better than you. This is a simple technique for dramatically changing how you feel. Try it!

POWER PLAY #32
Be in the Now

At any point in time, you're focused on one of three times: the past, the present, or the future. Each of these has different emotions associated with it, and when you're preparing to give a presentation, it's especially important that you put your focus in the right place.

How about the past? When most people think about presentations they've done, for some reason they tend to remember the ones that didn't go well more prominently than the ones that did. They think of being unprepared, or of audiences that didn't respond the way they were supposed to. This is true for me as much as the next guy. Although I've had thousands of fantastic presentations, the ones I remember best are those that didn't go as well. So if you're getting yourself ready for today's presentation by remembering one from the past that went incredibly well, that's great, but you want to avoid poisoning your mind with any past experiences that could shatter your confidence.

Most people focus on the future as they're getting ready to give a presentation. They're usually busy trying to think about and remember all the things they're going to say in the next thirty minutes. The problem with projecting yourself into the future is that it tends to create anxiety. The only time I like to think about the future is when I'm visualizing my presentation having gone incredibly well—I project myself to the time *after* the presentation. This gets me excited about it!

Right before your presentation, **the best place to be focused is on the here and now.** The present is really all there is anyway. Plus, you can handle the here and now. It's right in front of you, and it typically doesn't create the anxiety or uncertainty that the future and past create. Take a breath, stand up tall, look at your audience, and know you're getting ready to help them.

POWER PLAY #33
The Miracle Minute

Watch the typical presenter as they prepare to give a presentation, and they're usually furiously going through the slide deck trying to remind themselves of all the things they need to say to give the perfect presentation. Don't do this! It's a surefire way to psych yourself out, and it's a huge momentum killer. Right before you start, you don't want to be thinking about what you're going to say fifteen minutes into your presentation. If you do, expect to have some anxiety (as we learned in the previous Power Play). On the other hand, I'm not saying that you don't want to focus on any of your content right before you start. Instead, I believe that you should *focus mostly on how you think and feel*.

So, which part of your presentation will have the greatest impact on your confidence for the entire presentation? *The first sixty seconds*. That's right—**the first minute of your presentation is so crucial in getting you ready to present and creating momentum with your audience that I call it the "miracle minute."** If you struggle with what to say in that first minute, it tends to make the entire presentation a struggle. However, if you get on a roll in that first minute, it carries over into the rest of your presentation.

So as you prepare to begin and think about your content, focus only on how you're going to open up the presentation, how you're going to kick it off and get the audience's attention. You want to be feeling right about that first minute, and if you do, it'll fill you with confidence and give you the excitement you need to get up and go. Plus, once you nail that first minute, all the ideas you want to share will flow much more easily as you get into your presentation.

POWER PLAY #34
Focus on Them, Not You

Right before your presentation, are you thinking more about your audience, or about yourself? If you're thinking about yourself and how you're going to do, you can expect to feel nervous. Nervousness is actually a selfish emotion, because it comes from worrying too much about yourself. So what's the cure? One of best is to **put your energy and focus on your audience.** When you focus on them, you calm down. Every one of us does our very best when we feel that we're helping others. We rise to the occasion, and it makes us feel good. So one tip to make sure you feel your best is to look out at the audience before you begin speaking and remind yourself to give them everything you've got.

POWER PLAY #35
All You Can Do is Your Very Best

I only have one hard and fast rule when it comes to giving presentations: I have to give my very best. It's the same rule I had when I was a football player in high school and college. Most of the time, giving it all you have will be more than enough, but some of the time you'll give it all you have and still fall short. In my book that's okay, because you did your very best.

There were a few football games where I played my heart out and our team still lost, but to be honest with you, I still felt good. It wasn't the same feeling I would have had if we had won, but there was a sense of satisfaction in knowing I left everything I had on the playing field. That's the same feeling you should have when you give a presentation. **You've got to give it everything you have!** To do this, you have to be willing to exert a level of effort beyond what most presenters are willing to give.

The fact of the matter is that somebody is going to have to work hard during your presentation. Either your audience will have to work hard because you're not putting enough effort and energy into your presentation to make it interesting, or you'll have to work hard to keep them engaged. The reality, though, is that no audience is interested in working hard. If you're not giving it everything you've got, they will tune out. So there's really only one choice. It's got to be you. You've got to give it everything you have and then see where the chips fall. Even if you fall short, you have the satisfaction of knowing you gave all you had, and you'll be able to learn from what you did and get even better for your next presentation.

POWER PLAY #36
Outcome, Identity Statement, Four, Three, Two, One

You've read about several mental and emotional preparation techniques, so now I'll help you put them together in a routine you can use time after time to achieve spectacular results. All great performers have a routine that helps them consistently be at their very best, and you should have one, too. "Outcome, Identity Statement, Four, Three, Two, One" is a routine that makes getting ready for your presentation a simple process.

- **Start with a "6-2-7" clearing breath.** (Power Play #24)

- **Then, focus on your *outcome*.** In this step you simply focus on the outcome you have for your presentation. Remember to see the outcome as already accomplished. You want to make sure that you remind yourself why you're there: not just to deliver a presentation, but to deliver a presentation that moves your audience to action and achieves your outcome.

- **Next, remind yourself of your *identity statement*.** This is the two-part statement that describes your strength that will allow you to be great and what you will accomplish. (Power Play #25)

- **Next, focus on *four* optimal performance thoughts.** Remember, these are the powerful thoughts that help you accomplish your outcome. Thoughts are going through your head all day, but now is the time to choose the perfect thoughts to put in your mind. (Power Play #26)

• **Then, focus on the *three* optimal performance emotions.** Tap into the feelings you must have to deliver your best presentation. (Power Play #27)

• **Now, fire off your top *two* superchargers.** Your superchargers will give you an instant burst of energy and confidence. (Power Play #28)

• **Finally, focus on the first *one* minute of your presentation, your miracle minute.** With this, you know how you're going to kick off the presentation, and you're feeling ready to go. (Power Play #32)

• **End your preparation with one more "6-2-7" clearing breath.** (Power Play #24) Before every single presentation, I use "Outcome, Identity Statement, Four, Three, Two, One," and it works like magic. I recommend that you print a sheet or card that has your identity statement, four optimal performance thoughts, three optimal performance emotions, and two superchargers written on it. These should be the same from presentation to presentation. The parts that might change will be the outcome and the miracle minute, as these could vary depending upon your audience. In addition to the printed card, I also write down my outcome and a thought or two for my miracle minute. It's easy for me, even in the midst of chaos, to be able to go over my mental game plan in just a few short minutes because it's become so routine. You should be able to do this, too. But if there's too much distraction in the place where you're waiting before a presentation, don't be afraid to leave the room and go to a quieter place if you need to. Do whatever works best for you, but I can't recommend the "Outcome, Identity Statement, Four, Three, Two, One" process strongly enough.

POWER PLAY #37
Tap Into the Power of Your Subconscious Mind

I'm always on the lookout for the latest and greatest techniques for increasing performance. Several years ago I began experimenting with self-hypnosis and I experienced the awesome power of being able to tap into my subconscious mind and reprogram it to help me achieve success faster and easier.

If the word "hypnosis" makes you think of staged magic shows or mind control, don't worry. It's actually a powerful technique for creating new habit patterns that's being used by doctors, therapists, and consultants with great success. People use it in dental surgery or during childbirth to reduce pain, and when trying to change habits like smoking or overeating. It's also a great took for becoming a better public speaker.

You don't need a magician in a long black cloak to hypnotize you—you can do it all by yourself. Self-hypnosis simply means you move yourself into a trance-like state of focused concentration and deep relaxation, which allows you greater access to the subconscious mind, which is where many of our unhealthy and unhelpful habit patterns live. You can use muscle relaxation, breathing control, sound, or imagery to create the hypnotic state.

When I started experimenting with self-hypnosis, I was so excited by my results that I wanted to create a product that other people could use to accelerate their success as presenters. I found a man by the name of Dr. Paul Scheele, who had come up with a process that could take my ideas on presenting and put them into a hypnotic audio recording that helped people relax and reprogram their subconscious with ease. Together we created the CD, *Talking To Win*. All this technique requires is that you take a few minutes in a quiet setting and listen to the *Talking To Win* audio recording with a set of headphones. The results of the people who have used *Talking To Win* consistently has been outstanding. If you would like to obtain a copy of *Talking To Win,* you can order it now at http://tommccarthy.com/success-store/parliminal-cds/.

PART TWO SUMMARY:
Feel Like a Winner!

POWER PLAY #16: Feel Like You're on a Mission
Remember a time when you felt motivated to do whatever it took to succeed. Capture that feeling and bring it into every presentation, and you'll be unstoppable.

POWER PLAY #17: It All Starts with Connection
Connection with your customer is the most powerful core emotion you can have in communication—combine connection with passion or confidence, and the result is magical.

POWER PLAY #18: You Determine How You Feel
Don't look to the audience to make you feel good. It is your job to make sure you feel great and then deliver your presentation with an energy that changes how the audience feels.

POWER PLAY #19: Feel Great for Every Presentation
Make no excuses based on circumstances. Hold yourself to the highest standards and commit to feel great for every presentation.

POWER PLAY #20: Prepare Like an Athlete
Just like an athlete, presenters must perform under pressure, so warm up your body by stretching, and warm up your mind by visualizing success.

POWER PLAY #21: Cancel Thoughts You Don't Want

Take control of the negative thoughts that inhibit peak performance by immediately saying to yourself, "Cancel thought!" and then replacing it with a corresponding positive thought.

POWER PLAY #22: Interrupt Poor Mental Patterns

When your mental system is not performing well, reboot it by making a radical physical or mental shift, like jumping up and down or shouting, "Yes!"

POWER PLAY #23: Use Your Power Move

Engaging your whole body in a powerful gesture can create an instant increase in energy and get you emotionally ready to do your presentation.

POWER PLAY #24: Breathe Your Tension Away

A simple 6-2-7 clearing breath before your presentation can lower your heart rate and blood pressure and ease the unhealthy tension in your body.

POWER PLAY #25: Change Your Identity

Create an identity statement that will pull you to new heights as a presenter.

POWER PLAY #26: Think Your Very Best Thoughts

Open yourself up to growth by leaving yesterday's limiting thoughts behind and asking yourself, "If I knew that my presentation went perfectly, what would I be thinking?" Think at least four of these optimal performance thoughts before every presentation!

POWER PLAY #27: Feel Your Very Best Emotions

The audience will feel whatever you feel, so discover your own top three optimal performance emotions and practice being able to create them instantly.

POWER PLAY #28:Use Your Superchargers

Discover which short phrases provide instant energy for you and say them emphatically before you begin your presentation.

POWER PLAY #29: Get on the Friends and Family Plan

Overcome the discomfort and negative feelings that you project to an audience full of strangers by imagining that the audience is full of friends and family.

POWER PLAY #30: It's Just a "Presensation"

Give your presentations as if you were having a wonderful conversation with a group of coworkers or friends, and you will be "presensational"!

POWER PLAY #31:Visualize Your Audience Below

Imagine your audience sitting on a lower level. This will give your brain the feeling that you are helping your audience and have something to share with them.

POWER PLAY #32: Be in the Now

Focusing on the past tends to bring to mind our failures, and focusing on the future tends to cause anxiety. Right before your presentation, focus on the here and now.

POWER PLAY #33: The Miracle Minute

During the first sixty seconds of your presentation, it is crucial that you build momentum with your audience, so in the moments before a presentation you should focus mostly on how you think and feel, and how you are going to open your presentation.

POWER PLAY #34: Focus on Them, Not You

Right before your presentation, shift your focus off yourself and your nervousness and onto your audience and how much your presentation is going to help them.

POWER PLAY #35: All You Can Do Is Your Very Best

If you give your presentation everything you have, even if it doesn't go well you have the satisfaction of knowing you did your best.

POWER PLAY #36: Outcome, Identity Statement, Four, Three, Two, One

Combine Power Plays #24, #25, #26, #27, #28 and #32 into one technique by focusing first on the outcome of your presentation, then on your identity statement, then on four optimal performance thoughts, then on three optimal performance emotions. Fire off two superchargers, and lastly focus on the on the first one minute of your presentation.

POWER PLAY #37: Tap Into the Power of Your Subconscious Mind

Use the self-hypnosis audio *Talking To Win* to reprogram yourself to become an outstanding presenter.

PART THREE:
Energize Your Audience

Mohandas K. Gandhi had it. John F. Kennedy had it. Martin Luther King, Jr. had it. Mother Teresa had it. Ronald Reagan had it. Oprah Winfrey has it. Bill Clinton has it. Colin Powell has it.

And you have it, too! What am I talking about? *Charisma.* Even if you've never felt it, I guarantee you've got charisma buried inside of you. And I want to show you how you can get it out. First, let's take a look at what charisma really is.

Charisma = Presence + Power + Warmth

Once you understand this charismatic equation, you can begin to tap into it. I've never met former President Bill Clinton, but I know several people who have and whether they cared for his politics or not, all their stories are similar. They talk about being in a crowd, yet when they exchanged even a few words with Clinton, they felt as if the two of them were the only people in the room. They said he had a way of making them feel important: **he looks you right in the eye** as he talks to you and you talk to him. He's **not distracted** by anything going on around him. You can feel his *presence*, which is the first component of charisma, by the way he maintains eye contact. He also uses his voice qualities, like tonality, pace, and volume, along with his body language, like gestures and facial expressions, to communicate. People who use their **full range of voice qualities and body language** to communicate give off an aura of *power*, which is the second component of charisma. Finally, Clinton comes across as if he's **talking with a long-time friend**, even when he's meeting someone for the first time.

Because of this, the person he's with feels his *warmth*, the third component of charisma.

There you have it: all you have to do is work on being more present, more powerful, and warmer whenever you communicate. This third section of the book is filled with tips and techniques that will allow you to be more present, amplify your power, and be warmer with people during your presentations. I know they work, not only because they work for me, but also because they've worked for thousands of people just like you whom I've had the privilege of teaching. Growing up, I was probably the least charismatic person you'd ever meet. So if I can learn how to bring out my charisma, I know you can learn to do it, too.

POWER PLAY #38
Start Before You Start

Is there a way to warm yourself up for your presentation so that you can ease into your presentation almost effortlessly? Yes, there is: As I mentioned in Power Play #4, you can "start before you start" by engaging in conversations with people in your audience *before* your actual presentation. Before most presentations, the average presenter is completely wrapped up in PowerPoint or making sure the projector works, and they end up separating themselves from the audience. The net result of this is that they start their presentations without much of a connection to their audience.

If, on the other hand, you greet people in your audience, ask them questions about themselves, and create a warm conversation, it leads you into your presentation with a ready- made connection. **Because you've engaged them in a private conversation, they already feel receptive to you.** They're much more likely to listen to you and maybe even care about you. In addition, you'll feel better about them. They're not just nameless faces. These are people who've shaken your hand, and you've learned a little bit about them through your conversations. Since your presentation is really just a conversation, these conversations before your presentation lead you perfectly into having extended conversations with them throughout your presentation. (And as we learned in Part One, it also empowers you to tell a great story.)

Bonus: start before you start not only with live audiences, but also in webinars. With webinars, you're not literally shaking hands, but when participants log on, you can notice their names and start a conversation with them. This is a powerful technique, because most people who participate in webinars immediately put themselves on mute and start multitasking. When you engage them in a conversation, it changes their behavior and makes them much more likely to engage with you.

POWER PLAY #39
Create a Series of Connected Conversations

Instead of trying to talk to your whole audience at once, pick one person at a time to focus on and imagine you are having a conversation with him or her. Do this again and again throughout your presentation, and you'll do the single most important thing for engaging your audience: creating a series of "connected conversations." This is the Holy Grail! If you do this one right, you can't help but have charisma.

When you do create a series of connected conversations, you change from being a scripted presenter into a person who seems totally at ease, comfortable with your content and your audience. If you've ever seen a presenter who seems completely natural and confident in front of an audience, I can guarantee that he or she has been using this technique and talks to just one person at a time. If you've done the opposite, and tried to talk to an entire group without connecting with an individual, you already know how extremely unnatural it feels. We human being just aren't built for that! Our eyes are meant to focus on one person as we speak, and our nervous systems respond to and feed off their body language. So when you're speaking to an audience of any size, you want to be like a waiter at a table in a restaurant. A waiter focuses on one person and takes the first order. After the connection is made and the order is taken, the waiter goes to the next person, and so on, and so on.

How long should you stay with each person? There is no hard and fast rule, but most presenters don't stay long enough.

The ideal timeframe is about five or six seconds. You want to be there long enough to make a connection, but not so long that other people feel neglected. One of the things that happens when you get into connected conversations is that you break your audience down to a manageable size: one! Then one by one, you start pulling them into your presentation.

Many years ago in Australia, I was doing a five-city speaking tour over the course of six days. The first three engagements in Perth, Brisbane, and Sydney had gone exceedingly well, but in Melbourne, we hit a snag. I was scheduled to speak for two hours, with another presenter preceding me who was scheduled to speak for thirty minutes. At this event, the person speaking before me didn't connect with the audience, and they didn't warm up to him at all. This speaker became uncomfortable, and rather than finish his thirty-minute presentation, he caught me by surprise and ended it about ten minutes early.

He introduced me when I thought I still had several minutes before it was my turn, but what could I do? I quickly got up on the stage and started speaking without any time to prepare. Like the speaker before me, I had zero connection with the audience, especially after I'd seen how unresponsive they'd been to him. After two or three minutes, I could see they weren't responding to me, either. To be honest, though, it wasn't their fault. I was speaking a million miles an hour, and—you guessed it—I was trying to talk to all of them at the same time.

Then I remembered my golden rule of creating a series of connected conversations. So I looked at one gentleman in the fourth row, and I started talking to him. As I did, I could see him nodding at what I was saying. I then looked at someone to my left in the twentieth row and had a conversation with that person. Then I found someone to my right in the very first row, and I talked to that person for a few seconds. As I did this, I could feel myself settling down and creating a powerful flow. The more connected conversations I created, the more my audience started responding to me. They went from being a distant group of disinterested strangers to being people I'd love to speak with every day of the year.

The power to connect begins with one person and builds from there into a series of connected conversations. When you're using this technique, you don't want to be too predictable, though. If there are six people sitting at a table, you don't want to start with the person closest to you and then work your way around. That's boring. Mix it up. Connect with someone to your right. Then talk to someone in the middle. Then you can go over to your left. **The key is to be in the moment and be inclusive.** In small groups like this, try to connect with everyone. In larger groups, you'll want to divide the room into sections. You probably won't end up talking to every individual person, but you'll be looking at one person in a section, and everyone sitting around that person will think you're talking to them.

I can't stress the importance of this technique enough, and the beautiful thing is that you can practice it all day long. You don't have to wait for a presentation! You can practice it with your family at dinner. (Just be careful, though; your spouse or children might get a little freaked out that you're actually making eye contact with them!) All you need is a couple of people. Just remember to look them in the eye and, in a caring way, share an idea with them. The more you do it, the more comfortable you'll get with it, and then it will become easy to bring this technique into every presentation.

POWER PLAY #40
Catch and Release

I'm not much of a fisherman, but I do know what *catch and release* means. You aren't angling to bring home the fish but instead to catch it, reel it in, and then let it go. This is a good metaphor for what you want to do when you're having a series of connected conversations with your audience. When you make eye contact with someone in your audience, it's similar to casting your fishing line and setting a hook. Once you set the hook, you want to make sure you reel them in. **In other words, you want to solidify the connection.** Once that connection is solid and you know you've brought them into the conversation, you can release them and go create your next connection. Even though you've let go of eye contact with them, the connection you built in that short conversation will continue as you move to the next person.

POWER PLAY #41
Get Them Smiling and Laughing

A couple months ago, my son had committed to getting his homework done at a certain time, and when I found out that he'd been playing on his computer instead, I was very upset and started to launch into a forceful lecture. I was building steam and getting more intense, trying to get my message across, and then all of a sudden he said something in a funny voice that made me laugh. I tried to recover and get back in my serious mood, but he got me again by saying in that same funny voice, "Dad, are you laughing?" When he said it, primarily because of the way he said it, it made me laugh again. He threw me off my game, and we ended up having a good discussion before he went on to finish his homework.

What had he done to me? He got a hostile audience, me, to totally change the way I was feeling. This allowed me to open up and have a great conversation with him. Smart boy! I use this technique with every audience, because it's true: **whether they're excited to hear you speak or not, if they're smiling and laughing, they'll be more open to what you have to say.** Sometimes you can get other people smiling just by smiling when you look at them. Other times you might need to inject some humor. I'm not saying you have to be a comedian, because I'm certainly not. But I do think of myself as playful and fun, which allows me to bring that energy to my audience. The last thing an audience wants to hear is an overly serious presentation. So if you can get them smiling and laughing, you're already halfway there to winning the persuasion game.

POWER PLAY #42
Remember the Cookie Rule

My brothers and I had the good fortune of growing up with a mother who was an amazing cook. I still remember one day when my two brothers and I were out playing, and Mom called out to us that she had just made chocolate chip cookies, one of her specialties. We immediately ran for the kitchen. I was the oldest, so I won the race to get the first cookie. And which one did I want? The biggest one, of course. But there was a slight problem. The biggest cookie was on the bottom, covered by smaller cookies. To get to my prized cookie, I touched a smaller cookie to move it out of the way. Unfortunately, my mom noticed this violation of the rules of etiquette; she pointed to the smaller cookie and asked if I had just touched it. She had seen me touch it, so the only thing I could do was admit to it. As soon as I did, she invoked the cookie rule.

She told me, "You touch it, you eat it."

It's the same with connected conversations. **Don't let your eyes fall on somebody and then immediately go somewhere else,** as if they weren't important enough to warrant your full attention. We want people in our audience feeling like the biggest, most desirable cookie, not the small one. So when your eyes connect with someone, stay there for a few seconds, finish the conversation, and then move on to your next conversation.

POWER PLAY #43
Look 'Em in the Eyes

The coach with the most wins in college basketball is Mike Krzyzewski, whose teams have won more than 940 games and four NCAA championships. In addition to that, he's led the USA basketball team to two Olympic gold medals! Coach Krzyzewski has only one rule for his players when it comes to communication: **when you're talking with people, you have to look them in the eye.**

When it comes to presenting, Krzyzewski's rule is critical. I don't mean just looking in their direction—I mean looking in their eyes! The difference between the two is extraordinary. When you simply look in someone's direction, there's no power or presence in your gaze. Conversely, when you look someone in the eye, your eyes light up, and your facial expressions come to life. It's as if your energy becomes magnified many times over. You can practice this in the conversations you have throughout the day and then remember to bring it into the connected conversations you have when you're giving your presentation.

POWER PLAY #44
Move With Purpose

If you heard the voice of a friend calling you from behind, what would you do? Would you continue in the direction you were headed, away from your friend? Of course not. That would be rude, and your friend would be offended. The polite and respectful thing to do is to turn around and walk toward your friend so you can have a conversation.

Well, guess what? This is the same thing you want to do when you're giving a presentation. I call it *movement with a purpose*. To create purposeful movement within your series of connected conversations, make eye contact with someone in the audience and then move in his direction until you find a comfortable place to stop and have a conversation with him. A simple way to remember this is to think, ***Look, then move.*** Let your eyes find the person you'll talk to, then move in his direction until you get to a place where you can have a friendly conversation with him.

This kind of movement is charismatic and increases the confidence you project to your audience. It even makes you feel more confident, because you're not wasting energy. Everything has a purpose. Movement with a purpose also helps you eliminate things like fidgeting or rocking that distract your audience and detract from your presentation. These go away because you're directing yourself purposefully into conversations, the same way you would when talking to a friend in an everyday setting.

POWER PLAY #45
Close the Gap

Next time you watch a presentation, notice how big the gap is between the presenter and the audience. From what I've observed, most people's comfort zone is several feet of separation from the front row of the audience. This may create a perceived "safety zone" for the presenter, but it can be disastrous for the presentation, because it creates a me-versus-you environment. The audience feels this way and so does the presenter. Put yourself in this situation, and they won't connect with you—and you'll feel disassociated from them. All in all, it's a bad situation.

The solution is simple, though. Close the gap. I'm not saying you should stand right on top of them or violate their personal space, but **stand at the same distance you would when talking with a friend, which is just a few feet away.** It may seem like a small thing—perhaps moving only two or three feet closer to your audience—but when you practice this technique, you'll feel completely different about them, and they'll feel differently about you, too.

So stop standing in the middle of the stage or back against the wall, and move closer to your audience. It's one of the quickest ways to increase your presence and charisma.

POWER PLAY #46
Get in the Handshake Position

To exude charisma, the way you stand is important. Check this out for yourself in front of a mirror: Pull your left foot back about six inches while keeping your right foot planted. Then lean back slightly and put most of your weight on your left foot, as if you're leaning away from the mirror a little bit. How do you come across? Now put both your feet right under you and stand straight up. How does that look? And last, put your right foot just in front of your left again, extend your right hand, and lean in slightly, as if you're going to shake someone's hand. Notice how that looks.

This last one is the handshake position, the ideal stance for any presenter when speaking to someone to the right or in the middle of the room. If you're speaking to someone on your left, you simply reverse your foot position and lean into your left foot.

How do friends talk with each other? By leaning back? No way! They lean in. That's what you want to do when you're talking to a person in your audience. It creates friendly energy that everyone will feel, including you. Plus, it will increase your confidence and even make it easier for your brain to function. Think of leaning backwards as putting on the brakes and leaning forward into the handshake position as stepping on the accelerator.

POWER PLAY #47
Vary Your Energy

There's one profession in which, to be successful, you have to master the art of speaking in a way that puts people to sleep. It's the profession of being a hypnotist. But when you're speaking to your audience, I'm sure the last thing you want to do is bore them or put them to sleep. Think about how hypnotists put people into a sleep state. They do it by talking at the same pace with the same tonality and virtually no body language. We call this speaking in a monotone, which means talking the same way for an extended period of time. When a person is exposed to too much of the same thing, the brain starts to tune out. Even if you're talking in an excited tone, if that's all you do, it will become boring after a while.

So how can you keep your audience engaged and keep them from ever being bored? Think just like the director of a television show. It doesn't matter what kind of show it is—comedy, drama, or even a sporting event—the director knows that every five seconds or so, they have to change the camera angle, or the audience gets bored. So if you're watching two people in a conversation on a TV show, the camera won't stay on the same shot the entire time. It might start focusing on two characters, but then it will shift to a close-up of one person's face, then go to the other, and then shift again in another five seconds.

You can do something similar in the way you communicate. Think about the tools you have to get your message across: You have your *content*, or the words you're going to say. You have your *voice qualities*, which are things like pace, volume, and tonality (We'll be focusing more on this tool in Power Play #51). And you have your *body language*, which includes facial expressions, gestures, posture, and movement (We'll take a closer look at how to activate this in Power Play #48). When you communicate, you use all of these things to get your message across. In studies on communication, it was determined that only 7 percent of what your audience picks up comes from the meaning of the words you say. Thirty-eight percent comes from the voice qualities you use when you're saying those words. And 55 percent comes from your body language. In fact, body language is so powerful that you can send a message with it without saying anything at all. (Think about the last time you cut someone off on the freeway, and they signaled you back with a powerful gesture. They were probably saying, "I love you!")

Use your words, voice qualities, and body language in a way that a fascinating storyteller would. Great storytellers have a way of creating variety in the way they communicate. When appropriate, they may talk fast and loud and use expansive gestures and quick movement. Visually, they have high energy. But great storytellers also have the ability to use a more moderate pace and volume, with gentler gestures and facial expressions. Finally, storytellers can also speak in an intentionally muted volume and tonality, with even softer facial expressions and gestures, when it fits the story.

Everyone has a preferred modality, the one that makes them most comfortable both for listening and speaking. For instance, when I'm not giving a presentation, my energy tends to be moderate. Other people I know are extremely high energy. They always seem to be talking a mile a minute. And I also know people who are much more careful in their speech, taking their time to communicate what they're saying. It really doesn't matter what your normal style is, because I guarantee you can "turn on" all three.

The key is not to fall into the trap of using just one. To add color to your story, you have to be able to communicate with high, moderate, and muted energy. This will bring vibrancy to your story, and it makes it even more fun to be a storyteller. If you've ever read a story to a child, you know that you need to vary your voice and body language to make it interesting. The minute you stop doing that, the child either becomes bored or falls asleep, and your audience is the same way. So remember to mix up the energy by changing your voice qualities and your body language. The good news is that the more you can lose yourself in the telling of the story, the more naturally you'll be able to vary your energy and fully captivate your listeners.

POWER PLAY #48
Wake Up Your Body Language

How lively is your body language when you're delivering a presentation? How expressive is your face? Do your gestures engage people as you tell your story? Remember, your body language comprises 55 percent of your communication, so you'll want to do your best to wake it up and get it fully into the game.

If you need help figuring out how to do this, think of someone you know who's an expert at telling stories. How do they use their facial expressions and gestures? Do they look like they're forcing it, or are they naturally expressing themselves? Great storytellers are able to naturally use their body language, because they're fully invested in the story. You can be like this, too! What keeps most people from using their body language in powerful ways is that they become too self-conscious and hold back, which immediately puts the brakes on their ability to communicate.

One thing you should do before every presentation is warm up your body language. You don't want any tension in your body. I recommend you actually **spend some time stretching your body and even your face.** You might laugh if you saw me getting ready for a presentation. In a secluded place where no one can see me, I'm contorting my face and flapping my arms and making sure I get as much tension out of my body as possible, because I know that when I let go and fully engage my body language, it magnifies the power of my message. I'm not saying you have to go through my crazy routine of waking my body up, but if you want to be outstanding, you'll have to figure out your own special way to get your body language in the game.

POWER PLAY #49
Use Your Eyes to Tell a Story

Over the years, I've taught thousands of people the importance of not just looking people in the eye (Power Play #39), but using their eyes to tell a story. This is a critical component of your communication because your eyes, maybe even more than any other part of your body, tell a story. **When you watch someone speak, you can hear what she is saying, but if you watch her eyes, her story truly comes to life.** If a presenter has dull, lifeless eyes, it really doesn't matter what she's saying, because no one will really hear it. On the other hand, when a speaker has lively, sparkling eyes, people will listen all day long.

To make sure your eyes are ready, have a conversation or two before your presentation, and imagine that there is energy being transferred to the other person through your eyes. Open your eyes wide, and use them to deliver your message. When you do this, your eyes will start to come alive. The eyes are one of the biggest factors in transferring energy from you to your audience, so go into every presentation with your eyes wide open and full of energy.

POWER PLAY #50
Your Mouth Forms the Words

Arthur Joseph, one of the most famous voice coaches in Hollywood, often gives his clients this startling piece of advice: *use your mouth to form the words you are saying*. Okay, that may sound obvious, but when the average person talks, the words just tumble out of their mouths. Yet when a masterful presenter talks, it's as if the mouth takes on a life of its own. **The tongue and the lips actively work to bring life to each word.**

Try saying the following sentence the way you normally talk: *The sunset magically turned from orange to pink as it danced along the sky over the ocean.* Now, say it again while consciously focusing on using your mouth to form the words.

From your audience's perspective, two things happen when you consciously use your mouth to form the words: one is that your speech becomes clearer to them, and the other is that they are able to receive a greater amount of energy and power from you. This is a technique you can practice all day long and in every conversation.

POWER PLAY #51
Vary Your Voice

There are so many ways to vary your voice. You can vary your pace. You can vary your volume. You can vary your tonality. The key to varying your voice is to make it sound natural and conversational.

I've seen people do it in ways that seem rehearsed, almost like a canned presentation, which almost certainly will backfire on you. So how can you vary your voice in a way that sounds like it's really you? I was definitely not a natural at this when I first started. I had to study it. I remember watching a friend of mine, who is an amazing storyteller, and his voice seemed to naturally change in pace, volume, and tonality as he told his stories. I was so jealous! I thought his skill would be unattainable for me. By contrast, when I told stories, I remember seeing people's eyes glaze over because my voice was stuck in the same pace, the same volume, and the same tonality. In effect, I was hypnotizing them. I didn't know if I could make the change back then, but I committed myself to working on it. To be honest, it didn't feel great right away, but I began consciously working on varying my voice in every story. Rather than being stuck in monotone mode, I'd focus on speaking faster and louder when I was telling the part of a story that had some excitement to it. I also would bring my volume, pace, and tonality down when the story called for it. After a while, I became more and more comfortable with the new variety of speaking modes I was practicing.

For you to master varying your voice, it's going to take practice. But don't wait for your next presentation to practice. **Practice at the dinner table tonight with your family or at**

lunch tomorrow with your coworkers. Sure, it's going to feel weird if you're not used to doing it, but think about this. When you vary your voice and create more variety in the way that you bring your message across, you're not really doing it for you—you're doing it for your listener. You're giving them a beautiful gift, the gift of you at your best when you're communicating with them.

POWER PLAY #52
You Better Be Enjoying it

Is it possible for your audience to enjoy listening to your presentation when you're not enjoying *giving* the presentation? I don't think so. If you're not enjoying it, they're going to pick that up, and they won't enjoy it, either. So remember your mental preparation (see Part Two), and **program yourself to enjoy giving your presentation.** When I watch presenters, the telltale signs of whether they're enjoying themselves are their facial expressions. Are they friendly? Are they smiling? If so, there's no doubt they're enjoying their own presentations.

I genuinely hope this book has made the point that a presentation simply means talking to people in your audience the same way you'd talk with a friend. And that's certainly something you should be enjoying! Stop thinking of giving a presentation as something you have to dread. Start thinking of it as your opportunity to help people with an idea, product, or service that can improve the quality of their lives. And most importantly, start thinking of it as something that you'll love doing—a win-win for you and your audience. Now that's something we can all look forward to!

PART THREE SUMMARY:
Energize Your Audience

POWER PLAY #38: Start Before You Start

Before your presentation begins, engage members of the audience in private conversation, and you will find that the audience already feels receptive to you when you begin your presentation.

POWER PLAY #39: Create a Series of Connected Conversations

Instead of trying to talk to the whole audience at once, look just one person in the eyes and pretend you are having a personal conversation for five or six seconds, then move to another person in another part of the room. Try to do this with every person in the room, and your presentation will become a series of connected conversations.

POWER PLAY #40: Catch and Release

As you are creating a series of connected conversations, solidify your connection with each individual and make sure you have drawn them into the conversation before you release them and move on to someone else.

POWER PLAY #41: Get Them Smiling and Laughing

Be playful and fun. An audience that is smiling and laughing will be much more open to what you have to say.

POWER PLAY #42: Remember the Cookie Rule

If you make eye contact with a person, stay with them until you finish the conversation, or you will make that person feel like you are sifting through the small cookies looking for the big cookie.

POWER PLAY #43: Look 'Em in the Eyes
Follow Coach Mike Krzyzewski's only rule of communication and look people in the eyes when you talk to them.

POWER PLAY #44: Move with Purpose
Look, then move. After you make eye contact with someone, move naturally and purposefully in their direction until you find a comfortable place to stop and finish your conversation.

POWER PLAY #45: Close the Gap
Move closer to your audience to create a personal connection. Aim to be as close as you would be if you were talking to a friend, which is just a few feet away.

POWER PLAY #46: Get in the Handshake Position
Lean in when you talk to your audience, as if you were about to shake their hands. Think of leaning back as putting the brakes on your presentation, and leaning forward as stepping on the accelerator.

POWER PLAY #47: Vary Your Energy
Vary your content, voice qualities, and body language throughout your presentation, and combine those changes in a way that a fascinating storyteller would.

POWER PLAY #48: Wake Up Your Body Language
Spend some time stretching your body, even your face, so that you will feel comfortable using the full range of body language during your presentation.

POWER PLAY #49: Use Your Eyes to Tell a Story

Have a conversation or two before your presentation and imagine there is energy being transferred to the other person through your eyes. Then go into your presentation with your eyes wide open and full of energy.

POWER PLAY #50: Your Mouth Forms the Words

Rather than just letting the words tumble out, consciously bring each word to life by actively forming the words with your tongue and lips.

POWER PLAY #51: Vary Your Voice

Vary the pace, volume, and tonality of your voice. Practice this in your normal conversations with people until it feels natural.

POWER PLAY #52: You Better Be Enjoying It

If you are not enjoying your presentation, you can bet that your audience isn't either. Use all of these Power Plays to program yourself to enjoy giving presentations!

CONCLUSION

I hope that you have found the ideas and techniques in this book helpful. They represent some of the best advice I have found in helping people become superstar presenters. Do you need to master every single one of these Power Plays to win the presentation game? Of course not. Find a couple that resonate with you and master them. One thing I would caution you against, though, is only picking those that come easy for you. Sometimes the techniques that are the hardest and most uncomfortable for you will create the most dramatic results.

As I stated at the beginning of the book, I am absolutely certain that YOU can become an outstanding presenter. I may not know you personally, but I know what you're made of and I know the potential you have inside of you. Your version of greatness may not look exactly like someone else's, but it will still be great.

Thank you for taking this journey with me and I hope that I can continue to help you on your journey to being the best you can be.

In everything you do, don't just settle. Live Your Dreams!

ACKNOWLEDGMENTS

Tom McCarthy: When I was six years old I was standing too close to my five-year-old brother, who was swinging a golf club, and on his follow-through the club hit me square in the mouth. There wasn't much flesh damage, but the golf club chipped my right front tooth down to the root. My father was an Army officer who had been killed in Vietnam a couple of years earlier, so Mom, me, and my two brothers were subsisting on a small government pension. Needless to say, expensive cosmetic dentistry was not in our budget. So my mom took me to an Army dentist who sealed the root and put a gold band around the tooth. Nowadays, it might be hip to have a gold tooth (I think they're called grills), but for a little, self-conscious six-year-old, it was devastating. When I look back at my school pictures, I was never smiling, and I was terrified to even open my mouth and talk. Now I make a living by getting up and speaking in front of crowds large and small, but I couldn't have done it without several people who helped that six-year-old boy with a gold front tooth transform into a more confident and charismatic communicator.

The first person I would like to thank is my mom, Berenice McCarthy, who passed away in 2002. My mom believed in me way more than I believed in myself when I was young, and her confidence and love inspired me to think big. She was also an expert at putting me in situations where I had to step up and become more confident.

Growing up, I idolized my grandfather, Charles McCarthy. He was an amazing storyteller and enthralled me with stories about his experiences with Franklin Roosevelt, Harry Truman, Dwight Eisenhower, and Winston Churchill during World War II. His stories were fascinating, and he used his whole voice and body to make them come to life.

I first saw Tony Robbins speak at a seminar when I was twenty-four. He blew me away with the way he energized the entire audience, including me. I thought there was no way I could ever do anything like that, but with his support I learned how to use some of the techniques he had mastered. He showed me that miracles are possible when a presenter is truly connected with their audience.

I met Brandy Weld at a seminar I was teaching in Newport, Rhode Island, and she mentioned that she thought I could help the company she was working for, Cisco Systems. Brandy brought me into Cisco Systems and helped launch a major opportunity for our FIRE-UP Your Presentations training.

David Hutchison has been a friend of mine since the seventh grade. Little did I know back then that we would be in business together so many years later. David is a superstar presenter whom audiences absolutely love, and his energy and commitment inspire me daily.

I was having dinner with author and speaker Jack Canfield one night when he asked me what percentage of the average book did I consider memorable and usable. I think I said 20 or 25 percent and then I asked him what he thought. He responded that in his opinion only 15 percent of the average book was truly memorable and if that were the case then only that 15 percent needed to be written. That has stuck through me over the years and in this book I tried to pare down what I wrote to only the most important and memorable things I could share with you. Only you can be the judge of whether I succeeded or not, but I am grateful to Jack for his sound advice.

My wife Stacy probably didn't know what she was getting herself into when she married me back in August 1991. With my job I am often traveling, which leaves her at home taking care of kids, animals, and everything else while building her own successful business (www.yoganamastacy.com) in the health, fitness, and yoga industries. Her love and support have been essential in any success I've achieved and I am immensely proud of her and her amazing success as a mother and businessperson. I am so fortunate to have her as my wife, partner, and best friend.

One of the mental tricks I used to use to inspire myself when I was giving a presentation was to imagine that my children, Kylie and Tommy, were in the back of the room watching me. My goal was to perform at a level where to them I would be an example of someone playing full out and giving his very best. I feel like my most important job is being the best father I can be, and I love my children more than words can say. My daughter Kylie was initially very shy like I was as a child, but she has matured into a wonderful, confident young lady who is going to make a huge impact on the world. My son Tommy has always had the energy and charisma that I wish had come more naturally for me. Every day he's becoming more and more of a leader, and he has a spectacular future ahead of him.

David Hutchison: My parents were my first role models and teachers on public speaking. As a child I vividly remember my dad giving military briefings or volunteering as a lector for Sunday mass. He was brilliant at taking content and making it fascinating by varying his delivery. He is so engaging that he pulls you into his story and moves you to act by his energizing delivery. My mom is the best on how to connect and build rapport with your audience, when she walks into a room of strangers she instantly connects with everyone with her warm heart and smile. My parents both played a large part in developing my confidence as a child by feeding me stories like "I can do anything that I set my mind to", "there is no such thing as the word can't", "you are going to do great things", and many more...

In business my first role model as an outstanding presenter

is Tony Robbins. He is probably one of, if not, the best dynamic speaker on stage. I was so blown away by his charisma and energy while watching him at a seminar in 1987 that I went to work with him after I graduated from college.

I have known Tom McCarthy for over 40 years. He has played a large part in influencing me as a man because of the high standards he sets and achieves for himself. He is a quality individual in all areas of his life and an inspiration to be around. Tom is an impact player and I also credit him for taking my presentation game to another level. He is more than a great friend and business partner, he is a brother!

My brothers Bill, Mike, and John are my biological brothers and best friends. No matter where we are or what is going on in each of our lives, we always make it a point to connect. We are always there for each other and I am blessed to have them in my life.

My loving wife Lisa has been at my side since June 1994 and that is something to marvel at because that's not easy with my schedule. I have flown well over a 100,000 miles a year the entire time we have been married, with no stopping in the near future. Thank you for your love and support, I could not do what I do without you. I'm very proud of my daughters Kristin and Rachel— they are amazing women. Their talents are immense and they are destined for greatness.

To all of you, thank You and I love you very much!

ABOUT THE AUTHORS

For more than two decades as a corporate consultant, speaker, author, trainer, and coach, *Tom McCarthy* has successfully taught hundreds of thousands of people how to dramatically increase their level of performance in business and life. He has presented more than 1,500 seminars, workshops, and training programs to corporations and associations in more than twenty countries around the world. Tom's seminars and books have been translated into ten languages.

Tom not only speaks about success in business; he's lived it. After graduating from the University of North Carolina in 1983, where he was a member of the nationally ranked football team, Tom became the youngest stockbroker ever hired by a prestigious Wall Street firm. By his second year there, Tom had become one of the highest producing brokers in the entire firm.

In 1986, when one of the country's largest training organizations was looking for a leader to coach, energize, and train the Robbins Research sales force, Anthony Robbins chose Tom McCarthy. As its first National Sales Trainer and National Sales Manager, Tom provided leadership, management, and training, more than doubling the company's sales each year. Tom then became one of the first people Anthony Robbins personally selected to lead his prestigious Mastery University seminars.

In 1993, Tom founded Thomas McCarthy & Associates, a thriving training and consulting firm, which works closely with clients ranging from new ventures to Fortune 500 companies. In addition to coaching and training peak performers in business, Tom has also worked with four Olympic Gold Medalists, as well as several World Champion athletes and teams.

Tom resides in Rancho Santa Fe, California, with his wife, Stacy, and their two children.

For over 20 years as an author, executive coach, professional speaker, strategic business catalyst, and trainer, *David Hutchison* has successfully helped thousands of people improve both their professional and personal lives. He has delivered seminars, and training programs to corporations, and individuals around the world.

David received his BA from the University of North Carolina in 1987. He began his career in personal development, professional training, and speaking when he joined Anthony Robbins Companies as the National Sales Director and Global Sales Trainer. While there, he led the company to record growth for 5 consecutive years and he was one of the principal instructors for Tony Robbins programs. He has also held several executive sales management positions with high tech companies where he helped them experience explosive growth and break all previous sales records.

He is currently a managing partner at FireUp Training & Development- a specialized training company that provides the highest quality, most useful and innovative training and coaching services that educate, challenge and inspire people. The training platform is based on decades of research, real world material and everything taught comes from years of experience and it's what he uses on a daily basis.

David is the author of the book "Speaking Mastery: 7 Keys to Delivering High Impact Presentations", and he is a certified professional behavioral (CPBA) & values analyst (CPVA).

David resides in La Costa, California, with his wife, Lisa, and their two children.

CPSIA information can be obtained
at www.ICGtesting.com
Printed in the USA
FFOW05n1115020717

9 780996 498906

Acknowledgments

Many thanks to

My husband, Frank

You encouraged me from the moment I
told you about this challenge.

My daughter, Jessica Kitts

You prompted and encouraged me, proofread, made corrections,
and walked this journey right beside me.

My sweet friend Adriane Lawrence

God used you to "prompt" me, more than once, to accept this
Challenge; then you too walked this year-long journey with me.

The Lord gave me each of you to walk this journey with me.
Without the three of you, this book would not exist.

Introduction

Do you set aside a certain time to meet with the Father each day? A "quiet" time devoted just for the two of you? There was a time I didn't. I guess I went with what you'd call the hit-and-miss method. If I woke up early enough, I'd have time with the Lord before work, and if I didn't, I'd try to have it sometime before going to bed that night. Needless to say, if I didn't wake up early enough to have that time before work, it usually didn't happen. I came to realize I would have to make an appointment with Him, much the same way I make appointments for other things that are important in life. I mean, nothing is more important than spending time with the Lord, right? For me, it means having that time in the morning, while the house is still quiet and the day hasn't even started waking up yet. I realized, for me to have that time every morning, it meant setting my alarm to wake me up, even after I retired!

I want to encourage you to make a daily appointment with the Father in this new year. You may not do well to make your appointment early in the morning. You need to pick the time that works best for you, whether it's morning, afternoon or evening. The time of day doesn't matter. *Making* the time is what matters. You may think you don't have time in your busy day. I get it, I understand. I once thought that way too. That is why I want to *challenge* you to make time and *encourage* you to set your appointment, show up for the appointment and watch as He begins to honor your commitment. I know, from personal experience, what a difference it makes and how He will see to it that you still have time for the other things you need to accomplish. Just remember—sometimes, the things we think we need to accomplish aren't the things He thinks we need to accomplish. I have also learned, over time and through personal experience, to let go of my agenda and be more open to His agenda and what He would have me accomplish each day.

At the end of 2018, God challenged me to let Him give me a devotion each morning for the upcoming year. It took me a few days to accept it, but I did accept it. I have always liked to encourage others, so I thought I could write something encouraging every day, and I figured it would get me into the Word deeper, as I search for things He wants to show me.

My prayer is for this collection of devotions to challenge, encourage and grow myself and anyone else reading them. Be forewarned though: as you allow Him to do this in you, you will find yourself moving out of your comfort zone and loving it, even though it is a little scary sometimes.

Don't panic. I'm with you. There's no need to fear
for I'm your God. I'll give you strength. I'll help you.
I'll hold you steady, keep a firm grip on you.

—*Isaiah 41:10 (MSG)*

January 1

Challenging Encouragement

One morning, as I was sitting at my desk having my quiet time with the Father, I saw a note I had jotted down—"Collection of Encouragement." I thought to myself, *Some days, it may be more challenging than encouraging*, and that is when I heard, "Sometimes, to be encouraged, you must first be challenged." Whoa! How powerful and true I have found that statement to be. As I was contemplating whether or not I was truly hearing from Him about writing my own devotions for the coming year, He sent me encouragement from several different avenues—friends, messages, scriptures, etc.

Let me encourage you to be sure you make time for listening in your time alone with Him. Pour your heart out to Him, give Him thanks and praise and make your requests known to Him—just don't forget to be quiet and listen for Him to respond to you. You may not feel Him speak to you every time. He may speak differently to you than He does to me. If you think you've never experienced Him speak to you, trust me, He will, and you will know (John 10:27). He will continue speaking the same message to you in different ways, as I mentioned above—friends, messages, scriptures, etc.

Sometimes, He will challenge you too. Decide now how you want to respond to those challenges. Do you always want to fight against them, or do you want to accept them and see what He does with your acceptance of them? Encouragement will come from or out of those challenges. He will never give you a challenge without a purpose. Sometimes, He may challenge you simply to see if you are willing and available to do something new for Him. No matter the reason for each challenge, His challenges will, ultimately, be to grow and stretch you beyond anything you ever thought you could do!

Today's Prayer

Father,

Please use these devotions this year not only to encourage us, but to challenge us as well. Help us learn to trust You, no matter what, and to rely only on Your Word.

Amen.

Trust the Lord and His mighty power. Worship Him always.

—1 Chronicles 16:11

January 2

New Perspective

I've noticed all the posts on social media the last few days about the coming new year and all the different goals for the new year and how some are ready to bid adieu to the old year and start fresh and new in the new year.

Normally, I'm one of those making that kind of post, but every time I would start to write something, I felt a stirring in my spirit, preventing me from writing anything. I believe it's because He was giving me a new perspective.

We get so caught up in all the hype of a new year and wanting to start fresh and new. We forget we don't have to wait for a new *year* to do that! We get a fresh, new start every morning, when God chooses to wake us from our sleep. If He wakes us, then He has a purpose for us that day. He wants us to join Him in doing something He has specifically chosen for us to help Him get done. His mercies are new and fresh every single morning!

So, if yesterday was a bad day for you, don't get caught thinking you have to wait until next week or next month or next year to start fresh—START FRESH TODAY! That's why God has granted you the precious gift of today! He wants to walk with you through today and shower you with His new mercies and grace for this day. He wants you to catch the new perspective of starting fresh and new every morning as He wakes you. Let's join Him and make the most of today! If we feel, at the end of the day, like we missed it or messed up or made a bad choice or two (or three or more), we know we can give it all to Him before we go to sleep and start fresh again the next day. So, HAPPY NEW DAY!

Today's Prayer

Father,

    May we all remember to treat each new, glorious morning as the gift it is from You and start fresh and new. May we give You praise and thanks each morning and look for the path You would have us take this day.

    Amen.

The steadfast love of the Lord never ceases; His mercies never come to an end; they are new every morning; great is Your faithfulness.

—Lamentations 3:22–23 (ESV)

January 3

Captive Thoughts

Just because you have a thought, doesn't mean it came from you, and it certainly doesn't mean it is true! We have thousands of thoughts every day that come from many different avenues. It's what we do with those thoughts that make a difference. We may not be able to control what thoughts come into our mind; however, we can choose what we do with them. We can invite them in to stay a while, or we can slam the door in their face! In the words of Martin Luther, "You can not keep birds from flying over your head; but, you can keep them from building a nest in your hair."

In order to slam the door in the face of thoughts the enemy throws at us (you know, those "fiery darts" talked about in Ephesians 6:16), we must stay in God's Word. Every thought you have, good or bad, is subject to what you choose to do with it. It is up to you to take every thought captive and make it obedient to Christ. Take every thought and compare it to scripture to see if it is truth or a lie from the devil.

It truly is easier than you think to deal with all the thoughts that assail us on, sometimes, a daily basis. I am attacked way too often with thoughts of not being "good enough" or "no one wants you around," "why do you think that person would want you as a friend?" and other such nonsense. I can say nonsense now because I have learned where such thoughts come from, and they don't line up with God's Word, so I refuse to dwell on them. They must answer to Christ, and when I take them to Him, He dismisses them—every. single. time! So, I encourage you to learn to do the same. Do not invite those unhealthy, false, lies-from-the-enemy thoughts in for a party—throw them out immediately!

Today's Prayer

Father,

No thought attacks us that You don't already know about before it happens. Help each of us to determine in our hearts to take every thought to Christ, our Savior, and make it obedient to Him before we accept it as truth.

Amen.

We destroy arguments and every lofty opinion raised against the knowledge of God and take every thought captive to obey Christ.

—2 Corinthians 10:5

January 4

Immediately

Anyone else, besides me, have a problem with that word? I can remember, as a child, my parents asking me to do something, and my response, probably 99 percent of the time, was "In a minute." That response was seldom met with approval from my parents. They would, inevitably, say something along the lines of "I didn't ask you to do it 'in a minute,' I told you to do it *now*." Anyone else relate to what I'm talking about?

How do you respond when God asks you to do something? Especially when He asks you to do something—horror of horrors—outside your comfort zone? Unfortunately for me, I have to admit, I am still not to the place where I immediately respond the way He would like me to respond. Instead, I tend to start asking a million, bazillion questions, including the all-time favorite: "Are You really asking *me* to do that, or is this thought coming from somewhere else?"

Recently, He put the word *immediately* in front of me three times in three different ways from three different people in one day! Do you think He was trying to tell me something? Yes! What could we release if we will ever allow Him to get us to the place where our *immediate*, automatic response is, "Yes, Lord. Here I am. Send me, use me"? Might He be able to use us in so many more ways to further His Kingdom and point more souls to Him than we could ever imagine? I believe the answer to that is *yes*! He doesn't need us, yet He chooses to allow us to join Him in His plan, if we are simply willing to join Him. Are you willing? Am I?

Today's Prayer

Father,

Please help us get to the place where, instead of questioning You, we simply say, as Isaiah did, "Here am I, Lord. Send me." Use us, Father, to shine the light of Jesus into this ever-darkening world. In the name of Jesus Christ of Nazareth. Amen.

And I heard the voice of the Lord saying, "Whom shall I send and who will go for us?" Then I said, "Here I am! Send me."

—Isaiah 6:8

January 5

When Anger Is Okay

I recently became aware of the mistreatment of an individual by the very people she should have been able to trust for help. She found herself in a scary situation, yet when she reported the incident to law enforcement, it was brushed off and not taken seriously.

The more I thought about the situation, the angrier I became, which led me to prayer. I was, literally, crying out to God, asking Him to help me stop feeling so angry, when He stopped me in my tracks! I immediately felt in my spirit a resounding *no*! What? Why would You not take away my anger, Father? "Because I want *you* to help fight this battle, and I want you to share with others that, sometimes, anger is okay." That was the answer I heard. Not in an audible voice, but in my spirit.

So I began to search His Word, and He led me to many places. Psalm 7:11 talks about the wrath of God, Mark 3:5 speaks of Jesus's anger, 2 Samuel 12 speaks of David's anger, and in Ephesians 4:26, He tells us, "In your anger do not sin." When we get angry over the mistreatment of others, it is not a sin. Jesus got angry over the sins of the people, but His anger was directed at the sinful behaviors and injustice. He gets angry at injustice, and it is okay for us to be angry at injustice too!

Remember to keep your anger directed at the injustice and not individuals. Bring the injustice to light and then let God handle it from there. Once brought to light, the mistreated individual (if that's the case) won't have to say a word. God will handle it His way—and He just might use *you* to help.

Today's Prayer

Father,

Please help us to learn the difference in righteous anger and just getting angry because of how someone treats us. Show us when we need to speak up and speak out against injustices and help us allow You to lead us in these situations.

Amen.

God will fight the battle for you. And you? You keep your mouths shut.

—Exodus 14:14 (The Message)

January 6

Leave Christ Out

Did she really just say that? Yes, I did, and I'll tell you why. Those are the words I heard from the Holy Spirit last night, just before bedtime. Yes, I believe God was speaking those words to me. Here's why.

Every December, maybe even earlier, we begin to feel all the joy that's in the air in anticipation of the coming of Christmas. Then, December comes and goes and, unfortunately, so do our joyful attitudes.

We go back to the daily grind of day-to-day living and seem to completely forget about everything we were just celebrating only days before. I admit I'm guilty of doing the same thing, but I'm also here to tell you, we can choose not to do that! Just because we have to get back to daily schedules and the busyness of daily life, doesn't mean we have to forget all the thankfulness and joy we were just feeling a few days ago.

Christmas doesn't have to be just a season for us. We can carry Christmas with us all year long. How? By choosing to remember the joy and excitement we felt. We feel that joy and excitement because of the One we were celebrating—not because of the time of year.

So, I say to you again, leave Christ out. When you put away all your Christmas decorations, which most of you probably already have, don't put Christ away with them. Leave Him out. Allow Him to continue to shine through you and shed His light into a world that is growing darker every day. Keep the joy and keep Christ as the center of everything you do. Try it—I bet you'll like it.

Today's Prayer

Father,

Please help us remember the reason for the joy of the season we just closed. Help us each remember to keep Jesus in our hearts and let His light shine, pointing others to You, in this dark world we live in.

Amen.

> *You are the light for the whole world. A city built on top of a hill cannot be hidden and no one lights a lamp and puts it under a clay pot. Instead, it is placed on a lampstand, where it can give light to everyone in the house. Make your light shine, so others will see the good you do and will praise your Father in Heaven.*

> *—Matthew 5: 14–16*

January 7

Unsearchable

Not long after my husband and I were married, the Lord led us to a verse in the Bible that He has continued to bring us back to many times since. In the version I read, there is a word He suddenly brought to my attention a few months back: *unsearchable*.

In the past, when talking with someone about the answer to something, I have said, "Hey, just Google it. Google knows everything." Now, we may find that funny in today's time; however, maybe I should have followed it up with, "But, seriously. Let's pray about it and see what God says." In this day of googling everything for answers, only God can give me—and you—the truly important answers!

Yes, Google is a wonderful thing, and, yes, it is a wonderful tool we can use. However, when it comes to the important things our Father wants us to know, He is the only search engine we need to come up with the correct answers. His answer isn't always what we want it to be—that's when we have to remember Isaiah 55:8, "For My thoughts are not your thoughts, neither are your ways My ways, declares the Lord."

So, for earthly answers, use the Google search engine. However, when it comes to matters of true importance in life, remember to use the *God* search engine. You may not always get the answer you want, but, then again, sometimes even Google doesn't give you the answer you want. Am I right? I can promise you this: the answer you get from God will *always* be the right answer because His plan for you is *always* the best plan!

Today's Prayer

Father,

Help us remember to always come to You for the answers we need. You are ever so faithful and will always show us Your way. Maybe not in our time and not how we would choose, but remind us we can trust Your timing and Your way to always be the best!

Amen.

*Call to Me and I will answer you and tell you great
and unsearchable things you do not know.*

—Jeremiah 33:3 (NIV)

January 8

For Giving

What are some things you like to give? Did your mind go immediately to some product or gadget? We are just coming out of a season of giving (and receiving), and it makes me wonder how many of us got caught up in giving tangible items—like the latest gadgets etc.—and how many of us remembered to give some of the greater, less-tangible gifts—like grace, mercy, kindness, goodness, love, caring?

Those nontangible gifts, in my opinion, are worth so much more than we could ever imagine. The effects of those gifts are far more reaching than our minds could ever imagine! They have the same effect as a small pebble that has been thrown into a lake—the ripples continue out far beyond where the pebble went in the lake.

What about forgiving—you know, one of those greater, less-tangible gifts? What does it mean to you? Have you ever thought much about the word *forgiving*? Honestly, I never had until I found myself writing the words "for giving" in my prayer journal one morning, and I just stopped! I've written those words many times before, but this time, God stopped me as soon as I wrote them! He spoke to my spirit: Forgiving isn't something we do for others. It is something we do *for giving* ourselves peace of mind! Forgiveness is not about the other person at all! When we choose to forgive someone, we are freeing ourselves from bondage, and who doesn't want to be free? The enemy can no longer use against us what we have chosen to forgive!

Remember, when we go to God and ask forgiveness for our sins, we can only receive that forgiveness if we have chosen to forgive.

Today's Prayer

Father,

You are the One that makes any forgiveness possible. We cannot forgive in our own strength, but with You, we can choose to forgive. Help us make the choice, daily, to forgive so we may be forgiven.

Amen.

Instead, be kind and merciful and forgive others,
just as God forgave you because of Christ.

—Ephesians 4:32

January 9

Building Walls

It seems everyone's minds are occupied with building walls lately, and this got me to thinking. In Bible times, city walls were built and usually included gates, watchtowers and a ditch around the outer perimeter of the wall, which could be filled with water. When I searched for "scripture about building walls," I found one article that had fifty-eight scripture references on the subject!

Think for a minute, though, about walls we build that aren't brick-and-mortar walls. Many of us tend to build walls around our hearts in an effort to keep from being hurt. We think we are protecting ourselves, but in reality, the opposite is true. We must not allow the enemy to convince us building walls like that are okay, because they are not!

However, Proverbs 4:23 tells us, "Above all else, guard your heart, for everything you do flows from it." So, how do we guard our hearts without building walls? I believe we build a wall of a different nature. I believe we are to build a wall, with Jesus as our Watchman, to protect us from the attacks of the enemy, to help keep our hearts pure and free to love everyone as Jesus did, while at the same time, keeping the enemy at bay.

The wall we need to build is also to help us keep our self-control. Yes, we must let Him build the wall that keeps the enemy out, while at the same time, allows us to be free to love the ones we see as unlovable. We have to be able to protect ourselves and, also, share what we have with those who need it as bad as we once did and still do.

Today's Prayer

Father,

I feel there was so much more to say on this subject. I am asking You to use this short devotion to simply touch the reader enough to encourage them to dig deeper into this subject on their own. Help us all learn how to protect and guard our hearts the way You would have it done—to not only protect our relationship with You, but to be able to share it with others.

Amen.

Losing self-control leaves you as helpless as a city without a wall.

—Proverbs 25:28

January 10

Godfidence

I've heard, many times, "You need some self-confidence," but how can I have that? Self-confidence is "a belief in one's own ability, power, judgment, etc." The enemy had convinced me I had no ability or power. I now realize no one needs *self*-confidence. Yes! We need *confidence*, which, according to *The New Combined Bible Dictionary and Concordance*, is "full trust, belief in the reliability of a person or thing." According to Strong's #3982, the word *confidence*, as an intransitive verb, means "to be convinced, be confident, have inward certainty, trust." But, our confidence must be in God—not in ourselves! Author Renee Swope is the first one I heard call it "GODfidence."

I couldn't find one place in the Bible where it said to have confidence in one's self, but I did find where it tells me to have confidence in God, in the Lord, in Him: Psalm 65:5, Psalm 40:4, Psalm 118:8–9, Isaiah 57:13 and 1 John 5:14. I also found scripture that specifically tells me not to have confidence or trust in man: Jeremiah 17:5, Philippians 3:3 and Isaiah 31:1.

So, it isn't *self*-confidence we need—it is *Godfidence* (God-confidence)! *God*fidence will give us the boldness He wants us to have to do His work. He did not create us to be in doubt or to be afraid or timid or shy. He created us to have confidence in Him and to be bold in Him! Just as these scriptures tell us: 2 Timothy 1:7a, 2 Chronicles 32:7a, Deuteronomy 31:6, Ephesians 3:12, Proverbs 28:1, Hebrews 4:16, Ephesians 6:19, Hebrews 13:6, Philippians 1:20 and Hebrews 10:19. So, when we put our trust and confidence *in* Him, we no longer have to fear. We can be bold in Him!

Today's Prayer

Father,

Help us take the scriptures You have given us as weapons to fight the lies of the enemy when he attacks us with fear and doubt. Help us to recognize his lies immediately and bring them straight to Your throne, where they will be demolished!

Amen.

I've commanded you to be strong and brave. Don't ever be afraid or discouraged! I am the Lord your God and I will be there to help you wherever you go.

—Joshua 1:9

January 11

Time's Up

"God woke me and has given me a fresh, new day. Twenty-four hours to do with what I choose"—have you ever said or thought those words? I know I have. Maybe not those words exactly, but the same idea—thinking, because God woke me this morning, I have a whole new day—when that isn't, necessarily, the truth at all! God has numbered our days (Job 14:5), down to the hours, minutes and seconds. Just because He woke me this morning, doesn't mean I have another twenty-four hours to live. He could call me home at any time—even while I am writing this sentence.

This morning, God showed me a note I had written a couple years ago: "Show me how best to use the time You've given me." That, coupled with the fact a relative (by marriage) left this earth (unexpectedly) a few days ago, has my mind whirling this morning. Am I living as if I meant what I said in that note? Do I daily seek what He would have me do with the time He has granted me? Now, don't get all "spiritual" on me and start thinking I'm talking about only reading His Word or sharing the plan of salvation with every person you see today or anything along those lines. Yes, reading His Word and sharing the plan of salvation are important things and, obviously, things He wants us to do. However, daily life goes on, and we all have "life" things to do. Using our time wisely simply means spending at least a little time with Father each day to seek out what He would say to us and asking Him to lead and show us what He would have us do as the day goes on and we find ourselves still here. He wants to use us in these "life" things throughout the day, if we will allow Him to do it. Ask Him, daily, to make you keenly aware of the divine appointments He has for you this day.

Today's Prayer

Father,

Remind us to seek You daily and open our eyes to the divine appointments You set before us each day. Remind us what we think of as an "interruption" may very well be our divine appointment for this day.

Amen.

Act like people with good sense and not like fools. These are evil times, so make every minute count. Don't be stupid. Instead, find out what the Lord wants you to do.

—Ephesians 5:15–17

January 12

Did I Do That?

I wonder how many remember the TV character Steve Urkel. He was a character on the *Family Matters* sitcom in the early 1990s. According to Wikipedia, he was "central to many of its running gags, primarily property damage and/or personal injury as a result of his inventions going awry or his outright clumsiness," and his catchphrase was, "Did I do that?"

Let's think of that phrase in a different light this morning. Think about yourself and how you allow God to use you in His plans, if you allow Him to use you, that is. Do you ever have a thought to do something completely outside your comfort zone, and you immediately dismiss the idea because it's something you could never do! Maybe, the more you think about it, the more you convince yourself you simply don't have the ability to do it.

Funny thing is, God only wants your availability. Once you say yes to Him, He gives you the ability to do what He's asked. He provides everything you need to complete the task. I know this to be true from my own, personal experience. Do you really think I believe I can write a daily devotion? Absolutely not! Yet, when He asked, I said yes, and here we are on day 12, and He hasn't failed me yet. He shows up every morning, ready to give me what I need!

God has used me in many ways I would have never imagined. This morning He reminded me of several of those ways, and thinking back on them, I found myself asking, "Did I do that?" Yes! Yes, I did, with God helping me and providing what I needed. All it took was me allowing Him to work through me. He wants to do the same with you. Say *yes* to Him today, and before you know it, you will find yourself asking the same thing, "Did I do that?"

Today's Prayer

Father,

We can't even take a breath without You giving it to us. Help us be willing to say yes to whatever You may ask and leave the rest to You.

Amen.

I can do all things through Christ Who strengthens me.

—Philippians 4:13 (NKJV)

January 13

Who Sets Your Standard?

Years ago, my daughter and I were riding together in the car. We were listening to some songs she had recorded, and she skipped a few, making the remark, "They aren't really bad, but you wouldn't like them." Then a song came on by Taylor Swift, and my daughter made the innocent remark: "Candace Bure listens to Taylor Swift's music, so it's okay." To be honest, I didn't think much about it in the moment, but that remark kept playing over and over in my head, and I realized it was because God was asking me, "Who sets your standard? The world or Me?" Wow!

My daughter had made a very innocent remark, and I'm sure we've all made similar remarks. We tend to think of people—famous or not—that we think "have it all together" or are "more spiritual" than we are, and we think that if they do or say something, then it must be okay. Can you relate to what I'm talking about? Have you ever caught yourself saying or thinking along these lines?

Truth is, we can't look to others to determine if something is acceptable or not. The same way we shouldn't use ourselves as a measuring stick, "We do not dare to compare ourselves with those who think they are very important. They use themselves to measure themselves, and they judge themselves by what they themselves are. This shows that they know nothing" (2 Corinthians 10:12 NCV). No, we need to measure ourselves by God's Word. His is the only standard that matters.

I challenge you to ask yourself these questions: Who sets my standard? Me? My peers? Or do I allow God to set my standard, as it should be?

Today's Prayer

Father,

Please help us remember to come to You and Your Word for our measuring stick and not to anything or anyone else.

Amen.

But we will not boast of things without our measure;
but, according to the measure of the rule which God hath
distributed to us, a measure to reach even unto you.

—*2 Corinthians 10:13 (KJV)*

January 14

An Issue of Blood

Do you ever read a scripture you've read many times before, and all of a sudden, God shows you something completely new about it, and you are just in awe? Do you remember the passage about the woman with an issue of blood? I never stopped to think about the fact she surely had many other issues as well. Yet, she put aside all those issues to make her way to Jesus. She had heard of the way He had been healing others, and she believed, if she could just touch even the hem of His garment, she would be healed.

We are much the same way, especially before we come to accept Jesus as our personal Savior. We all have many issues, but we must first deal with our issue of blood. God can handle all our issues, but unless and until we accept the blood of Jesus as atonement for our sin, He will not help us with them. The very minute we accept Jesus and trust that His shed blood covered all our sin, our lives will begin to change. Once we deal with our issue of blood, He will begin to help us with any and all other issues we may have.

Even though I've read this passage several times before, He showed me something else new too. I'm sure we would all agree that when God touches us, there is a change in us. But, the lady in this passage wasn't willing to wait for God to touch her—she was determined to touch Him! Oh, that we would have that same determination! Also, how wonderful to realize we don't have to wait for Him to touch us, we can touch Him! There is definitely a change when God touches us, but we are also changed when we touch God!

Today's Prayer

Father,

Take what You have shown me and use it to touch anyone reading this, that they would not only have the same realization You gave me, but that You may even use them to take it a step further!

Amen.

And a certain woman, which had an issue of blood twelve years and had suffered many things of many physicians and had spent all that she had and was nothing bettered, but rather grew worse, when she heard of Jesus, came in the press behind and touched His garment. For she said, "If I may touch but His clothes, I shall be whole." And straightway the fountain of her blood was dried up and she felt in her body that she was healed of that plague.

—Mark 5:25–29 (KJV)

January 15

Out of My Way

We live in a fast-paced, microwave world—hurry here, hurry there; gotta get this kid to that practice and pick up the other kid from here and take them over there; deadlines to meet at work; we want what we want, and we want it now! We certainly don't have time to fit anything else into our busy, jam-packed schedules—or do we?

Have you ever been on your way somewhere, and God puts an opportunity to help someone in front of you? Maybe you see someone on the roadside, obviously needing help, or maybe He puts someone on your mind, and you feel like you should go do something for this person? No, you think, you don't have time to stop and help right now, or you don't have time to go do that task He put on your heart to do. If you did either of those things, you'd be late for work or late for wherever you thought you had to be at a certain time, or doing either of those things would simply not be "comfortable" for you.

What might happen, though, if you chose to go out of your way and do what He put in your spirit needed to be done? Think about how differently your entire day could go, if you listened to the prompting in your spirit instead of listening to the enemy tell you, "You don't have time for that."

Remember the good Samaritan? Do you think that parable would be in the Bible if the message wasn't important? Of course not! Have you felt prompted to do something lately you thought you didn't have time to do, or maybe it was simply out of your "comfort zone"? I want to challenge you to go out of your way—even out of your comfort zone—and do it next time, then see what happens as a result.

Today's Prayer

Father,

Help us to slow down in this crazy, fast-paced world we live in and remember to take time to listen to Your voice.

Amen.

A man from Samaria then came traveling along that road. When he saw the man, he felt sorry for him and went over to him. He treated his wounds with olive oil and wine and bandaged them. Then he put him on his own donkey and took him to an inn, where he took care of him.

—Luke 10:33–34

January 16

A Ram in the Thicket

Do you find it hard to completely trust God for your needs? I have to confess, I am in that place right now and have been questioning. Not questioning that He will provide what is needed, but asking questions like, Do I need to pursue other avenues? Do I need to just be still and wait on You? Are You waiting on *me* to do something else before You move in the situation? We make it so hard on ourselves sometimes, don't we?

The good thing about it? He understands our hearts! He knows exactly where we are, and He always sends us what we need, right when we need it! Today, He reminded me of a song He gave me years ago, when I was seeking His direction on a decision I had to make. The song "Ram in the Thicket" was based on the Bible passage from Genesis 22:1–19.

> *Isaac said, "Father, we have the coals and the wood; but, where is the lamb for the sacrifice?" "My son," Abraham answered, "God will provide the lamb." The two of them walked on. (Genesis 22:7–8)*

He used a crazy dream and that passage this morning to remind me to continue to trust Him. He reminded me to be still and wait on Him. He knows what is best for me. He knows my need, and He will provide exactly what I need, just when I need it. Don't get caught up in the enemy's lies when he tries to tell you time is running out and you need to take matters into your own hands and do something. Stop! Stand still! Wait! And trust! You won't regret it, I promise! (Go to Google and type in "Brandon Hughes Ram in the Thicket," if you would like to listen to the song.)

Today's Prayer

Father,

When we are trusting You for provision, remind us it is okay if we ask You questions along the way. You can handle not only our needs, but You can handle our questions also, and You will speak to us in a way we will understand. Thank You for always providing exactly what we need at just the moment we need it.

Amen.

Abraham looked up and saw a ram caught by its horns in the bushes. So he took the ram and sacrificed it instead of his son. Abraham named that place "The Lord Will Provide" and, even now, people say, "On the mountain of the Lord it will be provided."

—Genesis 22:13–14

January 17

Clean Your Closet

I have a closet I've been wanting to get cleaned out for quite a while now, yet I still haven't even attempted to get started. Why? Several reasons, actually, but mainly because I feel overwhelmed by it. So, I just never get started. Can you relate to that way of thinking? The "Ugh! I'll never get it done, so I don't even want to start" mentality?

How many times do we do that with our lives? We *know* God is showing us something we need to remove from or change in our lives, but it seems like such a daunting task, we just ignore His nudging and refuse to even get started.

We simply need to reset our minds and change our way of thinking. Stop thinking about all the junk we know needs to be cleaned out and focus on one thing at a time—like the old riddle says: How do you eat an elephant? One bite at a time. Just ask God to help you clean out one thing this week. Whether it's spending too much time on social media or smoking a pack of cigarettes or needing that drink after work, wherever you want to allow Him to start—it's up to you! You will find your life is like an onion with many layers, and God doesn't expect you to be able to peel off all the layers at once. He simply wants you to allow Him to start working in one area and, when that area is well under control, move on to the next. Sure, you may have to come back and work on some of the same areas from time to time, but as long as you don't allow it to go unchecked for long, next time around won't be near as daunting.

Now, if you'll excuse me, I think I hear a closet calling my name. I think I'll get started on it today by removing one item at a time.

Today's Prayer

Father,

Help us to tackle our spiritual closets, with Your guidance, one item at a time. Reassure us that You are with us every step of the way and *You* will see us through, giving us the strength we need on a daily basis.

Amen.

To be made new in the attitude of your minds and to put on the new self, created to be like God in true righteousness and holiness.

—*Ephesians 4:23–24 (NIV)*

January 18

Crybaby

Do you cry easily? I cry at everything! I cry when I'm happy, excited, upset, angry, overwhelmed, hurt or sad for myself or for someone else. I can even cry and not even know why! I especially cry when I feel I am in the presence of God. Coming into the presence of a Holy God is so overwhelming, I can't do anything, except cry.

There's a song that comes to my mind, quite often, "Tears Are a Language God Understands." The words to the chorus are:

> *God sees the tears of a brokenhearted soul*
> *He sees your tears and hears them when they*
> *fall*
> *God weeps along with man and He takes him*
> *by the hand*
> *Tears are a language God understands*

Tears cleanse not only our eyes, but our very souls. Once, I was talking with a friend about this subject, and she said, "Tears are beautiful—cleansing to the soul—funny how Mary's tears cleansed her own soul more than Jesus's feet (Luke 7:38)." Yes, I agree and believe that our tears cleanse our very soul. As we are pouring our tears out to Him, He bottles them up and records every one, then pours more of His love straight into our heart.

I love how Psalm 56:8 is written in The Message: "You've kept track of my every toss and turn through the sleepless nights, each tear entered in Your ledger, each ache written in Your book."

So, the next time you find yourself shedding tears—whether on the outside or the inside—remember, they are never wasted. Your Father knows about and saves every one, and He knows every situation that caused each individual tear. He loves you with an everlasting love, and He will never leave you or forsake you (Deuteronomy 31:8).

Today's Prayer

Father,

Thank You for giving us tears to cleanse not only our eyes, but our souls as well. Help us feel Your encouragement through each and every tear we shed.

Amen.

You keep track of all my sorrows. You have collected all my tears in your bottle. You have recorded each one in Your book.

—Psalm 56:8 (NLT)

January 19

Stop! Drop! Roll!

According to Wikipedia, "Stop, drop and roll is a simple fire safety technique." While this technique is no longer taught to children for fire safety, let's take a look at a new way we could use it.

Stop! The next time you feel you are coming under attack or you just don't know what to do in a situation, take a minute to stop. Don't do anything, don't take a step, don't make any decisions—especially major ones—until you take a minute to stop. Then...

Drop! Drop to your knees, literally or figuratively, in prayer. Search the Scriptures and see what God speaks to your heart about what you are going through. Remember, when you are going through something, the key word is *through*—you will make it to the other side, you won't stay in this place forever and you will find you are stronger when you do make it to the other side of whatever it is. Once you have dropped, all that's left to do is...

ROLL! Roll on through this challenge, knowing you have God on your side; and no matter how many fires you may have to go through on your journey, the flames will not be allowed to harm you—remember those three Hebrew boys? Shadrach, Meshach and Abednego? (See Daniel 3:16–18 if you aren't familiar with their story.) They could teach us a lot, from personal experience, about going through the fire. Because here's the thing: it's just like they said—*even if* God should choose not to deliver you from whatever it is trying to overtake you, *even if*—you still win because you still get to be in paradise with Him forever and *can't nobody take that* away from you, as long as you are His child!

Today's Prayer

Father,

Thank You for this new perspective on stop, drop and roll. I had never thought of it like that before, but it truly does make sense. Help us each remember to stop, drop and roll the next time we are under attack or simply find ourselves facing a situation where we don't know what to do.

Amen.

When you cross deep rivers, I will be with you and you won't drown. When you walk through fire, you won't be burned or scorched by the flames.

—Isaiah 43:2

January 20

Be Still

As Christians, we know our Father will provide all our needs. Not just one or two of our needs, but all our needs. Why, then, is it so hard for us to believe Him? Do you have a problem believing He will provide or, sometimes, find yourself doubting? Do you ever think you have to figure it out yourself?

Remember the passage in the Bible where the father wanted help for his son that couldn't talk and had epileptic seizures? The father asked Jesus to "Help us, if you can!" Jesus told him, "Anything is possible to those who believe." Then, we read in Mark 9:24, "Immediately the father of the child cried out and said with tears, 'Lord, I believe; help my unbelief!'" I read an article once that stated, "When my mind is consumed with my bank account, I'm believing that money provides my security rather than my Savior. When I yell at my children for leaving a mess I need to clean, I'm believing that my comfort comes from an orderly house rather than from the God of all comfort." We don't think of that as "unbelief," but it is.

When you pray and ask God to provide your need, then you get up from that prayer and start "running around like a crazy person," trying to figure out what you need to do to meet that need—you have just said to Him, "I don't believe You can do this." All He wants you to do is *be still!* Trust! Those are very hard things for any of us to do in this hurry-up world we live in, isn't it? We are programmed to believe we must be busy doing something or we aren't being productive. We aren't worth anything if we aren't trying to go in a thousand different directions to take care of things. The world we live in today says, if you don't have that "get 'er done" mentality, then you are being lazy.

The next time you find yourself running around, trying to figure out what you need to do about something, do this instead: STOP! BE STILL! JUST TRUST!

Today's Prayer

Father,

We know from times past, You always provide what we need. We *do* believe. Help our unbelief! Remind us to be still and trust only in You. Then, when we do, we will see Your mighty power in supernatural provision.

Amen.

> *Be still and know that I am God: I will be exalted*
> *among the nations, I will be exalted in the earth!*

—Psalm 46:10 (NKJV)

January 21

On My Own?

I was a single mom for many years, so I understand the concept of being determined to "make it on my own" and take care of my daughter and myself. The enemy has convinced us all that we should be able to take care of ourselves, needing no help from anyone else. The truth of the matter is, though, God never intended for any of us to walk this road alone and "do it on our own." He designed us to have relationship, not only with Him but also with each other.

If you were in deep water, drowning, and someone came by in a boat to rescue you, would you tell them, "No, go on without me. I'll make it on my own."? I don't think so! Then don't turn down the Lord when He sends friends to walk this journey with you—no matter what that might look like!

It might be someone offering to keep your kids while you and your spouse (or just you, if you're a single parent) have an enjoyable day or evening. It might be someone offering you a ride to the grocery store or doctor's office or church or anywhere else. Realize that, if they offer, it's because God moved on their heart and asked them to do it. Don't allow the enemy—or yourself—to use pride to get in the way of a blessing God wants to send your way. You may not feel you deserve or want the help, but if God has moved on someone's heart to make the offer, don't you think He also has a blessing in store for them for being obedient and listening? When you refuse to let others bless you, you could be interfering with your blessing and theirs.

God's very nature is relational—He is three in one: Father, Son and Holy Spirit. He created us in His image; therefore, we are made to be in relationships! In other words, we are made to do life together.

Today's Prayer

Father,

Let us not get so caught up in wanting to "make it on our own" that we forget You are the only reason we are here. Remind us You designed us to be in relationship, not only with You, but also with our Christian brothers and sisters.

Amen.

So God created man in His own image; in
the image of God He created him.

—Genesis 1:27

January 22

Your Heart's Desire

Do you know the desire of your heart? As I was pondering my own heart's desire this morning and asking myself what is it I truly desire, I suddenly realized, I don't know! I know the Bible tells me God will give me the desires of my heart. How can He do that if I don't even know what it is I desire?

Let's look at Psalm 37:4 in a fresh, new way this morning. *Take delight in the Lord, and He will give you the desires of your heart.* What does it mean to *take delight in the Lord?* Remember your first love? You wanted to be with that person every chance you got. Most likely, you found yourself going places and/or doing things you'd never done before, because the person you loved enjoyed those things. In doing that, you may have even found you actually enjoyed those things too.

It works the same way with the Lord. When you accept Him as your Savior, you want to spend more time with Him. You want to do the things He loves and enjoys. Sometimes, He will stretch you beyond anything you've ever done before, and to your amazement, you find you enjoy it, even though it's a little scary! It makes you want to try more new things with Him, go more new places with Him, and before long, you discover you're doing things you never ever thought you would or could do! This morning, realization hit. This is what "He will give you the desires of your heart" means.

He didn't force me to change what I thought I wanted. He didn't force me to go anywhere or do anything with Him. He simply invited me and let me choose whether or not to go along. It was because of my love for Him that I chose to go and do and try these new things. In that way, He put the desire there. I allowed it because

I love Him. Will you allow Him to give you the desire of your heart today?

Today's Prayer

Father,

Thank You for giving us the desires of our hearts. Especially when we don't even know what they are. Thank You for inviting us to go new places and discover new things with You!

Amen.

May He give you the desire of your heart
and make all your plans succeed.

—Psalm 20:4

January 23

Just Trust

I'm sure you've seen the picture of the little girl holding tightly to her little teddy bear, saying, "But I love it, God," and God is kneeling in front of her with a really big teddy bear behind His back, saying, "Just trust Me." It came to mind this morning as God showed me something He had done for me.

A little over five years ago, I had to give up some things in order to accept the wonderful husband God had for me. I had to give up mistrust, fear of rejection, being so independent, and I had to give up my two cats. Long story short—both cats came back to me, by way of coming back to live with my mom. One had to be put to sleep about a week or so after she came back to my mom's house. She was almost fourteen and had developed diabetes, so it was the best thing for her. But God allowed her to come back to me before she had to go. The other one stayed at my mom's, and I got to see him when I was at her house. We lived close, so I saw him often. Then, my mom got promoted to Heaven, and my sweet, Godly husband said the cat could come live with us! I gave up something I loved very much (my cats) to accept something even better (my husband). Then God turns around and gives me back what He had asked me to give up in the first place! It may not always happen that way, but one thing I know: God always knows what is best for me, and I will trust Him with that.

If He asks us to give up something, it means He has something much better for us. Not just material things either, though that could be the case sometimes. He is the only One Who knows what is best for us, and we must learn to trust Him.

Will you trust Him today? Will you give up whatever it is you're holding so tightly to so He can give you something even better?

Today's Prayer

Father,

Please help the person reading this to loosen their grip on whatever it is they're holding so tightly to and trust You to know what's best for them.

Amen.

Those who know Your Name will put their trust in You;
for You, Lord, have not forgotten those who seek You.

—*Psalm 9:10 (NKJV)*

January 24

Such a Time

Have you ever found yourself in a place or situation wondering why you were there? I'm not talking about going from one room to another and forgetting what you were going after. I'm talking about when God moves you from one city to another, or maybe you lost your job or you changed jobs. It could be any number of reasons where you find yourself wondering, "Why did I have to be in this place at this time?" Maybe it's just for a day or a few hours, or maybe it's a whole new season of life. Did you ever stop to think it's because of God's design, His plan?

God will place us in situations to orchestrate His plans. Remember Esther? She was strategically placed, by God, in just the right place at just the right time so He could use her in His plan to save the Jews. She could have chosen not to take part in His plan. He still would have saved the Jews, but Esther and her family would not have survived had she chosen not to be a part of God's plan.

If you find yourself in a place or situation and you don't understand why you're there, go to the Father and ask Him. He will let you know, when the time is right, what He would have you do. If you are there by His design, He has something for you to do or say, quite possibly to help someone else. Be open to whatever it is He may be calling you to do. Choose to join Him in His plan because, quite possibly, He has placed you there for such a time as this.

Today's Prayer

Father,

Make us aware of the places and situations You place us in. Give us the willingness to join You in Your plan and the boldness to speak out when You are calling us to speak out, and grant us the wisdom to know when the time is right to do so.

Amen.

For if you remain completely silent at this time, relief and deliverance will arise for the Jews from another place, but you and your father's house will perish. Yet who knows whether you have come to the kingdom for such a time as this?

—Esther 4:14 (NKJV)

January 25

I Have the Power

You are a very powerful person, whether you realize it or not. The question for you today and every day is: will you choose to keep your power, or will you choose to flippantly give it away to someone or something else?

When you wake up in the morning, do you find yourself saying, "Good morning, Lord" or "Good Lord, it's morning!"? It's your choice how you start your day. If you choose the first greeting, you are choosing to keep your power. If you choose the second, you have just given your power to the morning.

There are many examples that could be given, but it all boils down to how I heard it stated many years ago. When you find yourself saying, "You make me soooooo _____" (you fill in the blank—mad, happy, aggravated, etc.), then you have just given your power to whomever or whatever you are saying it to. That person, or object, has absolutely no power over you until *you* give it away.

Are you suddenly remembering your drive in to work yesterday, when that person cut you off in traffic and your response was, "You make me so mad!" Or maybe you just remembered when you were sitting at your computer, waiting for the s-l-o-w Internet to start working, and your response was "This stupid computer makes me so aggravated!"

Are these words resonating in your spirit? If so, consider that your challenge from the Lord. He is the One reminding you of how you have given away what is yours, and He wants to help you take it back! With His help, you can!

Today's Prayer

Father,

We know it will take time, and we are all "works-in-progress," but help us to start taking back our power today! From today on, let Your Holy Spirit be quick to speak to us when we are about to give our power away. We realize our power comes from You. Let us use our power to be a light pointing others to You!

Amen.

But me—I'm filled with God's power, filled with
God's Spirit of justice and strength.

—Micah 3:8a (The Message)

January 26

A "Has-Been"

If you have given your life to Christ, you are a "has-been." You may not think of yourself as a has-been, but you are. In my search for something else this morning, I came across a poem I wrote twelve years ago (2007), and I want to share it with you. I didn't write it from personal experience, but hopefully it gets the point across.

A "Has-Been"

I have been an addict
Of alcohol for years.
I have been hooked on drugs,
Caused my family lots of tears.
I have been living
For the devil all my life;
But, now something is different.
I don't want all this strife.
Now the Lord has called me
And I've opened the door,
Invited Him to come in,
To change me forevermore.
Now I'm just a "has-been"
I guess you could say,
A "has-been" of the devil
And his wicked way.
He'll hound me for sure,
Now that I've told him goodbye;
But, he no longer scares me

With Jesus by my side.
He may bark, he may bite,
He may growl, hiss and moan;
But, I'll just call for Jesus
And he'll have to leave me alone.
Yes, I am just a "has-been"
And that's just fine with me,
'Cause, since I accepted Jesus,
I have truly been set FREE!

Before we come to Christ, we all have issues—sin issues—and, sometimes, we still struggle with these issues *after* we accept Christ. The difference is, once we have given our lives to Him, He will help us overcome these issues. We are made overcomers by the blood of the Lamb and the word of our testimony. So, share your "has-been" with others. Help someone else by sharing your story. You never know who you might help, if you are willing to let God use you.

Today's Prayer

Father,

Thank You for making us all "has-beens." Give strength to the one reading this so they will be willing to share their own "has-been" story.

Amen.

*And they have defeated him by the blood of the Lamb
and by their testimony. And they did not love their
lives so much that they were afraid to die.*

—*Revelation 12:11 (NLT)*

January 27

A Hurt So Good

Father speaks to my spirit at some of the craziest times—in the shower, for example! I need to tell you, when I take a shower, I want the water very hot—as in, I look like a lobster when I'm done! I had just got in, and the water was *so* hot, I was still trying to get used to it, and I had the thought, "How can something that hurts so bad, feel so good at the same time?" Then my mind went to my mom being promoted to Heaven last year and to a friend who had a twenty-five-month-old daughter promoted to Heaven, eighteen years ago. We hurt terribly because we miss our loved ones, yet we rejoice because we know where they are and that we will get to see them again one day. It seems our thought process when an older person dies is "Oh, how sad for the family, but, their loved one lived a good long life. They knew the Lord, and now they're with Jesus." However, when younger people, especially babies and very young children, die, it's "How awful! They had their whole life ahead of them." That's when I felt Father speak the following into my spirit:

> *Your thinking is all wrong. I am the only One Who knows the number of your days. I have a purpose and a plan for every person I breathe life into. Whether that purpose and plan takes eighty-one years or twenty-five months to fulfill, is not for you to say. Remember the poem "To All Parents" I showed you years ago by Edgar Guest? You need to remember and remind others that My timeline is all-knowing and always what is best for each person.*

Yes, the death of a loved one—at any age—can hurt really bad, but feel good at the same time. His Word tells us *the day of death is better than the day of birth* (Ecclesiastes 7:1). Just remember, when you are hurting, He knows, and He can comfort you, if you just call out to Him. Read Psalm 139 and let Him speak to you.

Today's Prayer

Father,

We humans can truly be backward in our thinking. Please forgive us. Thank You for knowing our hearts and understanding why we get things backward sometimes. Thank You for comforting us when we are hurting. Thank You for Your loving-kindness in all seasons.

Amen.

Your eyes saw my unformed body; all the days ordained for me were written in your book before one of them came to be.

—Psalm 139:16 (NIV)

January 28

Bugs and God

God can use the funniest things to teach us lessons. I got in my car once and noticed there was a bug, outside, on my windshield, directly in my field of vision. I thought, "Well, you won't be there long," and started on my way. I had driven for a few miles, distracted by my thoughts of how the enemy had been attacking me lately, when I noticed the bug was still hanging on to my windshield. It was as if the Lord spoke into my spirit, "See how that bug is hanging on for dear life to your windshield? I want you to hang on to Me like that. Don't give up. Don't give in. I'm here for you, and I will see you through this. But this is going to be a process, and you must be willing to hang on to Me just like that bug is hanging on to your windshield. I've got you. I'm not gonna let you go." Wow! Okay, Father. I'm hanging on, but I need Your help. Some days, I feel like the enemy is snatching me away, and I just can't hold on any longer. But as long as You have me in Your hands, I know I'll be okay. You will continue to give me strength and help me hold on.

After driving approximately twenty minutes, about ten minutes away from my destination, I was amazed at how that bug was still hanging on, and then…it let go! It got that close to the destination, and it was like something snatched it off! Again, I felt the Lord whispering to my spirit, "See? Don't be like that bug. Don't be so close to getting 'home' in dealing with this attack only to let go. I've got you, and I'm not letting go of you, so don't you let go of Me either."

So, no matter how hard the enemy may want to snatch us from the Father, he can't do it! As long as we hold on, Father will not let go of us. *Correction*: Even if we do let go of Him, from time to time, *He will never let go of us*!

Today's Prayer

Father,

Thank You for holding tight to us, even when we do let go of You, sometimes. Thank You for never leaving us.

Amen.

> *My sheep listen to My voice; I know them and they follow me. I give them eternal life and they shall never perish; no one can snatch them out of my hand. My Father, who has given them to me, is greater than all; no one can snatch them out of My Father's hand. I and the Father are One.*

> *—John 10:27–30*

January 29

Sweet Hour of Prayer

"Sweet Hour of Prayer"—now, that's an old hymn. Anyone else remember it? Look at the words in the first verse:

> *Sweet hour of prayer, sweet hour of prayer,*
> *That calls me from a world of care*
> *And bids me at my Father's throne*
> *Make all my wants and wishes known!*
> *In seasons of distress and grief,*
> *My soul has often found relief,*
> *And oft escaped the tempter's snare*
> *By Thy return, sweet hour of prayer.*

So much truth in that one verse alone! No matter what your day is like, no matter how you may have been hurting before, once you enter into prayer, it all melts away. He gives us the freedom to come to Him and lay it all at His feet! How wonderful is that? Knowing that He is ready, willing and more than able to give us what we need, what He knows is best for us, and all we have to do is ask for it!

Do you struggle with prayer? God is there with you. Feel like you don't know "how to" pray, as I feel so many times? It doesn't matter. Just speak what's in your heart, that's all He wants to hear. Share with Him your wants and wishes, frustrations and problems, and watch as He does miraculous things in your life. Ask Him to help you make His will for your life, your will for your life, then get ready for things to happen. He has brought me from someone that would never consider praying out loud with others to someone who, knowing it gives Him glory, is determined to press through.

If He can do this for someone like me, I know He can do huge things in your life today. He's just waiting for you to ask Him. Will you ask Him now? I challenge you to do it and see how your life changes.

Today's Prayer

Father,

Thank You for allowing us, through the blood of Your Son, Jesus Christ of Nazareth, to come boldly to Your throne. Thank You for helping us take that first baby step, hearing even our simplest of prayers and growing us into more than we could ever imagine!

Amen.

So let us come boldly to the throne of our gracious God. there we will receive His mercy and we will find grace to help us when we need it.

—Hebrews 4:16 (NLT)

January 30

Just Be Held

I remember, as if it were yesterday, the first time I ever allowed Jesus to hold me. It was July 20, 2006. I will always remember that date as the day I fully surrendered and began a relationship with Him, even though I had gotten saved as a teenager. At the time I got saved, it was more like being given a new set of "rules" to follow, rather than having a relationship.

On this particular night, I decided to try something different when I finished my Bible study lesson. I lay down on my bed, closed my eyes and imagined I was sitting in Father's lap, and He was just holding me. That was the night He told me He loves me, and I finally, truly understood.

Do you know Jesus loves you? Not just because others have told you it's true, but have you ever experienced it for yourself? If your answer is no, please get alone with Him today and let Him speak to your heart. Allow Him to hold you until you hear it. He may even whisper it to you. Maybe you knew it once, a long time ago, but over time you have forgotten. Maybe you just don't *feel* that He loves you. Remember, we can't go on our *feelings*. The enemy loves to use our feelings against us. When you don't *feel* His love, remember His truth, and the truth is that He does, indeed, love you. He would not have given His only Son to die for you if He did not love you!

Don't say you can't get away or don't have time to get alone with Him. Those are lies from the enemy. You make time for what's important, and nothing is more important than your relationship with Him, so make the time ASAP. You will never regret spending time alone with Him—only that you didn't make time to do it sooner.

Today's Prayer

Father,

Thank You for the sweet reminder of Your love for us today. Thank You for allowing us to know You love us, even and especially on days when we don't feel it. Thank You for reminding us we can't rely on feelings, we need to rely only on Your truth.

Amen.

For God so loved the world, that he gave his only begotten Son, that whosoever believeth in him should not perish, but have everlasting life.

—John 3:16 (KJV)

January 31

Resolve or Commit

Did you make a new year's resolution, or did you make a commitment? Resolve is a firm determination to do something, whereas commit means to carry out or perpetrate. Do you see the difference there? You can make a firm determination to do something and never actually carry it out. So, until you make the commitment, the resolution doesn't really mean anything. To resolve to do something means nothing until you truly commit.

Thirty-one days, and Father has honored my commitment every single one of those days. It still amazes me and has me in such awe of what He can and will do when I simply make myself available to Him.

Hopefully, you have accepted Jesus as your Savior, but have you committed your life to Him? Being committed to Him means you are willing to make sacrifices and deny yourself sometimes. There are many mornings (like this morning, in fact) when I want to turn that alarm off at 3:00 a.m. and turn over and go back to sleep! But I prayed and asked Him, long before I started this journey, to help me "stay focused and stay committed," and He has been faithful to honor that request. It is only by His power I am able to get up some mornings. It is because He has been faithful to me in the past that I know I can trust Him to be faithful in the present and in the future. Because I know He has done this for me, I can say to you today—He is faithful!

Which brings us back to the question—have you committed your life to Him? Are you willing to do what He asks, even if it means denying yourself something that means a lot to you? If you have yet to commit your life to Him, why not let today be the day?

Is there something you feel He has been asking you to do, but you have found yourself saying no because of the commitment involved? Commit today. Trust me, you won't regret it!

Today's Prayer

Father,

Thank You for being faithful to us and showing up when we honor our commitment to You.

Amen.

Then Jesus said to all the people: If any of you want to be my followers, you must forget about yourself. You must take up your cross every day and follow me.

—Luke 9:23

February 1

Wait—a Solution

When we are waiting on the Lord to move in a situation, we find ourselves *wondering* how He is going to work everything out.

We get *anxious* about deadlines, due dates for bills and plenty of other things.

Waiting makes some of us feel *intimidated*. We become fearful of what might happen or that we aren't doing our part to resolve the situation.

Waiting can make you feel *troubled*. We begin to doubt that God is ever going to move in our situation, fearing He has abandoned or forgotten us.

What happens if we replace the *wondering*, *anxious*, *intimidated*, *troubled* thoughts? God's Word can help us trade our thoughts for His thoughts.

> *The Lord says, "My thoughts and my ways are not like yours." (Isaiah 55:8)*

Trade the wonderings for *worship*.

> *Ascribe to the Lord the glory due His Name; worship the Lord in the splendor of His holiness. (Psalm 29:2 NIV)*

Turn anxious thoughts into adoration and *adore* Him.

> *Love the Lord your God with all your heart, soul and strength. (Deuteronomy 6:5 NIV)*

Instead of being intimidated, get *intimate* with the Father.

> *You, God, are my God, earnestly I seek you; I thirst for you, my whole being longs for you, in a dry and parched land where there is no water. (Psalm 63:1 NIV)*

Then, throw the troubled thoughts out the door and replace them with *trust*.

> *Trust in the Lord with all your heart and lean not on your own understanding. (Proverbs 3:5 NIV)*

Today's Prayer

Father,

Thank You for helping us to replace our thoughts with Your thoughts. Thank You for Your forgiveness when we sometimes forget. Amen.

> *But those who wait on the Lord shall renew their strength; they shall mount up with wings like eagles, they shall run and not be weary, they shall walk and not faint.*

> *—Isaiah 40:31 (NKJV)*

February 2

Don't Be a Frog

Are you one of the so-called "strange" breed that likes to have your bathwater or shower so hot you can hardly stand it? I confess, I am. In fact, I like it so hot that when I get out, I look like a lobster because I'm so red!

As I was getting in the shower one morning, recently, I found myself thinking the water was too hot, so I added a little cold water to the mix. Then, it was too cold. So, I slowly turned down the cold water until it was completely off again. The difference was, I had gradually turned down the cold water, and now the hot water didn't seem as hot as when I first got in. That's when I felt a quickening in my spirit—"Kind of like life, isn't it?"

We must be careful not to find ourselves becoming like the frog in the fable. The fable is that a frog can be put in tepid water and stay there, even as the heat begins to rise, because it adjusts its body temperature to what's going on around it, and it will boil to death. Satan likes to use the same tactics on us. He gets "small" changes made, just a little at a time, so we go along with it, accepting the changes as being "not so bad." Nothing could be further from the truth! Wrong will always be wrong, and God's Word needs to be our measuring stick! If God said something was wrong all those years ago, it is still wrong today—no matter who says it isn't!

We must keep our guard up at all times and stay in His Word so we can stay strong and not get caught up in the enemy's lies! That is satan's ultimate goal—to kill, steal and destroy; and we must stay on guard! Has the enemy had you under that "gradual change" spell? If so, get in the Word today and remind him what God says about whatever it is and tell the enemy you stand with God!

Today's Prayer

Father,

Let us not get complacent but help us stay alert, being ever watchful. Help us stay in Your Word and instantly recognize when satan is trying to slowly turn up the heat. May we be vigilant in keeping our minds stayed on You and remember to call out to You for help and guidance when we feel the heat rising.

Amen.

Be on your guard and stay awake. Your enemy, the devil, is like a roaring lion, sneaking around to find someone to attack.

—1 Peter 5:8

February 3

Free to Go

Everyone in the courtroom knows you're guilty, including you. The prosecuting attorney stands and begins telling the judge everything you've done. He is telling it all, not leaving out one tiny little detail.

You are bracing yourself for the judge's sentence. You know it will be harsh. It must be, after all you have done. You know there is absolutely no way you are walking out of this courtroom.

Your defense attorney rises to share your side of the story. Wait—what's that he's saying? He is agreeing with everything the prosecuting attorney said. He is agreeing you did all these things and more that the prosecuting attorney has accused you of doing.

But then, He turns to the judge and says: "It's all true. Everything my client is accused of is true. But, Your Honor, this one that did all these things, this one belongs to me. This one loves me, serves me and has accepted me. Because this one has accepted me, I have accepted this one. This one is covered by my blood and, therefore, is washed clean of all guilt."

The judge turns to look at you, ready to deliver his sentence. You are braced for the worst, and you hear him say: "I find you not guilty. You are free to go."

The prosecuting attorney is satan. The defense attorney is Jesus Christ, the Son. The judge is God, the Father.

Because you belong to Him, you are free to go. "Go and preach the good news to everyone in the world" (Mark 16:15)—at least your little corner of it!

Today's Prayer

Father,

Thank You for my salvation through Jesus, Your only Son, Who paid the price for my sin.

Amen.

If God says his chosen ones are acceptable to Him, can anyone bring charges against them? Or can anyone condemn them? No indeed! Christ died and was raised to life and now He is at God's right side, speaking to Him for us.

—Romans 8:33–34

February 4

Broken to Multiply

Have you ever felt like God has forgotten you? Like you were in a dark, dark place all alone? Going through a trial of some kind, and you, quite simply, felt like no one—not even God—cared! No matter how bad the situation you find yourself in, please be assured God does care. He *is* with You and He *will* see you through. The key word here is *through*. You won't stay where you are, you will get through it. As a friend, Alisa Coffey, once said, "The Lord will handle 'it,' whatever your 'it' is, He's got 'it'!"

If you are a child of God, I'm not telling you anything you don't already know. However, I want to share something I heard recently and hope it will be an encouragement, as it was for me.

Remember when Jesus fed the multitudes with the two fish and five barley loaves (Matthew 14:13–21)? Do you remember what He did with the bread? First, He blessed it—oh my! He just pointed that part out to me this minute! He *blessed* it, *then* He broke it and, this is the beautiful part I had never realized before, the more He broke it, the more there was to give! And plenty left over besides!

Let's be honest, none of us like being broken. Being broken is hard, certainly no fun and definitely not something we typically ask for. Yet, seeing the purpose of it in this new light makes me want to get to the place where I can honestly shout, "Break Me, Father, And multiply me!" I'm not there yet, but I hope I can get there one day. For now, I can be more thankful for my past times of brokenness and appreciate them in a new way. What about you?

Today's Prayer

Father,

Though it may sound strange, thank You for my brokenness! It's not something I enjoy, but I do want to be multiplied for Your use.

Amen.

Jesus asked his disciples to bring the food to Him, and He told the crowd to sit down on the grass. Jesus took the five loaves and the two fish. He looked up toward Heaven and blessed the food. Then He broke the bread and handed it to His disciples and they gave it to the people. After everyone had eaten all they wanted, Jesus' disciples picked up twelve large baskets of leftovers.

—Matthew 14:18–20

February 5

Bitter Cup

Several years ago, I decided to do a cleanse. This involved consuming one fiber drink a day, for ten days. The only way I was able to get and keep those drinks down was with the help of Jesus! I prayed over every one of those drinks—before, during and after I drank them!

In preparing to drink the last one, I began praying, as usual, then found myself praying something different from before, "Lord, help me drink the last bitter cup of this stuff." As soon as I prayed those words, I began to weep as I realized that the bitter cup I was about to drink was nothing compared to the bitter cup Jesus drank for me! Then the enemy hissed, "Yes, but He only drank it once"—to which, I felt, Jesus replied, "Had it required more than once, I would have drank it as many times as required in order to give eternal life to My darling daughter." I know He would have too!

Which begs the question, How many times do we make Him drink that bitter cup? Every time we reject any of His promises? When we choose not to believe what He tells us in His Word, do we cause Him to drink that bitter cup again? It breaks my heart to think about it, but I believe, in a sense, we do.

Obviously, Jesus doesn't physically go to the cross every time we reject Him. Once was all it took to give us our freedom, if we accept it. I'm speaking figuratively. Is the pain the same to Him when we don't allow His Word to be truth to our very marrow? Are we, figuratively, driving the nails into His hands and feet each time we disobey? How many times must we inflict this pain on Him before we understand what we are doing to Him?

Today's Prayer

Father,

Thank You for being willing to sacrifice Your only Son for us. Jesus, thank You for being willing to drink that bitter cup. Make us keenly aware of how we hurt You every time we turn away from You, and may that awareness convict us and remind us to turn back to You, accept Your forgiveness and move forward in Your hope.

Amen.

> *Going a little farther, He fell with His face to the ground and prayed, "My Father, if it is possible, may this cup be taken from Me. Yet not as I will, but as You will."*
>
> *—Matthew 26:39 (NIV)*

February 6

Complaining All the Way to Your Blessing

A while back, I volunteered as an encourager (prayer partner) at a women's conference. Part of the encourager's job was to walk around the arena and pray over everyone who would be attending and pray for the speakers and performers also. I had finished praying and was still in the auditorium, when two ladies walked in and asked if seats were reserved. I told them they were not and they could sit anywhere they wanted. They just could not get over it! One of the ladies kept going on and on about how she couldn't believe they were allowed to sit right up front! She said she had been complaining all the way to the event because they weren't seeing anyone else and were beginning to wonder if they'd been sent the wrong direction! "Then we get here and are blessed with front-row seats! I just can't believe this!" she kept saying.

Isn't that just like us, sometimes, in even bigger things? God has such a blessing for us on the other side of whatever circumstance we may be going through; but, we are so busy complaining about our situation, when we receive our blessing, we almost feel guilty!

Puts me in mind of how the people complained when Moses was leading them through the wilderness. Are you in a tough spot right now? Are you complaining? What if you are in this place because God is leading you to a huge blessing on the other side? We need to learn to praise Him in all our circumstances, as He tells us in His Word. Do you find yourself complaining too much? Do you, like myself, need to work on this area? Why don't we start today? Oh, the lady I mentioned at the beginning? She actually joined the volunteers as an encourager at that conference and received her ticket cost back in a certificate to be used at the product tables!

Today's Prayer

Father,

Thank You for allowing us to come to You and ask forgiveness for our complaining attitudes. We tend to forget, sometimes, just Who is watching over us and taking care of us. Thank You for being patient with us and loving us.

Amen.

Always be joyful and never stop praying. Whatever
happens, keep thanking God because of Jesus
Christ. This is what God wants you to do.

—*1 Thessalonians 5:16–18*

February 7

Prepare to Resist

I'm sure you've heard many times to resist the devil and he will flee. James 4:7 is where you can find it. We know God's Word is true. However, we can't just read part of a scripture and make it say what we want it to say. We must read the entire verse and even verses surrounding it to see what, if anything, we must do to be prepared. In this case, we must prepare to resist.

Look closely at James 4:7—most people skip over the part that says, "Submit yourselves to God." That is where we go wrong. We must prepare by submitting ourselves to God, which frees God to do His part. We must *submit ourselves to God*, first, then we will be prepared to resist when temptations come our way. Whether it be tempting dating situations, tempting work situations or any tempting situation. If we have truly submitted ourselves to God, He is free to do His part, and He will make the devil flee!

Resist

Everything that satan says
Is nothing but a lie.
So, if you are a child of God,
Look satan in the eye.
Tell him to get behind you,
That he has got to flee.
Or better yet, in Jesus's name,
Just put him under your feet!

The Lord gave me those words in 1996. However, being much more mature in my walk with Him now, I believe the last two lines should be changed to

> Then, in the power of Jesus's name,
> Put him under your feet!

Should you find yourself in a tempting situation today, are you prepared to resist?

Today's Prayer

Father,

Help us to remember complete verses and not just the parts we think suit our situation. Remind us that You give us a part to play, also, and only when we do our part are You free to do Your part.

Amen.

> *So, let God work His will in you. Yell a loud no*
> *to the devil and watch him scamper.*

> —*James 4:7 (The Message)*

February 8

The Comparison Game

Do you ever feel you aren't "good" enough to do something? Do you look at others thinking to yourself they "have it all together" and wishing you were more like them? Well, guess what? They are most likely looking at you and thinking the same thing.

It's a game the enemy loves to play—*comparison*—and it is chock-full of his lies and deceit! He gets us to compare ourselves to friends, family members and, sometimes, even people we don't know. This is dangerous because we can look at some and think, "Oh, I'm doing a lot better than they are," or we can look at others and think, "I could never do that! I'm not talented, gifted or whatever enough to pull that off." The only One we should be comparing ourselves to is Jesus! He is the One and only One to serve as our measuring stick, as it were.

The enemy uses all kinds of tactics and lies to entice us into playing his comparison game with the wrong people. He knows if we stop comparing ourselves to others and start comparing ourselves to Jesus, we will begin to realize the truth!

The truth is we are all on the same playing field in His eyes. There is not one that is more important than another. There are many different things He wants to accomplish through each of us, and He has us exactly where we need to be in order to get His work done.

So, when you feel Him calling or asking you to do something, be willing to do it. Just say yes, no matter what it is! He will definitely give you anything and everything you need to do what He has called or asked you to do. Are you willing?

Today's Prayer

Father,

Help us resist the temptation to fall into the comparison trap. Thank You for helping each one of us carry our own load.

Amen.

Do your own work well, and then you will have something to be proud of. But don't compare yourself with others. We each must carry our own load.

—Galatians 6:4–5

February 9

Forty Days

Did you know today is the fortieth day of the year? Forty days since I began this new journey of listening for Father to give me a devotion every morning. Forty days of being amazed every morning as He speaks another devotion to me. If it weren't for this journey, I wouldn't have even noticed today is the fortieth day of the year. I decided to do a little research on the significance of forty days in the Scriptures and found some interesting information. Did you know, to the Jews, the number 40 represents a time of probation or trial?

Eugene Peterson says, "Forty is a stock biblical word that has hope at its core. Forty days is a period for testing the reality of one's life—examining it for truth and for authenticity. The forty days in Noah's ark was used to cleanse centuries of moral pollution. The forty years in the wilderness was used to train the Israelites to live by faith in the promises of God. The forty days of Jesus' temptation was used to explore His calling and test His commitment. The forty days of Jesus' appearances after His death, was used to verify His resurrection and characterize the new life of God's kingdom."

I found myself getting caught up in trying to find some special, hidden meaning about today being the fortieth day, and Father showed me something to share through that. We must be careful about placing so much significance on trying to find a special meaning behind every number in the Bible. As I found in my Google research this morning, "God has not called us to search for secret meanings, hidden messages or codes in the Bible. There is more than enough truth in the plain words of Scripture to meet all our needs and make us complete and thoroughly equipped for every good work."

Today, let's focus on what He would have us to do this day! Oh—and don't forget to be on the lookout for your divine appointment today!

Today's Prayer

Father,

Help us not get so caught up in symbolism and hidden meanings that we miss the plain, simple truth of Your Word. Remind us we are here to do the work You have called us to do and nothing more. Help us remember to put the focus where it belongs—on You—and not on hidden meanings.

Amen.

God uses it to prepare and equip His people to do every good work.

—2 Timothy 3:17 (NLT)

February 10

Winds of Life

"Wow! This wind is blowing the car everywhere! I am having to keep both hands on the steering wheel to keep it under control." As soon as the thought went through my mind, it made me start thinking about life, in general. How many times do I allow things to "blow me everywhere" and get me off track from where God would have me to be? When I don't "keep both hands on the steering wheel"—the steering wheel being God—it is not only easy, but inevitable, that I will be blown off course by the "winds of life"—the enemy.

The fall after her high school graduation, my daughter started college, a couple hours from home, at a branch of the university she truly desired to attend. This was her first taste of freedom—being away from Mom and Mom's rules. I remember her stating once, "It's nice here. I like it. But one day I'm going to be at the 'real' university. I don't know how or when, but I'm going to be there." However, having her first taste of "freedom," she let go of God and let life's winds begin to "blow her around." She was blown around like a little limp rag doll until she finally realized where she had gone wrong. She grabbed hold of God again with both hands and a fierceness she'd never known before. Still, one more really strong wind caught her off guard and blew her around for a very short time. This time, though, she had not completely let go, and God held her tight and helped her get steady on her feet again when she called out to Him. She can certainly testify that when you give God complete control of your life and do your best to do what He has for you to do, He will give you the desires of your heart. Nine years after her statement, she graduated from that university of her dreams!

We can all learn from her about keeping our faith and holding on to God for our dreams. When we seek Him first, He will give us the rest—even if it's nine years later.

Today's Prayer

Father,

Protect us from the winds that would blow us around. Remind us to never waver in our faith and to always trust You and Your plan. Amen.

But when you ask Him, be sure that your faith is in God alone. Do not waver, for a person with divided loyalty is as unsettled as a wave of the sea that is blown and tossed by the wind.

—James 1:6 (NLT)

February 11

I Love You

Those three words seem to hold so much power over our lives. Three words we all long to hear. Little girls, especially, long to hear their daddy say it to them. Depending on whether or not they do can drastically change the course of their life. A little girl needs to know and feel her daddy loves and cares for her and that he is there to protect her.

Sometimes, even though we were blessed with having a daddy we know loved and cared for us, other things happen in life. Things that make it hard for us to believe anyone, especially God, could ever truly love us. We may have made some bad choices. Choices, we believe, so awful, no one—especially God—could ever forgive us! Nothing could be further from the truth. That is a lie the enemy loves to get us to believe, and unfortunately it doesn't seem hard to convince us, most days.

I challenge you to walk around today (and every day) with your eyes wide open, looking for the ways God is loving on you through-out your day. It could be the gentle breeze blowing across your cheek. It might be the way that person stopped to help you, just when you needed it. Maybe it's your small group from church driving nearly fifty miles to show their support for you as you help sing in the Christmas cantata at your sister's church. (Yes, my Life Group did that for me once!)

No matter what you may have done that you think is absolutely unforgivable and no matter how unlovable you may believe you are, please listen to me today: God loves you! You cannot go far enough away to get out of His reach. He will follow you anywhere and tell you He loves you and show you in so many different ways. Will you listen to Him today? Stop running! Be still (as we've talked about before) and bask in His love! Let it wash and cleanse you!

Today's Prayer

Father,

Love on each person reading this devotion today. Let them feel Your arms wrap them in a loving embrace and hear You whisper the words "I love you, My child" in their ear. Thank You for loving us so! Amen.

I have loved you, just as My Father has loved me.
So, remain faithful to My love for you.

—John 15:9

February 12

Share and Share Alike

When I was a child, we were taught to "share and share alike." This meant, whatever we had, we were to share with others, and whatever others had, they were to share with us, whether it was toys, food, whatever.

It was fun sharing the good things we each had. But, what about the bad things? Like, if one got in trouble, we all got in trouble? Did we still enjoy it then? Not so much, but that's the way it was, and you know something? It worked! Even though we didn't like it as much, it still worked. Sharing the bad times helped us enjoy the good times even more.

It's the same way in our walk with the Lord. When Christ walked on this earth, He felt all the same feelings we do today. He had some really good days, and I believe, He had some really bad days. He had many sufferings while He was here. He willingly went through all of it—the good and the bad—because He wanted us to be in Heaven with Him for all eternity.

Why is it then when we accept Christ as our Savior, we expect everything to, suddenly, be all peaches and cream, with nothing bad happening to us? Why would we expect to be any better than the One Who gave His lifeblood for us? Christ dealt with ridicule, rejection and more, because He loves us so much and wants to spend eternity with us. He willingly suffered it all for us!

Therefore, we must be willing to share not only the good things, but the bad things as well. It is only by sharing in His suffering we can truly appreciate sharing in His treasure—His blessings. Are you willing to share in His sufferings? Am I?

Today's Prayer

Father,

We don't like to think about sharing Christ's suffering. We only want to ask for a share in the treasures, the blessings. Please forgive us, and thank You for giving us the strength we need when those times of sharing in the suffering come to us.

Amen.

And since we are His children, we will share His treasures—
for everything God gives to His Son, Christ, is ours, too. But, if
we are to share His glory, we must also share His suffering.

—Romans 8:17 (NLT)

February 13

Broken Vessels

As I was listening to my husband preach a message, I felt Father began speaking more to my spirit. The message was based on the scripture from Mark 5:1–5. It's about the man called Legion (because he had many demons), who lived among the tombs. Verse 5 tells us, "And always, night and day, he was in the mountains and in the tombs, crying and cutting himself with stones."

God is calling us to come out from living among the tombs of our past. There is nothing we can do that is beyond His forgiveness. He wants us to stop believing the lies of the enemy and live in the joy Jesus gives! Let go of any bitterness we are holding on to and hold on to the hope of Jesus instead!

Are you feeling broken today? As my husband brought out in his message, some labels seem to be written in permanent marker on our lives: Shameful. Rejected. Fearful. Anxious. Addict. Adulterous. Depressed. Unstable. Neglected. Victim. Forgotten. Hopeless. Broken. The good news is those labels are covered by the blood of the Lamb when you accept Jesus as your personal Savior. Those labels are as far from you as the east is from the west. They are no longer anything but lies from an enemy who wants to keep you feeling down and broken!

When you are feeling broken, remember that God loves to use broken vessels! If we have accepted Christ as our Savior, then we are covered by the blood, and our past is no more. We are new creatures in Him! We are FREE INDEED (John 8:36)! We are REDEEMED (Isaiah 43:1)! We are RESTORED (Mark 5:15)! Yes, it's good to remember our past in sharing our testimony and letting others know that what

God has done for us, He will do for them too! But, we are no longer defined by our past.

Today's Prayer

Father,

Thank You for taking us, broken vessels, and molding us into mighty warriors for Your army. Continue molding us into the vessels You would have us to be.

Amen.

But the jar he was making did not turn out as he had hoped, so he crushed it into a lump of clay again and started over.

—Jeremiah 18:4 (NLT)

February 14

Commanded to Be Courageous

In my personal time with the Father this morning, I was thanking Him for things I have that aren't "things," and as I began to list some of them, He began speaking so many things into my spirit, I couldn't get them written down fast enough! But the one thing that caught me off-guard was when He dropped this question into my spirit, "Why do we only question God when life isn't going the way we think it should?"

Why *do* we only question God when life isn't going the way we think it should? Do we ever question God when life is going our way? Do we ever question Him about all the gifts He lavishes upon us every day of our lives? Do we ever question Him for giving us good health or blessing us with a promotion at work or bringing that special someone into our lives?

God didn't ask us to be strong and courageous *if* everything was going our way. No! He didn't *ask* us to be strong and courageous at all. He *commanded* us to be strong and courageous and to not be afraid or discouraged! Yes, He understands we are human, and we do get afraid and discouraged sometimes. He gave us the command to be strong and courageous because He knows we can't do it in our own strength! He wants us to be strong and courageous in the strength He alone can give us!

It's okay to question Him, He doesn't mind questions, at all! What's not okay is turning away from Him at the very time you need to be leaning in to Him and depending on His strength to get you through. Question Him, be mad at Him—it's okay—He can take it. But He is hoping you will do these things while pressing into Him and drawing closer to Him than you ever have before!

Today's Prayer

Father,

When we question You during our tough times, help us, also, to lean into You more than we ever have before and draw from Your strength.

Amen.

Have I not commanded you? Be strong and courageous.
Do not be afraid; do not be discouraged, for the Lord
your God will be with you wherever you go.

—Joshua 1:9 (NIV)

February 15

So Many Gifts

Can we, please, take a minute and think about all the gifts we have received? I'm aware Christmas is not long past, and yesterday was Valentine's Day. I'm sure many of you received lots of gifts at Christmas, and some may have even received gifts yesterday. Those aren't the gifts I'm speaking of though.

Do you ever take time to think about all the gifts Father has given you? Have you ever taken the time to realize He gives you some of these gifts every day? For instance, the breath you are breathing right now as you are reading this? Do you remember it is a gift from Him, or do you just take it for granted that you will be taking your next one?

I'm guilty of not remembering to thank Him as often as I should for these gifts. So, I thought today would be a good day for us to pause for a moment and offer up our thanks for at least some of our gifts. Maybe my list will help get you started thinking, and then you can continue with your own list, afterward—because I'm sure there will be some I forget!

We want to thank You today, Father, for Your grace; Your mercy; Your unconditional love; Your forgiveness; Your protection; Your provision; Your correction; Your One and only Son's blood covering our sins; Your selflessness in being willing to give up Your One and only Son so we can live with You for eternity; Your Son, Jesus, being willing to give His life for us to pay a price we could never pay; Your healing; Your touch; Your constant, 24-7 access; Your strength; Your wisdom; Your guidance and Your faithfulness.

Now, continue making your own list of the gifts He has given you, and keep it in a place where you will see it often. Every time you see your list, take a minute or two and thank Him again.

Today's Prayer

Father,

It feels good to simply say "Thank You" sometimes without asking for anything.

Amen.

Every good gift and every perfect gift is from above
and comes down from the Father of lights, with Whom
there is no variation or shadow of turning.

—James 1:17 (NKJV)

February 16

He Will Carry You

I was rudely awakened this morning, from a sound sleep, having to run to the bathroom and pleading with God to help me all the way there. It has been many years since I have thrown up, and I was unashamedly begging Him to take it away from me this morning—whatever "it" was—and to *please* keep me from throwing up! You know what? He did! I had a rough little while, waiting for all the "yuck" to go away from my throat, but He touched me in a very real way! I eventually made it to the couch and was able to rest in Him there. What is the purpose in sharing this in a devotion? (1) Because He told me to share it and (2) because you need to know that what He did for me this morning, He will do for you too!

He carried me in His arms this morning, and He held me, as I cried out to Him, thanking Him for loving me so much! Thanking Him for taking the stripes for my healing, thanking Him for being so good to me when I don't deserve it, thanking Him for His protection from my enemies!

He held me in His lap, let me rest my head on His shoulder, and He gave me sweet rest! Then, He lovingly woke me up for our special, quiet time together. As I was asking Him what He wanted to share with me for a devotion this morning, He showed me this verse in Deuteronomy. He said to share how He did this for me this morning and to remind others He will do the same for them, if they will just ask.

Are you being attacked by enemies today? Whether those enemies are sickness, finances, marital problems or whatever—cry out to God, run to Him for your hiding place and let Him carry you through. He will. He longs to, He's just waiting for you to ask!

Today's Prayer

Father,

Help us remember to cry out to You for help. You are always there for us, wanting to help, if we will just ask. Thank You for giving us Your strength! Thank You for destroying our enemies and making them run!

Amen.

The eternal God is our hiding place; He carries us in His arms. When God tells you to destroy your enemies, He will make them run.

—Deuteronomy 33:27

February 17

What Is the Altar For?

Our Father wants us to acknowledge Him, publicly, and let others know we belong to Him. The altar is a good place to do that.

It grieves my heart, not to mention the Holy Spirit, how we seem to have no regard for the altar anymore. While searching for information about the altar, I found this definition: *An altar is a sacred place for sacrifices and gifts offered up to God.* You may be thinking, "We don't offer sacrifices anymore." I agree, we, obviously, no longer offer up animal sacrifices, but aren't we to live our lives as a living sacrifice to the Father (Romans 12:1)? Doesn't He give each of us gifts we should offer up to Him—like a good voice to use in singing praise to Him, writing to tell others about Him, the gift of service to show Him to others and the list goes on. Shouldn't we, if for no other reason, be in the altar every chance we get thanking Him for our gifts and offering them back up to Him to be used by Him for the furtherance of His kingdom?

Our gifts aside, take a look at our country today! Maybe you feel you don't have a gift (sidenote: you do, you just may not have discovered it yet), but you could still hit the altar every time the chance is presented to pray for our country. There is so much evil going on around us today, what might happen if we all truly spent some time in prayer (2 Chronicles 7:14)? Stop worrying about what people might think if they see us going to the altar to pray and just do it in obedience to our Father? Yes, you can pray at home and in the pew where you sit on Sunday morning, but there is something special about going to the altar to pray. It shows others you aren't ashamed of the Father; it speaks volumes to the enemy, who you better believe is watching. More importantly, it touches the heart of the

Father to see His children honoring Him in that way! Will you find yourself in the altar at your next service? I hope so!

Today's Prayer

Father,

Give us the boldness to get back to the altars and spend time in prayer with You there.

Amen.

If you tell others you belong to Me, I will tell my Father in Heaven you are My followers. But if you reject Me, I will tell My Father in Heaven you don't belong to Me.

—Matthew 10:32–33

February 18

Discernment

Once again, Father has used a personal situation to show me what He wants to share on this subject. My husband and I recently posted something for sale on a social media site. I felt a connection in my spirit with one lady, something drawing me to her, as we discussed the item for sale. Through conversations, most having nothing to do with the item, she has become an online friend we are now praying for. She may never buy the item we are selling, but I believe God had a bigger purpose in mind anyway. Then, the flip side. Another "supposed" lady showing interest. Almost immediately, I felt a sense of something not being quite right. While she shared some things about herself, making me feel better for a moment, I still felt a reserve, or a check in my spirit, at the same time. I don't know yet what the outcome will be, but I still feel that reserve and the need to be extra cautious, so I will continue to ask my Father for discernment in the situation.

We are definitely living in a time that calls for us to be more aware than ever before. Christians, especially, must have and use discernment at every turn. We live in the social media age, a time where anyone can portray themselves to be anyone they want because their true self is hidden behind a screen.

When I searched *discernment* online, I found several prayers to use in different situations. This is an excerpt of a prayer for discernment in deception:

Father,

Thank You that I am already free from the bondage of sin and death and have my feet firmly planted on the Lord Jesus Christ—but I also ask that You would grant me discernment and an understanding heart to know what is good and true and to be able to identify and reject what is false and deceptive.

Using that prayer or one of your own, I urge you to daily, actively, constantly ask Father for discernment.

Today's Prayer

Father,

Speak to our spirits and let us know when we are being approached by a wolf in sheep's clothing.

Amen.

Watch out for false prophets! They dress up like sheep, but inside they are wolves who have come to attack you.

—Matthew 7:15

February 19

How Long Has It Been?

I remember that song from my childhood. It's a song full of questions about talking with the Father and praying through. Questions like, how long since you told Him your heart's hidden secrets? We know nothing is hidden from God, but we do hide things in our hearts from other people. I think, sometimes, we even try to hide things from ourselves!

How long since you knew that He'd answer you? How long since you stayed on your knees (literally or figuratively) until the light shone through? How long since you knew He would keep you the long night through? I think that's referring to more than an actual night. Sometimes, we are going through a tough, hard time that seems like forever to us, but it is just a night for Him, and remember, joy comes in the morning (a song for another day).

Since January 1 of this year, I have been following a plan of writing scripture every day. I wrote a verse this morning that I've read many times before; however, as I was writing it, I was suddenly struck by the words and the implication of it! I immediately knew He was speaking this morning's devotion to me in that one powerful verse! As I transitioned from my verse writing time to our devotion time, He brought the above song to my mind. I believe it's because this song goes right along with the implication of this verse—the woman in this account (Luke 8:40–48) knew, if she could just touch the "hem of His garment," she would be healed! That is exactly what we do when we pray fervently, earnestly! We touch the Father, and His power goes out from Him to us! But, not from our rote, every-day prayers like, "Father, bless sister so-and-so and be with brother so-and-so." Not that those prayers aren't good. But, I'm talking about the kind of prayers we pray when we are in a dark place or a hard time and we are earnestly, fervently seeking Him for answers. What might happen if we prayed those prayers more often—even when we aren't in a dark place or going through a hard time?

Today's Prayer

Father,

Lead us into prayer with You and help us stay there until we touch You and Your power goes out from You to us.

Amen.

But Jesus answered, "Someone touched Me, because I felt power going out from Me."

—Luke 8:46

February 20

Do Not Fear

Fear means to be afraid of someone or something as likely to be dangerous, painful or threatening. According to Wikipedia, fear is *an emotion that arises from the perception of danger.*

The time we live in today can be a really scary time. There are "wars and rumors of wars" (Matthew 24:6); mothers against daughters, fathers against sons (Luke 12:52–53). We see it in our everyday life, not to mention what we see and hear about if we turn on the news. The news is very conducive to producing fear in all forms.

Hate is being spread everywhere, and it seems most of the hate is being directed at Christians. Why does this surprise us? Do we not remember how they treated our Savior when He walked on this earth? They hated and despised Him because He went against all their "religiosity"! He didn't come to bring peace to this world, He came to make people choose sides (Luke 12:51)!

However, He came to make us choose sides between good or evil. We choose to serve Him or the enemy. He never intended for color to be against color or race against race—all those issues come from us! The enemy loves to see all this fighting and fear abounding everywhere! But, if we belong to the Father, have truly given Him complete control of our lives, we do not have to be afraid or live in fear. He wants us to call out to Him when we are afraid. He gives us many places in His Word to combat fear. In fact, did you know the words "fear not" are in the Bible 365 times! That is one for every day of the year (except for leap year)!

If He tells us 365 times in His Word that we don't need to be afraid or live in fear, I believe it's a message He wants us to get in our hearts, don't you?

Today's Prayer

Father,

When we find ourselves constantly being fearful or living in fear of what may or may not happen on any given day, remind us to call out to You and put our complete trust in You.

Amen.

When I am afraid, I put my trust in You.

—Psalm 56:3 (NIV)

February 21

What Are You Thinking?

Have you ever found yourself thinking about someone you haven't seen or talked to in a while, and then, soon after, you see that person or talk to them or hear something about them? Have you ever thought how crazy that seems?

A while back, my daughter shared something with me that she saw on Facebook. It was talking about how it is easy to find things when you are thinking about them. For example, it said it's easy to spot a certain color car when you're always thinking about a certain color car. It went on to list other things too, but the general idea was this: It is easy to find what you are always thinking about.

How amazing, then, would it be if we started always thinking about how we could serve others? I'm thinking we would find ways to do it every time we turned around!

What if we started always thinking about how we could show the love of our Father to others? Again, I'm thinking He would be showing us ways to do it at every turn.

Then, what if we started thinking about how blessed we are and how much we have to be thankful for? How might that change the way we look at everything? Instead of always looking for reasons to be mad, what if we were always thinking of reasons we have to be happy and joyful?

Do you realize what you think about is, basically, what you are seeking? He tells us to "seek His Kingdom first" (Matthew 6:33) and He will take care of everything else. Are you ready to start a new way of thinking today? It can change your entire life.

Today's Prayer

Father,

May we find ourselves turning our thoughts toward the positive things instead of the negative. Thank You for helping and guiding us into a new way of thinking.

Amen.

You will seek Me and find Me, when you seek Me with all your heart.

—Jeremiah 29:13 (NIV)

February 22

Love God—Love Yourself—Love Others

In Mark 12:31, we are told to "love others as much as you love yourself." Now, you may look at that, as I did for years, and think you are supposed to love others before yourself. Then, God showed me something thirteen years ago, and it is still as clear to me as if it happened yesterday.

Read that verse again. It says we are to love others *as* we love ourselves. Now, here's what He showed me: If I don't love myself, how do I think I can truly love others? For years, I didn't love myself, and to be honest, I still struggle with that sometimes. But God finally got through to me one night that He truly loves me *just as I am* and it is okay for me to love me. That is when I started finding it so much easier to truly love others.

I gave my heart to the Lord as a young teenager; however, in those days, you didn't hear much about a "relationship" with the Lord. It was all about "rules" and what *not* to do anymore. Praise God, He finally got through to me, and I began a true *relationship* with Him! God wouldn't have let His Son, Jesus Christ, die for me if I wasn't important to Him. And the same is true for you. He loves you so much, He gave His Son for you. Do you struggle with loving yourself? If so, I pray this helps you start a conversation with Him about it. Then, be open to allowing Him to show you just how much He loves you—just as you are. Know this though: He also loves you enough not to let you stay the way you are, and you are going to be so glad!

Today's Prayer

Father,

Some of us find it hard to love ourselves. Help us realize, until we can love ourselves, we can't truly love anyone else. Sometimes we forget how valuable we are, and we need You to remind us. Thank You for loving us and helping us to love ourselves, enabling us, in turn, to truly love others as You have commanded us.

Amen.

"What is the most important commandment?" Jesus answered, "The most important one says, 'People of Israel, you have only one Lord and God. You must love Him with all your heart, soul, mind and strength.' The second most important commandment says: 'Love others as much as you love yourself.' No other commandment is more important than these."

—Mark 12:28b–31

February 23

Are You Ready?

She was sitting on the porch, relaxing and taking it easy—just chillin', as we all say these days. She knew her mom was coming to pick her up sometime between ten and eleven. However, she was waiting for the phone call or text that would say, "Okay, I'm on my way," before she actually got up and got ready to go.

Then, as she was sitting there, her mom drove up, and the girl found herself hurriedly scurrying inside to get ready to go! *Oh no!* she thought, *She's here, and she never called or texted to say she was on the way! I've got to hurry and get ready!*

Are you living your life like that girl? Are you just chillin', biding your time, waiting for a "second call" to give your heart to the Lord? Maybe you've given your heart to the Lord, but you aren't fully surrendered to Him and His will for your life because you're waiting for "later" to do that. I submit to you "later" may come for you sooner than you think! You aren't promised your next breath, and in case you aren't aware, there is absolutely nothing else that needs to happen before the Lord steps out on a cloud to call His children home! All He is waiting on now is for the Father to say, "Son, go call My children home."

We no longer need to be looking for signs. The signs are all here. We need to be listening for that sound. The sound of the trumpet! And you better be ready before it sounds because once it does, it's already too late. You won't have time to "run inside" to hurry up and get ready! Are you ready right now? This very minute? If not, what better time to get ready?

Today's Prayer

Father,

Let us not be lazy or fall asleep, but remain ever watchful for Your coming. May we no longer be looking for signs but listening for the sound of Your trumpet call!

Amen.

So be on your guard! You don't know when your Lord will come. Homeowners never know when a thief is coming and they are always on guard to keep one from breaking in. Always be ready! You don't know when the Son of Man will come.

—Matthew 24:42–44

February 24

Whatever

Years ago, the word *whatever* became slang to take the place of an entire sentence. When used, it implied you were saying "I don't care" or "I'm not going to challenge what you say, but I'm not necessarily going to agree to it." This happened at a time when my daughter was young, so I heard her and her friends use this expression a lot—more than I care to remember, actually—but, I also heard adults using it.

Then, one day, God pointed out these verses to me and showed me this word in a brand-new light! Suddenly, this word had new meaning for me! It no longer bothered me when I heard someone say it, because as soon as I heard it, I would start saying these scriptures. It began to bring me amazing peace! Imagine that, just like it says in the verse itself—the God of peace was with me!

I don't think it's used as much today like it was back then. I'm sure something, probably even worse, has long since taken its place. Occasionally, I do still hear it, though, and I'm sure you probably do too. I would like to challenge you, from this day forward, when you hear the word *whatever*, let it serve as a reminder to you to think on these verses. Even if you have to look them up the first few times, take the time to do it. We all have phones, and we can easily look up scripture on our phones, so our Bible is easy to have with us at all times. Before long, you will have these verses memorized, and they will forever be in your heart.

Today's Prayer

Father,

From this day forward, every time we hear the word *whatever,* may it remind us of Your Word. May it remind us to think on things that are pure, lovely, admirable, excellent or praiseworthy; and may we put the things into practice that we have learned, received or heard from You or seen in You so Your peace will be with us.

Amen.

Finally, brothers and sisters, whatever is true, whatever is noble, whatever is right, whatever is pure, whatever is lovely, whatever is admirable—if anything is excellent or praiseworthy—think about such things. Whatever you have learned or received or heard from me, or seen in me—put it into practice. And the God of peace will be with you.

—Philippians 4:8–9 (NIV)

February 25

Homesick

Homesick, as defined by *Merriam-Webster*, is "longing for home and family while absent from them." I have a dear friend who posted the one-word Facebook status "Homesick" a few days ago. She is currently torn between two desires: She misses being home with her husband and other son, but she knows the best place for her right now is helping with the grandchild, so she has made the sacrifice to do that.

Her status hit me in a different way, though. It made me think of the old song "Beulah Land," which tells of being homesick for a country I've never been to before.

The older I become, the more this song rings true in my spirit. I find myself longing to go to that country, that place called Heaven; and yet, like Paul, I know God still has things for me to do here on earth. We know God has a plan, a purpose and things He wants to do in and through us, if we are still on this earth. Because, when our purpose is complete, He will call us home to Heaven.

So, whether you know it or not, you are here today for a purpose. Maybe your purpose today is simply to share a smile with someone. Maybe your purpose today is to be here for someone else who needs a listening ear. You may never know what your purpose each day is, and that's okay. Let it be enough to know God used you today, even if you never know how.

Today's Prayer

Father,

May we all come to see our own lives this way—happy to live for Christ while we are here, yet longing to be in our true home,

Heaven. Remind us that as long as we are still on this earth, You have a plan, a purpose and things to accomplish in and through us. Help us be aware of what those things are.

Amen.

For to me, living means living for Christ and dying is even better. But if I live, I can do fruitful work for Christ. So I really don't know which is better. I'm torn between two desires: I long to go and be with Christ, which would be far better for me. But for your sakes, it is better that I continue to live.

—Philippians 1:21–24 (NLT)

February 26

Living Aware

For a few seconds yesterday, which seemed like minutes to me, I thought I might be leaving this earth. I remember thinking, "I think I'm about to go to that country I talked about this morning." And do you know what happened to make me think that? It wasn't any larger-than-life scenario. Nothing extreme going on at all. What was I doing? I was eating lunch! Not a fancy lunch, just some toast with mac and cheese. Suddenly, there was a bread crumb, a teeny, tiny bread crumb, stuck right in my airway. I couldn't get it to go down, and I couldn't get it to come up. I could barely breathe and was coughing, gagging and praying for the Lord to help me. Then, *finally*, it was gone!

I share that with you as a reminder that life is short. We say it all the time. It is said a lot, "Your life can change in an instant," but I wonder if we ever realize the truth of it. No, we shouldn't walk around scared to death every minute or second of what might happen to us or someone we love. God doesn't want us living in fear. He simply wants us living aware. Aware of what He wants us to do, where He wants us to be, and aware that He can use us, even when we don't know it.

Are you living aware? Are you seeking Him in every detail of your life? He wants you to seek Him for guidance in every decision you make, big or small. Are you living each day ready to serve in whatever way He sets before you? Sometimes, those "interruptions" in your day, or in whatever you're doing, aren't interruptions at all— they are your divine appointments. Are you living aware of divine appointments?

If you haven't been living aware, let this be your call to action today. Begin by going to Him in prayer and asking Him to help you begin living aware.

Today's Prayer

Father,

You and You alone know the number of our days. Help us not to worry about how many we have, but instead to live with awareness. Please use our lives to glorify Your name.

Amen.

How do you know what your life will be like tomorrow? Your life is like the morning fog—it's here a little while, then it's gone.

—James 4:14 (NLT)

February 27

Sunrise

A sweet, precious friend of mine posts beautiful sunrise pictures, nearly every morning, on Facebook. Quite a while back, her status update one day said something about "the sun didn't rise this morning"; and as soon as I read it, I felt in my spirit, "The sun did rise this morning, you just couldn't see it for the clouds."

Do you ever feel the same way, like the sun didn't rise? Especially on those dark, dreary, rainy days when there are so many dark clouds? Yet, deep down, you know the sun did rise because it's a new day; it's just that all the dark clouds and rain have the sun hidden. Sometimes, it may even peek out from behind one of those dark clouds, during the day, as if to say, "I'm up here. I'm trying to break through these clouds."

Is the same ever true in your life? When you are going through dark days and it seems no one cares, not even God, do you begin to think there was no Son rise? You may be going through health issues or financial problems or relationship troubles, and you feel like there is no hope and God isn't with you. My friend, the Son did rise, and He is seated at the right hand of the Father making intercession for you.

Don't give up when all you see are dark clouds all around you. Remember, Jesus went through dark times too. He was tempted, beyond anything we could ever imagine, for forty days and forty nights, but He remained faithful and steadfast in His trial. On the cross, He faced the ultimate dark time when the Father had to turn His back on Him because He couldn't look at all the sin Jesus was taking on Himself for us. He cried out, "Father, why have You forsaken Me"—yet, He knew His Father was still with Him. He is with

You too. Don't give up—the Son has risen, and He will help you through!

Today's Prayer

Father,

In our darkest times, remind us You are still with us. Because Your Son died and rose for us, we can boldly come to Your throne, with Jesus as our covering, and ask what we need, and You will hear us.

Amen.

Therefore, He is able to save completely those who come to God through Him, because He always lives to intercede for them.

—Hebrews 7:25 (NIV)

February 28

Personalize It, Please

Would you like that personalized? Yes, please. I don't know about where you live, but here in the South, it seems personalization is all the craze! I'm even a consultant for a company that caters to making their products your own by personalizing them. I think that is actually what He used to get me thinking about this.

This morning as I was searching to see if there was a verse or passage in the Bible that talks about "personalizing" scripture, I couldn't find one. Even though there isn't a Bible verse or passage, per se, on the subject, we know in our heart that each and every word in the Bible is timeless and living. And, even though a particular passage may have been written for a specific group of people in a different time, the general message of it can still be applied to our own lives.

I was also shown a verse this morning that, in a way, relates to this. It is Deuteronomy 11:18 and talks about memorizing the scriptures, thinking on them and writing them down. Personalizing a verse could aid you in memorizing it, so that would be another benefit of personalizing scripture.

Do you have a favorite verse that speaks to you? Personalize it! Not long after we were married, my husband and I felt the Lord gave us a verse. He kept putting it in front of us in many different ways, and so we adopted it as our life verse, and we personalized it. It is Jeremiah 33:3 (NLT), and it comes to our mind anytime we see the numbers 333 together. I have several I like for myself. I will share one of my favorites to give you an idea.

Have I not commanded Kathryn? Be strong and courageous, do not be afraid; do not be discouraged, for the Lord, Kathryn's God, will be with Kathryn, wherever Kathryn goes! (Joshua 1:9 NIV)

Today's Prayer

Father,

You gave Your Word to each and every one of us, and You want us to make it and take it personally. Please, help us remember this as we are reading Your Word each day and use it to impact and change our lives even more. We ask it in the name of Jesus Christ of Nazareth. Amen.

Fix these words of mine in your hearts and minds; tie them as symbols on your hands and bind them on your foreheads.

—Deuteronomy 11:18 (NIV)

February 29

Leap Frog?

Did you know the *KJV Dictionary* definition of *leap* is "To spring or rise from the ground with both feet, as man, or with all the feet, as other animals; to jump; to vault; as, a man leaps over a fence, or leaps upon a horse"? Have you ever wondered or realized how often the word *leap* is used in the Bible? I did, and I went looking. I can tell you it was in there more than I thought!

The verse that came immediately to my mind was Luke 1:41, where the baby in Elizabeth *leaped* when Mary greeted her! You can also find the word *leap* used in these verses or passages: 2 Samuel 6:16, Isaiah 35:1–6, Luke 6:22–23 and Acts 3:8, as well as others. Can you imagine all that leaping, especially when you think about it in the way the *KJV Dictionary* defines it? How amazing would it be to witness such a thing?

We often hear about people taking a leap of faith, and while that isn't actually in the Bible, it is what we do when we put our trust in Him and believe in something that has no evidence for it. To take a leap of faith implies we are jumping in with both feet, fully trusting God to catch us, provide for us, to show us the way in what seems like darkness to us.

What about the phrase "leap for joy"? That's another phrase we hear often, but I wonder how often we actually do it. How often do we allow ourselves to get so overcome with His joy that we truly *leap*—as in, spring or rise from the ground with both feet?

This leap year, why not try it? Try getting so close to Him that you can't help but *leap* for joy, or you can't help but take a true leap of faith and completely trust Him. See what He might have in store for you when you allow yourself to play LEAPFROG—*leap* into *fully* relying on God. See if He doesn't take you higher than you've ever been and fill you with wonder and amazement!

Today's Prayer

Father,

This leap year, may we look for and find all the reasons we have to leap for joy in You, and may we sing to You our praises.

Amen.

The Lord is my strength and my shield; my heart trusts in Him, and He helps me. My heart leaps for joy and with my song I praise him.

—Psalm 28:7 (NIV)

March 1

Just Do It

Don't just read the words—they *mean* something. Today, as I was reading an entry in an old prayer journal, Father reminded me of that sentence.

This is what I wrote as "my version" of James 1:22–25: "God's message, His Word, is a message to *obey*! It is not meant to just be read or listened to, we *must* do what it says. *Then* God will bless us for our obedience."

Are you doing your best to put into action what you are studying in God's Word? He doesn't want you to just *read* His Word. His Word *means* something, and He wants you to study it and put it into action!

So, when He tells you something in His Word, you can be sure He wants you to follow whatever it is. When He tells you to love the unlovable, love them! Ask God to help you, He will!

If you are reading God's Word, and you read about serving others and you feel prompted to go buy a bag of groceries for someone He brings to mind—you need to do it! No matter how crazy it may seem. He may be wanting to use you to answer someone's desperate prayer. If you are in a church service, and you suddenly feel like you want to do something that seems crazy to you, do it! Again, it could be God using you to answer someone else's prayer. Anytime God asks you to do something, He has a reason. Why don't you try being obedient and see what wonderful things begin to happen? Stop just reading His Word, start *doing* His Word and be amazed!

Today's Prayer

Father,

May we not just read or hear Your Word, but realize they have meaning. Help us study these meanings and apply Your Word to our daily lives.

Amen.

Obey God's message! Don't fool yourselves by just listening to it. If you hear the message and don't obey it, you are like people who stare at themselves in a mirror and forget what they look like as soon as they leave. But you must never stop looking at the perfect law that sets you free. God will bless you in everything you do, if you listen and obey, and don't just hear and forget.

—James 1:22–25

March 2

Got Your Umbrella Handy?

Do you believe God can speak to you in many different ways and He can use anything or anyone He chooses to do it? If He can speak to Balaam through a donkey (Numbers 22:28), then I know He can, will and does speak to me any way He chooses—even a television show!

Faith is like a muscle, and it requires being used to be strengthened. If you never had any difficult times, how would you know to appreciate the good times? It is in those difficult times you have a chance to exercise that faith muscle, making it stronger and stronger each time.

Several years ago, He used a television show to drive home a point to me about my faith—or lack thereof. The episode He used was about a town going through a severe drought. They needed rain, and they needed it quick. As I remember—and it's been a few years, so I could be fuzzy on the details—tempers were short, and people were on edge; but, eventually, they all came together. They gathered at the church for community prayer, to pray specifically for rain. What spoke to me about this? Only one person brought an umbrella to the prayer meeting!

Wow! A whole town full of people coming together to pray for rain, and only one person brought an umbrella. He used that to drive home a point to me that I have never forgotten. When I pray for rain, do I have my umbrella handy?

In other words, no matter what is going on in your life that you are praying for or about, are you truly praying in faith believing He will answer? Or are you praying with a doubtful mind, thinking what you need will never happen?

Today's Prayer

Father,

Help each one of us exercise our faith muscle to strengthen it. When it looks like there is no way out, may we trust You with the answer. Help us to grab our umbrellas when we pray for rain.

Amen.

My friends, what good is it to say you have faith,
when you don't do anything to show that you really do
have faith? Can that kind of faith save you?

—James 2:14

March 3

Freedom

When you accept Christ as Your Savior and give Him complete control of your life, He sets you *free* (John 8:36)! However, you must be responsible in your freedom. Jesus didn't shed His blood for you to give you free rein to do what you want. He shed His blood for you to give you the gift of eternal life. He shed His blood to free us from the law, but while we are free from the old law, we still have other things to consider.

Just because you can do something, doesn't mean you should, necessarily, do it. Something that may be okay for you to do becomes not okay if it causes someone else to stumble in their walk with the Lord. You may not see anything wrong with drinking a glass of wine with your meal. Some, who aren't as strong as you are in your walk with the Lord will see you and think that must mean it's okay to drink, even if you're a Christian—or the one who hasn't come to know the Lord yet will see you and think, "I'm as good as they are. They drink just like I do."

It's not just drinking that we need to be careful with. There are so many other ways to cause a brother or sister to stumble in their walk or even to cause someone not to want any part of Christianity. It's the words we use, the attitudes we show, the way we treat others—all of this—in public and in private that we need to keep our guard up about. We don't need to help the enemy do his work, we need to keep our focus heavenward and keep our eyes on Jesus and be about His work!

Jesus said, "It would be better to be thrown into the sea with a millstone hung around your neck than to cause one of these little ones to fall into sin" (Luke 17:2—NLT). So, next time you want to do something "just because you can," will you, please, stop and think about the impact it could have on another?

Today's Prayer

Father,

Help us begin to realize the consequences we might face, if we knowingly do something that could cause someone else to miss out on an eternity with You.

Amen.

But you must be careful with this freedom of yours. Do not cause a brother or sister with a weaker conscience to stumble.

—1 Corinthians 8:9 (NLT)

March 4

Worrier or Warrior

Do you ever worry? In years past, I probably could have won the title for World's Best Worrier. Seriously, I don't think there was anything I didn't worry and fret over—almost to the point of making myself physically sick. What changed? Me! When did it change? Gradually, over a period of time.

Have you ever paid close attention to what is going on when you are worrying or find yourself anxious about something? Do you find yourself asking questions like "What am I going to do?" "What will I do if this doesn't happen?" "What will I do if that does happen?" "How am I going to pay this bill?" and on and on and on. Do you notice the constant in all those questions? The word *I*.

Have you noticed that *i* is in the middle of *anxious*? Now, what happens when you take the focus off yourself and put your focus on Christ instead? You must train yourself to rely on Him in your circumstances instead of trying to rely on yourself. Then, and only then, will you notice the worry and anxiety going away.

Wouldn't you rather be a prayer warrior than a frazzled worrier? Search out scriptures on anxiety. Print or write them out so you will always have them handy. When you find yourself beginning to worry or becoming anxious about something, grab those verses, meditate on them and give it all to God in prayer. The change won't happen overnight, but keep at it. Soon, you will find you have gone from being a worrier to being a warrior!

Today's Prayer

Father,

Help us not to worry and instead to pray. May we lift our prayers and requests to You. Because we belong to Jesus, bless us with Your peace that no one else understands and let this peace control the way we think and feel.

Amen.

Don't worry about anything, but pray about everything.
With thankful hearts offer up your prayers and requests to
God. Then, because you belong to Christ Jesus, God will
bless you with peace that no one can completely understand.
And this peace will control the way you think and feel.

—*Philippians 4:6–7*

March 5

Master of the Wind

Do you believe that God is always in control? Do you believe nothing takes Him by surprise? Do you believe everything that happens in your life has to pass through God's hands first?

These are hard questions to answer sometimes. Especially after events such as 9/11 or the Columbine Shooting or even after natural disasters such as hurricanes, floods or tornadoes. It all seems so senseless, and it can leave us wondering why it happened.

The truth of the matter is, we may never know the reason any of these things happen. Maybe what we need to focus on, instead, is seeing how God, our Father, will bring good from it. What about the way we all seem to come together after such disasters? People start coming together, pitching in to help each other, neighbor helping neighbor, strangers helping strangers.

Suddenly, it no longer seems to matter what color anyone is or what country they are from or if they believe exactly the same as we do. We are simply all coming together, supporting each other through the tragedy. Maybe instead of asking God why He would allow such a thing to happen, we should be asking ourselves why it takes such a thing for us to put aside our petty differences and come together to work in unity.

Yes, Jesus is the Master of the wind, and He can speak to it, and it will obey Him and become calm. But, if we have allowed ourselves to get to the place where it takes a "strong wind" before we come together, shouldn't we share in the responsibility, instead of blaming Him? Something to think about, right?

Today's Prayer

Father,

We know You are in control. Sometimes, though, in the middle of our tragedies, we don't understand. Please give comfort to our hearts during those times. Please forgive us if we have allowed ourselves to get to a place where it takes a disaster to bring us together in unity.

Amen.

So they went to Jesus and woke him up, "Master, Master! We are about to drown!" Jesus got up and ordered the wind and waves to stop. They obeyed and everything was calm.

—Luke 8:24

March 6

Will You?

Will you take this man to be your husband, to live together in holy marriage? Will you love him, comfort him, honor and keep him in sickness and in health and, forsaking all others, be faithful to him as long as you both shall live?

These words are widely recognized as traditional wedding vows. When we accept Jesus Christ as our Savior, we become part of the bride of Christ. Let's take a look and see the connection between these vows and what happens when we become part of His bride.

Will you take Him to be your husband, to live together in holy marriage? Will you love, comfort, and honor Him?

When you live together with Him, He is a part of every choice you make. You don't make an important or critical choice without consulting Him first. To love, comfort and honor Him is similar. You love Him by joining Him in what He is doing and allow Him to show you your part in it. He is comforted when you come to Him with any and all your problems, no matter how big or small, because it shows Him you trust Him to take care of it. You honor Him every time you point others to Him.

Will you keep Him in sickness and in health and, forsaking all others, be faithful to Him as long as you both shall live?

It's easy to love Him when you are well. But, what if you (or a loved one) receive news of a critical or terminal illness? Will you blame Him or lean on Him more than you ever have before? Stay faithful to Him by not turning your back on Him in the bad times. Keep loving Him through it all, and He will give you, daily, the strength you need.

So, will you still take this Man to be your husband? I hope you say, "I will."

Today's Prayer

Father,

Thank You for showing us our relationship with Christ in a new light. Help us remember to love and honor Him and to stay with Him through bad times as well as good times. Help us to never turn our back on Him, but should we have a weak moment when we do, thank You for granting us forgiveness the very second we ask for it. Thank You for loving us!

Amen.

For your Maker is your husband—the Lord Almighty
is His name—the Holy One of Israel is your Redeemer;
He is called the God of all the earth.

—Isaiah 54:5 (NIV)

March 7

Tell Your Story

Have you ever shared your testimony? You may be thinking, "Well, I grew up in church, and I don't really have a testimony because I got saved really young, and there wasn't any radical change." Maybe so, but each and every one of us has a story to share. The question is, are you willing to share your story?

Those who lived the "wild" life before coming to the saving knowledge of Christ may find it fairly easy to realize what their story is, and they will have no problem sharing it. They can tell about the dramatic difference Christ made when they accepted Him, and they are, generally, happy to do so.

For those who were brought up in the church and became Christians at a young age, don't listen to the enemy's lie that you don't have a story to share. Can you think of at least one thing God has done for you? Something that's happened in your life and you know it was nothing but Him? That is your story, that is what you need to share with others who may be facing the same thing. Hearing your story of what God did for you can encourage them and give them strength!

We all have a testimony—a story to share! In fact, some of us have many stories to share. He is constantly moving and working in our lives, and we need to be willing to share what He has done and is doing. What would happen if we shared our stories as passionately as we talk about the latest sports rivalry game? Are you passionate about what God is doing in your life? We will always share what we are passionate about, and there is no greater message than Jesus!

Will you keep your eyes and ears open and be willing to share your story when the opportunity is given?

Today's Prayer

Father,

Thank You for writing our stories. Please give each one reading this courage to share their own stories with others. Through sharing, we are made overcomers, we are strengthened and You can work through it all!

Amen.

I will praise you, Lord, with all my heart and tell
about the wonders You have worked.

—Psalm 9:1

March 8

Temper Tantrums

"Mom, please pray for me," my distraught, new-mom daughter pleaded over the phone, nearly in tears. It seems her six-and-a-half-month-old daughter was crying, to the point of screaming, in her playpen, for no reason other than she wanted Mommy to hold her. She had been fed, had a clean diaper and had plenty of toys to play with in the playpen.

I talked my daughter through it, as best I could, speaking to her in a calm voice and telling her to do the same with her daughter—to speak calmly to her, reassuring her that Mommy was still there and would be with her shortly. I told her to sing "Jesus Loves Me" to her, and before we hung up, my husband prayed over her and her daughter too.

How many times do we pitch our own temper tantrums with the Father? Ouch! I remember, vividly, the last time I pitched one. My husband and I recently moved to a new city, and as usual, expenses were incurred, so I decided to look for a part-time job. I received a call asking if I would be interested in a full-time position, forty-five minutes from our house. No! I was retired; now I wanted a flexible part-time job. (Insert pouting, temper tantrum here.) I did not realize it was God asking me if I would be willing to work full-time, for a while, to help us become debt-free again. Long story short, I finally agreed I would work full-time, grudgingly at first, if that's what I needed to do.

Amazingly, once I totally gave my heart and mind over to His will and not mine, He offered me a part-time, totally flexible, position barely five minutes from where we live and working with great Christian ladies! Sometimes, He just wants us to be willing to do what He asks before He gives us what we want and/or need. Do you remember your last tantrum? What did you learn from it?

Today's Prayer

Father,

Please, help us to recognize, quickly, when we are throwing a temper tantrum. May we, also quickly, ask Your forgiveness and then line up with Your Word and what You are asking us to do—or not do, as the case might be.

Amen.

Our desires fight against God, because they do not and cannot obey God's laws. If we follow our desires, we cannot please God.

—Romans 8:7–8

March 9

Imitation Faith?

Did you know that daily scripture writing was "a thing"? I only found out about it this year, and I'm so glad I did! The scripture to write yesterday was Hebrews 13:5–8. They were all good, but verse 7 spoke volumes to me. A friend has a close family member going through some trials right now.

We were talking a few days ago, and my friend was telling me this person confided in her that they didn't really know what to think about this "God" she kept talking about. My friend was able to tell her about the many different things God has done in her life and in her immediate family's life. She shared her faith by sharing these things, and that person is now being witnessed to, even silently, by my friend's life and her faith.

When I read verse 7 yesterday, the Lord showed me this is exactly what is happening with my friend! Her family member doesn't have faith right now because of the confusion from their upbringing. This scripture, to me, says that's okay! That person can listen to my friend speak the Word of God, and that person can also consider the outcome of my friend's life—how God has taken care of so many situations for them—and my friend's family member can *imitate* my friend's faith until she comes into her own faith!

That's how important it is to speak the Word of God to others and show them your faith! In so doing, they can imitate your faith until they find their own! I'm not saying, and this verse isn't saying, that anyone can imitate your faith and get to Heaven that way. Each person must make their own decision to accept Jesus Christ as their Savior; He is the only way. But, the same way a child imitates what it sees someone else do until he/she learns to do it themselves, is how someone imitating your faith can come to know Jesus for themselves, and then they have their own faith!

Today's Prayer

Father,

May our lives be an example of our faith to others that have no faith of their own. May they look at us and imitate, or copy, our faith until they come to You and gain their own faith.

Amen.

Remember your leaders, who spoke the word of God to you.
Consider the outcome of their way of life and imitate their faith.

—Hebrews 13:7 (NIV)

March 10

Unimaginable Love

Have you ever wished someone you love could just look straight into your heart and see how much you love them? I actually told my husband, a while back, that I loved him so much and wished he could look inside and see just how much! Well, you guessed it, that got me to thinking.

We all have someone we love "so much" that we feel we can't adequately express it in words or show it in deeds, right? Can you imagine that feeling of love multiplied by a number we can't even comprehend?

We sing songs about how great the Father's love is, and as children, we even sang about how deep and how wide that love is, but how many times have you actually stopped and really thought about it, really let it sink in?

Remember just a few days ago, when we were talking about personalizing scripture? Here's one we need to not only personalize, but meditate on for more than the quick second it takes to read or say it:

> *For God so loved [insert your name] that He gave His only begotten Son, that* when *[insert your name] believeth in Him,* she/he *should not perish, but have everlasting life. (John 3:16 KJV)*

Words not italicized were added for the personalization to make sense.

Would you take some time today to reflect on John 3:16? How does it make you feel when you allow yourself to stop and meditate on just how much God loves you? Do you feel unworthy of His love?

Without the blood of Jesus covering us, we are unworthy; but, if we are covered by Jesus's blood, He makes us worthy. Will you commit to living a life that points others to Him?

Today's Prayer

Father,

Our human, finite minds will never be able to comprehend exactly how much You love us. We simply accept that You love us more than we could ever imagine loving anyone, and we are so grateful for it! Help us to love You well by living in a way that points others to You!

Amen.

But because of His great love for us, God, Who is rich in mercy, made us alive with Christ even when we were dead in transgressions—it is by grace you have been saved.

—Ephesians 2:4–5 (NIV)

March 11

Write It Down

Do you journal? Do you write things out so you will remember them in years to come? Sure, there are a lot of things I can remember and can share with you that God has done for me, but I would venture to say there are a lot more things I don't remember. It doesn't have to be anything fancy. You may even find your journaling style will change from time to time, as far as what you are writing about. When I first started, it was like a diary entry; then, I began to write out my prayers, and now, it is a bit of a combination of the two. It's your journal—your story—write it any way you wish—just write it!

Writing things down is so important it is mentioned in the Bible several times! Jeremiah 30:2–3, Habakkuk 2:2, Joel 1:3, Proverbs 3:3–5 and Deuteronomy 6:6–9 all speak of writing things down or telling things to your children. What better way to tell your children, and be sure they remember, than by writing it out? What better way to be able to remember things yourself than by being able to look back at what you've written?

Your journal entry one day may be as simple as one or two sentences, and other days you may write a page or two. The only rule for journaling is simply to do it. After my mom was promoted to Heaven, I brought all her Bibles and church notebooks home with me. It was so special to find a couple of things my mom had written when she first got saved. There were only a few entries, but oh how they touched my heart, and oh how I wish she had continued writing. However, I will treasure the few things she did write.

If you don't already journal, I want to challenge you to begin today! I will even give you the first thing to put in it:

Lord, today I was challenged to begin a jour-
nal, so here I am.

Then, just write down one or two things that happened that day—or the day before, if you are writing early in the day.

Today's Prayer

Father,

Please help us to write things down so, in years to come, we and others can look back and remember things You have done for us. Let it serve as reminders of Your faithfulness to us in good times as well as bad.

Amen.

Now go and write down these words. Write them in a book.
They will stand until the end of time as a witness.

—Isaiah 30:8 (NLT)

March 12

Becoming an Oak

God is doing an amazing, awesome work in and through us. He is preparing us for something big, and I am so completely humbled to be a part of it. Our enemy, satan, is not going to like this. We must keep our eyes on the Father and stay prayed up and stay in His Word. Our strength will come from Him, but we have to be on high alert and recognize when the enemy is attacking and trying to destroy what God is doing! When we see it, we must remind each other what is happening.

It's not the time for us to get scared or run away and not be a part of this. Because, even though we know the enemy will attack (Duh! This is war—what else would we expect?), what we also know is our Father is on our side, and He will keep us safe, if we keep our eyes on Him! We are each responsible for staying prayed up and staying in His Word so we know what He is telling us and where He is leading us! The absolute safest place to be is in the center of God's will.

We must remember our true identity in the Lord. We aren't just overcomers going around stressed saying, "Whew! Barely got through that." We are victorious overcomers! We are our Father's warrior princesses!

What I'm telling you, ladies, is this is what I feel in my spirit: God is calling the *walking wounded* to *come forth* as the *princess warriors* He created us as so He can grow us into the *oaks of righteousness* He wants us to be!

We will discuss that statement further in tomorrow's devotion. Are you in?

Today's Prayer

Father,

Help us remember who we are in You—healed and whole—and show us how You want to use us to help grow Your kingdom. Transform us from walking wounded into mighty oaks of righteousness!

Amen.

To bestow on them a crown of beauty instead of ashes, the oil of joy instead of mourning, and a garment of praise instead of a spirit of despair. They will be called oaks of righteousness, a planting of the Lord for the display of His splendor.

—Isaiah 61:3 (NIV)

March 13

Walking Wounded

Walking wounded is an apt description of so many women these days. We listen to the lies of the enemy telling us we aren't as pretty, as smart, as financially stable, as skinny, as any number of other things! The enemy loves convincing us to play the comparison game because he knows it will keep us wounded. God doesn't want us joining in the comparison game. He wants us to start digging deep into His Word and remembering who He created us to be!

He didn't create us to be whiny, jealousy-driven women. No! He created us to be strong, love-driven women! He created us to be full of faith and to fight our battles on our knees, not with our social media or our fists.

Are you one of the many who think you aren't called to such things as prayer? You think you've done way too many awful things for God to use you in any way, shape or fashion? You feel absolutely unqualified to pray for anyone because you think you are a mess yourself?

I have news for you! If that is how you feel, you are the very one He can use the most! Who do you think knows exactly how to pray for someone who is going through an awful divorce or has battled abuse? Someone who has already been through it! Maybe that's you! Did you battle an addiction? You are the perfect person to pray for someone else dealing with that battle now!

We are all unqualified without Christ! But, when we give our lives to Him, He then qualifies us and wants us to be the princess warrior He created us to be, ready and willing for Him to help us grow into His mighty oaks of righteousness! Are you ready to start growing into a mighty oak?

Today's Prayer

Father,

    You created us to be princess warriors, and You want to grow us into oaks of righteousness. When the enemy attacks us with his lies, help us to fight back with Your truth!

    Amen.

> *They will rebuild the ancient ruins and restore the places long devastated; they will renew the ruined cities that have been devastated for generations.*

> —*Isaiah 61:4 (NIV)*

March 14

Be You

Yesterday, the Lord reminded us He wants us to dig deep into His Word and remember who He created us to be. He created you to be *you*. He doesn't want or need you to try to be your sister or your neighbor or that girl at the office or anyone else. He wants and needs you to be *you*. In fact, there is a quote that says, "Somebody somewhere is depending on you to do what God has called you to do." Another one is: "Be yourself. Everyone else is taken."

You can't do what God has called you to do if you are too busy trying to be someone else. You may think someone else has it more "together" than you do and maybe that person could do a better job. When you find yourself falling into that way of thinking, you need to get in the Word and remind yourself, God doesn't look on the outside, He looks at your heart (1 Samuel 16:7). If your heart is in the right place, that is the only requirement needed. God can work with, in and through you when your heart is right.

It took a lot of years for me to understand the concept of just being me. Honestly, some days, it is still a struggle. Those struggle days come less and less, though, the more I stay in His Word and stay in communication with Him. When I notice the struggle days coming more often, it reminds me I'm not doing what I need to be doing.

Do you have struggle days? Do you find you have them more often when you aren't staying in His Word and communicating with Him? Remember, there is absolutely no one else on this earth that can be you, so go be the best you that you can be!

Today's Prayer

Father,

Forgive us when we try to be someone other than who You created us to be. Help us learn to seek Your face and let You show us who You created us to be, and then help us be the best we can be at being ourselves!

Amen.

And I praise You because of the wonderful way You created me. Everything You do is marvelous! Of this I have no doubt. Nothing about me is hidden from You! I was secretly woven together deep in the earth below; but, with Your own eyes You saw my body being formed. Even before I was born, You had written in Your book everything I would do.

—Psalm 139:14–16

March 15

Get Out and Stay Out

Do you ever feel like you just don't fit in? I hope your answer is a resounding yes! The truth is, if you belong to Jesus, you shouldn't feel like you fit in here. Once you accept Jesus as your Savior, you belong to another realm.

We talk a lot about our comfort zones and, all too often, use it as an excuse for not doing something we know God is asking us to do. I believe I could win a prize for the way I always held on to my comfort zone and, for the most part, lived there. Then, He began to work on that area of my life.

A few years back, He began to gently nudge me into areas I had never ventured into before. He did it gradually, so it wasn't as scary. Before long, I began to realize that every time I said yes to something He asked, it was something that moved me, yet again, out of my comfort zone.

Are you in a cycle of being in and out of your own comfort zone? Recently, He revealed something to me, and though it probably shouldn't have, it kind of made me take a step back and say, "Whaaaaat?" Our pastor was speaking on the subject of sharing with others the truth of what God has done for us. He made the statement, "We are exiles here, walking by faith," and that is the moment I felt God speak to my spirit, "You aren't supposed to be comfortable on this earth. You need to get out and *stay out* of your comfort zone!" Wow! The more I thought on it, though, I realized it as truth!

I saw a quote that sums it up pretty well: "A comfort zone is a beautiful place—but nothing ever grows there." Are you willing to step out of your comfort zone for Him today and never go there again?

Today's Prayer

Father,

Help us remember we are foreigners in this strange land and we don't need to get "comfortable" here. Keep nudging us out of our comfort zones until we reach the point of realizing we aren't supposed to be comfortable here. Help us stay alert and open to Your calling on our lives.

Amen.

We are only foreigners living here on earth for a while, just as our ancestors were. And we will soon be gone, like a shadow that suddenly disappears.

—1 Chronicles 29:15

March 16

Wake Up!

I woke up before the alarm went off and got up, thinking it would give me extra time with the Father. However, as I was trying to write in my prayer journal, I couldn't seem to keep my eyes open at all! I kept falling asleep! That's when I felt in my spirit, "Wake up! Don't you realize what time it is? Can you not even spend one hour with Me?" What truth in those words! We, as a nation, have truly fallen asleep. Tragically, we (the nation) have not only fallen asleep, we have all but abandoned the One Who gave us our freedoms.

God tells us in 2 Chronicles 7:14, "If My own people will humbly pray and turn back to Me and stop sinning, then I will answer them from Heaven. I will forgive them and make their land fertile once again." Notice the qualifier to that promise? "If My people will humbly pray and turn back to Me and stop sinning"—He is telling us to wake up!

All we have to do is look around and see everything going on around us to know time is running out! We must wake up, spiritually, and turn our eyes back to Jesus! He is the only One Who can help us.

I can only speak for myself, but I know I let way too many things take my attention away from what I need to be doing. For one, I need to turn the television off and, instead, spend that time in His Word. Spending time in His Word is the only way I can ever hope to know what His will is for my life.

Have you allowed yourself to get lulled to sleep by the enemy? Does he have you spending time doing mindless things when you could be spending time with the Father instead? Are you ready to *wake up* and take back the time the enemy has stolen? Are you ready to spend even one hour with Jesus?

Today's Prayer

Father,

Let us not go to sleep in our faith and get lazy about doing the work You have called us to do. Let us turn our eyes back to You! Amen.

When Jesus came back and found the disciples sleeping, He said to Simon Peter, "Are you asleep? Can't you stay awake for just one hour? Stay awake and pray that you won't be tested. You want to do what is right; but, you are weak."

—Mark 14:37–38

March 17

Eeyore or Tigger?

Eeyore has been described as pessimistic, gloomy and depressed. But, even among those negative connotations is a positive attribute—he is loyal!

Tigger, on the other hand, is described as optimistic, exuberant and friendly. Tigger is also loyal.

Eeyore takes life matter-of-factly and is definitely dedicated. Tigger loves to bounce around from place to place and, sometimes, jumps in trying to help before knowing all the facts.

While Eeyore and Tigger are very different, they are still friends. They get along and work and play together. They recognize they are different, but instead of trying to change each other, they figure out how to work and play together with their differences.

What two better examples could we have for the way God wants us to live in harmony and peace? Also, two great examples of how God can use anyone. It doesn't matter what kind of personality you have, God can and wants to use you to accomplish things for His kingdom while you are on this earth. The things we do for Him and His kingdom are the only things that will last. Everything else is going to fade away and be no more one day.

What kind of world might we live in if we could all learn to work and play together with our differences instead of trying to change everyone to be like us? Think about it: if we were all exactly the same, that would be terribly boring, wouldn't it? How would we be able to learn from each other and grow?

Whether you are an Eeyore or a Tigger, would you be willing to pray and ask God to help you learn how to work together with others for His kingdom?

Today's Prayer

Father,

You made us each with different personalities for a reason. You want to use us individually and collectively to accomplish many things for Your kingdom. Help us to accept and love each other, even in our differences, and work together for Your good.

Amen.

The grass withers and the flowers fall: but, the word of our God endures forever.

—Isaiah 40:8

March 18

Grumbling or Praising?

I suppose it's something we can all fall into so easily—because it's always easy to follow our sin nature, right? It comes so naturally; it takes no effort at all. Problem is, God wants and expects us to hold ourselves to a higher standard than the world's. He wants and expects us to operate in our new nature—His nature.

We need to pay attention to what we are doing when we grumble and complain. We are opening the door to the enemy. Our grumbling and complaining doesn't just crack the door a wee bit for him to try to squeeze through; it flings the door wide open, and he can breeze right in, as if he owns the place, and that, my friends, is a devotion for another day. Today, however, let's keep our focus where we need it.

Perhaps we find it easy to grumble about other people and how they are behaving—or misbehaving, as the case might be—and we even try to justify it in our minds. It doesn't matter. If we are reading and studying God's Word the way we should be, we know there is no excuse for grumbling and complaining—especially against another. James tells us in chapter 5 and verse 9, "Don't grumble about each other, or you will be judged, and the judge is right outside the door."

Would you be willing to join me in a weeklong challenge? Starting today, every time you hear yourself grumbling or complaining, turn it into a praise instead. After doing it for one week, you will find it gets easier and easier to praise instead of grumble. After doing it for a week, keep doing it for a month. Before long, you will find that praise is coming more natural to you than grumbling or complaining, as it should be. Are you willing to try it?

Today's Prayer

Father,

We don't want to get caught up in the grumbling and complaining any longer. Help us, in the name of Jesus Christ of Nazareth, to work diligently to put it behind us and follow Your example. Just as you taught us to "turn the other cheek," help us to turn our thoughts away from grumbling and complaining.

Amen.

Do everything without grumbling or arguing.

—Philippians 2:14

March 19

Whatever Happened to Grace?

Grace is the unmerited, undeserving favor of God that many have come to expect for themselves, but few are ready to grant it to others. We have become so self-oriented and live in such a state of entitlement that we have lost sight of what it means to give grace. I would venture to say we may have even lost sight of what it means to receive grace.

Colossians 4:6 (NIV) says, "Let your conversation be always full of grace, seasoned with salt, so that you may know how to answer everyone." Is your conversation always full of grace? Is mine? I can't answer for you, but I know mine isn't. All you have to do is read a few posts on Facebook or Twitter or any other social media, and you will be able to plainly see there are far too many of us that seem to know—or show—little to nothing about grace.

Did you show grace to that person when they cut you off in traffic? You may not know that person just left a doctor's office where they received a bad report about their self or a family member. You may not know that person was just told, "I don't love you anymore," after many years of marriage. If you knew, would you be more willing to show them grace and understand why it was easy for them to be distracted? Why not show them grace anyway? Have you ever cut someone off in traffic when you didn't mean to?

That's just the example the Lord put on my heart, but we are given so many opportunities every day to show grace to someone. If He has given it to us in abundance, and His Word says He has, that tells me I have plenty to share. I just need to make more of an effort to do it!

Would you be willing to show grace to someone today? Even if it means curbing your anger or feelings of entitlement?

Today's Prayer

Father,

It is so easy for us to forget to give grace to others, yet we expect to receive it from You and others any time we need it! Change our hearts, Lord, and help us to be as quick or quicker to give grace as we are to expect it for ourselves.

Amen.

Grace and peace be yours in abundance through the knowledge of God and of Jesus our Lord.

—2 Peter 1:2 (NIV)

March 20

Intimacy

We live in a time where we are so easily connected to people all over the world, yet we have become the most disconnected generation. Do we even know how to be intimate anymore?

Whether you are married, single or in a relationship, there are people you need to be intimate with. *Intimate* is not a bad word, it simply means "closely acquainted, familiar, close." We all need intimate relationships.

Why, then, would we think God wants any less from us than an intimate relationship with Him? David wrote, "O God, You are my God; Early will I seek You; My soul thirsts for You; My flesh longs for You in a dry and thirsty land where there is no water" (Psalm 63:1 NKJV). How much more intimate can you be? "I can hardly sleep for thinking about You, and I wake up early to seek You. My soul is so thirsty for You, and I long for You in this dry and thirsty land where there is no water!" Are you, am I, seeking that kind of intimacy with God?

Do you get so excited about spending time with Him that you can hardly sleep? Are you excited to go to church on Sunday to see what word He wants to speak to you through the Message? Is your heart so thirsty for Him that spending time in His Word feels like a cold, refreshing drink of water on a hot, steamy, summer day?

If not, what must we do to get that kind of relationship with Him? Spend time in His Word and spend time in prayer—not only talking, listening to Him also. Are you ready to get intimate with the Father? He's ready to get intimate with you.

Today's Prayer

Father,

Help us come close to You so You can come close to us. Let us wash our hands and purify our hearts so that our loyalty is no longer divided between You and this world we live in.

Amen.

Come close to God, and God will come close to you.
Wash your hands, you sinners; purify your hearts, for
your loyalty is divided between God and the world.

—James 4:8 (NLT)

March 21

Praying the Scriptures

Did you notice how the prayer at the end of yesterday's devotion was nothing but scripture? Did you know there is no better prayer than that? It's not something that came natural to me at first. I only heard about it a few years ago, and I confess I sometimes don't think about it much. But, yesterday, as I found myself praying the scripture for us, I felt in my spirit that was what we needed to hear about today.

Do you ever find yourself in a situation where you, honestly, just don't know what or how to pray? Maybe you are so involved in the situation, whatever it is, you feel like you don't know how you should pray. Maybe, when you do pray, you feel your prayers are just bouncing off the ceiling. Well, now you have an answer for that! All you have to do is pray the scriptures, and you know your prayers will be heard.

Praying the scriptures is so important. When we find ourselves in that place—not knowing how or what we should pray about a certain situation—we can be sure praying God's own Word back to Him will get through!

We can rest and trust, knowing when we repeat His Word back to Him, we are not praying amiss. When we pray God's Word to remind Him what He has said to us or promised to us, we can know He hears us.

Are you reading this and thinking, "That sounds great, but where do I even start?" Well, you know the saying in today's world—there's an app for that? When it comes to praying scripture, there's a psalm for that! Yes, you can pray any scripture, but the Psalms is a great place to start! There are psalms for repenting, rejoicing and requesting! I'm sure you could even find an app for that too! Actually,

I just went and searched Google Play, and there are several apps for that! Let's get to praying the scripture today!

Today's Prayer

Father,

Thank You for the confidence we have in You, knowing You hear us when we ask according to Your will. Thank You for Your faithfulness!

Amen.

Now this is the confidence that we have in Him, that if we ask anything according to His will, He hears us.

—*1 John 5:14 (NKJV)*

March 22

Walk like a Christian

Remember the song from the '80s "Walk like an Egyptian"? That song makes absolutely no sense—to me, anyway! Maybe there is some hidden meaning in the lyrics, but if so, it's lost on this old lady!

So, how about if we walk like a Christian instead? What would that look like? You know, as I typed those words, I felt in my spirit, "Walking like a Christian might make no sense to some people." Wow! I wasn't expecting that thought!

Let's explore a little more. Walking like a Christian means to walk as Christ did, so how did Christ walk? He walked in love, understanding, grace, mercy, trust and faith in His Father.

As Christians, we should also walk in the same things. We should be quicker to show love, understanding, grace, mercy, trust and faith than we are to show hate, ignorance, cruelty, justice, doubt and self-sufficiency. To one who is not a Christian, that is why it might not make any more sense than the aforementioned song of the '80s.

Why and/or how can you love someone who just said something awful about you? or did something awful to you or a member of your family? Only through the power of Christ. How can you show grace and forgive that same person? Only through the power of Christ.

There is no better way to point someone to Christ than for them to see you living in a way they don't understand. For, when they see you living this way, they will question you, "How can you do that? How can you be kind to someone like that?" How can you… you fill in the blank; and when they ask those questions, you get to say, "I can't. But God living in me *can*," and then you get to share what He has done for you! Are you walking like a Christian?

Today's Prayer

Father,

Help us to live the way You would have us, as Your children, live—in a way that brings glory and honor to Your name!

Amen.

Therefore I, a prisoner for serving the Lord, beg you to lead a life worthy of your calling, for you have been called by God.

—Ephesians 4:1 (NLT)

March 23

Give Us This Day

Let's face it, the majority of us live from paycheck to paycheck, and I know *experts* say we shouldn't live that way. I even agree with those same experts from time to time. Then, I'm reminded of the passage in Exodus where Moses was leading God's people out of bondage. When they were in bondage, they could eat all the bread and meat they wanted (Exodus 16:3), but now they were starving in the desert. Let that sink in for a minute. Moses took the people's complaints to the Father, and He told Moses He would *send bread down from Heaven like rain* (Exodus 16:4). Then, He also told Moses to tell the people to gather only what they needed for that day. Only on the sixth day were they allowed to gather and cook twice as much, so they could rest on the seventh day.

Do you see what I see there? They had to trust God daily for their sustenance. They didn't get to gather up for days at a time, and if they did, anything they gathered over what they needed for that day was rotten the next morning anyway! So, would you rather be in bondage or be free?

I'm not saying it's wrong to have a savings account or to have a job where you make enough money that you aren't living paycheck to paycheck. I am saying it's wrong if you are living in bondage to those things. Are you placing your trust and hope in the money you make and have saved, or do you remember that without Him, you have nothing? The enemy is a very sly character, and he can easily lull you into thinking you are taking care of yourself, so you must be constantly on guard.

You may be living from paycheck to paycheck, and you may not have much of a savings account, if any, but one thing you need to remember is you can never go wrong by placing your trust and hope in God, our Father! Wouldn't you rather live paycheck to paycheck in freedom than be in bondage?

Today's Prayer

Father,

When we start trying to figure out everything on our own, remind us to stop and put our focus and trust back on You. Help us to trust You and to know that You will give us this day our daily bread!

Amen.

Give us this day our daily bread.

—Matthew 6:11 (KJV)

March 24

This I Know—God Is on My Side

Are you in a season of battle? Do you feel as if everything is closing in on you and you are being attacked from every side? If so, I have good news for you! God is on your side! He is fighting for you and protecting you.

Are people talking about you? Is someone going around telling lies about you? I know the natural human response is to fight back and try to defend yourself. But, how can you defend yourself from a lie? Why even try? Why not, instead, allow God to fight the battle for you? He tells us in Exodus 14:14 (The Message), "God will fight the battle for you. And you? You keep your mouths shut." So, the next time someone verbally attacks you, try keeping your mouth shut, let God fight for you and see what happens.

Maybe it's not a problem of people telling lies about you. Maybe you feel as if you are being attacked by other things, like finances or a situation at work. You just don't see how you're going to pay that unexpected bill that came out of nowhere. You don't know how to handle the situation at work because you simply don't see an answer or resolution to the problem—kind of like when the Egyptians were closing in on Moses and the others. Go back a verse and read what Exodus 14:13 says, "But Moses answered, 'Don't be afraid! Be brave and you will see the Lord save you today. These Egyptians will never bother you again.'" Remember, God is no respecter of persons; what He did for them, He'll do for you!

Trust me, I know from personal experience, it is not easy to do things this way. It's not natural! But, you see, we aren't "natural" if we belong to Him. We have access to a superpower called the Holy Spirit. When we allow Him to operate in and through us, it is amazing what happens! I challenge you to try it for yourself and see if you don't notice a change for the better.

Today's Prayer

Father,

Help us remember that our enemies will retreat when we call on You for help. If we will keep our mouths shut, wait and listen for instructions from You, we will be victorious because You will win the battle for us every time!

Amen.

My enemies will retreat when I call to You for help.
This I know: God is on my side!

—*Psalm 56:9 (NLT)*

March 25

Let's Have Church

Last night, my husband and I were back at the church we attended before our move. We arrived early and were both visiting with different people we haven't seen in a while. When my husband came to sit down, he told me one of the members told him they "had church" this morning. My immediate response was, "So did we." I felt prompted right then to write down the phrase "let's have church" because I could already feel something stirring in my spirit, and I knew God wanted to speak to me more about this.

Have you ever used that phrase, "Man, we had church!" when describing a particularly moving service you were blessed to be a part of? If I'm going to be honest—and I am—I know I'm guilty of doing that and never giving it a second thought. Until last night. That's when I felt the conviction of the Holy Spirit. Not in a "bad" way—just in an enlightening way. I mean, I could literally feel the scales fall off my eyes as the Lord revealed a truth to me that I'd never realized before.

You might be in a church where no one raises their hands in worship or shouts *amen* or *hallelujah* or claps along to a song they're singing, yet when the Word of God is given in a message, it goes straight to your heart, and you feel God's presence as if He were physically sitting right next to you. It may have been the quietest service in the history of services, but when God's presence is there and you feel it that strong, my friend, you just "had church"!

You may even be in your car or at your home, completely alone, except for the Father, and you can "have church" right then and there. God will send His spirit to meet with us any time, any place and any way. He is simply waiting for us to invite Him in. Will you "have church" today? I plan to!

Today's Prayer

Father,

Thank You for being willing to meet with us anywhere and everywhere. Thank You that we can invite the Holy Spirit in wherever we are. Thank You for Your presence.

Amen.

Peter replied, "Repent and be baptized, every one of you, in the name of Jesus Christ for the forgiveness of your sins. And you will receive the gift of the Holy Spirit."

—Acts 2:38

March 26

Even If

Do you have something you've been praying a long time for? Anything at all that you really want or think you need? Are you facing a mountain of some sort? Do you feel like God just isn't answering your heartfelt prayers?

The question I felt Him asking in my spirit yesterday is this: "Are they willing to serve Me, are you willing to serve Me even if _____?" So, I'm asking you this morning, "Are you willing to serve Him even if _____?"

Even if you don't get that promotion at work, even if you never get pregnant, even if you lose your job, even if you find yourself all alone, even if you never get married, even if your finances never change, even if you get a bad health report, even if all your friends abandon you, even if _____—whatever you fill in the blank.

Are you willing to serve Him, love Him and tell others about Him even if you feel like nothing is going your way? Are you willing to trust Him, no matter what, knowing He has only the best for you? Are you willing to say, "God, I know You can do this, but even if You don't, I will serve you anyway!"?

And, as if that weren't a tough enough question, what about when He takes it one step further and asks, "Are you willing to serve Me even if _____, and not be angry or upset or hurt?" Ouch! I don't know about you, but He has definitely given me something to think and pray about this morning!

If He is asking these questions, it is for a reason. If God isn't number one in your life, then whatever is number one has become your god! Our God is a jealous God; you must never put anyone or anything above Him (Exodus 20:3). So, are you willing to serve Him even if _____, and still be okay?

Today's Prayer

Father,

Give us the courage and boldness to not only say, but to truly mean from the depths of our hearts, we will serve You—even if!
Amen.

The three men replied, "Your Majesty, we don't need to defend ourselves. The God we worship can save us from you and your flaming furnace. But, even if He doesn't, we still won't worship your gods and the gold statue you have set up."

—Daniel 3:16–18

March 27

Peace Can Be Yours

Everyone wants it. A lot of people pray for it. Most believe it is unattainable. Unless you are a Christian. Even some Christians can't seem to fully grasp the concept of true peace. Oh, we know it's available, but do we really want to do what is required to have it? Sometimes, I think we are afraid to let go of what is holding us back from having the peace God offers.

Wait! Are you saying if I want the peace God offers, I'm required to do something first? Yes, that's exactly what I'm saying. Have you never noticed how many of God's promises require something from us in order for us to receive that promise?

God promises in Exodus 20:12 you will live a long time, but first, He says you must *respect your father and your mother*. I'm not sure we see a lot of that going on in the world we live in today.

So, what is required of us to have the peace God alone can give? You can find it in Philippians 4:6, "Don't worry about anything, but pray about everything. With thankful hearts offer up your prayers and requests to God."

You are going to have to get to the place where, instead of worrying about everything that comes around the corner at you, you simply pray and give it to God and then leave it there! Let Him take care of whatever it is that is coming at you. He already knew about it before you gave it to Him. It didn't take Him by surprise. He already has a plan in place to take care of everything, and He wants nothing more than for you to be able to trust Him so you can have the complete, unexplainable (to those who don't know Him) peace that passes all understanding. Will you choose to put your trust in Him and have peace?

Today's Prayer

Father,

If we truly want the peace You alone can give us, help us remember to first put our trust in You. Remind us to give everything to You in prayer, instead of worrying about it ourselves, so we may have the peace You offer to each of us.

Amen.

Then, because you belong to Christ Jesus, God will bless
you with peace that no one can completely understand. And
this peace will control the way you think and feel.

—Philippians 4:7

March 28

Act Justly—Love Mercy—Walk Humbly

Why do we want to complicate everything? As far back as when Jesus was walking on this earth, we were trying to complicate things. However, Jesus told the disciples in Matthew 18:3, "I promise you this. If you don't change and become like a child, you will never get into the kingdom of Heaven."

Micah tells the people, in chapter 6, to listen to what the Lord says. The Lord is telling them He has a case against them, and He is asking the people what He has done to them, how did He burden them? He reminds them that He brought them out of Egypt and redeemed them from slavery and how He sent Moses to lead them. He reminds them of their journey from Acacia to Gilgal when He, the Lord, did all He could to teach them about His faithfulness.

In response, the people start asking how they can please God. Should they come before Him with burnt offerings? Would He be pleased with a thousand rams, ten thousand rivers of olive oil? Should we offer our firstborn? Again, being a little overdramatic and trying to complicate things.

Micah reminds them—and us—that God has already shown us what He requires of us. He simply wants us to do what is right, to love mercy and to walk humbly with Him. Doing what is right is easy to understand yet hard to do because of our sinful nature. We *can* do it, though, with His help. Love mercy—what does that really mean? At the core of mercy is forgiveness; therefore, to love mercy means to love forgiveness! Walking humbly simply refers to the attitude of your heart toward God.

Today, let's try not complicating things, come to Him as children and simply do what He requires of us: act justly, love mercy and walk humbly with Him. Are you willing?

Today's Prayer

Father,

Please help us to stop trying to complicate things and simply take You at Your Word. Help us to do good, act justly, love mercy and walk humbly with You.

Amen.

He has shown you, O mortal, what is good. And what does the LORD require of you? To act justly and to love mercy and to walk humbly with your God.

—*Micah 6:8 (NIV)*

March 29

The Lord Is Near

Have you ever experienced the sick feeling you get in the pit of your stomach when you can't find someone you dearly love?

I remember an instance, many years ago, when my nephew was young. We had all gone shopping—I think it was around Christmastime—and we all experienced that feeling. Only, it lasted for more than a second. We suddenly realized that my nephew wasn't with any of us. Talk about going into panic mode, we did! The store we were in issued a Code Adam—google it if you don't know what that is—and everyone in the store was helping us search. We were calling his name and looking everywhere! After a few minutes, which seemed like an eternity to us, he was found under a circular rack of clothes. He was just sitting there, smiling and quite proud of himself for having found such a good hiding place! He wasn't upset at all. He had been playing hide-and-seek and didn't understand why we were so upset. Yes, we were able to laugh about it later and can laugh about it today, but we also remember that sick feeling we had when we thought he was lost or, worse, taken.

As I was reading today's verse, the Lord reminded me of that story. Sometimes, we get so involved in our circumstances and trying to figure things out on our own that we go into panic mode. We are running around trying to find a way to fix whatever is going wrong. Then, as a last resort it seems, we cry out to the Lord, asking Him, "Lord, where are You?" Unlike my nephew, who wouldn't answer when we were calling him because he was hiding, the Lord immediately answers, "I'm right here, child. I was simply waiting for you to call on Me for help."

Have you been searching for the Lord lately, wondering where He is? Have you been feeling like you must have lost Him somewhere because you don't see Him working or moving in your circumstances? He hasn't moved. He's in the same place He's always been. Call Him, and you'll hear, "I'm right here."

Today's Prayer

Father,

When we find ourselves going into panic mode, please remind us we only need to call on You and You are right here with us.

Amen.

The Lord is near to all who call on Him, to
all who call on Him in truth.

—Psalm 145:18 (NIV)

March 30

God Knows

Have you ever found yourself looking around at where you are, physically or spiritually, and realizing you have no clue where you are? You don't recognize anything around you, and you can't seem to figure out how you got there?

It always comes back to choices. You come to a fork in the road, literally or spiritually, and you have a choice to make. Sometimes, there is a right (good) choice and a wrong (bad) choice. Those are, generally, the easy choices to make when you are a child of God because you want to choose the right way.

Other times, the choices aren't necessarily between right and wrong, good or bad; it's simply a matter of which route you would like to take—the scenic route or the direct route. Do you want to take the scenic route, enjoying the beauty along the way, seeing some sights you might otherwise miss? Or, would you prefer to take the more direct route and get to your destination quicker without the extras?

Yet, even other times, the choices are so muddled it's hard to decipher which way is the best, and you feel as if you're left on your own to make the choice. Maybe that's how you find yourself wondering where you are and how you got there sometimes.

No matter how alone you may be feeling because of not knowing where you are, if you are God's child, you are never alone! Even when you don't know where you are, God does! He knows everything about you, and He will take care of you! He will always guide you and hold you close (Psalm 139).

Take comfort and know, even if you don't know where you are, God does!

Today's Prayer

Father,

Thank You for always being with us and helping us no matter where we go. Even when we wander, You stay right by our side, just waiting for us to come back to You. Thank You for always knowing where we are, both physically and spiritually.

Amen.

How precious are Your thoughts about me, O God. They cannot be numbered! I can't even count them; they outnumber the grains of sand! And when I wake up, You are still with me!

—Psalm 139:17–18 (NIV)

March 31

Name That Fear

Each of us have something we are afraid of, something we fear. The thing you fear may seem irrational to someone else, but when you fear something, it is not irrational to you. It is very real, and to some, their fear can be crippling.

So, what are you afraid of? I ask that question because God showed me something a few years back. Naming our fear(s) is the first step in gaining victory over them! One thing you can be sure of is this: whatever your fear is, it doesn't come from God, "for God has not given us a spirit of fear, but of power and of love and of a sound mind" (2 Timothy 1:7 NKJV). Naming your fear takes away the power it holds over you. It might not necessarily be gone in an instant, but you have taken away a lot of its power!

Once you name your fear, trust God with it. Give it to Him and let Him set you free from it. Don't ask Him to take it away, go ahead and give it to Him! He can't—and won't—pry anything out of your hands that you're holding to so tightly, but when you let go and give it to Him, He will gladly take it. It may not be gone in an instant. It may be an ongoing process, but once you put a name on it, 99 percent of the battle is won, and you only have 1 percent left to deal with! One percent is way more manageable than 100 percent, right?

It's not that easy, you say. I know. It seems really hard. But, let me share my experience with you. Eight years ago, I learned I needed to name my fear. I had lived with it since I was in fifth grade. The fear of rejection. Once I was able to name my fear, God set me free from it. Yes, I still struggle with it, from time to time, but it no longer has the power or hold over me it once did. When I feel it coming on now, I immediately give it back to Him, and He takes care of it for me. He has set me *free*, and He will do the same for you, if you allow Him. Will you name your fear and give it to Him today?

Today's Prayer

Father,

Thank You for being here for us. You never leave or forsake us, even and especially in our fears. Help us relinquish our fears to You so You can give us victory over them.

Amen.

I prayed to the Lord, and He answered me.
He freed me from all my fears.

—Psalm 34:4 (NLT)

April 1

Know Your Calling

Have you ever wondered why you are here? why you were put on this earth? Do you sometimes feel your life has absolutely no purpose? Do you ever feel somewhat "guilty" for having those feelings? Let me assure you, you are not alone.

Many people go through the same thing, whether they are a Christian or not. In fact, Christians may even struggle with it more than non-Christians. As a Christian, you may feel you should be able to figure things out better. While it's true you can go to the Father and ask for His help, you may not feel you are hearing from Him.

Sometimes, I think we can get our calling and our gifting confused. We are all called, and we are each given different gifts. If you look up 1 Corinthians 12:8–10, you can read what it says about all the different "giftings." There are many: wisdom, knowledge, great faith, healing, prophecy, discernment, the gift of other languages and telling what is being said in the other language.

Discovering your gifting can be quite troubling for some, but if you will go to God in prayer, He will show you which gifting is yours. You will begin to notice people commenting on what you do well, and when you do, pay close attention. Chances are, God is using them to reveal your gifting to you.

As for your calling—we are all called to the same thing: to make disciples in all the nations by telling them about Jesus and what He has done for you. It is the Great Commission, given to us in Matthew 28:16–20.

Now you know what you are called to do, let's get out there and do it!

Today's Prayer

Father,

When we find ourselves wondering why we are here on this earth, help us remember that the main reason we are here is to point others to You! Yes, we do each have different "giftings," but above all else, we are called to share the Gospel of Christ with everyone. Give us the courage to be bold in sharing His message!

Amen.

Go to the people of all nations and make them my disciples. Baptize them in the name of the Father, the Son, and the Holy Spirit.

—Matthew 28:19

April 2

Live at Peace

We have talked about forgiveness and how important it is for us to forgive others, whether they ask for it or not. We know forgiveness is not about the other person, but about keeping our relationship with the Lord where it needs to be.

What we haven't talked about is *asking* others to forgive us when we have done something to hurt them. Asking forgiveness can be a hard thing to do, whether you did something small or big to hurt someone. Humbling yourself to ask forgiveness makes you vulnerable, and it's made even harder when you feel fairly certain the person is not going to forgive you. But, whether they accept your apology and forgive you or not, is no concern of yours. You are simply responsible for asking forgiveness. Once you've done that—and done it sincerely—then you have done what God requires.

But what about when you've hurt someone without even realizing it? Maybe something you said was taken the wrong way by someone else, or maybe you hit your spouse while you were asleep. Maybe you didn't even say or do something that someone thinks you did. The fact you didn't mean to hurt the other person doesn't change the fact that you did, indeed, hurt them. A hurt is a hurt, and pain is pain, whether intentional or not, and whether true or not. I couldn't find anywhere in God's Word where He tells us we don't have to ask forgiveness from that person who misunderstood us or the one we unknowingly caused pain.

No, all I could find was instructions to ask forgiveness, no matter what. Someone once said, "An apology is not so much an admission of guilt as it is an acknowledgment of responsibility." Are you ready and willing to take responsibility and do what He is asking you to do?

Today's Prayer

Father,

   If we have done anything to hurt anyone, knowingly or unknowingly, help us be bold and responsible enough to ask that person's forgiveness and to ask Your forgiveness. Then, knowing we've done what is required, help us to walk in Your forgiveness and move forward.

   Amen.

If it is possible, as far as it depends on you, live at peace with everyone.

—Romans 12:18 (NIV)

April 3

Livin' the Life

"Wellllll, doggies!" I have no idea why, but as I typed the title of today's devotion, I could just hear the character of Jed Clampett, from *The Beverly Hillbillies*, saying that! I admit, it took me by surprise, but Mr. Clampett certainly knew how to "live the life" we're talking about today.

The life we want to talk about living today is the thankful life. Are you living a thankful life, or are you always complaining about something? Do you feel like there's always something going wrong? "Life would be so much better if only _____." You fill in the blank.

What about Colossians 4:2, Philippians 4:6, Colossians 3:15 and 17? These are just a few of the verses that talk about being thankful. How can we not be thankful when we think of what Jesus did for us? Is anything you are going through worse than what He experienced for you on the cross?

No, there is no way we could ever repay what He did for us. The reason He did it was because He knew it was the only way we would ever be able to live in Heaven with the Father. He knew we would never be able to pay the price that was required. He willingly gave up Heaven and His riches to come and live on earth to show us the way.

He modeled for us how to live a thankful life. What would happen if you began living your life as a thank offering to Him? Am I saying you should be happy about everything all the time? No, don't confuse being happy with being thankful. No matter what is going on, no matter how bad you think things are in your life, you can always find something to be thankful for. If you think there's no way you can find anything to be thankful for, you can be thankful Jesus paid the price you couldn't pay. In light of what He did for you, what can you find to be thankful for today?

Today's Prayer

Father,

Thank You for helping us live a thankful life. Thank You for reminding us to give thanks to You in *all* circumstances. No matter what is going on, we can be thankful You are in control!

Amen.

Give thanks to the Lord, for He is good; His love endures forever.

—Psalm 107:1 (NIV)

April 4

Are You Too Comfortable?

Why do you take Communion? I always did it because, as a Christian, it was something we were to do. Four years ago, God taught me something about Communion. A friend had asked if I could find a poem about Christ rising from the dead, and I told her I would try. Instead of finding one, I wound up writing one, which led me to a Communion service that night. It was at that service, Father revealed to me something huge about my relationship with Him. It hurt me to realize what I had been doing, and yet, even in His correction, which I was ready and willing to accept, I could feel His deep, deep love for me.

He showed me, as much as I love Him and as much as I thought I had been honoring Him, I was wrong. He took me back and showed me I had become too comfortable. Yes, He loves me, and yes, He tells me I can come to Him at any time with any problem, big or small; but He also reminded me I still need to keep my awe and reverence for Him intact. I can't let myself become so comfortable with Him that I forget what He did for me. How He sent His *only Son* to die for *me*! His Son didn't just die for me—He died a horrible, gruesome, cruel death, and He would have done it even if I had been the only person on earth! (By the way, He did it for *you* too.)

All I could do, as He was pointing these things out to me, was cry. I shed many tears of sorrow in the realization of what I had been doing. The whole time He was showing me what I needed to correct, He was also loving on me, and as I asked His forgiveness, He was lavishly giving it, just as He promised He always would.

I challenge you to ask God to examine your own hearts today and see if He shows you if you have lost the awe and reverence for

Him that He deserves. If He shows you, as He did me, that you have, ask His forgiveness and ask Him to help you get it back. I know, from personal experience, He will.

Today's Prayer

Father,

Help us get back the awe and reverence for You that You so deserve. May we never take for granted what You and Your Son did for us!

Amen.

Therefore, since we are receiving a kingdom that cannot be shaken, let us be thankful and so worship God acceptably with reverence and awe.

—Hebrews 12:28 (NIV)

April 5

Your Own Worst Enemy

Abuse is never good, whether physical or mental, and it has the potential to leave lifetime scars. If someone is abusing you in any way, you need to do everything necessary to get away from that person. But, what about when that person is yourself? How do you get away from yourself?

Why does it seem so much easier to give others grace and not ourselves? I know I'm guilty of mentally abusing myself, allowing the enemy to feed me lies that I take for truth. He did it for years and kept me bound without me even realizing it. Praise God, I finally saw it for what it was and allowed God to set me free! Yet, there are still days I find myself saying something derogatory to myself. Like, "I'm such an idiot!" or "How could you be so stupid!" It's easy to do, but the Lord has been making me more aware of what I'm doing when I talk to myself that way.

First, confess and ask the Lord to forgive you (1 John 1:9). Then, begin to immerse yourself in His Word and let Him speak *truth* to you and receive it! He doesn't want us talking obscene to anyone, including ourselves (Colossians 3:8). He wants us to be kind and compassionate (Ephesians 4:32). Don't look for self-confidence (we talked about that before); instead, get your confidence from Him (Jeremiah 17:7)! Let the words of your mouth be pleasing to Him (Psalm 19:14). Meditate only on things that are true, right, noble, pure, lovely and admirable (Philippians 4:8).

It's important for you to remember you have an anointing from the Holy One and you know the truth (1 John 2:20). Today I challenge you to look up all the scriptures mentioned here today. Use them as a starting point to get your mind on the right track.

Remember, *you are God's chosen, treasured possession* (Deuteronomy 14:2)! You are valuable! He would not have allowed His Son to die for you if it were not so!

Today's Prayer

Father,

Please help us learn to love ourselves and talk to ourselves the way You talk to us in Your Word. May we speak only life to ourselves as well as others.

Amen.

Because you are precious in My eyes, and honored, and I love you, I give men in return for you, peoples in exchange for your life.

—*Isaiah 43:4 (RSV)*

April 6

You Are Gifted

Yes, we all have spiritual gifts, but that's not what we are talking about today. We are talking about the other gifts God has given us. You may not feel like it, and/or you may not see it yet, but God has given you a gift that is all yours. You are the only one who can use the gift He has given you to do what He wants you to do with it.

What are some things you enjoy doing? Do you like to make people smile? Do you like to send cards to people to brighten their day and just let them know someone is thinking of them and praying for them? If you answered yes to any of those questions, do you realize that is the gift of encouragement?

Do you see others hurting and want to do whatever you can to help them? Do you see someone being mistreated and you want to correct the situation? Do you realize this could be considered peacemaking? Peacemaking is a gift!

Maybe you're good at singing or sports or math or English or just simply being friendly—all these are gifts! You may even have more than one gift, and that's okay! Are you beginning to see now what we're talking about today?

We all have different gifts, and your gifts are unique to you the same way mine are unique to me. Discovering your gift(s) is really not that hard. Just take some time to quiet yourself before the Lord and ask Him to show you—He will, and it will be easier than you think!

In addition to your spiritual gifts, you need to be using these other gifts God has given you too. He gave them to you for a purpose that only you can fulfill. If you haven't already been using your gift(s) for His glory, will you begin to do so today? Will you start being bold and loving and sensible with the gift(s) He has given you?

Today's Prayer

Father,

Please reveal to each of us those things we are good at, the things You have gifted us with, and help us to be bold, loving and sensible in using them for You!

Amen.

> *God doesn't want us to be shy with His gifts,*
> *but bold and loving and sensible.*

> —*2 Timothy 1:7 (MSG)*

April 7

Yes, You Can

I love how God uses the Holy Spirit to reveal things to me through His Word, especially when He uses a scripture that I've quoted so many times over the years to reveal something new!

Recently, I was reading Philippians 4:13, and He showed me a couple of new things I had never thought about before. Over the years, I've used that verse to encourage and remind myself and others that, because of Christ being in us, giving us strength, we can do those things that were hard. I still believe that, but now, it's also much more!

I remember praying and asking God to help me be able to learn how to do things that I kept saying "I can't," and that's when I heard in my spirit, "You are the one that keeps saying you can't, my child, defeating yourself before you even get started. I never said you couldn't. Remember the verse you always quote? I didn't mean you would just have strength to do, in your words, those things you felt were 'doable,' though hard. I meant you *can do all* things. *You* are the one who keeps trying to limit what I can do through you. Stop! You are listening to the father of lies instead of listening to Me. Release yourself to Me *completely* and watch what happens!" Wow! That certainly got my attention. How about yours?

Then, to top that off, He showed me something else about the same scripture that I had never noticed before. While it *is* Christ Who gives us the strength, it could also be saying, "We can do all things, *which strengthens us*, through Christ." Meaning, He will allow us to do things that will strengthen our walk with Him and our witness to others. Those are the things that are important anyway—our walk with Him and our witness to others.

What have you been saying "I can't" to lately? Are you ready and willing, now, to say, "It may not be perfect, but I can give it my best try"? You *can*!

Today's Prayer

Father,

Thank You for bringing Your Word to new life in us! Thank You for reminding us *we can* because of You!

Amen.

I can do all things through Christ which strengtheneth me.

—Philippians 4:13 (KJV)

April 8

Gather

On our way out the door last night for church, I simply noticed the plaque hanging near our back door and immediately felt the Holy Spirit stirring in me. Why have we suddenly started using this word so much?

Which started me on a quest this morning, searching out the word *gather* in the Bible. I had a certain gathering in mind, but I was surprised to see how often the word *gather* is used in the Bible! You should google it for yourself to see what I'm talking about.

We do need to gather together these days, more than ever before (just my opinion), but not just to have a good time. We need to be gathering in the name of the Lord, teaching as many as we can about the Father, Who loves us so much He sent His only Son, Jesus Christ, to die on the cross for us and our sin, to be resurrected three days later, go into hell and take the keys from satan before ascending to His rightful place at the right hand of the Father. And then sending the Holy Spirit to live inside us when we accept Jesus as our Lord and Savior. We need to gather together to worship and praise His name and point others to Him.

We don't need to gather for the simple sake of gathering and not accomplishing anything for the kingdom of God. One day, I believe very soon, that trumpet is going to sound, and God is going to gather all His children together for the most wonderful, amazing gathering anyone could ever imagine! That, my friend, is the gathering we need to be preparing for. Are you ready for that gathering? Are you telling your friends and family about it?

Today's Prayer

Father,

Let us come and gather together in Your name, seeking to do Your will and win others for Christ.

Amen.

Call them all together—men, women, children and the foreigners living in your towns, so they may hear this Book of Instruction and learn to fear the Lord your God and carefully obey all the terms of these instructions. Do this so that your children who have not known these instructions will hear them and will learn to fear the Lord your God. Do this as long as you live in the land you are crossing the Jordan to occupy.

—Deuteronomy 31:12–13 (NLT)

April 9

Spread

When Father put the word *gather* in my spirit yesterday, I had no idea what He was going to do this morning. As I was writing today's scripture from the scripture writing plan I'm using, verse 8 stood out to me.

It made me begin to question if these words could, truthfully, be said of me. Do I spread the Lord's message? Do people know that I have faith in God by looking at my life? What about you? I began to wonder what might happen if we truly realized and began to grasp the importance of spreading the Lord's message.

We are so accustomed to having His Word at our fingertips, any time we need it, no matter where we are, I have to wonder if we take it for granted. If your house is like ours, you probably have more Bibles in more translations than you could ever use. Not only that, but with all our smartphones, we now have access to the Bible in the palm of our hand, in just about any translation we could think of!

Yet, with all that accessibility, how many of us take advantage of it and use it to spread His message? How many times have you had someone talk to you about a problem they're having, and instead of getting out the Bible (I mean, it's right there on your phone) to find scripture to help them, you either listen, nod and say, "I'll be praying for you," or you try to give your own advice about the situation.

For so many years, we have heard *we are living in the last days* that I'm afraid we have become "immune" to it. I believe God is calling us to wake up and become aware! We must start spreading His message to others, or there will be many who are left behind! Would you share His message with at least one person today?

Today's Prayer

Father,

Help us to spread the Lord's message everywhere and have the news of our faith in You known all over the world without anyone saying anything about it.

Amen.

And because of you, the Lord's message has spread everywhere in those regions. Now the news of your faith in God is known all over the world and we don't have to say a thing about it.

—1 Thessalonians 1:8

April 10

Scatter

Don't you just love how God works? Two days ago, He put a simple word in my spirit—*gather*—and gave me a devotion about it. Then, as He was giving me that devotion, He gave me two more simple words—*spread* and *scatter*—and told me those would be the next two devotions.

Gather, spread and scatter—first, He spoke to us about gathering in the name of the Lord and reminded us of a gathering He is going to have one day soon, then He spoke to us about spreading His message to others. Today, He wants to speak about *scatter*ing the seeds. Today's word and yesterday's word are very similar, yet different. To spread something is to distribute over a period or among a group; to scatter is to throw in various, random directions.

Yesterday was more about being intentional in one-on-one or group situations, but today is about scattering the seed everywhere, much like Jesus talked about in the parable of the farmer. We scatter seed—good or bad—in many different ways.

You scatter seed everywhere you go, simply by your actions. When you show genuine love, compassion and caring for others while you are going about your day, you are scattering good seed. You aren't responsible for where it lands or what happens to it after you have scattered it. You are only responsible for which kind of seed you scatter!

Were you already aware of how you scatter seed everywhere you go? Did you know you are always scattering seed—good or bad? Are you scattering the good seed—the message of the hope of Jesus Christ? Will you spend some time in prayer today, asking God to help you scatter good seed?

Today's Prayer

Father,

Help us to scatter the seeds of Your good news! While some will fall and be stepped on for the birds to eat and some will fall among rock to wilt and die after it begins to grow, let us remember there are some that will fall on good ground, grow and produce a hundredfold crop!

Amen.

Those seeds that fell on good ground are the people who listen to the message and keep it in good and honest hearts. They last and produce a harvest.

—Luke 8:15

April 11

Be the Same

No matter where you go, if you are a Christian, a Christ-follower, your conduct should be the same. Period. Your actions, your speech, your demeanor, *everything* about you should scream—yes, scream—*Jesus*! If you don't conduct yourself the same, no matter where you are, how can you expect to be a witness for Him? When someone sees you in church, praising the Father, loving others and smiling, will they see the same you when they see you at work on Monday morning or in the grocery store or in traffic?

You can use all the excuses for your bad behavior you want— "You don't understand how incompetent the people are that I work with," "I don't know why they can't have more than one lane open. I don't have time to wait in this long line," "Did you see that car just pull out in front of me to go 5 mph?"—at the end of the day, they are just that, excuses.

Do you realize what you are using as an excuse for your bad behavior just might be God "sharpening" you a bit? Don't you think He knows exactly who you work with? Don't you think He knows how you hate to wait for anything? Don't you think He knows that car pulled out in front of you?

Maybe He wants you to be a light in that coworker's life, showing them the love of Jesus by being kind to them and helping them "learn the ropes." Maybe He wants you to wait in line, not only to teach you about patience, but so you can be a witness to the person you are waiting in line with, even without saying a word or just being a listening ear. Maybe He allowed that car to pull out in front of you to slow you down and keep you from being in a horrible accident on the road. Just a little something for you to consider and ponder over today. Are you the same Christian everywhere you go?

Today's Prayer

Father,

Help us not to conform to the way we acted before coming to know You, but to be holy in all our conduct, as You are holy.

Amen.

As obedient children, do not be conformed to the passions of your former ignorance, but as He who called you is holy, you also be holy in all your conduct, since it is written, "You shall be holy, for I am holy."

—1 Peter 1:14–16

April 12

He Arose

The Lord gave me this poem three years ago. Let the words sink into your spirit today as you read it. Do you truly grasp what He did on that cross, all those years ago? He did it for *you*! He loves *you*! Do you love Him?

All the talk about this Jesus
Religious leaders could not stand
They wanted to take His life
Not knowing they were part of the plan

Three nails held Him on the cross
Or at least that's what they thought
He willingly hung there
For by His blood we would be bought

His loved ones took His body
And placed it in a tomb
They were overcome with grief
Feeling nothing now but doom

A huge stone at the entrance
No one could go in or out
When they arrived on the third morning
They were puzzled and full of doubt

For the stone was rolled away
The tomb was empty, save for his clothes,
Two angels appeared and told them
"He is not here! He arose!"

Yes, He took our sins upon Him
When He died upon that tree
And because He rose again
You and I can now be free

Today's Prayer

Father,
Thank You for the sacrifice of Your Son so we could be set free!
Amen.

He is not here; He has risen, just as He said.
Come and see the place where He lay.

—Matthew 28:6 (NIV)

April 13

Don't Worry

You know it's coming, right? After the title of today's devotion, you must know it's coming—be happy! "Don't Worry, Be Happy," a cute little song released by Bobby McFerrin in 1988—cute, but oh so true!

If you're too young to remember the song, google it and listen or look at the lyrics. Since the Lord put that song on my heart as I listened for a title to today's devotion, I began to wonder if Bobby McFerrin was a Christian. I mean, he had to be, right? To be able to sing a song about not worrying, how could he not be? So, I did what everyone does these days, I went to Google. I was correct; he is definitely a Christian. He didn't "flaunt" his Christianity, but if you ask me, it certainly shone through in that song.

Don't worry. Be happy. Can you really live like that? There is so much meanness and hatred going on these days, how are you not supposed to worry about things? You could be driving down the road and get shot by someone who is just shooting for the thrill of it. You could be facing losing your job; how are you not supposed to worry about how the bills will get paid if that happens? You send your kids to school and wonder if they'll make it home at the end of the day or if there will be a school shooting at their school. You got a bad report from the doctor about those tests you had done. How are you not supposed to worry about that?

Jesus. The answer is that simple. And just like that, another song popped into my head—"Without Him." Look up the lyrics. If you belong to Jesus, you never have to worry about anything! Oh, you can choose to worry, but why? It will only make you sick. I challenge you today to give your worries to Him. You were meant to trust. Trust Him with all your worries, and see how much better you feel!

Today's Prayer

Father,

We are so thankful we can depend on You to bring everything together for good. Thank You for taking away our worrying when we give it to You. Thank You for allowing us to have You at the center of our life instead!

Amen.

Before you know it a sense of God's wholeness, everything coming together for good, will come and settle you down. It's wonderful what happens when Christ displaces worry at the center of your life.

—Philippians 4:7 (The Message)

April 14

Better Together

Recently, I've gone back to walking thirty minutes every day. It sure wasn't pretty or fast the first day or the next, but as the days went by, I saw a little improvement. I walk along the road that runs in front of our house. I go down our driveway, turn to the left and walk to the end of it, then turn around and walk back the other way. Coming back past our house and continuing on, there is a curve, and just around that curve, a slight incline begins going up a hill.

One of my first goals was to make it to the top of that hill before I turned around to head back to the house. I had no plan to go over that hill to the other side. I thought it was a long way over that hill to where the road curved around going out to a main highway. Finally, I made it almost to the top of the hill one day before I turned around.

A few days into my walking, my sweet husband started walking with me. As we approached the menacing hill, I told him about my goal to reach the top of it one day. He encouraged me to do it that day, and we did! Walking with him, I not only made it to the top of that hill, I made it over the hill, down the other side and around the curve, all the way to the end of that road where it ran into the main highway.

I wouldn't go over that hill by myself because I was scared of what was on the other side. So many times, the things we fear aren't really as bad as we're thinking. When we face things with others, it is so much easier. I know I wouldn't have conquered the hill that day and certainly wouldn't have gone all the way around on my own. But, doing it with someone else made it not so scary to face what was on the other side of that hill.

God never intended for us to walk this path of life alone. Who in your life inspires you to push forward and conquer your fears? Do you inspire anyone? Let's make it our goal to be a cheerleader for someone today. You in? I am!

Today's Prayer

Father,

Thank You that we are not meant to walk this road of life alone. Thank You for giving us friends and family to walk alongside us and encourage us along the way. Help us be an encouragement to someone today.

Amen.

Two people are better off than one, for they can help each other succeed.

—Ecclesiastes 4:9 (NLT)

April 15

Climb Your Hill

Remember the hill we talked about yesterday? God showed me something else about that hill too. Yes, it was very daunting, and I don't know when I might have conquered it had it not been for encouragement from someone else. With that encouragement, though, I did persevere and conquer it!

We never know what God is going to ask us to do. He was asking me to get to the top of that hill, and I knew He would help me get it done. I just wasn't ready to do it on my own yet, so He sent me encouragement to get it done.

It wasn't easy! It was one, slow, hard-breathing step at a time. But, as ugly as it must have been, I was making forward progress, and I made it! I not only made it to the top but, as I shared yesterday, went on down the other side and on down the road too.

What I didn't share yesterday was what happened coming back. As we began to approach the hill again, coming from the other side this time, I began to mentally prepare. As we got to the hill, I began asking the Lord to help me. I kept saying, "Help me, Lord. Push me if You have to. I know You will help me get back to the top of this hill again. We're almost there, Lord. Thank You for helping me." Then, there I was at the top of that hill again. And, as I was beginning the descent of that hill, I felt in my spirit, "The reward for walking uphill is going downhill!"

What is it that God is asking you to do? Is there something you've been arguing with Him about doing or resisting doing because you know it is going to be hard? I encourage you to stop arguing or resisting today. Start that uphill climb. Just take it one, slow, hard-breathing step at a time. He will be with you every step of the way, and then once you have done it, you get the reward of going downhill for a little while. Will you start climbing your hill today?

Today's Prayer

Father,

Help us persevere and do Your will so we may receive what You have promised us. It won't always be the easy thing You ask us to do, help us do it anyway, in the name of Jesus Christ of Nazareth!

Amen.

You need to persevere so that when you have done the will of God, you will receive what He has promised.

—Hebrews 10:36

April 16

The Ripple Effect

We all know about the ripple effect, how one small act spreads outward affecting many more. There are many different types of ripple effects, but today we want to focus on the ripple effect of kindness.

Do you ever give much thought to how everything you do causes a ripple effect? Wouldn't you rather be causing ripples of kindness than anything else? Do you know it doesn't take much effort on your part to do that? You can simply smile at someone today and start a ripple effect of kindness—one that you may never even know the extent of; but without you simply smiling at that one person, it wouldn't have happened.

The ripple effect is why every choice we make is so important, whether we realize it or not. Start making a conscious effort to do something kind. Try smiling at just one person today, even if you don't feel like it. Do you realize doing something when you don't feel like it is a sacrifice? So, smile at that person the enemy just used to try to make you mad; say something kind about the person who just cut you off in traffic. Hold the door open for someone when you're out and about today. Let someone go ahead of you in the checkout line at the store; entertain that energetic toddler while the frazzled mom checks out. Tell someone how their smile made your day better.

You may think these choices are too hard to make and you could never do it. I have to disagree with you. Would you be willing to at least try it first? Sincerely ask the Lord to help you with this and then just choose to do it. You will be surprised, the more you do it, how easy it becomes. Before you know it, you will be doing it without even thinking about it because it becomes second nature to you. God has already put something in your mind, an act of some type of kindness, He wants you to do today. Are you willing to take the challenge and do it? If you do, you will be encouraged, so what are you waiting for?

Today's Prayer

Father,

Please help us become more like Dorcas, full of good works and acts of charity. Let us be the start of a ripple effect of kindness and may we start it not just today, but every day.

Amen.

Now there was in Joppa a disciple named Tabitha, which, translated, means Dorcas. She was full of good works and acts of charity.

—Acts 9:36 (ESV)

April 17

Hand 'Em Over

Are you in a season of wondering how God is going to take care of everything? Are you facing financial loss in any form? Are you facing relationship issues, whether with a spouse, boyfriend or family member? Do you find yourself being tempted to worry?

My husband is a missionary, and we depend on partners to join with us, financially and prayerfully, in order for him to receive a paycheck. Due to circumstances beyond some of our partners' control, we have lost quite a few financial partners this year. To the point that now there isn't enough money in his account for him to receive any more paychecks, until it gets built up again. This could cause us to worry and fret about things. But, surprisingly, I am not at all concerned or feeling worried in any way! The only explanation I have for that is I know how God has always provided for us in the past, and I know He will continue to do so, even if He hasn't shown us how yet.

For instance, I was looking through my prayer journals the other day, and I came across an entry that made me realize again just how much more God cares for us than we could ever imagine! Three years ago, I was thanking God for providing us with a different house, even though He hadn't revcalcd it to us yet. I never could have imagined that house would come two years later, in a totally different city and in such a beautiful setting!

So, ask Father to help you refuse to be fearful about what will happen to you. You know He is faithful, and He will take care of you, if you trust Him. So, when you know you are in His will, push forward, knowing He will clear the path before you! Take the burden off yourself and place it on Him, the way He always intended it to be. He has always wanted to carry your burdens because they are much too heavy for you, but oh so light for Him! It is very freeing when you take off your burden and give it to Him! Would you do that today? Give it to Him and leave it there. But, if you pick it back up, give it to Him again. He will take it every time—even if you're handing it to Him every five seconds.

Today's Prayer

Father,

Thank You for caring about every aspect of our lives. Thank You that we can give everything to You and trust You to take care of us.

Amen.

God cares for you, so turn all your worries over to Him.

—1 Peter 5:7

April 18

Do You Love?

You would think it would be easy to love those who believe the way we do. Yet, there are those times or those brothers or sisters that make us realize it isn't so easy.

Think about your own family, for instance—especially if you grew up with brothers and/or sisters. Did you always love each other? Do you love each other as adults? Unfortunately, I know every family is not like ours. Not every family loves each other or even likes each other, for that matter! It was a sad time for me when I realized not every family loves each other the way ours does. Sure, my brothers and sister and I had arguments growing up, but at the end of the day, we knew we loved each other and would be there for each other when needed. The same is true, even more so, now that we are adults.

But, what about our Christian brothers and sisters? Shouldn't we love them even more? Shouldn't it be easy to love them? Sure, there are some that are easy to love, then there are those others…well, you know what I'm talking about. Don't you know God knew how it would be? Why do you think Jesus tells us in John 13:34, "But I am giving you a new command. You must love each other, just as I have loved you"? He isn't *suggesting* we love each other; He is *commanding* us to love each other. No. Matter. What. Period.

He doesn't say anywhere in that commandment that we won't disagree with each other or argue or have different opinions about some things. He simply says love each other. So, when we do disagree with each other or argue or have different opinions about things, we aren't to "get mad, take our toys, and go home." No, we are still to love each other, pray with and for one another and let Him work out the details. The world needs to see us loving each other; if we don't, how are we any different from them? Why would they want what we have if it's no different than what they already have?

Today's Prayer

Father,

Help us love each other so everyone will know we are Your disciples. And, as we love one another, help us love others and shine Your light into a dark world.

Amen.

If you love each other, everyone will know that you are My disciples.

—*John 13:35*

April 19

Strong Tower

There came a storm at our house last night. It was late when we were finally making our way to bed, and we were just beginning to hear rumbles of thunder outside. It took me a few minutes to relax, not because of the weather but because I had been baking all afternoon for a bake sale going on at work today. I was hurting between my shoulder blades and thought it would take me a while to go to sleep. I was wrong.

However, I can remember a time when I was so afraid of storms or bad weather, I couldn't go to sleep if it was storming. Finally, as a young teenager, I remember lying in bed one night, so scared of the storm going on outside, I couldn't sleep. My sister was in the bed, sleeping away; but I was so scared, I was wide awake! I have no idea why the song came to me—other than the Holy Spirit bringing it to my mind—but I started singing "There's Something about That Name" over and over in my head, and the next thing I know, I was waking up the next morning.

So, the next time it started storming and I was scared, I did the same thing. I'm not sure when it happened, but over time, I learned I could trust Him in the storm, and He would keep me safe, and I didn't even have to sing the song to calm my fear. Now, I love it when it's storming outside and I can sleep!

Do you know He will do the same for you? In stormy weather or even in the storms of life, do you truly know you can trust Him? Do you depend on Him completely? Do you run to Him and know He will keep you safe?

Today is Good Friday (2019), and it reminds me of just what Jesus endured in order to give me—and you—the chance to freely run to Him any time and, especially, in our stormy times. Will you begin to sing that song today and let Him teach you to completely trust Him, if you aren't there yet? He is and wants to be your strong tower!

Today's Prayer

Father,

Thank You for being our strong tower and for allowing us to run to You for safety. Help us remember to trust You in every storm, whether it's a storm outside or a storm in our life.

Amen.

The name of the Lord is a fortified tower; the
righteous run to it and are safe.

—Proverbs 18:10 (NIV)

April 20

The Day After

No hope. The One they thought had come to save them, to be their true and righteous King, was dead. All hope was now gone. Sadness overtook them, and they grieved. They grieved hard. They didn't understand when He told the Jewish leaders, "Destroy this temple sanctuary and I will raise it in three days" (John 2:19).

I find it interesting, as well as a little puzzling, we aren't told much about the day after Jesus's death on the cross. Why wouldn't He want us to know what His followers were thinking about or going through on the day after His death?

I imagine they were feeling like they had been gut-punched! Lower-than-low, sheer, utter hopelessness like they had never ever known before must have enveloped them. What were they going to do now? How could this be happening to them? They had trusted Him when He said He was the Messiah, only to see Him die a cruel, horrible death! I cannot even begin to imagine the depth of the pain or betrayal they must have felt.

Then again, I find myself thinking, "How could they not know? They walked with Him, they talked with Him, they knew Him as a man and had seen all He had done. How could they not know and understand what He had been trying to tell them?" How could they question His death and think that was it?

Then He gently reminds me of how I have walked with Him and talked with Him and seen all He has done in my life and the lives of others, and yet, I've gone through feelings of doubt and utter hopelessness myself. How is that any different?

What about you? Have you ever felt hopeless about anything? Have you ever felt completely, utterly alone? as if no one cared about you or what you were going through? Seek His face with all your heart and allow Him to show you just Who He is and how He loves you! And just wait until tomorrow.

Today's Prayer

Father,

Thank You for not hiding from us. All we have to do is call on You, seek You with all our hearts, and we will find You.

Amen.

You will seek me and find me, when you seek me with all your heart.

—Jeremiah 29:13 (NIV)

April 21

Sacrifice

He Is Risen! He is risen, indeed! Is there really anything else that needs to be said? Other than "thank You," which seems so small in light of what He did for us—for me! for *you*!

He paid a debt we could not pay, a debt He did not owe, because He knew that on the cross, we could never go! We could never be that spotless sacrifice that was needed, because we are all sinners from birth! He knew every sin we would commit, even though we weren't yet born, and He gave His life so we could be forgiven and have fellowship with Him, the Father and the Holy Spirit!

He paid the debt so I could be *free* to get up early every morning and have this special time with the Father! Even on the mornings, like today, when I struggle to stay awake! I give Him thanks for helping me stay faithful on these mornings when it is so hard, because as hard as it is for me, it is nothing compared to what Jesus did for me!

Do I really think I'm making a big sacrifice by getting up at three every morning? Compared to what He did for me, getting up early is easy! It's a cakewalk, as we say, yet I am thankful that my Father does see it as a sacrifice and He honors it.

What do you sacrifice for Him? one thing that you know is nothing compared to what He did for you, yet you are thankful He sees and honors it? Or should the question be, *do* you sacrifice anything for Him? Maybe you do, and you aren't even aware of it because "it's just something you always do."

If you aren't making any sacrifices, ask Him to show you something you can do as a sacrifice to Him. A sacrifice that He can honor and bless.

Today's Prayer

Father,

"Thank You" seems so little to say in light of what Your Son, Jesus, did for us. But, we do thank You for raising Him to life, and we ask You to help us live our lives as a sacrifice of praise!

Amen.

He isn't here! God has raised Him to life, just as Jesus said He would. Come, see the place where His body was lying.

—*Matthew 28:6*

April 22

All I Need

So, my hubby is about to be gone for a few days, leaving me here in this house, all alone, except for the cat. This is going to be a brand-new experience for me. Oh, he's had to be gone before and leave me at home, but it didn't bother me so much because I knew my mom was just right down the street. I knew if I got a little uncomfortable being alone, I could go spend the night with her, and all would be well. Now, don't get me wrong, I don't mind staying by myself. I rather enjoy it sometimes. But this will be my first time to stay by myself in a place that is still fairly new and my first time to stay in this "big" house by myself. However, God always has a plan.

He always comforts us right when we need it and gives us His Word at just the right time. The scripture writing for today came from Lamentations, and as I was writing verse 24, I felt such a huge peace! He reminded me that I am never alone! He is always here, He is always with me, He is all I need and I can depend on Him! I can depend on Him for comfort, peace, protection and so much more!

Lamentations, really? A book, I would imagine, that doesn't get read a whole lot. Yet, it is part of the Bible, so there must be important info in there, right? Just in the five verses I wrote out this morning, He showed me things I've always heard, and even quoted, but I couldn't have told you they were found in Lamentations! Things like "His mercies are new every morning" and "His love never fails"! He showed me I need to read this entire book—maybe these days alone would be a great time to do that!

Is there a book (or books) in the Bible you don't read very much? I challenge you to ask God to show you one He would like for you to explore. I promise He will not only show you, you'll be amazed at what you find there—especially when you read it in different translations! Has a book already popped into your mind? Why wait? Go start on it now and find the nuggets hiding there for you!

Today's Prayer

Father,

Thank You for being all I need, and thank You for reminding me I can depend on You! I know I can trust You to take care of and protect me.

Amen.

Deep in my heart I say, "The Lord is all I need; I can depend on Him!"

—Lamentations 3:24

April 23

Trust and Obey

Two words most people don't like to hear anymore. There are so many dishonest people in the world, and it seems to get worse with each passing day. We find ourselves in the place where we trust no one. How sad it is to say that, and even sadder that it is true.

As for the word *obey*, "Don't even go there" is what most people are thinking. It certainly has no place in a marriage ceremony anymore, according to the majority of people. Yet, at one time, it was one of the most precious things to promise to love, honor and obey. It seems in this "me" world we live in, no one wants to obey anyone; but they sure want everyone else obeying them!

Well, here's a cold, hard fact—actually, here's the absolute, loving *truth* found in God's Word: We either choose to trust and obey Him or we suffer the consequences. He is not going to make us trust or obey Him. Yes, He could, He has the power to do that. But, think about it, do you want someone to love you because you are making them love you, or do you want someone to *choose* to love you? Of course, we all want someone who chooses to love us—flaws and all. God is no different; He wants us to *choose* Him and to choose to love Him, honor Him, trust Him and obey Him.

When we make that choice, when we accept what Jesus did for us on the cross, His blood immediately covers all our sin—not just some of it, *all* of it! It doesn't mean we'll never mess up again or that we will be perfect, far from it! It does, however, mean that when the Father looks at us, He only sees the blood of His Son, and that makes us righteous in His eyes. We need only ask His forgiveness when we mess up, and He willingly gives it! He gives us grace beyond belief!

Have you chosen Him? Have you accepted Jesus as your personal Savior? I hope you have, but if you haven't, why not choose Him today? He's waiting to accept you with open arms.

Today's Prayer

Father,

Thank You for Your kindness and for reminding us we need to trust and obey You in order to receive it.

Amen.

The Lord is kind to everyone who trusts and obeys Him.

—Lamentations 3:25

April 24

Go Ahead, Make Your Plans

Remember a couple days ago I mentioned my hubby was going to be gone for a few days? Well, I made myself a list of things I was going to get done—or at least work on—while he was gone. Would anyone like to guess how many things on that list has happened? So far, none! And, you know what? I'm okay with that. Really, I am, because I know every day has been orchestrated by God.

It is good for us to make plans. God wants us to make plans. We have scriptures showing us plans were made: Acts 15:36, Romans 1:13, Acts 6:1–3, Matthew 10:5–15, Matthew 16:21 and Matthew 26:17–19, just to name a few.

The important thing to remember, when making plans, is to stay open to God's plan. When something happens that changes your plans or maybe takes them in a little different direction than how you had it mapped out, don't let it be a stress factor. Instead, let it be a bless factor. Be willing to go with whatever changes God makes, and you will be blessed, not stressed.

Don't look at those changes as preventing you from getting done what you wanted to get done. Realize that, while you may have had a good plan, God has the best plan. He always has the best for you in mind. You know what you *think* needs to be accomplished, but God knows what He actually needs you to accomplish.

What do you have planned for today? Are you willing to let God change those plans? Do you make your plans with the understanding God can change them and accomplish something greater than you could have ever imagined? Do you realize that something greater could simply be you taking time to show someone you care?

Go ahead, make your plans, but as the saying goes, "Write them in pencil, and let God have the eraser."

Today's Prayer

Father,

Thank You for allowing us to make our plans knowing, ultimately, You will show us what You want us to do or where You want us to go. It is good for us to make our plans, as long as we write them in pencil and leave the eraser with You. Thank You for caring about every detail of our lives.

Amen.

We make our own plans, but the Lord decides where we will go.

—Proverbs 16:9

April 25

Wait Equals Trust?

I found myself remembering the scripture writing from this morning. It was in Psalm 27. When I pulled up Bible Gateway to look at the scriptures again, I noticed the version I normally use (CEV) was not what I had used this morning! I had changed my Bible app to NIV last night at church; therefore, I wrote the scripture verses from the NIV instead of the CEV. (So you can see the inspiration behind today's writing, both versions are included at the end of today's devotion.)

Accident? I don't think so. I believe God wanted to show us how these words—*wait* and *trust*—are interchangeable. Have you ever thought about that before? You know that sometimes you need to wait for the Lord, and you know you need to always trust the Lord. Have you ever realized, though, how waiting on Him could also be the same as trusting Him?

If you are waiting on Him, truly waiting, then you are trusting Him with whatever it is you're waiting for—whether it's an answer to a prayer or showing you which road you need to take when you find yourself at a crossroads or a fork in the road or anything else.

If you are truly trusting Him, then you are waiting on Him, because if you are truly trusting Him, you aren't trying to figure out solutions to problems on your own. You aren't running around trying to "help" Him. Remember what happens when we try to "help" Him? It's never good, right? So, to trust Him and trust Him completely, you have to wait.

Wait and *trust*—has He challenged you to look at these words differently today?

Today's Prayer

Father,

Thank You for showing us how *trust* and *wait* can mean the same thing. Thank You for reminding us we can be strong and take heart and wait for—trust in—You.

Amen.

Wait for the Lord; be strong and take heart and wait for the Lord

—Psalm 27:14 (NIV)

Trust the Lord! Be brave and strong and trust the Lord.

—Psalm 27:14 (CEV)

April 26

My Time or His Time?

Normally, one of the last things I do before going to bed each night is check my phone to be sure the alarm for 3:00 a.m. is turned on. Last night I didn't do it. Hubby was finally back home after being gone for three nights, it was raining outside, we were both exhausted and not feeling well and I think we were both pretty much asleep before we even got in bed!

This morning I woke up and looked at my phone to see it was 4:15! I was about to let myself go into panic mode when I felt Him whisper to me, "It's okay. I got this." That's all it took to remind me—He knew I didn't set my alarm last night, and He woke me when He knew I needed to get up. I was able to immediately reverse my thinking and avoid the panic mode the enemy tried to put on me.

Then, He led me to the scripture below for today's devotion. I didn't realize it at first, but then He spoke to my spirit and allowed me to see it in a new light. How many times have you been in a tough spot, financially, and used this verse to remind yourself that He will take care of your needs? What about the times you're facing other difficult situations and this verse was a comfort to you, reminding you God would take care of it all?

Why, then, do we not realize it means He will take care of our time as well? When we oversleep, why not trust that He is the One that allowed it and He has a reason for it? I'm not saying use it as an excuse when you just chose to take your time getting ready to go somewhere and then find yourself running late. He still expects us to be responsible. But, when either things happen beyond our control or we honestly forgot to set an alarm or something, don't allow the enemy to place panic on you. God can and will redeem the time for you in those situations. His time is always the right time, don't you agree?

Today's Prayer

Father,

We are so thankful we can depend on You for anything and everything we *need*—not for our wants, Father, but for our needs. Thank You for so lovingly taking care of us and for knowing what we truly need better than we do. Please help us learn to trust You in and for *all* things!

Amen.

My God will use His wonderful riches in Christ
Jesus to give you everything you need.

—Philippians 4:19 (ICB [International Children's Bible])

April 27

Stay in Tune

Have you noticed how we are living in a "me" generation? It *seems* that—no, it's sad but *true*—a majority of the population today only wants to look out for themselves. "Look out for number one," they say, "because if you don't, nobody else will." Do you find it surprising, then, that is not what we are taught in God's Word? We are taught exactly the opposite. Then, why are we surprised at how the enemy has changed the way most people think?

He wants to keep everyone pitted against each other, tearing each other down. He wants everyone to say, "You do your thing, and I'll do mine," which is exactly opposite of what God wants us to do. It scares him to think of what we would be capable of if we all worked and pulled together!

Can you let yourself imagine, for a moment, what it would be like if, instead of us all going off and doing our own thing, we all came together and worked together to grow His kingdom? Can you imagine what that would mean, how that would look? Everyone pulling together for one cause—the cause of Christ—and sharing Him with everyone we come in contact with, whether in words or actions.

Yes, you can share Jesus without using even one word. In fact, whether you realize it or not, you are either sharing Jesus or the enemy every day of your life, every second of your life. By your actions and the way you treat others, you are either being a witness for the Lord or a witness for the devil himself.

Take a long, hard look in the mirror today and ask yourself, "Am I a 'me' person or a 'we' person? Do I want to work with others, or do I want to go off and do my own thing?" Ask God to search your heart and show you what is truly there. If you don't like what He shows you, He is right there, ready to help you change. Are you willing to let Him change you?

Today's Prayer

Father,

Please help us let the peace of Christ keep us in tune with each other. Remind us we need to work together for Your kingdom and not be trying to do things on our own. Also, remind us to be thankful in all things.

Amen.

Let the peace of Christ keep you in tune with each other,
in step with each other. None of this going off and doing
your own thing. And cultivate thankfulness.

—Colossians 3:15 (The Message)

April 28

Who Are You?

What is your first response to that question when someone asks you? Is it something like, "I'm so-and-so's mom, wife, daughter, sister," or do you maybe even use your job title to say who you are?

Maybe when you hear that question, you remember all the lies you've been told through the years—"You are so clumsy!" "You are so fat!" "You are so skinny!" "You can't do anything right!" "You are such an idiot!" I could probably make a list a mile long and still not get them all. However, we don't want to focus on those lies today.

Our goal this morning is to replace all those lies the enemy has fed you over the years with the truth of God's Word and who He says you are! The first three words that came to my mind this morning, as I contemplated that question, were *healed, whole* and *forgiven.* Then I also remembered *chosen* and *free*!

When you want to discover who you truly are, search the Scriptures and listen to who God says you are! It is time to stop listening to the enemy's lies and grab hold of God's truth and begin speaking it over yourself!

We (women) have listened to the lies long enough, and we need to change our way of thinking! Stop being run down by the enemy, speak out loud who God says you are and start living in those truths today!

Here are a few to get you started: you are *redeemed* (Ephesians 1:7), you are *loved* (John 3:16), you are *free* (Acts 13:39), you are *His* (1 John 3:1)! There are many other truths in God's Word about who He says you are. I challenge you to search them out today for yourself and see how many you can find. Then, write them out on index cards and post them around your house where you will be constantly reminded of them!

Today's Prayer

Father,

Thank You for reminding us today who You say we are. Help us remember to listen to Your truths and not the enemy's lies.

Amen.

Out of all the peoples on the face of the earth, the Lord has chosen you to be His treasured possession.

—*Deuteronomy 14:2 (NIV)*

April 29

Do You Wait Eagerly?

When Father asked if I would be willing to let Him give me devotions each morning this year, I think I expected it to be something new every morning—and, in a way, it is. However, *wait* and *trust* seem to be two words He keeps bringing up, though presented differently each time.

This morning, the scripture writing was Psalm 130:5–6. I'm writing the scriptures in a book called *Soul Scripts Journal* (purchased at Hobby Lobby), and it has scripture written at the bottom of every page. At the bottom of today's page was this scripture: "Those who know Your name will put their trust in You; For You, Lord, have not forsaken those who seek You" (Psalm 9:10), and that couldn't go along with today's scripture writing any better!

It seems to me, maybe He is asking if we are truly listening, if we are really understanding what He is trying to tell us. Are we truly waiting on and trusting in Him for everything? Not just what we call the "big" things, but even what we consider the "little," things and are we waiting and trusting eagerly?

Maybe you have read this scripture before, maybe you haven't, but have you ever thought of waiting on the Lord as *eagerly as a soldier on guard duty waits for the dawn*?

It must be important to know how eagerly he was waiting, since it was repeated. Do these scriptures have you wondering if you have learned to truly wait on and trust in Him? Are you waiting as eagerly as a soldier on guard duty waits for the dawn? Can you even imagine how eagerly that is? What about a woman about to give birth? Do you wait as eagerly as a woman about to give birth waits for her baby to be born? How about as eagerly as a child waits for Christmas?

Think of anything you may wait eagerly for, and ask yourself if you wait that eagerly on the Lord. If the answer is no, what can you do to change that?

Today's Prayer

Father,

May we be willing to wait for You more eagerly than a soldier on guard duty waits for the dawn—more eagerly than we wait for anything.

Amen.

I wait for You more eagerly than a soldier on guard duty waits for the dawn. Yes, I wait more eagerly than a soldier on guard duty waits for the dawn.

—Psalm 130:6

April 30

Anger Management

We live in a world of bitter, angry and rude people. It seems this trend has become worse over the years. I believe it's because there are so many people who are silently hurting. We all know that hurt people, hurt people. It's what they know, what they are comfortable with. Let's be more honest—we are, most likely, part of "they."

Someone hurt you in the past, and instead of dealing with it and allowing the Lord to heal you, you moved on as quickly as you could. Maybe pretending it didn't even bother you. Then, you hurt someone, and the cycle continues. I'm not talking about physically hurting someone as much as I'm talking about emotionally.

Until you stop running and hiding, the hurt and anger will control you. The enemy loves it when we allow that to happen. He delights greatly when you are bitter, angry, rude and hurtful. Nothing pleases him more than seeing you do exactly what he wants you to do, sometimes with absolutely no help from him.

What is the answer—anger management? Maybe, on a practical level for some. However, what about using today's verses as anger management? Keep these verses in front of you, at all times, and see what a difference they make in your life!

I challenge you to print these verses out, write them on sticky notes or index cards and place them around your house, your work area, your vehicle—anywhere you will be sure to see them *often*! Commit them to memory! Live by them and be amazed at the glorious, wonderful work He does in *you*. Isn't it funny how when we work on making ourselves better, everything around us seems to change for the better?

Today's Prayer

Father,

Help us stop being bitter, angry and rude people. Let us not yell or curse each other, but instead learn to be kind, merciful and forgiving—the way You forgive us because of Christ.

Amen.

Stop being bitter and angry and mad at others. Don't yell at one another or curse each other or ever be rude. Instead, be kind and merciful and forgive others, just as God forgave you because of Christ.

—Ephesians 4:31–32

May 1

Check Engine

That pesky little light that comes on in your vehicle when something isn't "just right." What do you do when it comes on in yours? Do you ignore it? Do you take it to the shop immediately to have it checked? Do you wait a while, thinking, "I'm really busy right now, so I'll take care of this later"?

Have you ever thought about your spiritual "check engine light" that comes on in your life? That's right, your life—it could come on in several different ways. Maybe you start noticing you're getting more negative than you were before, maybe you start noticing you're slipping into some bad habits, maybe you haven't been to church in a while to be filled with God's Word and the fellowship with brothers and sisters in the Lord, maybe you start isolating yourself again—not wanting to be around anyone, maybe it's your friends and/or family telling you things they are noticing that maybe you aren't.

What will you do—or have you done—when your spiritual check engine light comes on? Will you have it checked out immediately, put it off for a little while or completely ignore it? I recommend having it checked out as soon as possible! How do you do that? Go to God in prayer. Ask Him to show you where tune-ups or adjustments are needed, and then allow Him to perform the necessary work to get you back on the road again.

Remember me sharing how I felt God was nudging me to read the book of Lamentations last week while my hubby was gone? I never seemed to get around to doing it. Then, this morning He was gracious and kind enough to show me this other little gem hiding and waiting there for me. What am I going to do about it? Start reading it today!

Your challenge? Perform that spiritual checkup today, and allow Him to perform the necessary work to get you running in good, spiritual order again.

Today's Prayer

Father,

Make us aware when our check engine light comes on, spiritually. Help us take a good look at how we're living and reorder our lives to line up with You and Your Word.

Amen.

Let's take a good look at the way we're living
and reorder our lives under God.

—*Lamentations 3:40 (The Message)*

May 2

Persistence

Does anyone else have a cat—or any pet—that demands attention? My cat, Patches, will be fifteen years old this summer. I rescued him when he was just a couple months old, and he has always been a loving cat. When he wants "loving," he can be pretty demanding!

This morning as I was writing in my prayer journal, he jumped up on my desk, as he usually does, but this morning was a little different. Normally, he will lie at the top or to the side of my journal, where I can pet him with the hand I'm not writing with, or he will lie where he can rest his head on my arm while I am writing. Today, however, he kept getting right on top of my journal—we're talking plopping himself directly on top of it, covering the whole thing where I couldn't write. He wanted loving, and he was being a little pest about it, demanding attention!

I confess, I was getting more than a little aggravated with him when, suddenly, I felt in my spirit, "Are you as persistent with the Father as Patches is with you?" I immediately thought of the story about the woman begging for her daughter's healing and how even dogs are allowed to have the scraps that fall from the table. I suddenly realized Father was speaking this morning's devotion to me—persistence! We can't just ask the Father one time for something, especially something as important as someone's salvation, and then never ask again! No matter what it is you are praying for, as long as it lines up with God's Word, be persistent! Never stop asking! Keep praying those prayers—they will last and keep their power, long after you're gone!

Today's Prayer

Father,

Help us have the persistence of my cat and this woman in Matthew, never giving up asking for You to move in different situations, such as praying for the salvation of loved ones and for prodigals to return to You.

Amen.

Then Jesus said to the woman, "I was sent only to help God's lost sheep—the people of Israel." But she came and worshiped Him, pleading again, "Lord, help me!" Jesus responded, "It isn't right to take food from the children and throw it to the dogs." She replied, "That's true, Lord, but even dogs are allowed to eat the scraps that fall beneath their masters' table." "Dear woman," Jesus said to her, "your faith is great. Your request is granted." And her daughter was instantly healed.

—Matthew 15:24–28 (NLT)

May 3

Nothing More Than Feelings

How are you feeling today? Fine? Good? Hurting? Alone? Lonely? There is one thing I have finally started getting a better grasp on over the years, and that is this: You cannot go on your feelings! Your feelings will lie to you and deceive you in all kinds of ways! The enemy loves to use your feelings to mess with you, if you allow it. Don't!

If you can't depend on your feelings, what can you depend on? I'm so glad you asked that question because there is also one other thing I have gotten a better grasp on over the years: You *can* depend on the Lord! You can *know* He loves you, and you can know nothing can change that!

When you don't understand what's going on inside yourself or where some of your *feelings* are coming from, you know you can trust in the Lord! You know you can depend on Him! He is your rock! Your fortress! Your refuge! Your friend! He will never leave you or forsake you! No matter where you go, He goes with you! He is the One thing that never changes!

Your feelings will be up and down and all over the place, but He is your constant! Put your trust in Him! He is your everything! You can trust Him and Him alone! You may not understand some things, and sometimes you may question things or wonder *why*. Ask Him to help you turn your *why*s into *what*s! Instead of "Why are You doing this, Father?" ask "What are You doing, Father?" Ask, "What are You wanting me to learn through this?" or "What is going to help me grow from this?"

You may not have the answers, but you know the One Who does! You know all you have to do is keep trusting Him and keep believing! Even if it means you have to pray: "Father, I *do* believe!

Help me overcome my unbelief!" (Mark 9:24). Let that scripture be a help to you on the days you are questioning and your feelings are going all over the place! Forget what you're feeling, and choose to trust God instead!

Today's Prayer

Father,

We come before You today, asking You to help us not trust in our own hearts and feelings. Help us instead to trust in You and what You say!

Amen.

The heart is deceitful above all things and
desperately sick; who can understand it?

—*Jeremiah 17:9 (ESV)*

May 4

He Is Faithful

My morning routine—get up at three; have my quiet time with the Father, which is when I write in my prayer journal; then, I write my daily scripture writing; and, lastly, I get quiet and listen for Him to give me the devotion for the day. My prayers in my prayer journal are usually me thanking Him for various things He has done at different times. Some days, it gets to being more than that; other days, it's a struggle to get a paragraph written out. Not a struggle to pray—just a struggle to write things down sometimes.

This morning was no struggle at all! I was thanking Him for how faithful He has been to me in several different ways and the tangible ways He has shown His faithfulness. I was having no trouble praising Him for His faithfulness. I even make the comment, sometimes, "He remains faithful to me, even when I am not so faithful to Him."

I opened up my daily scripture writing plan to get the passage for today, then opened my Bible to it (1 Peter 4:1–6 CEV) and nearly fell off my chair as I read the title for this passage—"Being Faithful to God"—You could have knocked me over with a feather! Wow! Talk about a wake-up call!

What about you? Do you consider yourself faithful to God? I understand we are imperfect people, and as such, we are going to fail Him from time to time. But, do you try your best to be faithful to Him, or do you sometimes find yourself making excuses for your behavior. Do you say things like, "That's just the way I am. That's just my personality. He made me this way"?

No, He didn't make you that way, and if that's your personality (to be rude, gruff, mean, etc.), then maybe He wants you to allow

Him to change it! Do you want to do your best to be faithful to Him, or do you want to continue making excuses for your behavior? Are you willing to ask Him to change whatever needs to be changed in you to help you be more faithful to Him?

Today's Prayer

Father,

You know there are a lot of "get rich quick" schemes in this world today. Help us be faithful to You and Your Word and desire Your blessings over the riches of man.

Amen.

A faithful man will abound with blessings, but he who hastens to be rich will not go unpunished.

—Proverbs 28:20 (NKJV)

May 5

What Are You Expecting?

When you wake up each morning, do you find yourself expecting to have a good day or a bad day? Do you think of all the things that could go right, or are you constantly worrying about what could go wrong?

What about when you are getting ready to attend church? Are you doing it because it's Sunday and that's what you're "supposed" to do, or do you find yourself looking forward to the service and what God might want to speak to you there?

Do you realize that if you find yourself always expecting the worst, your expectations are coming from satan? It's true! God wants only to bless us and give us good things when we are doing our best to live a life pleasing to Him. Why, then, would we not want to get our expectations from Him instead of the enemy?

Yes, bad things happen to good people. We live in a sin-sick world, and we can't get around that. However, you can bring bad things on yourself if you are always expecting bad things. It goes along with the truth of "death and life are in the power of the tongue" (Proverbs 18:21). You can choose to let your expectations come from the Lord and speak good things, or you can let your expectations come from the enemy and speak bad things.

God doesn't want us to live our lives in fear of all the bad things that could happen. He wants us to get our expectations from Him and be able to experience the good things He has in store for us.

Wake up expecting to have a good day and, then, no matter what happens, see the good things! As you are getting ready for church, go with an attitude of expectancy, just waiting to see what

He wants to say to you through the message! Are you ready to start expecting good things?

Today's Prayer

Father,

May we all wait silently for You alone, and may our expectations come from You alone. Help us resist the natural tendency to expect the worst, and help us retrain our brain to expect Your goodness!

Amen.

My soul, wait silently for God alone, for my expectation is from Him.

—Psalm 62:5

May 6

Annoyances

Do you ever get annoyed, irritated or exasperated with anyone or anything? You probably do—at least now and then. I know I do. I'm not proud of it; I'm just being honest.

I've mentioned my cat, Patches, before, remember? I get amazed, sometimes, how God continues to use him to teach me things about myself. Patches is a rescue cat, so I don't really know what breed he is. It is very evident, however, from the beginning, that he must have some Siamese in him because Siamese cats are notorious for being very vocal. In other words, they meow a lot! Lately, it has gotten worse, though, and quite frankly, it can be extremely annoying sometimes—especially early in the morning.

I was sitting at my desk a few mornings ago, having my quiet time with the Father, and He spoke to me about this. Patches was lying right beside my prayer journal (his usual spot), and I was thanking Father, once again, for giving him back to me. I wrote, "Thank You for this beautiful, loving, sometimes extremely annoying cat— Ha! Ha! Even though he can be very annoying, I love him so much," and immediately I felt in my spirit, "Now you know how I feel! Ha! Ha!" Wow! What a revelation! We can annoy God sometimes, but not in the way we think of annoying someone. I think it's more of a loving annoyance. He wants so much for us to have complete and total faith in Him, it annoys Him when we don't. But only because He loves us so much and wants only the best for us.

Do you ever feel like you annoy God? Do you think He gets exasperated with you sometimes? If so, remember, He loves you and wants only the best for you. And, if I can never annoy Him enough to stop loving me, then you, my friend, have nothing to worry about! (Read Luke 9:37–50.)

Today's Prayer

Father,

How nice it is to know that even though You may get annoyed or exasperated with us from time to time, it is a loving annoyance or exasperation because You want only the best for us. Help us learn to exercise our faith more and our fears less.

Amen.

Jesus said to them, "You people are stubborn and don't have any faith! How much longer must I be with you? Why do I have to put up with you?" Then Jesus said to the man, "Bring your son to me."

—Luke 9:41

May 7

Encouragement Challenge

Merriam-Webster says the definition of *encourage* is "to inspire with courage, spirit, or hope." The *KJV Dictionary* definition of *encourage* is "to give courage to; to give or increase confidence of success; to inspire with courage, spirit, or strength of mind; to embolden; to animate; to incite; to inspirit." Therefore, an encourager is one who does those things.

Did you know encouraging one another is so important that God commands it? It may not be one of the Ten Commandments, but nonetheless, it is a command. Just look at 1 Thessalonians 4:18 and 1 Thessalonians 5:11 (listed below). One of my favorites is Hebrews 3:13 from the ICB (International Children's Bible) version:

> *But encourage each other every day. Do this while it is "today." Help each other so that none of you will become hardened because of sin and its tricks.*

I love that verse because it presents a challenge. When you feel prompted to send someone a card or a text or to call someone, this verse challenges you to do it *today*, because it might be just the thing that person needs today—not tomorrow! It could be as simple as a text letting that person know they are being thought of and prayed for that day.

Do you like to be around encouragers? They just seem to make you feel better, right? Do you consider yourself an encourager? Do you feel you can't be an encourager because you are going through so much trouble in your own life? If so, I challenge you to write out Hebrews 3:13 and put it where you see it every day! I challenge you to do something to encourage someone else every day for thirty days—even something as simple as a smile or holding a door for someone or letting someone go ahead of you in line at the store. You just might be surprised to realize, when you are encouraging others, your troubles seem a little less, and you will find you have encouraged yourself along the way. Are you willing to take the encouragement challenge?

Today's Prayer

Father,

Thank You for the sacrifice of Your Son so we can live with You. Help us encourage and build one another up as we travel this road of life.

Amen.

Christ died for us so that, whether we are dead or alive when He returns, we can live with Him forever. So encourage each other and build each other up, just as you are already doing.

—1 Thessalonians 5:10–11 (NLT)

May 8

What's In a Name?

Have you ever researched what your name means? I know a lot of couples, especially the ladies, who put a lot of time and research into a name for their expected baby. Names are very important and can easily define us and separate us from everyone else.

When you're talking with a friend or family member, and you begin discussing someone else, don't you find yourself saying things like, "You know, she is Emily Stone's daughter" or "Her husband is Joe Jones" or "She was a Johnson before she got married"? Yes, names are important.

We also have some given names that are considered "ordinary" or "average," meaning there are a lot of people with the same name, like *Mary, Tom, Sue, John*, etc. Even in our quest to find a "different" name for our child, those too become common at some point, and the "old" names are "different," once again.

Even in the days when Jesus Christ walked the earth as a man, there were a lot of common names. *Jesus* was one of those names. That's why when the disciples would pray, they would pray "in the name of Jesus Christ of Nazareth." They were making the distinction of exactly Whose name they were praying in. It wasn't just anyone named *Jesus*. No! They were praying in the name of Jesus Christ of Nazareth. Look at Acts 3:6.

> *But Peter said, "I don't have any silver or gold! But I will give you what I do have. In the Name of Jesus Christ from Nazareth, get up and start walking."*

When we pray, we also need to remember to pray in the name of Jesus Christ of Nazareth, because satan knows that name, and it is the only name he knows even he must obey! If you haven't already been praying this way, start today!

Today's Prayer

Father,

Thank You for giving us the power to pray in the name of Jesus Christ of Nazareth and to approach Your throne boldly in His name. It is only because of His blood covering us that we can come to You at all. Thank You!

Amen.

But there is something we must tell you and everyone else in Israel. This man is standing here completely well because of the power of Jesus Christ from Nazareth. You put Jesus to death on a cross, but God raised Him to life.

—Acts 4:10

May 9

Justify or Confess?

When you accepted Christ as your Lord and Savior, the Holy Spirit immediately came to live inside you. That doesn't mean, however, that Jesus is Lord of your life right away. It's more of an ongoing work in progress.

When you accept Christ, He comes in and cleans up your heart, getting rid of the junk in there. Then what? In Matthew 12:43–45, we read about what happens if you don't allow the Holy Spirit to take up residence in your heart. You leave yourself open to satan and his demons coming back in, taking over and making it even worse than it was before. Yes, you receive the Holy Spirit the instant you are saved, but if you don't allow Him to move into your heart and give Him full control, you could find yourself in a whole heap of trouble!

Why would you not want the Holy Spirit living in your heart? What keeps you from giving Him full control? Maybe it's because you enjoy your sin. You may not want to admit it or say it that way, but that's what it boils down to—you don't want to confess your sin because you enjoy it. You're comfortable with it. You find yourself trying to justify it instead of confessing it.

Maybe you're short-tempered or blunt with people when you speak. You try to justify it by saying, "Well, that's the way God made me. It's just the way I am, and I can't change that." Um, no, ma'am! God did not make you that way, and while you are correct in saying you can't change it, you can allow the Holy Spirit to change it!

Take a hard look at yourself today and ask God to show you which sins you are trying to justify instead of confess. I'm doing the same thing. Then, ask Him to forgive you, confess the sin(s) He shows you and allow the Holy Spirit to begin working. Doing this is one way to honor Christ and allow Him to be Lord of your life. It's an ongoing work, and He is happy to do it for you!

Today's Prayer

Father,

Let us allow You to not only sweep our hearts clean, but help us honor You as Lord of our life every day, allowing the Holy Spirit to live in our hearts. May we always be ready to answer anyone who asks us about our hope!

Amen.

Honor Christ and let him be the Lord of your life. Always be ready to give an answer when someone asks you about your hope.

—1 Peter 3:15

May 10

The Cost of Sacrifice

Everyone makes sacrifices for something. Some make the sacrifice of eating less so they can lose weight. Parents make sacrifices in order to try and give their children a better life than they had. Spouses make sacrifices because they love each other and want to put the other first.

A sacrifice, according to *Merriam-Webster*, is *an act of offering to a deity something precious*. There are many different ways you make sacrifices on a daily basis. But, the most important sacrifice(s) you will ever make are the ones you make for the Lord. He wants us to live every day as a sacrifice to Him (Romans 12:1).

Do you make sacrifices as a way of life, or do you find, sometimes, you are trying to make a sacrifice to make up for something you didn't do—or did do? For instance, you felt God asking you to do something, but you didn't do it, or you knew He was telling you not to do something, and you did it anyway. So, you find yourself trying to offer a "sacrifice" in order to gain forgiveness. That is not how it works (1 Samuel 15:22).

Have you ever given much thought to what you sacrifice for Him? Is there anything that means a lot to you that you are willing to give up for Him? Are you willing to sacrifice an extra hour (or two) of sleep so you can spend some time alone with Him in the mornings or in the evenings? Are you willing to sacrifice your pride and do that "crazy" thing He is asking you to do—knowing that crazy thing could be the answer to someone else's prayer?

Yes, your sacrifice will and should cost you something, whether that be in the form of money, lost sleep or something else. However, nothing you sacrifice will ever come close to what He sacrificed for you in order to offer you grace!

Today's Prayer

Father,

Thank You for reminding us there is a price to pay for the sacrifices we offer You. No price we pay could ever compare to that which Jesus Christ of Nazareth paid for us, yet You honor it the same. Thank You for accepting our humble sacrifices, and please use us to further build Your kingdom.

Amen.

But David answered, "No! I have to pay you what they're worth. I can't offer the Lord my God a sacrifice that I got for nothing." So David bought the threshing place and the oxen for fifty pieces of silver.

—2 Samuel 24:24

May 11

Weary in the Battle

This morning I was reminded of the story of Moses, Aaron and Hur. It has long been a favorite of mine. I'm speaking of where Moses commanded Joshua to fight the army of Amalek. He told Joshua he would stand at the top of the hill with the staff of God in his hands.

So, Joshua did what Moses commanded him to do and led his men out to fight the Amalekites. Moses, Aaron and Hur went to the top of a nearby hill, as Moses had said he would. As long as Moses was holding up his hands, Joshua and his army was winning, but when Moses's arms became tired, and he lowered them, the Amalekites started getting the victory. So, Aaron and Hur got Moses a rock to sit on, and then they held up his hands for him.

What an example for us to follow in our own lives! You know at least one person who is going through a rough time right now. The Lord just spoke a name to you, didn't He? That friend who loves and trusts the Lord but is growing weary in the battle of the moment. When you're the one in the battle, it seems like much longer than a moment. In fact, it can sometimes seem like the battle lasts for years! It could be any kind of battle—bad health or bad health report, financial, relationship, new parent, old parent—each battle comes with its own difficulties.

What could you do to 'hold up the hands' of the friend God has brought to your mind this morning? Could you offer to drive that friend to a doctor's appointment or maybe offer to take their child (or children) for an hour or two and give them a break? I'm sure God has already whispered something in your ear that you could do. I challenge you to do it today. Hold their hands high for them, until they can hold them up on their own again.

Today's Prayer

Father,

Thank You for giving us people to walk this journey with. Help us be aware when others are getting tired and weary so we may help them keep their hands lifted high to You and defeat the enemy—not in our strength but in Yours.

Amen.

Moses' arms soon became so tired he could no longer hold them up. So, Aaron and Hur found a stone for him to sit on. Then they stood on each side of Moses, holding up his hands. So, his hands held steady until sunset.

—Exodus 17:12 (NLT)

May 12

It's Okay to Be Afraid

Have you ever been afraid? I mean, seriously, genuinely frightened, possibly even to the point of death? I have been afraid many times in my life of many different things—one of which was becoming a mother. Is there anything scarier than that? Being responsible for another human life?

What if that fear is placed on top of a long list of other fears you already carry around? Fears like thinking you are expected to be perfect at everything, it's all up to you to make sure the house gets and stays cleaned, it's all up to you to be sure you are taking care of your husband and all that he needs on a daily basis, it's all up to you to make sure all the bills are paid every month, it's all up to you to make sure everything at your job is running smoothly, it's all up to you to keep it all together and not "lose it" because everyone, and I mean everyone, is depending on you to be the rock. Lions and tigers and bears, oh my! "Have pity, God Most High! My enemies chase me all day. Many of them are pursuing and attacking me" (Psalm 56:1–2). See? Even in the Bible, people were afraid!

When you are the one walking through this valley of fear, it isn't so easy to quote the Bible verses that speak to you about fear. When it's you in the middle of that valley, I dare say, you don't even really want to hear the verses. I mean, you do, but you don't. You simply want a chance to breathe and not have to be responsible for anything! Can't it just, please, be someone else's turn to have to deal with everything? Just for one day?

You already know the truth. You know God is the One ultimately in control. You know it matters what you speak over your own life, let alone other people's lives; but the enemy has been chasing you, pursuing and attacking you for so long, you aren't able to feel anything anymore, except defeat! Can I be honest with you? It's okay to feel that way. That's when you need your "Aaron and Hur" to hold your arms up for you, while the battle is raging. Will you let me be one of them for you today? Let me hold your arms up while the battle rages. Then, one day in the future, you do the same for someone else.

Today's Prayer

Father,

In the midst of all my anxiety and fear, help me keep trusting You with it all. Send my "Aaron and Hur" to help me until I am strong again.

Amen.

But even when I am afraid, I keep on trusting You.

—Psalm 56:3

May 13

Helping Others Helps You

Which one are you today? Are you a Moses, trying your best to do what you said you would do and keep your hands lifted to the Father, while the battle is raging all around you? Perhaps you are Aaron or Hur, and you are helping someone else keep their hands lifted while they are in the midst of a battle.

If you are a Moses, you may be feeling like you shouldn't need help from anyone. You may feel you should be able to keep your hands lifted to the Father on your own. You may feel less than or not good enough when you realize you need help keeping your hands lifted. Nothing could be further the truth. God gives us each other for these reasons. Look at Ecclesiastes 4:9, "Two people are better than one. They get more done by working together."

If you are Aaron or Hur, you may start to feel a little too important, if you're not careful. You might begin to think your friend couldn't do anything without your help. Be careful when God is using you as an Aaron or Hur for someone, and don't let your pride get the best of you, making you believe you are "all that and a bag of chips." Look what He tells us in Jeremiah 9:23, "This is what the Lord says: 'Don't let the wise boast in their wisdom, or the powerful boast in their power or the rich boast in their riches.'"

So, at different times in our lives, we are all either Moses or Aaron and Hur. We are either the one needing help to keep our hands lifted or we are helping to hold someone else's hands up. No matter which one you are today, God loves you just the same!

If you are in the place of Moses today, you may not feel you have anything to offer anyone. However, remember this: Praying for someone else who is in a battle of their own will oftentimes make your battle a little easier, simply because you are no longer focusing on your own struggles. Try it and see if it doesn't work that way. You may find yourself pleasantly surprised!

Today's Prayer

Father,

Even when we are going through our own struggles and need help keeping our hands lifted, help us also be interested in the lives of others. Sometimes helping someone else is the best way to help ourselves.

Amen.

Do not be interested only in your own life, but
be interested in the lives of others.

—Philippians 2:4 (ICB)

May 14

Simply Love Simply

A few mornings ago, during my quiet time with Father, He began to speak to me and give me so many ideas for devotions. I wasn't even asking for it, He just began speaking to me so fast and furious I could hardly keep up. Just in my prayer time, He spoke eight different devotion ideas to me.

One thing He spoke to my spirit—after giving me six new ideas—was this: I've given you so many ideas to choose from, but maybe not one of them is what I want you to use at the moment. Maybe I simply want you to share *love*. All these other ideas are important, and yes, I will elaborate on those when the time is right. But, for now, please, just share how important it is for them to simply love each other and to love simply because I ask you to do so.

Can it really be that simple? It should be. He commands us in His Word to do it. John 15:12 tells us, "This is my command: Love each other as I have loved you." Do you ever give much thought as to how Jesus loves you?

I believe the easiest way to understand how Jesus loves us is if we have children (or a child) of our own. It becomes so much more relatable then. You have no idea how deeply you can love someone until you have a child. Am I right, Moms? No matter what that child does and no matter how exasperated you may become with that child, your love goes much deeper than your exasperation! Just because you are exasperated for the moment, doesn't mean you no longer love your child.

Jesus loves us the same way, and it's how He expects us to love each other—with an overabundance of grace, mercy and forgiveness. Even when, in our minds, it is someone we have deemed as "unlovable" for any number of reasons. Today, reach out to one person you find it hard to love and just love them. Give them grace, mercy, forgiveness and, most of all, love, and see how it changes you!

Today's Prayer

Father,

May we all learn this simple truth, to sincerely love each other. When we finally get that part right, we will begin to see a huge change in our own lives.

Amen.

> *Most important of all, you must sincerely love each other, because love wipes away many sins.*
>
> —*1 Peter 4:8*

May 15

Brave

This word means different things to different people. According to *Merriam-Webster*, as a verb, it means "to face or endure with courage." It says nothing about not being scared, did you notice that?

Being brave isn't about not being scared. I know a lot of people, mature in their faith, who will tell you they get scared sometimes! We live in a scary world, after all.

However, being scared doesn't mean you can't be brave too! Being scared doesn't make you a weak person. It can, in fact, make you a stronger person than you ever thought you could be! We don't get bravery from ourselves! God is the One Who makes us brave!

Without Him, we are all nothing but cowards and easy prey for the enemy. When you find yourself about to be in a battle, do you find you begin praying more? When that doctor is giving you a bad report, do you feel brave from the minute you hear the news, or do you find yourself wanting to run away and not face the battle? Whether it's a health battle or a financial battle or a relationship battle or even just a personal battle within, brave isn't most likely the first thing you feel.

You may first feel scared or weak or even angry! That doesn't mean you can't be brave! I believe, sometimcs, being brave means being able to admit you're scared, weak or angry but, at the same time, depending on God to get you through the battle, knowing He will, in His time.

Rest assured, when He brings you *to* something, He will bring you *through* it also. You can be brave only because of Him and in His strength. He is all you need in any battle! Be brave in Him, soldier!

Today's Prayer

Father,

We want to be brave and strong. Remind us we can be, especially when we feel scared and weak. Remind us You are by our side and that You will never leave us.

Amen.

Be brave and strong! Don't be afraid of the nations on the other side of the Jordan. The Lord your God will always be at your side, and He will never abandon you.

—*Deuteronomy 31:6*

May 16

Milestones

Baby's first words, first steps, first day of school—these are all milestones we get so excited about and love to brag about. My oldest great-niece is graduating from high school tonight, so my mind is whirling at how fast time has gone by!

What about your own milestones in life? What have they meant to you? Did you do anything special for those times? Normally, there is a special event or, at the very least, a gathering of friends and/or family to help celebrate the different milestones in our lives like kindergarten graduation, high school and college graduation, all the way up to retirement! These are milestones in our natural lives.

What about the milestones in your spiritual life? Do you mark those with special events or gatherings? Do you remember the day you gave your life to the Lord? Granted, depending on how that happened, you may not have had a lot of family and/or friends present, but what about the milestones in your spiritual journey after that?

In the Old Testament, we read about several instances where monuments (usually consisting of piles of stones) were left to remind the people of the important events, whether good or bad. You need to do the same in your own spiritual journey. Whether you do it by keeping a journal or writing things on a calendar or putting it in your phone—there are many different ways you can do it these days—you just need to do it. It allows you to look back at where you once were and how God has used things to grow and stretch you. It is good to remember the many different ways He has blessed you along the way.

You don't need to live there—in the past—but you do need to remember where God has brought you from and all He has brought you through! It is good to see how He directs your steps and delights in the details of your life!

Today's Prayer

Father,

Thank You for directing our steps and taking delight in every detail of our lives.

Amen.

The Lord directs the steps of the Godly.
He delights in every detail of their lives.

—Psalm 37:23 (NLT)

May 17

Sin Is Sin

What a needed reminder in scripture writing this morning. In writing the passage, Galatians 5:19–26, God reminded me that sin is sin—period. There is no big sin or little sin, the way we try to make it out to be.

When you hear of an adult who has hurt a young child, you may say or think something like, "How awful!" or "They should have the same thing done to them." Yes, it is awful, but it is sin. Plain and simple.

When you hear of someone living a homosexual lifestyle, you might wonder how in the world they could do that! Don't they know it is a sin against not only God, but themselves? How horrible! Yes, it is horrible. Sin is horrible. Yet again, it is sin. Plain and simple.

When you hear someone use offensive language, especially taking the Lord's name in vain, you may wonder how they could talk in such a way. You don't like it, but do you say anything about it? It is sin. Plain and simple.

When you are eating and realize you are full, but, oh, that scrumptious dessert is just calling your name, so you devour it also. Even though you were already full, and now you are so extra full you are miserable. Do you know that is gluttony? Gluttony is a sin. Sin is sin. Plain and simple.

You don't like to think of yourself on the same level as a murderer or a homosexual or even someone who uses offensive language. However, if you will take a second to be honest with yourself and let God speak to you about this subject, you have no alternative except to admit sin is sin.

We tend to see things as big sins or little sins when, in fact, it doesn't matter. Sin is sin, and not one of us is any better than another. We are all sinners saved by grace. Don't take offense with me over this devotion; take it to God and ask Him if this is truth or not. Then read Galatians 5:26 again.

Today's Prayer

Father,

In our humanness, we tend to forget that sin is sin to You. Help us not to be conceited or think we are better than anyone else. Help us learn to simply love one another and give grace as You give to us.

Amen.

But don't be conceited or make others jealous by
claiming to be better than they are.

—Galatians 5:26

May 18

Pick Me! Pick Me!

Did you grow up in a time when children actually played games outside? Even if you lived out in the country and didn't necessarily have neighborhood kids that played together, you likely played games in elementary school. Outside games like red rover or kickball or baseball or football—you get the idea.

Games where the teacher would choose two captains, and they would take turns picking their team. Some of the kids were shouting, "Pick me! Pick me!" and some of the kids were silently praying they wouldn't be picked at all and maybe not have to play, and some were secretly shouting "Pick me!" because they just wanted someone to want them on their team.

Maybe you were a captain who got to choose your team members, maybe you were one of the ones always chosen first, maybe you were one the captains always fought over, or maybe you were the one nobody wanted on their team. Maybe you were the one who always felt hurt and rejected, thinking you weren't good enough to be chosen or popular enough to be chosen.

Maybe those feelings of rejection carried over into adulthood, and you still struggle with wanting to be chosen or accepted by your peers—at work or at church. I have great news for you. There is One Who has chosen you—yes, you! He chose you before you were even known to anyone on this earth. "For you are a people holy to the Lord your God. Out of all the peoples on the face of the earth, the *Lord* has chosen you to be his treasured possession" (Deuteronomy 14:2 NIV), and in John 15:16a, "You did not choose me. I chose you."

You have been chosen, picked by God to be on His team throughout this life and on into eternity. He chose you; He wants you on His team. If you haven't already accepted, will you accept His invitation and join His team today?

Today's Prayer

Father,

Thank You for choosing us. Thank You for loving us and wanting us to spend eternity with You, holy and blameless in Your sight because of what Your Son, Jesus, did for us.

Amen.

For He chose us in Him, before the foundation of the world, to be holy and blameless in His sight.

—Ephesians 1:4 (HCSB)

May 19

He Is Your Strength

Last year, God moved my husband and me to a new city. We moved in March, but I still had to go back and forth to fulfill a job commitment, which ended in May. So, I feel as if I actually moved to the new city in May.

This year, the month of May has a lot of "one year ago today" memories. My mom moved to Heaven last May, we closed on our house and started moving in, my daughter's baby shower and other things.

Have you ever moved to a new city where you know absolutely no one? It's a hard thing to do—especially when you can't call Mom and tell her about everything that's going on! But, I know God's timing is perfect, and I know He is the One looking out for me. I never could have made it through this move without Him. I certainly couldn't make it through this month of "one year ago today" memories without Him.

Are you going through an especially tough time right now in your own life? Maybe you didn't have to move to a new city where you don't know anyone, but it could be something just as "traumatic." Have you recently lost a loved one? Moved to a new place? Going through a divorce you didn't see coming? It could be any number of things that have you feeling like you just can't go on. You want to cry your eyes out, go to bed, pull the covers over your head and try to make the world go away and leave you alone.

My friend, this is the time you need to lean on God. Let Him be your strength through this time when you are weak. Lean on Him and allow Him to help you take the next step and the next. If you will truly give it all to Him and depend on Him 100 percent for everything, you will begin to notice it gets a little easier to take that next step. He's waiting for you to call out to Him and let Him be your strength. Will you do it today?

Today's Prayer

Father,

Thank You for being our strength when we are weak. Thank You for helping us and filling our hearts with joy. Help us trust you with *all* our heart and our hurts until we burst out in songs of thanksgiving.

Amen.

> *The Lord is my strength and shield. I trust Him with*
> *all my heart. He helps me, and my heart is filled*
> *with joy. I burst out in songs of thanksgiving.*

> —*Psalm 28:7 (NLT)*

May 20

Are You Listening?

Are you a good listener? Do you know what it means to truly listen? I believe most of us like to think we are good listeners, but yesterday, I took an honest, hard look at myself and realized I haven't been a good listener at all!

If someone asks you to listen and you start giving advice or try to "fix" their problem, you aren't listening at all! If they share with you how they are feeling and you start telling them why they shouldn't feel that way, you are, in essence, walking all over their feelings and not being helpful or a good listener at all! They just want you to listen—not talk or try to fix their problem or tell them how they should feel—just listen!

As a mom, it is very hard to truly listen to your children—no matter how old they may be! Moms, I believe, are hardwired to try to fix everything and make all things right again, especially when it comes to our babies, am I right?

You don't realize you are actually hurting the situation or making the problem worse when you try to fix it. Even—maybe especially—when your child is an adult in their own right and they want to come to you, simply to pour out their thoughts and feelings. They aren't wanting you to fix it, they just want you to listen and that is so hard for us to do—but oh so necessary!

I've always heard, "God gave you two ears and one mouth for a reason—He wants you to listen twice as much as you speak." I don't know if that's true or not, but it does make sense! I know He wants us to learn to truly listen. Stop listening to try and fix the problem or to tell someone how they should or should not feel—start truly listening, just so the one talking has someone to hear, maybe a shoulder to cry on for a moment, with no judgment or advice or any talk at all. Just someone they can trust to be quiet and listen. Will you be a good listener for someone today? Are you willing to at least try it?

Today's Prayer

Father,

Help us be quick to listen and slow to speak or get angry. Remind us what it means to listen and that it does not mean to offer our advice or try to fix things for others.

Amen.

My dear friends, you should be quick to listen
and slow to speak or to get angry.

—*James 1:19*

May 21

True Joy

One of the saddest things I hear these days is the phrase "I seem to have lost my joy." We live in a "me" society, so it should come as no surprise when people begin losing their joy. Everywhere you turn, everyone is telling you to think of yourself and what you want first. Look out for number one—nobody else is going to!

Nothing could be further from the truth! The problem is many of us have *joy* and *happiness* confused. You don't have to be happy to have true joy. The enemy loves to tell you different, but he is a liar!

Your joy comes from the Lord, not your circumstances! You can be sad for a while and still have true joy! Stop listening to the enemy's lies and realize you can have true joy even in the middle of not-so-joyful circumstances.

If you want to have true joy, you must put Jesus first! If you are truly giving Him first place in your life, you can make it through anything! No, you may not feel happy all the time, but remember, you don't have to be *feeling* happy to have true joy! When you put Jesus first, others second, and yourself last, you will begin to see your *joy* returning.

You were born into this world a sinner and, as such, being selfish comes easy. However, when you give your life to the Lord, you are no longer living for yourself. You must learn to put Jesus first, above everything else! When you do, you will begin to notice a big difference, and you will realize you have *joy* in the middle of your circumstances, no matter what they are!

How can you begin putting Jesus first if you aren't already doing it? Would you let someone ahead of you in line at the store? Would you be willing to pray for that person who really knows how to get under your skin or push your buttons? Put Jesus first in at least one thing today. The more you do it, the easier it becomes. Before you know it, you'll have your joy back!

Today's Prayer

Father,

Thank You for this day You have given us! We will rejoice and be glad today!

Amen.

This is the day that the Lord has made. Let us rejoice and be glad today!

—Psalm 118:24 (ICB)

May 22

Friendly Fire

Chances are, when you hear the term *friendly fire*, you think of the military. We all know friendly fire is what it is called when someone is wounded—or killed—by someone on their side. Today—a different perspective of that term.

Do you ever find yourself talking bad about anyone? Not necessarily someone you know, just some random person? I imagine you might be saying—or thinking, "What? No! That's crazy! Why would I talk bad about someone I don't even know?" I have to ask, then, what did you say about that person who grabbed the parking space you had been sitting there waiting on for fifteen minutes? What did you say when you heard on the news about the person who had committed that heinous crime? Would your comments be considered friendly fire?

It's bad enough when we talk bad about someone we don't know, but how many times have you talked bad about someone you love? Did you know your hurtful (evil) words have the potential for killing someone? You have the ability to build someone up or crush their very spirit, in essence killing them with your words—your "friendly fire."

Your tongue is one of the most dangerous, deadly weapons you will ever possess. If you don't believe that, do a Google search on "scripture about controlling your tongue" and see what you find! I saw a T-shirt once that had this printed on it: "Lord, keep Your arm around my shoulder and Your hand over my mouth!" He can keep His hand over your mouth *if* you will allow it, but it certainly won't come easy. You must stay in constant prayer in order to allow Him to work in and through you, including your tongue.

If your tendency is to speak hurtful, rather than helpful, words, start changing that today by going to Him in prayer. It won't be easy; you may not change overnight, but you *can* change, if you will allow His power to work in and through you. Will you begin, today, to submit your tongue to Him?

Today's Prayer

Father,

May we speak words that heal and give life and not evil words that crush the spirit.

Amen.

As a tree gives us fruit, healing words give us life. But evil words crush the spirit.

—Proverbs 15:4 (ICB)

May 23

Confucius or Solomon?

"Confucius say…" That was a popular thing when I was a young teenager. Don't hear it much anymore, but, apparently, it's a huge part of Chinese culture to this day.

Confucius seems to have been a wise man, but he was no Solomon! While Confucius seemed to believe human beings were naturally good and that selfish interests could be controlled by adherence to virtue, we know the exact opposite is true! Each of us entered this world a sinner! Unless and until we give our hearts to Jesus, we are naturally bad and will act bad.

Once we give our hearts to Jesus, though, and allow the Holy Spirit to guide us, we can learn how to be and do better. A lot of the scripture writing this month has been from Proverbs, and I found myself pondering these teachings. Have you read much from the book of Proverbs? If not, I highly encourage you to do so.

Did you know the purpose of the book of Proverbs is contained in chapter 1, verse 2? Not sure the purpose is so plainly given in any of the other books or not.

Confucius may have been a seemingly wise man; unfortunately, it doesn't appear he knew the Lord. If he had, he would have known we are all inherently bad and not good. Would you rather learn from the teachings of a man who didn't know the Lord or from one who knew Him? There are thirty-one chapters in Proverbs. I challenge you to read one chapter a day for a month. Don't just read them— act on them! Apply them to your life, and notice the change that begins to take place! Let the wise teachings given to you through Solomon from the Lord, begin to reshape your entire way of living and thinking!

Today's Prayer

Father,

While Confucius may have had some good teachings, let us look, instead, to the wise teachings of Solomon and learn about wisdom and discipline there. Let us receive our instruction and gain knowledge from the wise sayings You speak to us through Solomon's teachings.

Amen.

The purpose of these proverbs is to teach people wisdom and discipline and to help them understand wise sayings.

—*Proverbs 1:2*

May 24

Never Have I Ever

I've heard that phrase many times through the years, but never have I ever realized it is, apparently, primarily a drinking game! I do know the enemy loves to take Godly things and offer an evil version of it, so today we will take the enemy's game and turn it into a Godly version.

Never have I ever seen one of God's children lacking anything they need. If you are a child of God and you are truly living your life for Him and trusting Him for everything, He will supply your every need—not your wants, but your needs (Philippians 4:19).

Never have I ever known of any prayer to go unanswered. You probably hear people say sometimes, "Thank God for unanswered prayers," but I cringe every time someone speaks those words. God answers every prayer in one of four different ways—three of which you probably already thought of: yes, no or wait. Just because He says no or wait doesn't mean the prayer is unanswered. It only means He didn't answer the way you wanted it answered. Remember though— He knows what is best for us! Tomorrow, we will look into the fourth way He answers prayer.

Never have I ever known of God turning anyone away! He wants and accepts everyone who comes to Him (John 6:37). Yes, He chooses you, but at the same time, He gives you the free will to either accept or reject Him. If you come to Him, He will not turn you away.

Do you get the idea? There are so many other examples of *never have I ever*, but there isn't room in this short devotional. In fact, you could probably fill another book with them! Take some time today to get quiet and let Him show you even more "never have I ever" statements you could make about Him. He may surprise you and show you something you never ever thought about before!

Today's Prayer

Father,

Never have I ever seen one of Your children abandoned or begging for bread. Thank You for showing us a whole new way of looking at the phrase "never have I ever." We give You all the honor, praise and glory!

Amen.

Once I was young, and now I am old. Yet I have never seen the Godly abandoned or their children begging for bread.

—*Psalm 37:25 (NLT)*

May 25

I Can't Hear You

As promised, today we are talking about the fourth way God answers prayer. The fourth way is by saying, "I can't hear you." I had never thought of this before, but during my research yesterday, I came across it in an article and, immediately, knew it was truth! It's backed up by God's Word, so I know it is truth.

Have you ever watched Gomer Pyle? Remember how Sergeant Carter was always bellowing, "I can't hear you!"? Well, our Father doesn't yell the way Sergeant Carter did, but He does, sometimes, have to say, "I can't hear you."

If you haven't accepted Jesus as your personal Savior yet, that is the first step you need to take. If you are already His child, it certainly doesn't mean you are suddenly perfect (Romans 3:23). We all sin daily in some way, whether it is intentional or not. I believe it is always best to confess your sin as soon as the Holy Spirit convicts you and you know you've done something wrong. I don't know about you, but if I wait until the end of the day to confess my sins, I'm most likely going to forget something!

Having unconfessed sin in our lives creates a roadblock between us and the Father, and we can't get through to Him until that roadblock is cleared away. Just look what happens when we clear that roadway:

> *But God did listen! He paid attention to my prayer. Praise God, who did not ignore my prayer or withdraw His unfailing love from me. (Psalm 66:19–20 NLT)*

Do you have unconfessed sin in your life today? Stop right now and pray, asking Him to forgive you. This clears the roadway, and you are free to approach His throne boldly, where you will be treated with undeserved kindness, and you will find help (Hebrews 4:16),

While His answer to you might still be no or wait a while, instead of yes, at least the roadway will be clear for you to get to Him and for Him to hear you.

Today's Prayer

Father,

Even as Your children, we know we still sin. Please remind us to daily confess our sin to You, empowering You to hear our prayers. Amen.

If I had not confessed the sin in my heart,
the Lord would not have listened.

—Psalm 66:18 (NLT)

May 26

Battle Cry

Are you in a battle right now? Remember Joshua and the Battle of Jericho? Joshua was to have his entire army march around the city once a day for six days. On the seventh day, they were to give a mighty shout—a battle cry, if you will. I offer you the following battle cry for your battle:

> You must humble yourself under God's mighty power, and in His good time, He will honor you. You must give all your worries and cares to Him because He cares about what happens to you. You have got to watch out for attacks from the devil—your great enemy—because all he wants to do is devour you, but you must take a firm stand against him and be strong in your faith. You must remember that you are not the only one suffering. Your Christian brothers and sisters all over the world are going through the same kind of suffering you are. You must remember that God, in His kindness, called you to His eternal glory by Jesus Christ, His Son. After you have suffered a little while, He will restore, support and strengthen you, and He will place you on a firm foundation. All power is His forever and ever!

Confession: I certainly did not write that battle cry. I took it straight from His Word—1 Peter 5:6–11—simply personalizing it and putting it in paragraph form. I actually gave that battle cry myself ten years ago. I came across it in my prayer journal and felt Him nudge me to share it. He actually put the words *battle cry* in my mind because those words weren't in my prayer journal. Ten years ago, I didn't realize it was a battle cry. I only knew I was going through a tough time, and He spoke to me through those scriptures.

Is He speaking to you today? Is He giving you this for your battle cry? Be faithful and diligent. He will give you the victory! Even if that victory doesn't look the way you think it should. Honestly, mine sure didn't look like I thought it would or should! And that's a devotion for another day.

Today's Prayer

Father,

Give us the strength to circle around as many times as You ask and help us hear when You tell us to give the battle cry, for You are handing "the city" over to us!

Amen.

The seventh time around, the priests blew the rams'
horns and Joshua told the army, "Give the battle cry,
for the Lord is handing the city over to you!"

—*Joshua 6:16 (NET)*

May 27

Victory

Yesterday, we gave a battle cry. Today, let's talk about the victory we receive! As a Christian, you don't fight your battles alone. In fact, if you give it to God in prayer, you don't really have to fight at all! You just do whatever He might require (or ask) of you, then sit back and watch Him work.

Whatever your battle is, if you will leave it in His hands, He will take care of it for you. You must remember this, however:

> The Lord says: "My thoughts and my ways are not like yours. Just as the Heavens are higher than the earth, my thoughts and my ways are higher than yours." (Isaiah 55:8–9)

I shared yesterday how my victory didn't look like I thought it would or should. Let me explain—ten years ago, I was in a battle for my marriage. I began praying for my marriage, like never before. I did everything I felt the Lord was asking me to do. I even spent the day before our divorce hearing in the prayer room at my church—yes, the entire day, from eight to five! I just *knew* God was going to do a miracle and my marriage would not end in divorce!

I was wrong. My marriage did end in divorce, yet I still got the victory! No, I didn't realize it then, but God had a plan. He always has a plan! After the divorce, God started me on a journey of restoration—with myself. He showed me, nearly a year later, that just because one had chosen to walk away from His plan didn't mean He had abandoned me (Jeremiah 18:9–10)! A little less than two years after that, He brought the most amazing, Godly man to me, and we have now been married for almost five and a half years! Yes, indeed, I got the victory!

So, you see, God is always in control; and, sometimes, when it seems everything is falling apart, it's really all just falling into place. Trust Him to fight your battle and trust Him with the victory—even if it looks different than you had in mind. Will you trust Him today for your victory?

Today's Prayer

Father,

Thank You for going with us and fighting for us against our enemies! Thank You for giving us victory—even when that victory doesn't look like we thought it would.

Amen.

For the Lord your God is going with you! He will fight for you against your enemies and He will give you victory!

—Deuteronomy 20:4 (NLT)

May 28

Stir the Embers

When you accepted Christ as your personal Savior, the Holy Spirit immediately came to live in you. He set your soul on fire, and you were burning bright, like a big, huge bonfire! You couldn't help but share what He'd done for you with everyone who gave you half a chance, and even those who didn't.

Over time, that roaring fire dies down, and you don't have that burning desire to share. You get caught up in the daily routine of life, and the fire that was once a roaring blaze is now nothing but a glowing ember.

So, what do you do about it? Do you ignore it until it completely goes out? Do you just walk away from it wondering why you ever thought that blazing fire was so great anyway? Do you get lost in the day-to-day routine of life and decide the fire wasn't for you, after all?

Or do you realize what's going on and begin to feel that stirring in your spirit? You begin to see where you started ignoring the flame, where you quit working at keeping it going. You begin to realize you no longer find yourself in the altar praying, and you are simply too busy to take time to read in His Word every day and spend time talking with Him and listening for His guidance for your daily life.

You begin to start blowing on those glowing embers by realizing you must take time to spend with Him each day. You fan those embers by finding yourself back in the altar, crying out to Him for even the smallest things going on in your daily life. You begin to see those glowing embers becoming small flames again as you get back to attending church regularly and regaining the fellowship with Christian brothers and sisters.

Before you know what's happened, the fire is roaring again, and revival has come to your own heart and can now spread to others! Are you ready to start that revival in your heart today?

Today's Prayer

Father,

Help us stir the embers and get the fire going full blaze again, then help us use it well for Your kingdom.

Amen.

So I ask you to make full use of the gift that God gave you when I placed my hands on you. Use it well.

—*2 Timothy 1:6*

May 29

Slaves No More

Confession: I was struggling with hearing from the Father this morning. I sat here praying and listening and couldn't seem to hear anything in my spirit. So, I took a break to go brush my teeth. That's when He showed me the lyrics I have taped to my bathroom mirror. I see them every morning, but sometimes I don't really "see" them, if you know what I mean.

This morning, however, I heard in my spirit, "Remind yourself and the others you don't have to be a slave to fear anymore." The song lyrics on my bathroom mirror? "No Longer Slaves" (aka "Child of God"). He used this song to give me victory in October 2016. I remember it well. I was having a little trouble getting into it when it began because the rhythm of it just seemed off to me, so I wasn't really singing along. Then, the words began seeping into my soul, and before I knew it, I was weeping! Tears streaming down my face!

If you struggle with fear of any kind, you need to know that fear comes from the enemy! You do not have to fear anything or anyone when you are God's child! Don't misunderstand, I'm not saying you will never be afraid of anything—only saying you don't have to let that fear rule you! God gives you the power to conquer and overcome these fears, even if you have to do it on a daily basis. You do not have to be a slave to any fear! Just call out to Him and remind your fear Who you serve and Who takes care of you and Who fights your battles for you!

The song didn't change me overnight—the song didn't change me at all. The song was simply a tool the Father used to remind me of something I had forgotten—He has already conquered all my fears, and He has done the same for you! I still have days I struggle with certain fears, but I'm quicker to give them to Him now. You can do the same thing. You don't have to live your life as a slave to fear. You are God's child, and He will help you, if you'll let Him. Whatever your fears may be, will you give them to Him today?

Today's Prayer

Father,

Thank You for adopting us and welcoming us into Your family! Thank You for all Your promises and for reminding us we no longer have to fear or live in bondage like slaves.

Amen.

You are no longer slaves. You are God's children and you will be given what He has promised.

—Galatians 4:7

May 30

Don't Get Mad—Get Even

Is that the motto you live by? Hopefully, if you answered, "You bet!" you were only joking. It is most definitely our basic, human nature to live that way—you hurt me, I'm going to hurt you—but it isn't how God calls His children to live. Because we are His children, He expects us to know a better way and to live in that way.

That way is to repay evil with good, hatefulness with kindness. He wants you, His child, to live in a way that is honorable and to do your part to live in peace, as much as you can. He tells us He will take vengeance and repay those who deserve it (Romans 12:17–19). Oh, how we like to balk at that one!

When someone does you wrong or treats you bad or they wrong someone you love or treat badly someone you love, your natural response is to strike back, right? However, when you became a child of God, you received the Holy Spirit, and if you are allowing Him to control your life, you will allow Him to help you respond in a way that is totally opposite to your "natural" one. Will you trust Him to know who deserves what better than you ever could?

If an enemy of yours is hungry or thirsty or has a need of any kind you can meet, are you willing to meet that need? That's what His Word instructs us to do (Romans 12:20). Will you do it?

There are a lot of good life lessons packed into these few verses (Romans 12:17–21). Is this something that is hard for you to take in and digest? Does it turn your stomach to think of doing something good or kind to someone who has done evil to you or a loved one? Is leaving vengeance to the Lord the last thing on your mind in any of these situations?

If you answered yes to any of those questions, drop to your knees (literally or figuratively) and ask God to forgive you and to help you learn how to live your life this way. It isn't something you can do on your own, but with the help of the Holy Spirit, you can do it!

Today's Prayer

Father,

Help us not repay evil with evil, but to repay evil with good and leave the vengeance to You.

Amen.

Don't let evil defeat you, but defeat evil with good.

—Romans 12:21

May 31

God's Will

How do I know God's will for me? How do I know what His plan is for my life? I've always heard the safest place to be is in the center of God's will, but how do I know if I'm there?

Are these questions you ask yourself from time to time? I have asked these before—and still do, sometimes. But, I'm finding the answers to these questions are not as difficult or hard to find as I once thought they were.

Do you know the answer to every one of those questions is waiting for you in His Word? All you have to do is read His Word, meditate on His Word, and He will show you His will for you and your life.

The answer may actually surprise you because it is so simple. When you discover the answer, you may find yourself thinking, "That's it? That's all? Are you sure? Surely, there has to be more to it than that."

It is God's will that your honorable lives should silence those ignorant people who make foolish accusations against you. (1 Peter 2:15 NLT)

God's will, put simply, is for you "to act justly and to love mercy and to walk humbly with your God" (Micah 6:8 NIV).

Those are just a couple of the verses that tell you what God's will is for you. Once you realize how simple it is to know His will, and you begin to walk in that, allowing Him to change the way you think about things, you will begin to see how wonderful it is to live in the center of His will. Oh, there will still be challenges, but you will have everything you need to make it through every battle.

Today's Prayer

Father,

Let us not behave like worldly people, but transform us and help us change the way we think. In doing so, we will know Your will for us, which is good, pleasing and perfect.

Amen.

> *Don't copy the behavior and customs of this world, but*
> *let God transform you into a new person by changing the*
> *way you think. Then you will learn to know God's will*
> *for you, which is good and pleasing and perfect.*

—Romans 12:2

June 1

The Battle Is Over

May was a hard month for me this year (2019). As hard as it was, though, the Lord saw me through. I couldn't have made it without Him.

At the beginning of Psalm 18, it says, "A psalm of David, the servant of the Lord. He sang this song to the Lord on the day the Lord rescued him from all his enemies and from Saul." When I read Psalm 18:1–3 this morning, it washed over me like a tidal wave of absolute relief! It's as if I've been struggling to breathe for a month, and suddenly, the air just filled my lungs!

Do you ever feel completely overwhelmed with life? You find yourself wondering how you are going to make it through another second, let alone another day? You are not alone! He is with you through every trial, every time you feel like you're going under for the last time; He will raise you up again and give you the strength to carry on, to put one foot in front of the other just one more time, and then another and another.

Then, one day, you wake up and realize the battle you were in is over, and He has given you the victory! You know other battles will come your way, but for today, for this minute, you can relish in the victory, savoring it the way you would your most favorite food. But, this is better than any food you could ever put in your mouth! Once again, He has seen you through, He has delivered you and, somehow, you are even stronger now than before! To God be all glory, praise and honor, for without Him, you would have been defeated long ago. Take time to enjoy whatever your victory is today—and, if you are still in a battle, hold on and remember Who is fighting for you and know your victory is on the way!

Today's Prayer

Father,

We love You and thank You for being our strength, our rock, our fortress and our Savior. We thank You for protecting us, for being our shield and our stronghold. We call on You, Lord, for You are worthy of praise, and we thank You for saving us from our enemies!

Amen.

I love you, Lord; You are my Strength. The Lord is my Rock, my Fortress and my Savior; my God is my Rock, in Whom I find protection. He is my Shield, the Strength of my Salvation and my Stronghold. I will call on the Lord, Who is worthy of praise, for He saves me from my enemies.

—Psalm 18:1–3 (NLT)

June 2

Chosen

"The Lord rescued him from all his enemies and from Saul." Did that line stand out to anyone else yesterday besides me? It didn't grab me when I read it in my Bible, but as I was typing it in the devotion, I felt a stirring in my spirit, and I knew He was showing me something else.

"From all his enemies and from Saul"! I realize this is not actually in God's Word, it is just a heading, but still something worth exploring a little more. Was Saul not one of David's enemies? Why would Saul not be included in "all his enemies"? Why did he have to be singled out?

When King Saul learned from the prophet Samuel that David had been chosen by God to replace him as king, he became filled with jealousy and envy. He had once loved David, his son-in-law, but now his one goal was to kill him.

Do you have a King Saul in your life? Someone who once loved you deeply, but now, for some reason, they are so jealous and envious of you, their main goal is to harm you?

Don't fall into their ways. Your friends, as David's friends, may be whispering to you, "Now's your opportunity! Today's the day." You may even begin to think, just for a moment, this is exactly what you will do. You may have even "crept forward and cut off a piece" of their "robe" (1 Samuel 24:4).

Stop! Remember what David said (1 Samuel 24:6), and remember your time will come, if you continue to obey God instead. King Saul was God's chosen, until he chose to disobey God. Continue to obey and honor God and allow Him to lift you up in His time. Hold on, it's coming!

Today's Prayer

Father,

Help us not fall in the trap of jealousy and envy, but let us remember You created each of us for our own specific purpose. May we not attack anyone, especially Your anointed ones, which is anyone who belongs to You. You have chosen each of us, and we thank You. Amen.

> *He said to his men, "The Lord forbid that I should do this to my lord the king. I shouldn't attack the Lord's anointed one, for the Lord Himself has chosen him."*
>
> —*1 Samuel 24:6 (NLT)*

June 3

Head, Shoulders, Knees and Toes

The same way the human body needs all the parts to work together, the body of Christ needs all its parts to work together too. You are one of those parts. Whether you are a head or a shoulder or a knee or a toe, it doesn't matter. No matter which part you are, it is important that you do whatever it is you're designed to do. That is what makes the body of Christ work well—when each one does what they were designed to do.

Do you enjoy a nice, warm fire in the fireplace during the winter? Or do you like to grill outside in the summer? The body of Christ is like the wood or the charcoal in those fires. You stack the wood or the charcoal all together in a pile, light the match and watch the flames get bigger and bigger.

But what happens if a piece of wood or a charcoal briquette falls away from that pile and is off to itself? Either will still glow brightly for a while; however, the longer it is away from the rest of the wood or charcoal, the colder it gets, and it can't burn anymore. If you separate all the wood or spread the coals out where they aren't touching, that roaring fire you had going will soon die out.

You see, that's how it is with the body of Christ. We need each other to stay on fire. We need each other for comfort, encouragement and so much more. Don't remove yourself from the fire when the going gets tough, for that is when you need to be surrounded. Don't separate yourself from your Christian brothers and sisters. In fact, you need to get even closer than ever before because you will be strengthened and be stronger than ever! On our own, we can't do much; but together, we can take a roaring blaze and set this world on fire for God!

Today's Prayer

Father,

   Thank You for creating us to all work together as one body. Show each of us what our work is and help us to do it well. Thank You for giving us each other to do "life" on this earth with, and remind us we do need each other, as sometimes we forget.

   Amen.

Just as our bodies have many parts and each part has a special function, so it is with Christ's body. We are all parts of His one body and each of us has different work to do. And since we are all one body in Christ, we belong to each other and each of us needs all the others.

—Romans 12:4–5 (NLT)

June 4

Going Home

Last year, God moved me from an area where I spent nearly fifty years of my life. He planted me in a city I had barely heard of and knew no one (except my husband). I love our new home, and we are getting to know more people. Today I had to make a quick trip back "home."

As I was approaching the exit, I began to cry—okay, I began to sob! It was kind of a happy cry, I guess, because the thought going through my brain was, "I'm here! I'm home! It feels so good to be back where I know people and they know me! I know we live in the other place now, and I love it, but this is *home*!" Then, as I was going down the off-ramp and turning on to the road that would take me into town, God spoke to my spirit and said, "This feeling you have right now? *This* is how you are going to feel when you *really* get *home*!" Oh my! The tears started flowing freely again, and the very next thought I had was, "And this is how Mom already feels about being *home*!" and I cried even more!

As a Christian, you have no doubt heard this world is not our home. It seems I've heard it all my life. Today He let me experience what it will feel like! I so wish I could put this feeling in each of you so you could "know in your knower" how wonderful it is! But, I can't.

I know this isn't the "normal" devotion; I just know He wanted me to share it with everyone! I don't know when He's coming back or if my time or yours here on this earth will be over before He does. I only know that when we leave here—through death or the rapture—we will have such an overwhelming, wonderful feeling of being *home*!

More food for thought: As I was approaching the exit to come back to our new home, the radio station played the song with the lyrics "All I know is I'm not home yet, this is not where I belong." The name of the song is "Where I Belong" by Building 429—needless to say, tears and praises flowed again!

Today's Prayer

Father,

Thank You that this world truly is not our home and we have a much better place to look forward to with You!

Amen.

For this world is not our permanent home; we are looking forward to a home yet to come.

—Hebrews 13:14 (NLT)

June 5

Taken for Granted

Nearly all of us have someone we tend to take for granted. We may not want to admit it, but it's the truth. Especially when that person is there for us all the time! We may not even realize we take them for granted until something happens, and they aren't—or can't—be there for us.

In my prayer time this morning, I told the Father, "I still get so amazed and overwhelmed at the things You show me!" Then my mind went to how I usually follow that with, "I know it shouldn't still amaze and overwhelm me, but it does." This morning, however, when I thought that, He gently spoke to my spirit and said, "Yes, it should."

Have you ever been thinking of all He's done for you and wonder why you are still amazed at how He does it or that He does it at all? Do you ever find yourself saying, "I don't know why it amazes me so much, but God has done it again!"?

My friend, if you still find yourself amazed, overwhelmed, almost in disbelief at how He did something or how He moved in your life or someone else's, be thankful. You are still on the right track, as the saying goes. Because, if you still feel this way, it means you most definitely are not taking Him for granted.

Where would your heart and soul be if you were not amazed and/or overwhelmed when He moves? Quite possibly, it could mean they aren't where they should be, don't you imagine?

Yes, continue to have faith He will take care of everything and take care of you. Having faith is different than taking Him for granted. He just doesn't want you to forget the many blessings He has given you. Take time to remember and appreciate Him, and you won't have to worry that you're taking Him for granted.

Today's Prayer

Father,

May each of us always love You with all our heart, soul and strength because when we do that, we won't take You for granted.

Amen.

So love the Lord your God with all your heart, soul, and strength.

—Deuteronomy 6:5

June 6

Date Night

You hear a lot about how important it is for couples to have date nights even after they're married (especially after they have children). Most "experts" agree on the main reasons date night is important. Those reasons are even more important when thinking about them in relation to a date time with the Lord.

It doesn't matter what you call it: date time, quiet time, alone time—*whatever* time, it only matters that you make time! The same reasons it's important to make time for you and your spouse (or boyfriend or fiancé) is why it's important to make time to spend with the Lord.

A preplanned evening—or morning or afternoon or whatever time works for you. Jesus sometimes had His quiet time late at night (Matthew 14:22–23), and sometimes He had it early in the morning (Mark 1:35). It doesn't matter when you have it, it only matters that you purposely plan the date and keep it! Only, instead of once a week or once a month, it needs to be a daily date!

Communication—communication is an important part of any intimate relationship! If you never, or hardly ever, spent time talking with your spouse, how could you have an intimate relationship? How can you expect, then, to have an intimate relationship with the Lord if you don't make time to communicate with Him? Time that involves you listening as well as talking! Not just time for you to give Him a list of needs and/or wants!

It gives you time to relax and take a break from your daily stress. It will help you grow closer to Him and rekindle the fire you had when you first came to know Him. It will increase your commitment to Him, and you will be teaching others by example—whether it's your children, spouse or friends. Do you already have a set daily time to spend with Him? If not, would you start today?

Today's Prayer

Father,

    May we each find time to draw near to You and confess our sins. May we learn to follow You and not the world. Make our thinking pure, Father, as we spend quality time with You.

    Amen.

Come near to God and God will come near to you. You are sinners. So clean sin out of your lives. You are trying to follow God and the world at the same time. Make your thinking pure.

—James 4:8 (ICB)

June 7

It's about Time

As you were reading yesterday's devotion, some of you were probably thinking, "That's a really great concept, and I wish I could do that, but I just don't have time for it in my schedule." Challenge: Do you really not have time, or are you simply choosing not to make time?

The saying "We make time for what's important to us" is true. If spending time alone with the Lord is truly important to you, you will *make* the time to do it. Again, it all comes down to choices. You can give a thousand excuses, but at the end of the day, it all comes down to one thing—you *chose* not to make the time for Him (Luke 12:34).

He is still there for you, no matter how much you ignore Him! He isn't a petty God, Who says, "Oh, you didn't have time for Me this morning, so I don't have time for you now." No, He loves you and will always be there for you. But, He is a jealous God (Deuteronomy 4:24).

How much better could your day go *if* you chose to spend even five minutes with Him? Just you and Him, alone, for five minutes. It doesn't mean you won't have problems during the day. It doesn't mean the baby won't start demanding your attention during those five minutes or that the phone won't ring or a text won't come through or a social media notification. What it does mean, though, is when you *choose* to give Him time, even five minutes, to put Him first, then you are seeking His kingdom, and everything else will take care of itself (Matthew 6:33).

If you have that much to do, how do you *not* have time to spend with Him? If you will give Him just five minutes, He will honor your commitment, and eventually you will begin to notice a huge difference in your days!

Today's Prayer

Father,

Let us not get worried and upset about too many things. Let us remember the one important thing—spending time with You—that will never be taken away from us.

Amen.

But the Lord answered her, "Martha, Martha, you are getting worried and upset about too many things. Only one thing is important. Mary has chosen the right thing and it will never be taken away from her."

—Luke 10:41–42 (ICB)

June 8

Think, Speak, Do

How are your thoughts, words and deeds lining up with each other? How are they lining up with God's Word? That is the true measuring stick, right? We've talked before about our thoughts and how not every thought we have comes from the Lord.

So, how do we know which thoughts we should linger on and give more attention? If a thought doesn't line up with the Word, you can be sure it isn't from the Lord, and it needs to go! Ask God to search your heart, to test you and know your anxious thoughts. Ask Him to point out anything in you that offends Him and lead you along the path of everlasting life (Psalm 139:23–24 NIV).

What words are you allowing to come out of your mouth? Remember, out of the abundance of your heart, the mouth speaks (Proverbs 4:23). So, a big part of making sure you speak life is to guard your heart, first and foremost! Let your words and your thoughts be pleasing to Him (Psalm 19:14 CEV), and when they are, you know your words are lining up with Him.

Last, but not least, what about the things you do? Do you do the right thing? Probably not all the time, but if it is your goal to always do the right thing, He knows your heart, and He will help you, if you let Him. Psalm 15:1–2 (NLT) asks, "Who may worship in Your sanctuary, Lord? Who may enter Your presence on Your Holy hill?" Then it goes on to give the answer, "Those who lead blameless lives and do what is right, speaking the truth from sincere hearts." The only way you can lead a blameless life is through the blood of Christ covering your sins!

What you think, speak and do are important, and it is important they line up with God's Word. Are your thoughts, words and deeds lining up today?

Today's Prayer

Father,

Thank You for the blood of Christ, covering our sin and making us blameless before You. Help us do what is right in Your eyes and speak only truth from sincere hearts.

Amen.

Who may worship in Your sanctuary, Lord? Who may enter
Your presence on Your Holy hill? Those who lead blameless lives
and do what is right, speaking the truth from sincere hearts.

—Psalm 15:1–2 (NLT)

June 9

Essential Oil

Everyone seems to use essential oils these days, my husband and I included. It seems you're always hearing, "There's an oil for that!" When you hear of how an essential oil helped someone, you must take that information at face value, as every individual is different. An oil, or combination of oils, that helps one person may not necessarily help another the same way. You simply have to try it to see if it will help you the same way it helped someone else.

There is one essential oil, however, that will do the same thing for each and every one of us! It is the only true *essential* oil there is. It is the oil of the Holy Spirit! The very day you accepted Jesus as your personal Savior, God anointed you with the oil of the Holy Spirit! When you hear someone testify of what *God* has done for them, you don't have to try it or wonder if He will do the same for you. You know He will! God is no respecter of persons; in other words, He doesn't show favoritism (Romans 2:11). What He does for one, you can *know* He will do for you!

There is no better essential oil in this world today than the essential oil of the Holy Spirit. It empowers you to do the things God calls you to do, such as taking the good news to those who need it and comforting those with broken hearts and/or lives. But, how can you proclaim that captives will be released and prisoners freed? Captives and prisoners aren't always being held in brick-and-mortar buildings. Sometimes they are being held captive or prisoner in their minds, by the enemy. Show them how they can be released and freed, the same way you were released and freed from your own captivity and prison. You can use the oil of the Holy Spirit to help them break those chains! Allow the Lord to use you as a vessel to pour out the *true* essential oil!

Today's Prayer

Father,

Thank You for anointing us with the oil of the Holy Spirit to take the good news to the poor, comfort the brokenhearted, proclaim that captives will be released and prisoners will be freed. Give us each the courage to do what You have anointed us to do.

Amen.

The Spirit of the Sovereign Lord is upon me, for the Lord has anointed me to bring good news to the poor. He has sent me to comfort the brokenhearted and to proclaim that captives will be released and prisoners will be freed.

—Isaiah 61:1 (NLT)

June 10

No Fishing

Do you ever find yourself asking God to forgive you for something that you have already asked forgiveness? There was a time I did that a lot!

Do you realize what He tells us in His Word doesn't go along with that at all?

> *Repent, then and turn to God, so that your*
> *sins may be* wiped out, *that times of refreshing may*
> *come from the Lord. (Acts 3:19 NIV)*

I emphasized the words *wiped out*. Let those words sink in for a bit.

When you repent—ask forgiveness for your sin—He wipes it out completely. Imagine He wipes it out completely. Imagine your sin was written on a dry-erase board. When you confess it to Him and ask Him to forgive you for it, He doesn't just take the eraser and wipe it off where you can still see traces of it there. He gets out the dry-erase board cleaner, sprays it on and completely wipes it out where you can't tell there was ever anything there!

Look at Micah 7:19, "Lord, You will have mercy on us again. You will conquer our sins. You will throw away all our sins into the deepest sea" (ICB). Think of that as the sea of forgetfulness. Because, once He has forgiven it, He forgets it so completely it may as well be at the bottom of the sea. He throws it into that deep, deep sea, and then He puts up a No Fishing sign, and you are not allowed to go fishing there! He doesn't want you to keep asking forgiveness for it because He won't have any idea what you are talking about. Once He forgives, He forgets. It's hard for our minds to comprehend because we have a hard time forgetting things.

Okay, some of us are easier at forgetting things than others, but you know the drill. When the enemy starts whispering to you about that sin, you just say, "What sin? That has been forgiven and forgotten!"

Today's Prayer

Father,

Thank You for Your forgiveness of our sin and for choosing not to remember them anymore, once we have confessed them to You. Thank You for reminding us we only have to confess once because after that, You remember no more.

Amen.

Then He says, "I will never again remember their sins and lawless deeds." And when sins have been forgiven, there is no need to offer any more sacrifices.

—Hebrews 10:17–18 (NLT)

June 11

The Only Way

The enemy has blinded a lot of people in this world we live in. He is very cunning and deceitful, which should not come as a surprise to us (Christians), since we are told in God's Word about him (1 Peter 5:8).

A lot of people believe in God and will talk about God with you and don't mind if you talk about God. Romans 10:2 (NLT) says, "I know what enthusiasm they have for God, but it is misdirected zeal. It is misdirected because, as verse 3 says, they don't understand God's way of making people right with Himself." They don't believe in Christ, and without Christ, no one can come to God.

Romans 10:9–10 (NLT) says, "If you openly declare that Jesus is Lord and believe in your heart that God raised Him from the dead, you will be saved. For it is by believing in your heart that you are made right with God and it is by openly declaring your faith that you are saved." And verse 11 goes on to say, "As the Scriptures tell us, 'Anyone who trusts in Him will never be disgraced.'"

So, you see, if you don't believe in and accept Christ as your personal Savior, you have no way of coming to the Father. You cannot approach His throne until you have accepted Christ. Because, you see, the Father doesn't see you when you approach Him. He only sees the blood of His Son, Jesus Christ, covering you. If you don't have that blood covering you, it's as if you aren't even there.

Remember from yesterday: once you accept Christ and ask His forgiveness, your sins are gone! Then and only then, "my friends, the blood of Jesus gives us courage to enter the most holy place by a new way that leads to life! And this way takes us through the curtain that is Christ Himself" (Hebrews 10:19–20).

So, you see, my friend—Jesus *is* the *only* way! Have you come to Him yet? If not, would you do it today? He is waiting for you with open arms!

Today's Prayer

Father,

Thank You for willingly giving Your Son, Jesus Christ of Nazareth, to die for our sin so that we may boldly come to You in His name.

Amen.

"I am the way, the truth, and the life!" Jesus answered.
"Without me, no one can go to the Father."

—*John 14:6*

June 12

The Rainbow Covenant

What is a covenant? Simply put, a covenant is an agreement. The definition in *Merriam-Webster* states it is "a written agreement or promise usually under seal between two or more parties, especially for the performance of some action."

Have you ever heard of the Rainbow Covenant? Maybe you have and you've just never heard it called that? Some years back, the Lord revealed something to me that I had never ever noticed before in His Word.

Have you ever read chapter 9 of the book of Genesis? That's where you can find the Rainbow Covenant. You have probably read it before, many times, just as I had. We all know the rainbow is a sign from God that He will never flood the entire earth again, right? And, maybe, your question is, "Then why do we still have floods today?" Read it again (Genesis 9:12–16), paying special attention to verse 15. It doesn't say there will never be another flood. It says there will never be another flood to destroy *all* life.

But the part that stands out is in verse 16—where He says the rainbow will be a reminder to *Him* of the covenant! Now, you know God doesn't forget any of His promises. In fact, the only thing God forgets is your sin, once you have confessed it! So, why would He say the rainbow is a sign to *remind* Him of the covenant?

Because He wants you to know that He remembers. He knows when you're in a storm—literally or spiritually—and He gives the rainbow to assure you He hasn't forgotten His promise! True, we can use things to make our own rainbows, but the most beautiful, meaningful ones are the ones He makes!

Have you ever noticed some of the brightest rainbows come after some of the worst storms? Maybe that's a devotion for another day.

Today's Prayer

Father,

Thank You for the beautiful Rainbow Covenant. Thank You for remembering Your agreement with us that continues forever.

Amen.

*When the rainbow appears in the clouds, I will see it. Then
I will remember the agreement that continues forever. It
is between Me and every living thing on the earth.*

—*Genesis 9:16 (ICB)*

June 13

A Storm and a Rainbow

Storms and rainbows—it really does seem the brightest rainbows come after the fiercest of storms. This morning in my personal prayer time, I felt God was speaking to my spirit about finding your rainbow (encouragement) through the storms (challenges).

You know there are ways to create a rainbow on your own, right? All you need is a prism, or something to work like a prism, and some light, and you can "manufacture" (create) your very own rainbow, any time you want. But it still isn't the same as that vibrant, bright rainbow only He can create in the sky, right?

I have a friend who has been going through a storm (challenge) for a little over two years now. Two years and three months to be exact! In those two years, he and his wife have been given a few rainbows (encouragement), enabling them to stay steady throughout this storm. Every time it seems the storm is just about over, it starts up again. This is a storm that is definitely out of their control. There is no way they can "manufacture" or create their own solution. Only God can speak to their storm and tell it to be gone. Only God can give the brightest of rainbows at the end of this storm, assuring them He is always with them and He remembers His promise to them. When that day comes, the rainbow will be so bright it will outshine the sun, and they will have many friends and family rejoicing with them!

But, you know, sometimes you go through storms (challenges) that you try to calm on your own. For instance, you might be having some difficulty in your finances, and instead of trusting God and giving it all to Him, you try to find a way to solve it yourself. Maybe God has promised you something and you don't see it happening. So, like Sarah, you try to figure out how to make it happen. Stop! Trust God to give you the perfect, brightest of all rainbows in His time— not yours. Be assured, the rainbow He will create is better than any you could ever hope to!

Today's Prayer

Father,

Thank You for being our strong tower, our shelter from the storms of this life and a place where we are safe from our enemies.

Amen.

You are a strong tower, where I am safe from my enemies.

—Psalm 61:3

June 14

The Downhill Struggle

When you are going uphill, it's likely you are going a little slower and being more intentional about every step you take. You think you can't take another step, but you push through and tell yourself, "Just one more step, you're almost at the top of the hill, then you'll be able to breathe easier, you'll be able to relax and enjoy the view." At times, your financial struggle, work struggle, relationship struggle or whatever struggle you are in can seem like such an uphill battle. You feel like you are going so slow. However, you are seeking the Lord with every step you take, asking Him to help you just put one foot in front of the other one more time. You feel like you are going so slow, just trying to make it to the top of the hill.

Then, you reach the top of the hill, and you think, "Thank You, Jesus! You helped me make it!" and then, as you start going downhill, you think, "Thank You, Father, for downhill!" It's so much easier going downhill than it is going uphill—or is it?

You start walking a little faster, stepping quicker and quicker, to the point you're almost running! Wow! This is so much easier than going uphill! Crash! What was in your path? Something caused you to fall, and you find yourself sprawled out on the pavement, hurting and confused! What happened? Maybe it was just a little too easy to put one foot in front of the other. Quite possibly, once you started downhill, you thought you could do it on your own, and you forgot to ask the Lord for guidance.

You have just learned a valuable lesson. Never run—or walk—ahead of God. He doesn't want us running ahead of Him or lagging behind Him. He wants us by His side, seeking His guidance for every step—especially when the path seems easy! Remember, uphill or downhill, you need His guidance both ways.

Today's Prayer

Father,

Help us not to run ahead of You but to continue in the teaching of Christ so we may have both You and Him. Especially when we are walking downhill.

Amen.

Anyone who runs ahead and does not continue in the teaching of Christ does not have God; whoever continues in the teaching has both the Father and the Son.

—2 John 1:9 (NIV)

June 15

Speak, Breathe, Repeat

Those may seem like simple instructions, but when you are in the middle of a battle, they can be some of the most important instructions to keep you going. Let's take a look at what those simple instructions are really saying.

Speak: "Death and life are in the power of the tongue: and they that love it shall eat the fruit thereof" (Proverbs 18:21 KJV). So, while you are in a battle, remember to speak *life* over your situation. You can talk yourself into defeat, or you can talk yourself into a victory! The choice is yours.

Breathe: "Then He breathed on them and said, 'Receive the Holy Spirit.'" Take time to breathe in the Word of God and His presence. Breathe in the Holy Spirit. Allow yourself time to take a break from your battle, whatever it is. Don't retreat or shrink away from it, but give yourself some time to get your focus back on God, and remember He is the One truly fighting your battle for you, even though you are a soldier in the battle.

Repeat: Be sure you repeat steps 1 and 2 as often as you can. If you will take time to repeat those two steps daily, you will be amazed at how much easier the battle becomes. Why? Because you are allowing Him to fight it for you in a way you could never imagine or hope to! He tells us in Joshua 1:8 to "keep this Book of the Law always on your lips; meditate on it day and night, so that you may be careful to do everything written in it. Then you will be prosperous and successful." You are probably even more familiar with verse 9, which says, "Have not I commanded thee? Be strong and of a good courage; be not afraid, neither be thou dismayed: for the Lord thy God is with thee whithersoever thou goest."

So, the next time you are in a battle, remember these simple instructions:

SPEAK, BREATHE, REPEAT: "This I know:
God is on my side."

Today's Prayer

Father,

Thank You for being there the minute we call for help in defeating our enemies. Thank You for always being on our side.

Amen.

*On the day I call for help, my enemies will be
defeated. I know that God is on my side.*

—Psalm 56:9 (NCV)

June 16

Sometimes Right Is Wrong

Do you ever find yourself saying the right thing at the wrong time? Unfortunately, a lot of us, myself included, can do this and not always be aware of it. If something is right and true, how can it be wrong? The Lord taught me a lesson in this just a few days ago.

Social media is a wonderful tool, as it allows you to stay in touch with friends as well as acquaintances, no matter where life may take you. It is much faster than sending a letter through snail mail (and much cheaper); however, it is also lacking in many areas. If not handled correctly, it can be an easy way to cause hurt, disappointment and/or other negative feelings. When you type a response, a comment or a message, you cannot inflect the tone of your voice. There isn't a way to type on a computer screen if you are being sarcastic, criticizing, joking or loving. Oh, I know there are a lot of emojis out there in cyber land to try to compensate for this, but it still isn't the same as *hearing* how it is being said.

Saying something that's right at the wrong time is still wrong. If your words cause hurt to someone, then it is wrong to say them. Especially on social media! You may not know what has gone on in that person's life over the last hour or day or the last week. You don't know what pain or heartache they may currently be dealing with. So, even if you are saying something to them that they already know, and you are saying it in a kidding or joking kind of way, they can't *hear* that on social media, and your words could cause them to be hurt. Therefore, your words are wrong!

The lesson the Lord taught me was more of a reminder, and one we could all use. Always be prayerful before saying anything to anyone. Whether you are saying it in person or on social media. Maybe, when saying something on any social media, you should even be extra prayerful. If you, like me, can't stand the thought of having caused someone to feel hurt or criticized, you will be glad you spent a little extra time in prayer before speaking.

Today's Prayer

Father,

We not only need You to take control of what we say and guard our lips, but we also ask You for wisdom in knowing when the time is right to speak and when we should just keep quiet.

Amen.

Take control of what I say, O Lord, and guard my lips.

—Psalm 141:3

June 17

Mentoring

The younger generation used to look up to the older generation for guidance in everything; the older generation took time to teach the younger generation the important things of life. It's called mentoring, and we need it again!

Paul speaks to us about this in the book of Titus. Specifically, in chapter 2, he tells Titus the older women need to be mentoring the younger women and the older men need to be mentoring the younger men.

As a member of the older generation these days, I have felt God's nudging about the importance of mentoring. I wish I had known someone who could mentor me when I was younger, trying to raise a daughter, basically, on my own and not having a clue how to truly manage things.

Remember the movie *War Room*? It was all about older mentoring younger, and everyone raved about it! Yet, as much as everyone raved about how great it was, still no one seems to want to follow the guidelines it set out for us.

Younger women today don't seem to want older women giving them advice about anything, especially not about how to love their husband or children. How many marriages might have been saved if only there had been someone mentoring them—teaching them the ways of the Lord when it comes to marriage and/or raising children?

Everyone wants to go their own way, it seems. It's the mentality of "I can do it myself, and I don't need your help!" that makes it so hard for anyone, including God sometimes, to get through. I believe He wants us to take a closer look at mentoring and what it means. Are you willing to learn?

Today's Prayer

Father,

Thank You for clear instruction in Your Word for the older women to be mentoring the younger women. Help us get back to a place where we put this into practice—older women teaching the younger women to live wisely and be pure, to do good and to be submissive to their husbands.

Amen.

These older women must train the younger women to love their husbands and their children, to live wisely and be pure, to work in their homes, to do good and to be submissive to their husbands. Then they will not bring shame on the word of God.

—Titus 2:4–5 (NLT)

June 18

The Blood Covering

Have you noticed there are a lot of people who believe in God and have no problem with anyone talking about Him? However, take those same people and try talking to them about Jesus Christ of Nazareth, and they suddenly become offended, or worse, and are trying to silence you.

We need to get one thing perfectly clear before we go any further with these devotions: Without the blood of Jesus Christ of Nazareth covering you, you can*not* approach the throne of grace, the most holy place, our Father, and expect to be heard or even seen!

Before you even think about entering into God's presence, you must first accept His Son, Jesus Christ of Nazareth, as your personal Savior and ask Him to forgive your sin! There are many places in His Word that speak of this. One is in Ephesians 2:13 (NLT), "But now you have been united with Christ Jesus. Once you were far away from God, but now you have been brought near to Him through the blood of Christ."

You know, you can talk about God as much you want, and the enemy doesn't really care; but, start talking about the blood of Jesus Christ of Nazareth, and he will do anything and everything to stop it! Since beginning to write what I feel God is giving to us this morning, I have been interrupted no less than three times, and I'm home by myself!

There is power in the blood of Jesus! Just look at Revelation 12:11 (NLT), "And they have defeated him by the blood of the Lamb and by their testimony." It is only with the blood of Jesus covering you that you can approach the Father. When you do, He doesn't see you, He sees the blood of His Son, and that is the only thing that makes you worthy. Are you covered by the blood of Jesus?

Today's Prayer

Father,

Thank You for Your Son, Jesus Christ of Nazareth, Who was willing to pay the ultimate price so that we, being covered by His blood, may boldly come into the most holy place and approach Your throne of grace.

Amen.

And so, dear brothers and sisters, we can boldly enter Heaven's Most Holy Place because of the blood of Jesus. By His death, Jesus opened a new and life-giving way through the curtain into the Most Holy Place.

—Hebrews 10:19–20 (NLT)

June 19

A Willing Vessel

That's all God wants—willing vessels, to do what He wants to do here on this earth. Does He need us to accomplish anything He wants done here? Of course not! He chooses to let us join Him in His plan, if we want to participate. Feeling qualified is not a prerequisite to Him using you.

When He asks You to join Him in something—to be an active participant, all He wants is your availability, not your ability. In fact, the more unqualified you feel, the better. If you feel you are capable or qualified to do something, you might think you are doing it under your own power and not His.

I've shared before how I do not feel qualified to be writing these devotions. However, I have been faithful to show up every morning to meet with Him, and He has been faithful every morning in giving a devotion for that day. It may not be one that resonates with me on that particular day, but I trust it will one day, or it will resonate with someone else, and that is why He needs it to be written—to reach that one! You can do what I've done this year. Not necessarily write devotions, but whatever it is you feel He is asking you to do. Accept His offer, enjoy the challenge and praise Him every time He does it through you by letting others know it is Him! Be a willing vessel!

Even Jesus told us He was only doing what His Father wanted Him to do. Look at John 6:38, "I came down from Heaven to do what God wants Me to do. I did not come to do what I want to do" (ICB).

No matter what you may have done in your past, God can and will use you. In fact, I am convinced He likes to use the most broken ones to actively participate in what He wants to do! Will you do what

He asks? Will you be a willing vessel? Then, if anyone should ask, let them know it is Him doing what you do because you could never do it on your own!

Today's Prayer

Father,

Thank You for reminding us that when we live by Your truth, we gladly come to the light so others will know that anything we do is not really us doing it, but it is You doing it through us.

Amen.

But everyone who lives by the truth will come to the light, because they want others to know that God is really the one doing what they do.

—John 3:21

June 20

Every Minute Counts

Procrastination, in my opinion, is one of the enemy's favorite tools. If he can get us to put things off, instead of just getting them done, he knows we will begin to feel overwhelmed at some point, become frustrated and—figuratively, if not literally—throw our hands up and say, "Forget it, I quit!"

Do you ever get caught in his trap of procrastination? If we're honest, we probably all have to answer "Oh yes!" to that question. As I was sitting here praying and, literally, crying out to God, asking Him to give me this morning's devotion, He began speaking softly to me. He had me thinking about the project I've been working on this week while my husband is away at a conference. I leaned in to hear Him more clearly, and I began to hear the word *procrastination*.

So, I looked up scriptures about procrastination, and my eyes immediately fell on Ephesians 5:16, and I knew I was on the right track. There are plenty of scriptures about this subject though. Ecclesiastes 11:4, for example, says, "If you worry about the weather and don't plant seeds, you won't harvest a crop." There are plenty of others too. Just google it and see what comes up!

Do you find yourself putting things off, for one reason or another, saying you'll get to it tomorrow? Are you aware that tomorrow never comes? I'm pretty sure it was my mom who told me that. I know she used to say it a lot! The reason tomorrow never comes, in case you haven't figured it out, is because when tomorrow gets here, it is no longer tomorrow—it's today! You've probably heard the saying, "Yesterday is *history*, tomorrow is a *mystery*, but today is a *gift*—that's why it's called the present."

Today truly is a gift God has given us, and He wants us to use our time wisely. I confess I haven't been doing that for probably the last couple of years. Today, I ask forgiveness for the sin of procrastination and make the choice to strive to put it behind me. Will you do the same today? Don't put it off until tomorrow.

Today's Prayer

Father,

We are definitely living in evil times, and we come before You today asking You to help us make every minute count.

Amen.

These are evil times, so make every minute count.

—Ephesians 5:16

June 21

Even If You Don't

Last night I was reminded of a scene from the movie *Facing the Giants*. The one where the woman comes out of the doctor's office, yet again, with the news that she is not pregnant. She is heartbroken and sad, yet she prays simply and sincerely, "Even if I never get pregnant, I will serve You anyway." That may not be the exact line—but the meaning is the same.

What are you longing for right now? Are you sick and longing to be healed? Are you still waiting for that special someone to spend the rest of your life with? Are you, like the lady in the movie, still longing for a baby to be added to your family? Are you praying for loved ones to come to the Lord?

You know God can do all those things and more. The question is, will you serve Him even if He doesn't? Will you choose to praise Him even if He doesn't answer your prayer the way you want Him to? Are you truly willing to love and serve Him even if you never received another blessing?

You know God can bring your loved one to salvation, but God is a gentleman, and He will not force anyone to love or accept His Son or Himself. He will not override man's (or woman's) free will. He only wants those who choose to love and serve, no matter what.

Have you ever stopped and thought maybe God is simply wanting to know you are okay with whatever He has for you? Maybe He is waiting for you to sincerely pray the same simple prayer the lady in the movie prayed, "Even if I never [*you fill in the blank*], I will love and serve You anyway!" Can you pray that prayer today and mean it sincerely from the bottom of your heart? Are you willing to place your son or any other desire on the altar, the way Abraham did, trusting God and being willing to love and serve Him no matter what?

Today's Prayer

Father,

We know You can heal us from our sickness, give us the baby we long for, send us that special someone to share life with or any other number of things, but, Father, even if You don't, we will worship and serve You anyway! We know that Your way is the best way.

Amen.

The God we worship can save us from you and your flaming furnace. But even if He doesn't, we still won't worship your gods and the gold statue you have set up.

—Daniel 3:17–18

June 22

Me Too

How many times have you given a scripture to a friend, assuring them God would provide for and take care of them? Philippians 4:19 is one we tend to use a lot, right? And, it's true! God will provide for and take care of all our needs.

What I'm wondering this morning, though, is a little different. A few days ago, during my personal prayer time with Father, He showed me something about myself that I never realized before. I was praying for two special people in my life, thanking God (in faith) for bringing them back to Him. I have no doubt He is putting people in their paths to point them straight to Him and that He will remove the blinders from their eyes, and they will come running to Him! As I was praying that, He gave me one of those Holy Spirit nudges—a revelation about myself, actually!

He asked me, "Why do you find it so easy to have confidence I'll do things for your loved ones, and yet you struggle, sometimes, with having the same confidence that I will do it for you?" What! Wow! He really called me out on that one! Thing is, I know He was speaking nothing but truth! That's all He can speak—truth!

Are you, like me, guilty of praying for something for yourself, wanting to believe He will work in your life, when, at the same time, you find yourself thinking, "That would never happen for me."? Aren't you His child too? Doesn't He love you just the same as He loves everyone else?

He wants you to know today that He will do the same for you! He is no respecter of persons. Choose to start telling yourself, "What He did for that person, He will do for me too!" Start walking in that truth today and see how it changes your entire life! As we Southerners like to say, He will bless your socks off! Practice saying, "What He did for them, He'll do for me too."

Today's Prayer

Father,

Thank You for reminding us You will take the same care of one of us as You do another. You created each one of us, and we can trust You to carry us and keep us safe.

Amen.

I will still be the same when you are old and gray and I will take care of you. I created you. I will carry you and always keep you safe.

—*Isaiah 46:4*

June 23

Do You Have a Second?

"Nobody's listening to anything the preacher says after twelve anyway." Oh, how that statement hurts my heart and makes me cringe inside! It's one thing to joke with a pastor about how long his sermons are, but to make a statement like that in a serious conversation? That is troubling in more ways than one.

First of all, do you realize the pastor is God's servant? He is the one God uses to deliver a message to *you* each week. Yes, you! The message this week may not be as specifically for you as it is for another. However, you should be praying so intently for the message to be reaching the one(s) it is meant for that you have no idea of the time. Also, just because it may not be speaking about something you are personally dealing with at the moment, every message you hear *is* for you, or God wouldn't have you there to hear it. He knows what you are going to be dealing with in the future, and He may be giving you a heads-up on how to deal with it ahead of time!

Secondly, who are you to put God on a timetable? Do you go to church with the attitude, "Okay, God. You have thirty minutes to speak to me, and then it's time for me to think about lunch and what I have to do after church is over"? Don't you know God doesn't work on your timetable? What if the part of the message He had for you isn't spoken until ten minutes after twelve? What might you be missing because you stopped listening at twelve?

Thirdly, do you understand making a statement like the one above is saying to God your time is more important than His? Do you understand the One you are trying to put on a time schedule is the very One Who schedules your time? He grants you the next second, or He could, just as easily, call you home instead. What might happen if you leave your timekeeping device at home for the next service? Or, keep it where you can't see it until after the service?

Take time to search your heart today and seek Him. It will be time well spent, no matter how long it takes. He promises! So, do you have a second? Or sixty?

Today's Prayer

Father,

Help us to seek and find You when we search for You with all our heart! Time we spend seeking You is never wasted!

Amen.

And you will seek Me and find Me, when you
search for Me with all your heart.

—Jeremiah 29:13 (NKJV)

June 24

The Supernatural

Would you describe yourself as an introvert or an extrovert? Do you consider yourself to be very outgoing naturally, or would you prefer to stay more to yourself and not be around a lot of people?

Is it natural for you to talk with strangers and carry on a conversation, as if you've known each other for years, or do you find yourself at a loss for words and being not so good at the small talk?

Naturally, are you an extrovert or an introvert. I am an introvert, by nature. A couple mornings ago, the thought went through my head, "I guess I'm just naturally an introvert," and immediately God spoke to my spirit, saying, "But I have called you to live in My *super*natural, not in your natural!"

There's our challenge and encouragement for today! Whatever you consider yourself to be, naturally, whether extrovert, introvert or something else you struggle with, remember God has called you to live in His *super*natural! How do you do that? Glad you asked. By the power of the Holy Spirit!

> *For the Kingdom of God is not just a lot of talk; it is living by God's power. (1 Corinthians 4:20 NLT)*
> *Now all glory to God, who is able, through His mighty power at work within us, to accomplish infinitely more than we might ask or think. (Ephesians 3:20 NLT)*

The power comes from the Holy Spirit living inside us! Whatever struggle you are facing in the natural, whether it's being an introvert or something else, remember that God has given you the power to live in the *super*natural!

Will it be easy? Probably not. I've always heard, though, anything worth having is worth fighting for, and I believe it! Just remember 2 Timothy 1:7 (KJV), "For God hath not given us the spirit of fear; but of power and of love and of a sound mind." So, are you ready to start living the *super*natural life?

Today's Prayer

Father,

Thank You for filling us completely with joy and peace when we trust in You, and thank You for the overflowing confident hope we can have through the power of the Holy Spirit.

Amen.

I pray that God, the source of Hope, will fill you completely with joy and peace because you trust in Him. Then you will overflow with confident hope through the power of the Holy Spirit.

—Romans 15:13 (NLT)

June 25

How to Pray

First of all, I ask you to pray for everyone. Yes, everyone! The people you love and, especially, the people you have a hard time loving. Ask God to help and bless them all. Even your enemies? Yes, maybe even more so for your enemies. It is easy to pray for those you love, but when you pray for your enemies, you are acting like your Father in Heaven (Matthew 5:44–46). When you pray, tell God how thankful you are for each of them.

Pray for kings and others in power. In other words, pray for everyone—from the president of the United States all the way down to your local government. God is the One Who placed them in their position, so we need to pray for them. We don't have to agree with everything or anything they do, but He does command us to pray for them so that we may live quiet and peaceful lives as we worship and honor God.

This is the kind of prayer that is good, and it pleases God our Savior. Sometimes, in our humanness, it's easy to forget that we are all just people. Those in authority are no different than us. We must remember they need prayer as much as, if not more than, we all do.

God wants everyone to be saved and to know the whole truth. What truth? There is only one God, and Christ Jesus is the only One Who can bring us to God. Jesus was truly human, and He gave Himself to rescue all of us.

Today's instructions on how to pray come straight from 1 Timothy 2:1–6. The challenge is for you—and me—to begin praying this way. The encouragement is, when you begin praying this way, God will honor it, and you will begin to see great and wonderful things happen in your world.

Today's Prayer

Father,

Thank You for reminding us we are to obey the people in authority over us. You are the One Who gives them authority and puts them in their place of power. If we oppose our authorities, we are opposing You, and we can expect punishment.

Amen.

Obey the rulers who have authority over you. Only God can give authority to anyone and He puts these rulers in their places of power. People who oppose the authorities are opposing what God has done and they will be punished.

—Romans 13:1–2

June 26

Harvesting Destruction or Life?

"I think it's a lack of commitment." That's a statement made about why people don't show up for things at church. It is so true—sad, but true. What has happened to cause this lack of commitment? Is everyone really so busy with their own lives they don't have time anymore?

You will make time for what's important to you. So, what it comes down to is, how important is your relationship with the Lord? You are already saying, "My relationship with the Lord is very important to me. I just don't have the time I used to have." Then you go into a long list of excuses as to why you don't have time to spend with the Lord or doing His work.

That's all they are—excuses—and when it comes down to it, excuses are just choices. They are choices you make not to spend time with Him. You choose to put other things ahead of your relationship with Him. It's a matter of priorities as well as commitment. Are you married? How would your spouse feel if you paid as much attention to him/her as you do to your relationship with the Lord? Would he/she put up with you only spending an hour or two a month with them? How would they react if you were always telling them, "I love you, but I can't spend time with you today because I have to _____ [you fill in the blank with one of your excuses]."

Married or not, doesn't really matter. You cannot have a relationship with anyone unless you are willing to make sacrifices to spend time with that person and cultivate the relationship. Why do you think your relationship with the Lord could be any different? If you don't spend time with Him, how can you get to know Him? If you don't spend time doing things with Him, how can you get close to Him?

Are you ready to recommit to your relationship with the Lord today? Are you ready to fall in love with Him all over again? Will you choose to put Him first?

Today's Prayer

Father,

Help us not to follow our selfish desires of doing what we want, only to reap destruction, but help us to follow Your Spirit and do what You would have us to do so we may reap eternal life with You.

Amen.

If you follow your selfish desires, you will harvest destruction; but, if you follow the Spirit, you will harvest eternal life.

—Galatians 6:8

June 27

True to Who?

"To thine own self be true" was the singsongy phrase that flitted across my mind this morning. Why? What does that even mean, Lord? Full confession here—I've never read *Hamlet* or watched any movies or plays of *Hamlet* and had no idea that is where the phrase comes from—act 1, scene 3 to be exact. Some guy named Polonius was, apparently, giving advice to his son. From what I was reading, it has become quite the catchphrase. In fact, a lot of people think it is in the Bible—it is not!

Is that really the kind of advice you would want to give your son or your daughter? On the surface, you might think there's nothing wrong with it. The challenge is to look deeper. What is that phrase really saying? Be true to yourself; put yourself first, don't worry about anyone else or what they are saying or doing or feeling.

The exact opposite of what the Lord says in Matthew 22:37–40. He says the first and most important commandment is for you to love the Lord, your God, with all your heart, soul and mind. The second most important commandment is to love others as much as you love yourself!

The world screams, "Be who you are!" God gently tells us to become who we should be—Christlike. The world's way is the easy way, but it comes at a high price! God's way is harder, but it comes with great rewards!

Who would you rather listen to? Polonius or God? Who would you rather follow? The world or Jesus? When it comes to the seriousness of this decision, I pray you will choose Jesus. I challenge you to try it His way for thirty days—put others ahead of yourself, and see what happens. You just might be in for a big surprise!

Today's Prayer

Father,

Help us to forget about ourselves. It's the exact opposite of what the world teaches, and it goes against our human nature. But, Father, we want to have Your nature and be like You. Help us take up our cross and follow You in all we do.

Amen.

Jesus then told the crowd and the disciples to come closer and He said: If any of you want to be My followers, you must forget about yourself. You must take up your cross and follow Me.

—Mark 8:34

June 28

All It Takes

Do you know what it takes to have a quiet time with God? Do you know which devotional you need? Do you need pens, markers, a journal? What kind of pens, markers and journal do you need?

Do you need to get up extra early in the morning? Do you need to stay up extra late at night? Do you need to spend an hour or more? How long does your quiet time need to be? What do you need to pray about? How long do you need to pray? Who do you need to pray for? How do you even begin to pray? Do you need to try to remember everyone by name?

What about that journal? What are you supposed to write in it? Do you have to draw pictures too? What colors do you need to use? Do you need to write a paragraph, a whole page or two or more pages?

At this point, you may be quoting the old commercial, "Calgon! Take me away!" (Google it if you're too young to know what that is!) You may be thinking it just isn't worth it. There are too many things you need that you don't have and you don't have the money to buy them. You don't really like to write or draw, and you really don't have time anyway because every hour of every day is already spoken for and then some!

Relax. Take a breath, and listen to this. I will tell you exactly what all it takes to have a quiet time with God, and you may find yourself amazed! All it takes is you and God. Yep! That's it! All those other things are fine and dandy, if you have them. But all you really need is you and God. Even if it's in your car as you're driving around doing errands. Even if it's only a few seconds at a time. *Any* time you spend drawing near to Him, He will draw near to you. Could you give Him just five seconds today? He's ready and waiting.

Today's Prayer

Father,

Let us come near to You, Father, so You can come near to us. Help us clean sin out of our lives and stop trying to follow the world and You at the same time. Make our thoughts pure, Father.

Amen.

Come near to God and God will come near to you. You are sinners. So clean sin out of your lives. You are trying to follow God and the world at the same time. Make your thinking pure.

—*James 4:8 (ICB)*

June 29

Friendship with God

In cleaning out some screenshots from my phone yesterday, I came across one of a Facebook post I had made on May 13, 2013. Apparently that morning, my scripture reading was in Romans, the verse used at the end of today's devotion, to be exact. Do you ever really think about God as being your friend?

How often do you think of God as friend? More often than not, you probably think of Him as your Father, your provider, your protector, your healer and a host of other things. But, how often do you think of Him as your friend?

Full confession—God knew I needed that reminder yesterday, even though I didn't realize it at the time. Yesterday was a hard day. One of those days where I was crying every time I turned around, and the hardest part? Not really knowing why. Yes, the enemy was messing with my mind, but even though that's what I *thought* was upsetting me, I still sensed something deeper, something I couldn't quite put my finger on. Until today, when I realized it was a feeling of mourning—though I don't know what I was mourning. I only know that during my prayer time, He turned that mourning into joy, and I was praising and worshipping Him! And I felt Him speak to my spirit to share the post from 2013 with others to encourage them!

Post from May 13, 2013:

When I read this verse, three words really struck me: FRIENDSHIP WITH GOD—I don't know why it hit me like it did. I know God loves me and cares for me and all that—but I guess

I never really thought of it in terms of "friend-ship." I can't even begin to describe the peace that flooded through me, realizing I have a FRIEND-SHIP with God! What more could any of us ask or hope for?

If you are having a bad day today or a day of mourning, just turn to your friend God, and He will turn your mourning into joy!

Today's Prayer

Father,

Thank You for restoring our friendship with You at the great cost of the death of Your Son, even while we were Your enemies. Thank You for saving us through the life of Your Son.

Amen.

For since our friendship with God was restored by the death of His Son while we were still His enemies, we will certainly be saved through the life of His Son.

—Romans 5:10 (NLT)

June 30

His Word Never Changes

We all have our opinions on things, and it seems we love to put them all over social media! Do we ever stop and ask ourselves, though, if this is our opinion of something, or is this what God's Word says about something?

There is nothing wrong with having your opinion about things, but where do you get the basis for your opinion? That is very important to consider. Do you base your opinions on the Word of God, or do you base your opinions on views of the world?

Who would you rather follow? Would you rather follow God or man? Let's see what Paul says in 2 Corinthians 13:7–8 (NLT).

> *We pray to God that you will not do anything wrong. We pray this, not to show that our ministry to you has been successful; but, because we want you to do right, even if we ourselves seem to have failed. Our responsibility is never to oppose the truth; but, to stand for the truth at all times.*

You see, Paul was telling them they should do right, even if the ones in authority over them were not doing right. Even Christians are going to fail at doing the right thing sometimes, but we can get forgiveness the minute we ask for it. Seeing a Christian do something wrong isn't your excuse to do the same thing. You can't say, "Well, so-and-so did it, and I know they are a big Christian, so it must be okay"—no way! Two wrongs don't make a right—never have, never will.

You see, it doesn't matter what you think about anything. The only thing that really matters is what God says in His Word. If He says something is wrong, then it's wrong! It doesn't matter how many laws man passes saying otherwise. If God says it is wrong, then it is still wrong, no matter what!

The world's opinion on things or God's Word—the choice is yours to make!

Today's Prayer

Father,

Even though the flowers and grass will fade away, thank You for reminding us that Your Word always stays the same—it never changes. What was wrong yesterday is still wrong today, no matter what man says.

Amen.

Flowers and grass fade away, but what our
God has said will never change.

—Isaiah 40:8

July 1

The Chosen Few

The governor's son is getting married, so invitations were sent to many of their finest friends. However, when the big day arrived, and everything was ready, all those friends turned down the invitation to attend. They had better things to do. They couldn't waste their time going to a wedding!

The governor was so upset! He called some of the hired help together and sent them out, telling them to go and invite anyone they could find to come to the wedding. So, they did. They went to the streets and invited everyone they could find—good and bad alike! They all showed up, and the governor's mansion was filled with guests for the big wedding and reception. They had all dressed up in the finest wedding clothes they had and come to take part in the big celebration. Except for that one...

When the governor came in to meet the guests, he noticed that one who wasn't dressed up at all. That one who was still wearing the same clothes he had on when he was invited to join the celebration. When the governor asked him why he hadn't dressed for the occasion, the man had no answer. The governor had him removed at once! For many were invited, but only a few were chosen.

Did any of that sound familiar? That was my version of the wedding feast parable found in Matthew 22:1–14. You may read verse 14, "For many are called; but, few are chosen," and think God already has His chosen picked, and you may not think you are one of those.

Here's the thing, though—God has chosen everyone! However, not everyone will choose Him. When you accept His Son, Jesus, you are dressed in your finest wedding clothes. The one who wasn't dressed in his finest clothes was the one who wanted to come to the celebration, but didn't want to accept Jesus as His Savior. God has already chosen you. Will you choose Him?

Today's Prayer

Father,

Thank You for giving us all to Jesus, if we accept Him. When we accept Him, then He is able to accept us, and we can freely come to You.

Amen.

The Father gives Me the people who are Mine. Every one of them will come to Me, and I will always accept them.

—John 6:37

July 2

Whatever It Takes?

Full confession: At this moment in time, I am not willing to pray, "whatever it takes." God is dealing with me about this, and I believe He wanted me to share it here for others who may be feeling the same way.

Prayer comes with a lot of responsibility and consequences. I am thankful for the privilege of prayer, and I know I can completely, totally trust Him with it all. But, do you fully understand what it means to pray "whatever it takes" prayers?

Are you a little afraid and not willing to go quite that far yet? To be honest, not that long ago, I used to pray "whatever it takes" prayers because I only thought of how it might affect my life. Don't get me wrong—I'm no martyr by any stretch of the imagination—I was simply willing to go through whatever *I*, personally, needed to in order for God to be able to use me.

Just a few days ago, in my prayer time, God showed me I had changed. I found myself writing these words:

> *I also know I'm not where I should be when it comes to prayer. I'm not to the place where I can pray "whatever it takes" yet, because I admit to You it is still scary to me. I know it shouldn't be; but, in my humanness, it is.*

I changed because I started thinking about my beautiful, new baby granddaughter and then my daughter and my son-in-love and my husband. If I pray that "whatever it takes" prayer, am I ready for what it might cost them, as well as me? Am I ready for what it might cost me, in regards to them? For instance, am I ready if "whatever it takes" could mean losing one of them? I want to be there. God knows my heart, and I know He understands my fear. I also know He wants me to relinquish that fear to Him and be brave enough to pray the "whatever it takes" prayer, knowing He knows best and He will help me through whatever it might take.

If you are in the same place I am today, take comfort in knowing you aren't alone, but let's also pray for each other to get past the fear and be bold in our prayers. He will give us mercy and grace to help us.

Today's Prayer

Father,

Help us get past the fear and be able to come boldly to Your throne, where we will receive Your mercy and find grace to help us when we need it most.

Amen.

> *So let us come boldly to the throne of our gracious*
> *God. There we will receive His mercy, and we will*
> *find grace to help us when we need it most.*

> *—Hebrews 4:16 (NLT)*

July 3

You Are His

If you have accepted Jesus as your personal Savior, you are His. No ifs, ands or buts about it, as they say. Once you are His, you are His forever. Yes, you could choose to turn your back on Him, deny you ever knew Him and walk away from Him. But, He will never turn His back on you, deny He ever knew you, and He will most certainly never walk away from you—no matter what you do!

He loved you from the beginning of time. You didn't do anything to make Him love you. You didn't say anything to impress Him to make Him love you. He simply loves you because you are here. He loved you *before* you accepted Christ as your personal Savior, and He will love you always.

Even after my full confession of yesterday, I know I am still His. I still belong to Him, and He still loves me just the way I am. However, He also loves me enough not to let me stay the way I am. He will continue to grow and stretch me beyond anything I ever imagined I could do.

And He still loves you—no matter what! You may think you've done too many awful things for Him to love you, but that is a lie from the pits of hell and satan himself! You are never beyond God's reach; you can never do too many awful things for God to ever be able to love and forgive you.

Paul tells us in 1 Timothy 1:16, "But for that very reason I was shown mercy so that in me, the worst of sinners, Christ Jesus might display His immense patience as an example for those who would believe in Him and receive eternal life." Even though Paul called himself "the worst of sinners," the truth is we are all the same. God doesn't see big sin and little sin. He simply sees sin—until you accept

Christ. Then all He sees is the blood of His Son that has washed you clean and made you white as snow!

Today's Prayer

Father,

Thank You for creating us, for forming us. Help us learn not to be afraid because You have saved us, called us by name and made us Your very own. Thank You that we are Yours!

Amen.

Now this is what the Lord says. He created you, people of Jacob. He formed you, people of Israel. He says, "Don't be afraid, because I have saved you. I have called you by name, and you are mine."

—Isaiah 43:1 (ICB)

July 4

Giving Up Independence

We currently live in a free country and are able to enjoy many freedoms because of it. However, those freedoms were not free. A long, bloody battle was fought to gain our independence from England.

Did you know the Declaration of Independence was not a set of laws but a statement of principles? And, like it or not, they were (are) biblically based, Godly principles. A lot of people these days seem to have forgotten that. Too many people are wanting to take God out of everything!

Bring it down to a more personal level: You like your independence, don't you? When you were younger, you couldn't wait to "grow up," get out on your own and have your independence so you could "do whatever you wanted," or so you thought. Then you found out that independence comes with a price, right? You had to get a job to pay for that independence, right?

While many men and women fought—and still fight—for you to enjoy your freedom and independence, some of them paid the ultimate price for you to have it: they paid with their life. They willingly went and continue to go into battle and face the possibility of never returning so you can continue to enjoy the freedoms you have—many of which you take for granted every day.

There is One, though, Who fought for you by not fighting at all. No amount of man power could have put Jesus on that cross, except for the fact He was willing to pay that price so you could have eternal freedom of a different kind: freedom from having to pay the cost of your own sin. He was willing to pay that price for you to give you access to the Father and eternal life.

So, are you willing to give up being independent and be dependent on God for everything? You can trust Him to take care of your every need.

> *And this same God who takes care of me will supply all your needs from His glorious riches, which have been given to us in Christ Jesus. (Philippians 4:19 NLT)*

Today's Prayer

Father,

Thank You for this land You have given us. Not by our own strength, but by Your power and because of Your favor. We, as a nation, need to turn our hearts back to You, Father, or be willing to pay the price.

Amen.

> *They did not conquer the land with their swords; it was not their own strength that gave them victory. It was by Your mighty power that they succeeded; it was because You favored them and smiled on them.*

> *—Psalm 44:3 (NLT)*

July 5

A New Day

Every morning is a fresh start, a new beginning. Even His mercies are new every morning (Lamentations 3:22–23). Early in the morning, while it is still dark outside, everything is quiet, the world is still sleeping and it is a wonderful time to sit and listen for His still, small voice.

It is a wonderful time to learn more about His love and come to Him in prayer, asking for His guidance (Psalm 143:8). Maybe that is why this early morning time means so much to me. Honestly, yes, there are some days I would love to turn that alarm off and go right back to sleep. But, then I remember He is waiting for me, and I can hardly wait to see what He has for me each morning.

It is wonderful to tell about His love each morning and to announce how faithful He is each night (Psalm 92:2). So, even if early morning isn't a good time for you to meet with Him, that's okay. He will meet with you any time, any place, for five seconds or for an hour or more.

His mercies are new every morning, but they last all day. He will always have plenty of mercy and grace for you, no matter what time of day you meet with Him.

Every day is a new beginning, a new chance to be a better you than you were the day before. A fresh start, no matter what time your day starts. A chance for a new perspective on things. Another day to learn how to trust Him more and gain strength from Him. Let Him fight your battles this day.

When you begin to take life in daily increments, realizing every day is a brand-new day, and you learn to look at it through His eyes, you will see things in a whole new light! Life won't be so overwhelming. Stop trying to live in the future and *be* in the present, realizing that is all you have. You never know when the new day you've been given is the last new day you'll get. Spend at least a part of it in prayer and ask Him to guide you through your day. He will meet you whenever, wherever, and your day will be better because of it.

Today's Prayer

Father,

Thank You for letting us know Jesus woke early in the morning, while it was still dark, and went to a place where He could be alone and pray. While some of us may not be able to do that, help us see the importance of having time alone in prayer.

Amen.

Early the next morning, Jesus woke and left the house while it was still dark. He went to a place to be alone and pray.

—*Mark 1:35 (ICB)*

July 6

Before Day One

While it has been a rough week, emotionally speaking—being in a strange place, knowing nothing about the history of it or the people in it, I felt a stirring in my spirit this morning. He reminded me that He knew me before day one! He knows my history as well as my future! He has a plan, not to harm me but to prosper me, *when* I search for Him with all my heart (Jeremiah 29:11–13).

No matter where He places you, no matter where you go, He is always with you! He knew you before you were born. He made all the delicate, inner parts of your body, and He put you together in your mother's womb (Psalm 139:13).

It gets even better than that. He not only knows you and your history—He knows your future! He knows every heartache and joy you've experienced to make you who you are today. He knows every time you've walked with Him, and He knows the times you've walked away from Him.

Even in the times you walked away from Him, He never walked away from you. He never left you. He may have stayed silent, knowing you didn't want Him around, but He never left you. He was waiting with open arms when you realized what you'd left and came running back to Him. He had forgiveness, mercy and grace all waiting there for you, and He gave it all to you as He wiped your tears of regret away and said, "Welcome home, my child, welcome home."

If you are in a strange, new place, and you don't know the history of it or anyone you meet, it could be, quite simply, God placed you there because someone there needs to hear and know your story. Then again, maybe you need to hear the story of someone there. Either way, He is with you. He will never leave you or forsake you

(Hebrews 13:5). Let Him stretch you outside your comfort zone. It's really not so bad—in fact, it can be very rewarding!

Today's Prayer

Father,

Thank You for being with us since before we were born. Thank You for ordaining all our days before even one came to be. Help us to live each of those days for and with You.

Amen.

Your eyes saw my unformed body; all the days ordained for me were written in Your book before one of them came to be.

—Psalm 139:16 (NIV)

July 7

Going Back

Do you remember a time when there was right and wrong and you knew the difference? A time when it was easy to tell if someone was a Christian or not? Do you remember when the laws were based on principles from the Word of God? A time when man didn't make laws to suit his own wants or needs?

Do you remember when a man's word and a handshake were as binding as any fifty-page legal document it might take today? Do you remember a time when people were honest because it was the right way to be? A time when marriage was a man and a woman making vows before God, family and friends, and it was much more than just a piece of paper that could easily be wadded up and thrown away if things don't work out?

Do you remember a time when children could play in their own yards without fear of being taken by someone? Do you remember a time when a neighborhood was like family and everyone watched out for each other? A time when life was simple and neighbors helped each other make it through the hard times?

What happened to those days? When did everything suddenly become so hard? How did things evolve into this "me" generation we live in today? A day where neighbors only help each other if there's something in it for them? A day when selfies are all the rage because, after all, isn't it all about self?

Everyone talks about moving forward, the times they are a changing, we have to keep up. Yes, the times are changing, but what if in order to move forward, we need to take a few steps back?

Are you ready and willing to go back? Back to living by God's Word and striving to live the way He has outlined for you there? Are you up for the challenge? Are you willing to go back to living by His truth?

Today's Prayer

Father,

We don't want to be lukewarm Christians that You spit out of Your mouth. We want to be on fire for You and live in Your ways. Help us get that fire back and let our lives point others to You.

Amen.

But since you are lukewarm and neither cold nor
hot, I will spit you out of My mouth.

—Revelation 3:16

July 8

Hope and Peace

There you are, sitting in your nice, quiet house, early in the morning, no one else awake or stirring around yet, and you have such a peaceful feeling. You are soaking up all you can with Jesus and the Father before the busy day begins, and you are thinking it doesn't get any better than this when, all of a sudden, you hear this loud, horrendous noise!

What was that? Your mind begins darting around to all the scary places it can think of, and before you know it, that peaceful, contented feeling you had just a second ago is completely gone! You are wondering how someone got in your house without you knowing it and wondering what is about to happen, and your mind is still racing, racing, and your heartbeat is getting faster and faster and then...

You realize it was the ice maker dumping ice in the freezer! That was the big, scary noise you heard! It was nothing! It was a noise you hear often in the daytime and never think anything of it. Yet in the quiet, early morning hours, it sounded much scarier!

Then you realize the enemy does things like that too. You are sailing smoothly along from day to day, knocking away the little darts he throws at you—when, seemingly out of nowhere, the waves get rough, and you feel you're being tossed around to the point you're afraid you are going to crash into something or, worse yet, sink to the bottom...

Until you remember—you have an anchor you can throw out. Not just any anchor, you have *the* anchor, your hope in God, to hold you steady and get you through whatever storm (financial, health, relationship, etc.) has come your way and tried to shake you. Sure, the enemy scared you for just a second there, but his tactics are useless against the hope and peace you have. You *do* have that hope and peace, don't you?

Today's Prayer

Father,

Thank You for the peace we can have in You. Thank You that we no longer have to be worried or afraid once we come to You. Thank You for helping us not to be worried or afraid.

Amen.

I give you peace, the kind of peace that only I can give. It isn't like the peace that this world can give. So, don't be worried or afraid.

—John 14:27

JULY 9

The First Mission Trip

I wonder if I would have been willing to go on that very first mission trip... would you? Would you be willing to do it today, should He ask? How much do you truly want to serve Him?

Would you leave your home, taking nothing with you? No food, no money, no hotel reservations, no phone, no computer, not even a change of clothes? I think, in our "Christianity", we would all like to think our answer would be a resounding YES.

However, if we were to get really honest with ourselves, how many of us would have to not only answer very quietly; but that answer might even be that we'd say "I don't know if I'm there yet" or "I'm not sure I'm ready for that kind of commitment yet."

Would we ever even ask Him to help us get to the place where we would be willing? Maybe it's something we'll never know unless or until He does ask. You (and I) definitely need to spend time in prayer, searching, to see if we are ready for whatever He might ask of us.

Would you be willing to go on a trip of self-denial? If He asked you to lose your life for others and trust Him for your safety and needs, what would you answer? He commanded the disciples to go. They even had to depend on others for their shelter.

The very first mission trip was to teach the participants about self-denial and the provision of God. I can't help but wonder, how many of us would eagerly sign up to go on a mission trip like that first one? Would you be willing to go? Would I? Much to think about today, my friend. Much to think about...

Today's Prayer

Father,

you instructed the disciples to take nothing but a few basic items on their trip and they went. Help us be willing to lay down all our "stuff" if You ever asked it of us.

Amen

This is what Jesus told them: "Take nothing for your trip except a walking stick. Take no bread, no bag, and no money in your pockets. Wear sandals and take only the clothes you are wearing.

—Mark 6:8-9 (ICB)

July 10

Hindrances

"Throw off everything that hinders." Wow! Did that grab your attention the way it did mine? It certainly gives you a lot to think about, wouldn't you agree? Since I only know about me, let's use me for an example today.

What hinders me? My past and the fear of rejection. I continue to allow my past to shadow my present. I don't like it, but I'm just being honest. I have become much better at recognizing when it is happening, and I'm also getting better at shutting the enemy down when he uses this tactic on me.

Still, there are times I envision what I want to happen, how I want to be in given situations—crowds, mostly—but then the enemy steps in, and I freeze. I give in to what was in the past instead of pushing through and moving on to what can be in the present.

I'm suddenly aware, though, of just how far God has brought me in this. Yes, I still struggle sometimes, but those times are getting fewer and further between. It is because I finally gave that part of my life to God. I find myself listening to Him and believing what He says about me more and more. Well, I've always believed Him, it's just that now I am beginning to allow it to permeate through me. Maybe that's what it means by "throw off"—I've thrown it to God. Now, I believe, He wants me to help others do the same thing!

So, ask yourself what it is that hinders you. What is holding you back from being all God wants you to be? Would you be willing to give it to Him today and let Him perform the change to allow you to run the race He has for you? Will you begin to truly trust and rely on Him to do in you the same thing He's done in me? It might not be easy—it will be worth it though!

Today's Prayer

Father,

Many people are watching us, so help us get rid of anything that hinders and the sin that so easily draws us in. Help us run this race with perseverance and be able to hear, "Well done, thy good and faithful servant," when we are done.

Amen.

Therefore, since we are surrounded by such a great cloud of witnesses, let us throw off everything that hinders and the sin that so easily entangles. And let us run with perseverance the race marked out for us.

—Hebrews 12:1 (NIV)

July 11

Release of the Butterfly

Have you ever been set free from something and not accepted it? I have. But I didn't realize it until yesterday. He showed me that He set me *free* from something nearly three years ago, yet I've still been walking around in bondage, talking about how these chains have me bound! I have continually repeated the devil's lies about being bound, and people would look at me like I'm crazy because they couldn't see any chains!

Imagine a person who is in prison and has been there for many years. One day, they tell him, "You are free. You can go out these doors and go wherever life takes you." So, the prisoner leaves, but he goes home and lives as if he were still in prison—is that person truly free? There are no longer any bars or doors actually keeping him confined, but he lives as though there are. So, is he truly free? Of course not!

Are you still walking around in bondage to something, even after God set you free from it? Maybe you are and you just don't realize it. Ask Him if you are doing the same thing I was doing. I promise He will let you know! Stop using the "struggle" as an excuse!

Stop giving the enemy so much credit, saying something is the way it is because of him, when in reality, it's your own self getting in the way! Take some time to get quiet and alone with the Lord and ask Him to show you what you need to see.

A couple of weeks ago, June 29 to be exact, as I was getting in bed to go to sleep for the night, I heard in my spirit, "From a turtle to a butterfly." I wasn't exactly sure what that meant. I got my answer when He whispered to me last night, "The butterfly has been released"!

How long are you going to wait before you accept what He has given you?

Today's Prayer

Father,

Thank You for making us new in You. Thank You for throwing our past into the sea of forgetfulness, never to be remembered again by You, and thank You for making us new!

Amen.

Anyone who belongs to Christ is a new person. The
past is forgotten and everything is new.

—2 Corinthians 5:17

July 12

The Struggle Is Real

That phrase is heard a lot these days. It seems people apply it to just about anything they say or do. Why do we have to struggle in this life?

Look at Jesus and His life—do you think He didn't struggle? He was tempted by satan three times (Matthew 4:1–11). Do you think you are any better than Jesus that you should not have to struggle? I'm fairly certain we all know why we can expect to have struggles in our lives.

Psalm 27:10–13 says, "Even if my father and mother should desert me, You will take care of me. Teach me to follow, Lord, and lead me on the right path because of my enemies. Don't let them do to me what they want. People tell lies about me and make terrible threats, but I know I will live to see how kind You are." These verses definitely speak of someone who is struggling, yet this person also remembers Who is in control!

Those verses remind you not to fear because you know the Lord is taking care of you. He is watching out for you. Whether the struggle you are in is because of a choice(s) you made, life in general, or even if your current struggle is straight from the Lord Himself—the thing you must remember is this: He has never left you, He is with you everywhere you go, in everything you do, and He hears everything you say (as well as what you don't). Sometimes the words you don't say are more powerful than the ones you do!

Why must you struggle in this life? There must be a purpose for it, right? Consider the butterfly for a moment. Aren't they one of the most beautiful insects you've ever seen? Before the butterfly is made beautiful, though, it is an ugly bug! A caterpillar! The caterpillar is the one who works and surrounds itself with a cocoon. In order to get free of the cocoon, the butterfly must struggle hard. You see, the struggle is real, but it is the struggle that makes the butterfly beautiful, and your struggle will make you beautiful!

Today's Prayer

Father,

When we are in the midst of a struggle, remind us to wait on You, to stay strong, be encouraged in You and wait for You. Remind us of the struggle the butterfly endures before it emerges as a beautiful creation.

Amen.

Wait for the Lord; be strong and take heart and wait for the Lord.

—*Psalm 27:14 (NIV)*

July 13

The Ugly Parts

I've never been a huge fan of butterflies. Well, not a fan of being up close and personal with them anyway. Their wings are beautiful, but when you get up close, you see the "ugly" parts—the icky-looking body, that was once a bug, and the spindly little legs and antennae, and, well, I've just never been a fan of bugs, what can I say?

Before the butterfly becomes a beautiful insect, it is an ugly, ugly bug! As that ugly bug grows, it begins to wrap a cocoon around its body. While it is inside this cocoon, many, many changes take place. By the time it emerges as a butterfly, the transformation is unbelievable!

Instead of an ugly bug, from a distance, you see a beautiful creature. A beautiful, colorful, wonderful creation of the Lord. Only He could take an ugly bug, like the caterpillar, and turn it into something so beautiful for your eyes to behold. But, wait! What's that? As you look closer at the butterfly, you see this ugly-looking body, and what about that ugly head and the antennae? What is that about? How can something so beautiful have something so ugly be a part of it?

Isn't that a beautiful reminder of your own life? Even though you become a new creature in Christ and He turns you into a beautiful soul, those ugly parts are still there too. But, the ugly parts are what helped you become so beautiful. In fact, they were a vital part of you becoming the beautiful creature you are. If it weren't for the ugly parts, you wouldn't be the beautiful creature you are now. So, don't be ashamed of the "ugly" parts. Show them off and tell others how God can and will do the same thing for them, if they will allow Him to work in their lives.

Today's Prayer

Father,

Thank You for giving us beauty for our scars and turning our mourning into joy. Thank You for giving us a garment of praise to replace the heaviness and for planting us as trees of righteousness so that anything we do may bring glory to You!

Amen.

To appoint unto them that mourn in Zion, to give unto them
beauty for ashes, the oil of joy for mourning, the garment of
praise for the spirit of heaviness; that they might be called trees of
righteousness, the planting of the Lord, that He might be glorified.

—Isaiah 61:3 (KJV)

July 14

The Forgotten Gifts

There are many different occasions when people give/receive gifts—birthdays, anniversaries (of all kinds), Valentine's Day, graduations, weddings, new baby, Christmas and the list goes on. Which do you prefer: to give gifts or receive them?

When it is your turn to be on the receiving end, what are some things that come to your mind to request? The answer to that question, most likely, depends on the identity of the giver. Obviously, you would probably request something much more personal from your spouse than you would from a good friend.

Let's look at some gift ideas most people don't think about. What about giving the gifts of love and compassion? That small child who lives near you, the one who is always "pestering" you when you're outside or wants to come in and visit when you're at your busiest? Maybe that child needs your love and compassion. Would you be willing to take a few minutes to give it?

That person in your neighborhood who lost their job—could you maybe spare some groceries from your overstocked pantry and fridge? We live in a world today where gifts like that are seldom thought about, yet the most desired!

What about the gift of prayer? Yes, praying for someone is one of the greatest gifts you could ever give, and having someone pray for you is one of the greatest gifts you could ever receive!

The next time a special occasion comes around, and you are to be either the giver or the receiver, try to think about giving or requesting from this list of forgotten gifts—time, love, prayer, compassion, friendship. Whether you are the giver or receiver of this kind of gifts, the rewards are more than you could ever imagine! Don't believe me? Try it and see what happens.

Today's Prayer

Father,

Thank You for the reminder today to help others and share what we have with them. May we do so generously and with a pure heart so we may be pleasing to You with our sacrifice.

Amen.

But don't forget to help others and to share your possessions with them. This, too, is like offering a sacrifice that pleases God.

—*Hebrews 13:16*

July 15

What Will You Give?

When the subject of giving comes up, your mind automatically goes to money, right? Did you know there are many other ways to give?

The Lord brought an old hymn to my attention yesterday morning at church. We didn't sing it—it was across the page from one we did. "Trust Me, Try Me, Prove Me" is the name of it. It's also known as "Bring Ye All the Tithes into the Storehouse."

Yes, you should be giving 10 percent of any money God blesses you with back to Him. It's all His anyway, right? And He only asks for 10 percent back. Why? He doesn't need your money. He does, however, want your obedience and trust. When you put your trust in Him and do as He asks, you are going to receive so much more back!

But, there are other ways you can give too. Look at 2 Corinthians 8:12, "If we can encourage others, we should encourage them. If we can give, we should be generous. If we are leaders, we should do our best. If we are good to others, we should do it cheerfully." So, you see, whatever your talent is that He has given you, use it to give back to others.

In fact, a line from the song mentioned above says, "All your money, talents, time and love. Consecrate them all upon the altar." In other words, dedicate those things to the Lord, for His use. When you do, you will be amazed at what begins to happen! He will begin multiplying everything you give to Him! Whether you are giving Him your talent, your time, your love or your money—it doesn't matter. As long as you are doing it with the right attitude, your return will be much more! Tomorrow, maybe, we'll talk about the right attitude.

Today's Prayer

Father,
   When we bring to You the first tenth of what You have given us, we will receive so much more back from You we won't have room for it all! May we give generously, above what You ask, and may we do it with a cheerful, willing heart.
   Amen.

"Bring to the storehouse a tenth of what you gain. Then there will be food in My house. Test Me in this," says the Lord of Heaven's armies. "I will open the windows of Heaven for you. I will pour out more blessings than you have room for."

—*Malachi 3:10 (ICB)*

July 16

The Right Stuff

I may have the gift of prophecy; I may understand all the secret things of God and all knowledge; and I may have faith so great that I can move mountains. But even with all these things, if I do not have love, then I am nothing. (1 Corinthians 13:2, ICB)

Remember how we talked about giving with the right attitude? Love is the right attitude!

Paul tells us, "Each of you must make up your own mind about how much to give. But don't feel sorry that you must give and don't feel that you are forced to give. God loves people who love to give" (2 Corinthians 9:7). Yes, it is important to give, but the first thing you need to do is make sure you are giving out of love! God loves a cheerful giver. If you are giving out of a sense of obligation or duty, you may as well keep whatever it is you are giving.

This applies not only to your financial giving, but also to your talents, your time—anything you have that you can give. Are you giving out of a generous heart, or are you giving only because you feel obligated? When you give anything to God with a cheerful heart, it will be returned to you in greater ways than you could ever think about!

Giving out of love, simply because you enjoy blessing others or being obedient to the Father, is one of the greatest feelings you will ever experience. Giving without expecting anything in return is also important. If you give 10 percent in tithes, time or talents only because you are expecting a huge return, your heart isn't in the right place. Yes, God will bless you when you give, no matter the intention of your heart. But, would you rather get minimal blessings from obedience or abundant blessings because you are giving out of genuine love?

It's a fine line that is sometimes hard to explain or even understand. Yes, God wants you to know He will bless your generosity, but He doesn't want that to be the reason you are generous. I pray you understand the difference.

Today's Prayer

Father,

May our hearts be in the right place today. May we do all we do out of love, for without love, we gain nothing.

Amen.

I may give everything I have to feed the poor. And I may even give my body as an offering to be burned. But I gain nothing by doing these things if I do not have love.

—1 Corinthians 13:3 (ICB)

July 17

Best Gift Ever

Well, after salvation, that is. Thanks to Facebook memories, I was reminded of this sweet, precious gift we have been given. However, it made me start wondering how many of us receive it.

How many gifts have you been given that you have never opened? Most of us open any and all gifts we are given, right? I mean, who receives a gift and just leaves it there, never to be opened and enjoyed the way the giver intended it to be?

If nothing else, aren't you too curious to see what is inside to just leave it sitting there? Wouldn't you at least have to open it and see what was inside? Now, how many gifts have you opened and set aside after seeing what it was? Maybe you thought you had no use for it, or you had no place for it, or it just wasn't something you wanted or needed. Only to discover, later, it would be just perfect for something you never thought about before.

I hope you have accepted the gift of salvation, which is probably the most precious gift you will ever receive. Then, I hope you will accept this gift—peace of mind and heart—that the Lord offers. We live in very troubled times these days, but you don't have to be troubled or worried or wonder what might happen next.

If you will accept this gift He offers, you can have a peace that won't be understood by those who don't know Him. To be honest, even some that do know Him, sadly, won't understand. They won't understand because they have never accepted this gift from Him, and they are always troubled and afraid. Wouldn't you rather live in peace than in worry? All you have to do is say yes and accept the gift. Don't just open it and set it aside—embrace it!

Today's Prayer

Father,

Thank You for the best gift we could ever get—peace of mind and heart. Help us not be troubled or afraid in these times we live in. Help us, instead, to remember to give everything to You.

Amen.

I am leaving you with a gift—peace of mind and heart. And the peace I give is a gift the world cannot give. So, don't be troubled or afraid.

—John 14:27 (NLT)

July 18

Love Wins

But I am giving you a new command. You must love each other, just as I have loved you. If you love each other, everyone will know that you are My disciples. (John 13:34–35)

Wow! This is one command we all seem to want to forget about, right?

Some people just make it hard to love them, don't they? Are You telling us we're supposed to love everyone? Like *everyone*? Read the verses above again. Yes! He is telling you (and me) to love every single person. You may not *like* the things they do, but you (we) are still commanded to love the person. Surely you've heard it said, "Love the sinner, not the sin."

You know we've discussed before the fact there is no big sin or little sin in God's eyes. In His eyes, sin is sin. So, yes, we are to love that person we heard about that robbed the store at gunpoint. Yes, we are to love that person who lives next door to us that has the loud parties, late at night—and the list goes on—yes, love that person who cut you off in traffic!

Is it easy to love everyone? No, He never said it would be easy, only that it is necessary! It is only by loving others that we can demonstrate to them, on a very small scale, how God loves us. It's easy to love those who love us, it's a whole different thing to love those who hate us. Yet, He tells us we must do that also. Just look at Matthew 5:44 or Luke 6:28.

Then, look at Proverbs 25:21–22 and see what it does to those who hate us when we show them love. Wouldn't you rather do as the

Father asks and let Him take care of your enemies? Do you realize that every time you say you hate someone—anyone—that He created, you are denying Jesus?

The next time you find yourself about to say—or even think—you hate someone, remember 1 John 4:20 and ask God to help you love instead.

Today's Prayer

Father,

Help us to love each other the way You have commanded. Help us love those we can see so we may better love You, whom we can't see.

Amen.

> *But if we say we love God and don't love each other,*
> *we are liars. We cannot see God. So how can we love*
> *God, if we don't love the people we can see?*

> *—1 John 4:20*

July 19

When God Says Yes!

Have you ever wanted to do something so much, you thought you would just die if you didn't get to do it? Have you ever had that desire burning in your heart, your very being?

Have you ever had someone tell you that you couldn't or wouldn't do something? Well, if God has told you yes, don't even spend time to listening to anyone else, especially the enemy. The enemy will tell you all sorts of lies about why you can't do something, but that's only because he is so scared of you! The enemy knows that if you trust and follow God, then he will have no power over you, and that scares him! The enemy wants to keep you bound, unable to move or afraid to move—he wants you to think you aren't good enough or strong enough or that you've done too many awful things in your past to do anything good now; but, he is nothing but a liar and deceiver of the truth!

The enemy knows when you are set free and you accept that freedom, he is done for! You will be a strong force to be reckoned with when you are so free realizing that God is in control and fighting all your battles for you! Not that he won't keep trying, but he will know he is fighting a losing battle when he sees you are always calling on the Lord to help you and to fight your battles for you. The enemy knows that war has already been won and you are the victorious one! It isn't you that is powerful; rather, it is Christ *in* you that is powerful, and once you accept and receive that and begin to walk in it, you will see how wonderful it is to live truly free!

Then you will truly realize that when God says *yes*, no one else can say no! God's Word is true, and He is unchangeable! If He says something is going to happen, it will happen. If He says you are going to do something, you will do it, no matter what man says. Man might try to bring you down, but if God wants you to do something, it doesn't matter what mere men say. As long as you are willing, God will use you to do what He needs done.

Today's Prayer

Father,
   Thank You for never breaking Your Word to us. Thank You for reminding us that when You say yes, no one else can say no!
   Amen.

My covenant I will not break, Nor alter the
Word that has gone out of My lips.

—Psalm 89:34 (NKJV)

July 20

Did It Really Come to Pass?

You've heard that phrase, "This too shall pass," many times, right? Especially when you are going through something hard. Well-meaning friends and family members will throw it out to you as if it's a Bible verse. Did you know, in fact, it is not?

Several people think the phrase "This too shall pass" is in the Bible. Do you know they are mistaken? That phrase is nowhere to be found in the Bible. Now, you will read the phrase "and it came to pass." But, truly, when you read that in the Bible, it is really only saying, "The next thing that happened was…"

Please understand I am not trying to bring you down or make you think the hard time you are going through is never going away. On the contrary, I only want to remind you that your peace is found in Jesus. No matter what trouble you might be facing on this earth, you know you can depend on Him to see you through, and while the phrase "This too shall pass" is not in the Bible, it is a great reminder that He is going to see you through to the other side.

Satan will always be coming at you with one problem or another—and, sometimes, the difficulty you are facing is because of choices you made yourself. Either way, it doesn't matter. Because even when our difficulties come from our own choices, He still takes care of us and sees us through.

So, no matter why you are under attack, just remember He is always with you! He is your strong tower, your refuge, your shelter in every storm, your peace, your chain breaker, your waymaker, your provider and so much more! He will always love you, unconditionally, and He knows your heart! Accept the peace He alone can offer you and rest in Him, knowing He has already defeated the world for you!

Today's Prayer

Father,

Thank You for the peace we have in You. Even though we may go through tough times on this earth, we can take comfort in knowing You have already defeated the world!

Amen.

I told you these things so that you can have peace in Me. In this world you will have trouble. But be brave! I have defeated the world!

—John 16:33 (ICB)

July 21

Getting in Tune

According to Simple English Wikipedia, tuning an instrument means getting it ready so that when it is played, it will sound at the correct pitch: not too high or too low. Wikipedia goes on to say that when two or more instruments play together, it is particularly important that they are in tune with one another. This means that when they play the same note, it is indeed exactly the same note. If the two instruments are not in tune with each other, it will sound unpleasant.

Some instruments can be tuned by the person playing them. However, the piano or organ must be tuned by a specialist in tuning. In fact, if an orchestra is going to be playing with a piano soloist, they must tune to the A of the piano because the piano has already been tuned by the piano tuner.

If the orchestra tunes their instruments to the oboist or the violinist when they are playing with a piano soloist, they may not be tuned just right with the piano. Then, when they start trying to make the beautiful sound of an orchestra, they will be off-key. It will not be a pleasant sound to hear at all and could, quite possibly, hurt the ears of those having to listen to it.

The same could be said of you (and me). You have to be tuned by the Master Tuner in order to work together, or individually for that matter, to make the correct sound or impression. You must allow the Master Tuner, Jesus, to tune your heart, or you could possibly hurt the ears of others listening.

If you are not tuned by the Master Tuner, how can you play in the orchestra with other Christians? If you are not in possession of a heart tuned to the Word and to the Father and what He wants, how can you be of help to the orchestra of the Christian family? It takes us all working together, all being tuned by the Master Tuner, to be truly effective. Sure, you can work alone, and sometimes He will ask you to, but He still wants you to be in tune with Him so He can also use you to work with others. Has your heart been tuned, lately, by the Master Tuner?

Today's Prayer

Father,

Thank You for Your word today. Help us to guard our hearts, keeping them in tune with You and Your Word.

Amen.

Guard your heart above all else, for it determines the course of your life.

—Proverbs 4:23 (NLT)

July 22

The Life of a Prayer

A lot of people think about their prayer life, but have you ever thought about the life of your prayers? Have you always thought when you prayed a prayer, that was the end of it, and it goes no further?

Rest assured, my friend, it definitely does not end there, especially if you are remembering to pray God's Word back to Him. We talked about that before—about how important it is to pray God's Word so we know we are praying powerful prayers. It doesn't even have to be word for word when we pray His Word. For example, He tells us in 2 Peter 3:9 that He wants everyone to be saved, to turn from sin, and that He wants no one to be lost.

Therefore, when you are praying for the salvation of a loved one, you can be sure you are praying His Word and His will. However, don't just pray one time and think it's done. Remember the parable of the widow in Luke 18:3–7? She kept coming to the judge, asking him for justice until he finally gave it to her. Jesus told them in verse 7, "Even he (the unjust judge) rendered a just decision in the end. So, don't you think God will surely give justice to His chosen people who cry out to Him day and night?" Yes! Of course, He will!

Never give up when you are praying! God always answers prayer. He may say yes, no or wait, but He always answers. Remember Daniel 10, when Daniel prayed for twenty-one days? What if he had given up on day 19 or 20?

And what about Elijah? He had prayed for the drought, and when it was time for the drought to end, he prayed seven days for rain. What if he had stopped praying on day 6? That is why you should never give up—you never know when the answer is coming.

Even though you may not live to see the answer to your prayer, your prayer will go on living long after you're gone, and it will be answered. Yes, the life of a prayer is infinite—it goes on and on because God's words last forever. So, keep praying His Word until you get the answer or until He calls you home.

Today's Prayer

Father,

Thank You for teaching us to pray Your Word back to You. We can be assured when we do, our prayers will last forever—even to the point of outliving us, if necessary.

Amen.

The sky and the earth won't last forever, but My words will.

—Luke 21:33

July 23

Close to the Source

In our house, the guest bathroom and the master bathroom are both very close in proximity to where the water heater is located. The kitchen, however, is much farther away. If you go in either of our bathrooms and turn on the hot-water side of the faucet, you will have hot water very quickly. However, if you go in the kitchen and turn on the hot-water side there, it will seem like you wait an eternity before it gets hot!

My husband used that demonstration in his message this past Sunday. He was talking about how it seemed you have to wait forever for the water to get hot in the kitchen and was using it to demonstrate the power of waiting. God used it to speak something else to me. As my husband was giving his demonstration, God spoke to my spirit, "It's because it's farther away from the source"! Whoa!

The reason it takes longer for the water to get hot in the kitchen is because it is farther away from the source of power that makes the water hot (the water heater), while the bathrooms are very close to the source of power.

The closer you are to the power source, the quicker you get the results you need! We live in the days of people talking about being "plugged in" because we have so many electronic devices. You also hear people talk about going on a vacation, just so they can "*unplug*" and get back to the basics of living life with each other and truly reconnecting.

How close are you to the most important power source of all? When you got saved, you received the Holy Spirit. You will never have any more or any less of the Holy Spirit than the day you got saved. But, do you live in the *power* of the Holy Spirit daily? Sadly, not many of us can answer yes to that question.

What might happen if you got plugged in to the power of the Holy Spirit and truly began to operate your life in that power? The source is close to you. How close are you to the source? Do you need to move a little closer today?

Today's Prayer

Father,

Thank You that we can be strengthened with power through the Holy Spirit, if we will allow it. May we all begin choosing to operate in the power of the Holy Spirit!

Amen.

I pray that out of His glorious riches He may strengthen you
with power through His Spirit in your inner being.

—Ephesians 3:16 (NIV)

July 24

Thirst Quencher = Spirit Griever

Remember a time when you were working outside in the heat of a summer day and you were so thirsty you could hardly stand it? You couldn't wait to take a break and get a drink of ice-cold water to quench your thirst! That's a good thing to do. When you are working out in the heat, you definitely need to keep pouring in the water, not only to quench your thirst, but to keep hydrated as well. However, do you know there is a thirst you never need to quench? The thirst you get from the Holy Spirit doesn't need to be quenched.

It doesn't get any plainer or easier to understand than 1 Thessalonians 5:19 (NKJV): "Do not quench the Spirit." Plain and simple, right? The minute you are saved, the Holy Spirit comes to live inside you. That doesn't mean you are automatically, magically, made perfect! Far from it! It means you have the *power* to live in a whole new way, *if* you choose it. It is a daily choice you have to make, and while it seems it would be an easy one, it can really be a struggle!

Confession: I am guilty of quenching that thirst and grieving the Holy Spirit, as recently as two nights ago, in our living room no less! It's easy to do when you are in a church service or anywhere with a group of people. The enemy loves to whisper in your ear, "Don't raise your hands! People will just think you are doing it for attention!" and other such lies. But, y'all! This was in our own living room—just me and my husband there! Something happened that made me want to shout "HALLELUJAH!" but because my husband was there, I didn't! God very quickly made me aware of what I had done and have been doing for far too long! I asked forgiveness right then and even confessed it to my husband. I told him, "I know you are used to me being quiet, but I'm just letting you know things are changing." I refuse to be a thirst quencher, "Holy Spirit griever" anymore! At least, not on the norm. There may be some times I miss it or forget and don't do as I feel led, but the new normal is going to be to go with the Holy Spirit, however He leads! Are you with me?

Today's Prayer

Father,

Help us break free from anything that holds us back from allowing the Holy Spirit to have control in our lives. May we not be guilty of quenching or grieving the Holy Spirit, but, instead, live in total freedom!

Amen.

And do not make the Holy Spirit sad. The Spirit is God's proof that you belong to Him. God gave you the Spirit to show that God will make you free when the time comes.

—Ephesians 4:30 (ICB)

July 25

Victory Is Yours

Do you trust God? You go to church on Sunday, and you've heard many messages about how trustworthy He is. Do you believe it? Has someone in your past hurt you and left you with the scar of distrust, so you find it hard to trust anyone, including God?

Think back for a moment. Do you remember a time when you believed God so strongly for something you didn't even realize what you were doing? Maybe even think back to when you were very young and you suddenly found yourself dreaming about something you never thought you would dream about.

Maybe you found yourself dreaming about attending your favorite college one day—even though you knew your parents wouldn't be able to afford to send you, no matter how badly they might want to. You never let go of that dream, and then, even though you had some twists and turns before you got there, He gave it to you! You not only attended, but graduated from that college, and you always told everyone how great God is!

Life happens, things go wrong sometimes and you seem to forget about the trust you had in Him. The enemy has you convinced He doesn't do things like that for you, at least not anymore. But, that's a lie from the pits of hell!

The enemy wants to keep you convinced that God won't do things like that for "someone like you," but he is a liar and a thief! All he wants is to hold you back and keep you from trusting God because he knows what God can do for you! He wants to steal your joy, your trust and anything else he can get his filthy hands on! Don't let him! Stop him right now, today!

Tell him you will no longer listen to his lies! Remind him this day Who has taken care of you in the past and Who will take care of you in the present and the future! Take back the trust he has stolen from you and GO FORTH IN VICTORY! GOD SAYS YOU HAVE THE VICTORY IN HIM!

Today's Prayer

Father,

Thank You for reminding us we can trust You. You are our helper and protector! You *will* provide exactly what we need at just the time we need it, and sometimes You will go beyond anything we could ever hope for!

Amen.

You people who fear the Lord should trust Him.
He is your helper and your protection.

—Psalm 115:11 (ICB)

July 26

Where Is He Calling You?

Nearly six years ago, a song came out that truly touched my heart in a deep place. I loved to hear it, and I loved to sing it; but more than anything, I wanted to be able to *live* it. The song? "Oceans (Where Feet May Fail)" sung by Hillsong United.

It talks about being willing to go wherever God calls you, trusting God without any borders, which, to me, is saying you choose to trust Him no matter what! In the good times, in the bad times, in the in-between times—*all* the time! It is saying you want to serve Him anywhere He might take you and that you trust Him to take care of you, wherever that may be.

Yes! Who wouldn't want to be in that place? The place where you truly trust Him that much! Like I said, I wanted to be able to *live* it. Was I ready for that six years ago? Looking back, I have to say no, I wasn't. But, He has definitely brought me a long way in my journey since then.

In the last six years, He has shown me what it is like to truly trust Him. It has been a little scary sometimes, but He has always proven true to His Word and has never left me lacking or wanting for anything I needed. So many of us today, though, get needs confused with wants. It's natural to think your want is a need when, in reality, you know it is not.

In the last few weeks even, He has helped me grow in understanding of what it means to truly trust Him with everything. To turn it over to Him and trust Him with whatever happens, knowing He wants only the best for His child.

With all that has transpired over the last few weeks, I believe I am closer to living that song than I ever have been. What about you?

Where do you feel He is calling you? Are you ready to trust Him with it today and say, "Yes, Lord"? Are you willing to go wherever He might lead? If not, are you willing to ask Him to help you get to the place where you are ready?

Today's Prayer

Father,

May we be willing to go wherever You may call us, knowing if it is You calling us, You will keep and protect us from harm. The safest place we can ever be is in the center of Your will. Let us hear Your voice clearly.

Amen.

Peter replied, "Lord, if it is really You, tell me to come to You on the water." "Come on!" Jesus said. Peter then got out of the boat and started walking on the water toward Him.

—Matthew 14:28–29

July 27

Powerful Prayers

What kind of prayers do you pray? Do you pray safe prayers, or do you pray bold prayers? There's not anything wrong with safe prayers, really; but, I believe God wants us praying bold, scary, audacious prayers! The kind of prayers Jabez, Joshua and Hezekiah prayed, just to name a few.

Jabez—A few years back, it seemed all the talk was about the Prayer of Jabez. There was merchandise of all kinds about it; then, it seemed to fade away. The commercial, merchandising part of it, anyway. Jabez's prayer did not fade away. His prayer can still be found in 1 Chronicles 4:10, and it is still a powerful prayer to pray. Why not try it? Ask God to enlarge your territory, whatever that might mean for you. What would that mean for you? Is it something that scares you? Good!

Joshua—In Joshua 10:13, he asks God to make the sun stand still! Steven Furtick actually wrote a book called *Sun Stand Still*, and it is definitely a good read. If you haven't read it, you definitely should. Joshua was in a battle, and he needed it to stay daylight until they could defeat their enemy, the Amorites. The Lord was helping them, and Joshua prayed his bold, audacious prayer asking the Lord to make the sun stand still and the moon as well.

Hezekiah—Look at his prayer in 2 Kings 19:15–19. The king of Assyria sent a note to Hezekiah telling him not to trust his God. But Hezekiah simply laid that letter before the Lord and prayed boldly!

Do your prayers scare you? If your prayers don't scare you, they aren't scaring the enemy either—have you ever thought about that? God already knows what you need—your prayers allow Him to release His angels to bring the answer to you. Though they may be delayed due to having to fight (see Daniel 10:12–14), your answer is on the way the minute you begin praying. If you haven't been praying bold, audacious prayers, why not start today?

Today's Prayer

Father,

We know it is only because of Your Son, Jesus Christ of Nazareth, we can come boldly to Your throne with our requests. Thank You for giving us mercy and grace when we need it most.

Amen.

> *So let us come boldly to the throne of our gracious*
> *God. There we will receive His mercy, and we will*
> *find grace to help us when we need it most.*

—Hebrews 4:16 (NLT)

July 28

Homecoming

The church we have been attending, for almost a year, is having their homecoming service today. It got me to thinking about homecoming, and what is homecoming anyway?

Homecoming, as defined by *Merriam-Webster* is "a return home or the return of a group of people usually on a special occasion to a place formerly frequented or regarded as home." Homecoming is a celebration—a time of reflection on both the happy and sad, the good and the bad. Thinking of all the loved ones who have passed through the doors of your church and those who have passed through the gates of Heaven.

Homecoming is also seeing friends we haven't seen in a long time and being able to catch up, but most importantly, for homecoming, you are in God's house. A place where you should always feel welcome, secure, at peace, able to be yourself. A place where you might meet God for the first time or find your way back after veering off the path for a while. It's a time to turn that spark back into a fire and get your batteries recharged. It's a time to celebrate being together again to worship and fellowship with Him and each other in His house.

It's also a time when we should come together and tell each other what God has done for us and how good He has been to us. Just like the former demon-possessed man that wanted to get in the boat and go with Jesus. He was told no. Jesus told him, instead, to go home to his family and to tell them all that He had done for him. Sometimes, our family is the hardest to witness to, don't you agree? But, I believe that is exactly what this man was supposed to do.

Your family can be the hardest to witness to, because they see you like no one else does. But they are also the most important for you to witness to. Will you share with your family what He is doing/ has done in your life?

Today's Prayer

Father,

Help us to tell our own families how much You have done for us and how good You are to us.

Amen.

> *When Jesus was getting into the boat, the man begged to go with Him. But Jesus would not let him. Instead, He said, "Go home to your family and tell them how much the Lord has done for you and how good He has been to you."*
>
> *—Mark 5:18–19*

July 29

Cracked Pots

This morning I sensed the Father was wanting to remind us of how He uses what we consider "broken." He reminded me of a story I heard a long time ago about two pots a man in India used to carry water. He used a long stick with a pot on each end, and he had to walk a long way to the stream to fill the pots with water. One pot was perfect, but the other pot had a crack in it.

The cracked pot, after a long while, began to apologize to the man for not being able to carry his full load. Due to being cracked, by the time the man got back to the house, the cracked pot was only half full. The man, however, told the cracked pot to notice the flowers on its side of the path as they walked back to the house. He told the pot he knew about the crack, and he took advantage of it, planting seeds along the path on the side of the cracked pot. Every day, the cracked pot watered the seeds, and the beautiful flowers grew, so the man had beautiful flowers to put on his Master's table every day because of the cracked pot.

So, you see, even with its flaws, the cracked pot was used to its full potential. Let's face it, we are all cracked pots with our own unique flaws; but, the Lord knows our flaws and can use each of us in our own unique way to bring something beautiful to the Father's table, if we will allow Him to use us.

Instead of being ashamed of your flaws, your past or whatever "ugly parts" you think are so horrible, boast in those flaws, those weaknesses, and allow the power of Christ to work through you.

Even when you may think you aren't carrying your "full load," remember that Christ is working through you, and He may be, unbeknownst to you, watering the seeds along your path to grow beautiful flowers in His garden—souls that, without your water (your witness), may never have sprouted at all! Will you let Him use your flaws to help someone today?

Today's Prayer

Father,

Thank You for Your Son's grace. Thank You for using His power in our weaknesses. Let us remember to gladly boast (witness) about our weaknesses and brokenness, which allows Your Son's power to work through us.

Amen.

Each time He said, "My grace is all you need. My power works best in weakness." So now I am glad to boast about my weaknesses, so that the power of Christ can work through me.

—2 Corinthians 12:9 (NLT)

July 30

Reminders

I bought two bracelets from the group that sang at our homecoming service this past Sunday. They are leather bracelets with string tied in a way for you to slide and make the bracelets smaller or larger. On each bracelet is a piece of some type of metal with a word carved in it. One has the word *courageous*, and the other has the word *freedom*.

Both bracelets made me immediately think of the work God has been doing in my own life over the last few weeks. I thought these bracelets would go perfectly with the dog tag necklace I've been wearing for the last few weeks. These words are written on the necklace—"I am in Christ, a Child of God, Greatly Loved, a New Creation and Overcomer." I wear this necklace to remind me what God has done and is doing in my life.

As I was putting the bracelets on Monday morning, I heard, "Tie it on your wrist and wear it as a reminder." It made me think of the verse in the Bible that talks about "tying them on your hands." That is why I wear these bracelets and this necklace. I don't care what anyone else thinks about them; these simply serve as my reminders.

Reminders of what God has done and is doing in my life every single day. They remind me who I am in Him, and when the enemy starts spouting his lies, they remind me to remind him Who I belong to! They could also be great conversation starters. It's a great way to share what He has done and is doing.

Do you have anything special that reminds you of what God has done and is doing for you? Are you able to share with others when they ask you about it? How do you fix His words in your heart and mind? You may not have something that actually *ties* on your wrist. Maybe what you have is simply your smile, and when people ask how you can smile like that, it's a perfect opportunity for you to share. Who will you share with today?

Today's Prayer

Father,

Thank You for helping us fix Your words in our hearts and minds by giving us bracelets, necklaces and more to remind us and keep Your words ever before us. May these things not become mere fashion pieces, but truly serve as reminders for us.

Amen.

Fix these words of Mine in your hearts and minds; tie them as symbols on your hands and bind them on your foreheads.

—*Deuteronomy 11:18 (NIV)*

July 31

New Things

I was reading Jeremiah 18:9–10 this morning and thought my devotion for today was going to come from that scripture. You see, God showed me that scripture a few years back to let me know He wasn't done with me just yet and that He still had a plan for me.

Have you ever been through a tough time and wondered why you had to go through it? The tough times, the hard times, that's when you really grow. You are seeking God daily, possibly like you never have or haven't in a long time. He has your full and complete attention. What might He be able to do in you if He had your full and complete attention all the time—even in the good times?

Your test becomes your testimony, your mess becomes your message and your testimony and your message are ever changing—or should be—because you are always going through different things. Not even necessarily bad things. God can use good things to grow you too. He wants to do a new work in you every day!

How much do you want to seek Him and seek out what new thing He wants to do in you? What do you feel bubbling beneath the surface? Anything? Do you sense an excitement of any kind anymore? Remember when you first came to know the Lord how excited you were about each new day?

You wanted to tell everyone you met about what He had done for you! You wanted to share your excitement, even with strangers! Do you still have that excitement, or has life gotten in your way? It's easy to get busy with the daily task of living and working, but why must you let it steal your excitement?

If you have lost yours, get it back! The enemy is the one who stole it, so make him give it back in the name of Jesus Christ of

Nazareth! Ask God every day what new thing He wants to do in you today. You will be amazed at what will happen, and your excitement will return! Let's get all excited!

Today's Prayer

Father,

Thank You for doing new things even in us. Thank You for our road in the wilderness and our river in the desert.

Amen.

Behold, I will do a new thing, now it shall spring forth; Shall you not know it? I will even make a road in the wilderness and rivers in the desert.

—Isaiah 43:19 (NKJV)

August 1

Hard Decisions

Life is full of hard decisions. Who do you turn to when you have a hard decision to make? Your parents? Your best friend? Your spouse? What about God? Shouldn't He be the first One you turn to for direction?

It's not always a question of doing what's right, either. Sometimes, it's simply a matter of knowing what would be best. If it were only a case of doing the right thing as opposed to the wrong thing, it wouldn't really be a very hard decision to make, right?

Look at today's verse from Isaiah 41. Have you ever thought of that verse when it comes to making decisions of any kind? I never had until this morning. I found myself face-to-face with a hard decision to make, and I went searching in His word to see what He would tell me, and He led me straight to this verse.

At first, it didn't make sense. Then, it clicked—no matter what hard decision you are facing, you don't have to be afraid because He is always with you! He will never leave you to make a decision on your own, He wants to help you.

He will make you strong. In other words, He will give you the strength to carry out your decision when you make it with His guidance. He will not only make you strong, He will protect you. But, look at the next sentence and really grasp what it means!

He will give you *victories*! Not victory, singular, but victories, plural! He will give you multiple victories! For instance, the decision you have to make might be an ongoing thing, like losing weight. This part of this verse tells you that's okay. Because He will be with you every step, giving you small victories along the way! Every day that you make good choices is a day of victories!

What decisions are you facing today? Rest assured He is with you and ready to help. All you have to do is call on Him.

Today's Prayer

Father,

Thank You for being with us in the hard decisions. Help us not to be afraid and to trust You to give us strength and protect us as You give us victories.

Amen.

> *Don't be afraid. I am with you. Don't tremble with fear. I am your God. I will make you strong, as I protect you with My arm and give you victories.*

> *—Isaiah 41:10*

August 2

Fearless Freedom

Father spoke to me this morning something that is so sad: Too many of His children are walking around thinking they are free when, in reality, they are tightly bound by the enemy!

He told me to look for the verse on freedom that He wanted me to share. He didn't tell me where it was, just that I would know when I found it. So, of course, I took to Google. I searched "verses about freedom" and read several verses. Each time, I would think, "That's good, but I don't think that's it," so I kept searching and reading.

Then He took me to Isaiah 61:1. As soon as I read it, I knew it was the verse! Yesterday, He kept speaking the word *freedom* to me and had me speaking freedom over several people, and He did the same thing again this morning.

Yes! He has most definitely called me to speak freedom to those who are bound! Even and maybe especially to the ones who *think* they are free but are actually bound tightly by the enemy! Freedom to those bound by sexual sin; freedom to those bound by addictions; freedom to those who are already free and don't realize it! Freedom to those bound by unforgiveness; freedom to those bound by generational curses, freedom to those bound by depression! Freedom!

I cannot stress enough the importance of this message of freedom! God wants His people *free*! *Freedom* is breaking out everywhere! Oh, how He wants His people truly *free*! This is all so new to me, I don't truly understand it. I don't have to understand it, though. You don't have to understand it. All you have to do is surrender to it! Surrender to Him! Surrender all your fears to Him and watch what He will do in your life and in the lives of those around you!

Are you ready to be free? Are you ready to see what He has in store for you?

Today's Prayer

Father,

Thank You for the spirit of the Lord taking control of us! Thank You for choosing us to tell the oppressed the good news, for using us to heal the brokenhearted and for announcing freedom to prisoners and captives!

Amen.

The Spirit of the Lord God has taken control of me! The Lord has chosen and sent me to tell the oppressed the good news, to heal the brokenhearted and to announce freedom for prisoners and captives.

—Isaiah 61:1

August 3

Too Tired?

She's lost, hurting, all alone. She has no hope left. She's been living in the streets too long. She just wishes she could find somewhere to go, someone who would care, maybe take her in and show her what real love is. She remembers seeing that church when she was walking in town the other day. She thinks to herself, "Maybe I'll go there and see if I can find any hope." She walks the three blocks to get there and, when she arrives, finds the doors locked—not for security, but because no one is there. She turns away, feeling dejected, more alone and forgotten than ever before. Maybe there really isn't anyone who cares, she thinks. "Why do I even try to keep going on? Maybe it would be better if I just wasn't here anymore…"

How many souls have been lost because we (Christians) were "too tired"? How many church services have been cancelled because we were "too tired" or not enough people come anymore? How many souls feeling all alone, lost, deserted by everyone and having no hope left came searching for something and found our doors closed because we were too tired to be there?

God is calling His people to WAKE UP! He needs His people to be living in freedom, but how can you live in freedom if you aren't even awake? He isn't talking about the natural—He is talking about the spiritual! Do you think the enemy's demons get tired doing his work? Yet, they are relentless, they never rest! What would happen if you were as tenacious as they are? How many lives would you impact? Probably way more than you realize! You have no idea how many people you impact every single day with your life! Oh, you are working all right! The question is, who are you working for? Are you ready to wake up and get busy working for the Lord, even when you feel tired?

Today's Prayer

Father,

Help us wake up! Help us become stronger before we (the church) die off completely. Show us what we need to be doing. Remind us of what we received and heard. Give us the strength to obey it. Change our hearts and lives! If we don't wake up, Your coming will surely surprise even us!

Amen.

Wake up! Make yourselves stronger while you still have something left and before it dies completely. I have found that what you are doing is not good enough for my God. So do not forget what you have received and heard. Obey it. Change your hearts and lives! You must wake up or I will come to you and surprise you like a thief. And you will not know when I will come.

—Revelation 3:2–3 (ICB)

August 4

All the Same

Have you ever seen the wonders God does in the lives of people around you and think to yourself, "That's great for them, but He doesn't do stuff like that for people like me"? That is a lie from the enemy himself!

God is no respecter of persons. When He saw the widow give the two pennies, He said she had given the most of all. While the others were giving what they didn't need, the widow gave all she had! That's what He wants from us; He wants us to give it all. When we give all we have with a sincere heart, He sees and He knows and He will bless you!

Even more wonderful, beautiful and unbelievable than that is the fact that He loves to bless you! It's simply Who He is! He sees you making an effort, doing your best to love Him the best way you know how, going to worship Him with fellow believers on Sundays and all the other little things you are doing—some of them, maybe, even secret, hidden things you do for Him that you don't want anyone else to know about. Like the day you paid for the person's order behind you in the drive-through lane and the clothes you gave to that couple who needed them for their newborn baby.

You have probably heard—and recited—the passage Matthew 7:1, "Judge not, that ye be not judged." You probably always think of that in terms of judging people around you. But, did you know it also means you don't need to judge yourself? You are the worst judge of yourself! There is only one person who can judge you, and that is God! He knows your heart; He knows the true meaning behind why you do the things you do.

So, stop telling yourself the lie that God does things for others that He would not do for you! God is no respecter of persons (see verse below), and He loves to do great and wonderful things for His children. He loves to be lavish! All He asks in return is for you to worship Him and do what is right. It doesn't matter where you come from or how badly you messed up in the past!

Today's Prayer

Father,

Thank You for loving us all the same and accepting all of us who worship You and do what is right. No matter where we come from! Amen.

Peter began to speak: "I really understand now that to God every person is the same. God accepts anyone who worships Him and does what is right. It is not important what country a person comes from."

—Acts 10:34–35 (ICB)

August 5

Are You Prepared?

What is a typical Sunday morning like for you? Is it waking up, wrestling with the kids to get them ready to go to church? Playing referee when the kids start fighting and getting into an argument with your spouse? Maybe you aren't married and you live alone. Do you wake up with just enough time to get ready for church? Do you keep hitting the snooze button and then find yourself hurrying and scurrying to get ready on time?

When you finally arrive at church, kids in tow, and you get them settled in kids church, you walk into the sanctuary breathing a sigh of relief that you made it, praise the Lord! Or you arrive at the church by yourself, flying into to the parking lot with barely a minute to spare, and you rush inside, find a seat in the sanctuary and let out a deep sigh, thinking, *Whew! I made it without getting a speeding ticket!*

But, think back to what happened before Sunday morning. What was your week like? Did you take time to spend time with the Father each day—on your own and as a family? Did you spend time in prayer with Him? Thanking Him for all the many things you have to be thankful for?

Did you know you could prepare for Sunday morning by starting on Monday morning and continuing throughout the week? Did you know, when you go to church on Sunday, you can go expecting God to do something incredible? Did you know that if you go expecting God to move, He will?

I challenge you to start preparing for Sunday on Monday morning and continuing through the week by spending time with Him and expecting something from Him daily. Does it mean you, your kids and your spouse will suddenly all get along with no arguments and everything will go smoothly come Sunday morning? No. But, if you've been preparing all week, you will be better equipped and prepared to handle what the enemy throws out.

Today's Prayer

Father,

Help us clear a path and make a straight road for You each day of the week and not wait until Sunday morning.

Amen.

Someone is shouting: "Clear a path in the desert!
Make a straight road for the Lord our God."

—Isaiah 40:3

August 6

Are You Expecting?

Did you grow up going to church every Sunday and Wednesday and any other day the church doors were open? If so, you most likely didn't get very excited about it. Most likely, it became more of a chore for you than anything else.

Now, as an adult, it's just what you do. You don't question it, and you certainly don't get excited about it; you just do it. You get to church on Sunday morning and wait to hear the songs and the message and see if they speak to you. You probably keep a check on your watch the whole time you're there because you really just want to get back home to your recliner and relax while watching something on TV. You leave church that morning thinking, *Well, that was a waste of time. I got nothing out of that.*

Maybe you didn't grow up going to church every Sunday. Maybe you became a Christian later in life, and at one time, you were excited about going to church every time the doors were open. Then, as time moved on, you simply got tired. Now, it seems, you don't hear the Lord speaking to you, and you leave the church no different than when you arrived.

What might happen if you went to church expecting? Not expecting the pastor or the worship leaders to make you "feel good," but expecting to hear from God? What if you spent time with Him all week and you could hardly wait to get to church Sunday morning to see what He has waiting for you there?

It's not the pastor's job or the worship leader's job to get you excited or "feeling good." Their job is to do what God puts in their hearts for each service. It's your job to prepare all week and come expecting something from Him and Him alone!

Challenge yourself this week to go to church Sunday morning with a different attitude—go expecting God to show Himself to you in a new and real way! He won't disappoint you. He may even give you more than you imagine!

Today's Prayer

Father,

May we look to you the same way the lame man looked at Peter and John, with expectancy! May we prepare ourselves for You to move in our lives and live in daily expectation, not just on Sundays! Amen.

And Peter, fastening his eyes upon him with John, said, "Look on us." And he gave heed unto them, expecting to receive something of them.

—Acts 3:4–5 (KJV)

August 7

Inmate or Soldier?

Soldiers are made to feel special. They have to make quick decisions in an instant. They are admired by most and know they are doing a great service to their country. They must be prepared for battle at all times! They must be in shape and have sharp minds!

Inmates are made to feel worthless. All decisions are made for them. They are looked down on by others and repeatedly told what a disgrace they are. They are beat down, sometimes literally, and made to feel worthless.

You don't have to be behind concrete walls and iron bars to be living in a prison. The enemy loves to put you in the prison of fear and doubt, the prison of depression, the prison of unforgiveness and many more.

Your mind is a battlefield! It is where the enemy attacks you the most and the best, and you better be prepared! Second Timothy 1:7 tells us, "God's Spirit doesn't make cowards out of us. The Spirit gives us power, love and self-control." You cannot have a spirit of fear and be prepared for battle! Look at Ephesians 6:17 (KJV): "And take the helmet of salvation and the sword of the Spirit, which is the word of God." Why would you need a helmet to protect your mind if it wasn't constantly being attacked?

Where do you stand today? Are you a soldier or an inmate? Do you listen to the Father when He tells you how special you are, simply because He created you? Or do you listen to the enemy's lies and allow him to hold you in one or more of his many prisons? Even if you are, literally, in a prison due to choices you made in your past, you can still live in more freedom than anyone on the outside, simply by choosing Jesus! He is the only way any of us can truly be free!

The choice is up to you. Soldier or inmate? You must have the mind of a soldier and not of an inmate, if you want to live in true freedom anywhere!

Today's Prayer

Father,

Remind us to put on our full armor every morning so we will be able to defend ourselves throughout the day and still be standing firm at the end of it.

Amen.

So put on all the armor that God gives. Then when that evil day comes, you will be able to defend yourself. And when the battle is over, you will still be standing firm.

—Ephesians 6:13

August 8

Silly Teenage Girl

She was a silly, teenage girl, scared of her own shadow, feeling like she didn't fit in anywhere. But this night, this night she knew what she wanted. She turned to her friend standing next to her and asked if she wanted to go, but her friend said no. She decided she didn't care if she went all alone, she was going. Something in her told her she *had* to go. So, she stepped out from the pew where she was standing and began walking down that aisle, straight to the pastor to give her heart to Jesus.

Little did that teenage girl know what life held for her. She certainly didn't see herself being married years later, having a daughter of her own, then divorced and on her own with a daughter to raise. She surely didn't see herself, years later, married again, only to be divorced a second time a short while later.

She didn't see herself moving from an area where she had spent pretty much her entire life and settling in a place she had barely heard of and certainly had never been, not knowing even one person there with the exception of her third husband. No, she hadn't seen that (third husband) coming either. But it did, and she couldn't be happier about it. She didn't see all God would do for her in this new town—introducing her to new friends, a new church family, and, eventually, drawing her into the community.

Had that teenager been able to see all that was in front of her, she might never have taken that first step to give her heart and life to Jesus. She wouldn't have been able to see how He used all those things to grow her in her faith and reliance upon Him. She wouldn't have seen all the times He carried her through. But, if you ask her today, some forty-six years later, she would tell you she wouldn't change a thing.

She would tell you she'd do it all over again simply to get to the place she is now. More alive and free in Him than she has ever been in her entire life! And she would ask you, "What are you waiting on?" Surrender to Him and His will today and watch what happens in your own life.

Today's Prayer

Father,

Thank You for teaching us to follow You and helping us to obey Your truth. If we saw Your plan for us too soon, it would scare us to death! Help us simply to remain faithful to You and take one step at a time, as You lead us.

Amen.

*Teach me to follow You and I will obey Your
truth. Always keep me faithful.*

—Psalm 86:11

August 9

It Can Happen

Did you ever see the movie *Angels in the Outfield*? I love how the little boy was always praying—what adults thought were outlandish prayers—and saying, "It could happen!" What faith that little boy had!

It makes me wonder what would happen if adults would pray with the same expectation. Are you one that knows and believes God is in control? If so, does the way you live your life confirm that? Do you truly trust God to take care of you and all your needs, or do you find yourself rushing around trying to make it happen all by yourself?

You can't be double-minded. You either trust Him or you don't. It really is as simple as that. James 1:8 says, "Such a person is double-minded and unstable in all they do." If you say you trust God, then why are you still trying to fix whatever you think is wrong or trying to control how things go in your life?

Do you have times in the past where you had to totally rely on God? If you do, then do you not remember how He came through for you when nothing you were trying worked? If He did it for you once, don't you think He will do it again? And again and again—as many times as He needs? Or do you believe you already used up all your blessings from Him?

If this is your first time to ever have to truly trust Him with something, then use it as a great starting place to begin trusting Him completely. Do you know, sometimes, He wants you in a place where you have no one to rely on but Him? As the old Nike commercials said, "Just do it!" Just let go of everything and watch Him work. It *can* happen, but not until you completely surrender it all to Him.

Then, when it's over, and you're on the other side of whatever it was, don't forget to thank Him and give Him all the praise, honor, and glory He is due!

Today's Prayer

Father,

May we never ever forget to thank You and sing praises to You for all that You do, have done and will do in our lives!

Amen.

> *When one of them discovered that he was healed,*
> *he came back, shouting praises to God.*

—Luke 17:15

August 10

A Proverb a Day

You've always heard "an apple a day keeps the doctor away," right? Well, what about "a proverb a day keeps the enemy at bay"? What? You never heard of that one? Neither have I—until it just came to me as I was praying, asking the Lord what He wanted to tell me today.

Do you know there are thirty-one chapters in Proverbs? That means you could read one a day every month, and for the months that only have thirty days, you have an extra. Do you realize how much truth and power are packed in these thirty-one proverbs? For example, since today is the tenth of the month, I looked at Proverbs 10. There are thirty-two verses in that chapter, and I realize He could give each one of us a devotion with every single verse! That's thirty-two devotions in one chapter alone!

What is a proverb? A proverb is a short, wise, easy-to-remember saying that calls a person to action. These proverbs teach us how to live, if we pay attention to them. Proverbs 1:3 (NLT) says, "Through these proverbs, people will receive instruction in discipline, good conduct and doing what is right, just and fair." Maybe if everyone could read at least one chapter a day in Proverbs, we would start to see a difference in our home, then our neighborhood, then our city and on to our country. You know the other saying, "It only takes a spark to get a fire going!"

When you read these proverbs—when you read any part of His Word—take it slow. The Bible is not a book to be rushed through just so you can say you read it. Slow down, meditate on what you are reading. Take one verse at a time, if necessary, and let it really sink in to your heart. Then move on to the next verse. There is a lot of wisdom in these proverbs. If you are praying for wisdom, start reading the book of Proverbs—slowly, deliberately, and soak it in!

Today's Prayer

Father,

Thank You for giving us the book of Proverbs. Thank You for teaching us wisdom and discipline and for helping us understand the wise things.

Amen.

The purpose of these proverbs is to teach people wisdom and discipline and to help them understand wise sayings.

—Proverbs 1:2 (NLT)

August 11

Pray for Who?

Prayer is a hard subject for some to talk about. Some people think they don't know how to pray. Some people think prayers have to be long and full of all these big, fancy words. However, did you know prayer is not only a privilege and honor, but it is your responsibility as a Christian?

Yes, one morning as I was ending my prayer time and thanking God for allowing me the privilege and honor of praying for others, I suddenly found another word coming out of my mouth—*responsibility*! I hadn't thought about that, but God showed me very clearly that it is not only a privilege and honor to pray for others, as a child of the King and daughter of the Most High God, it is my responsibility!

It is your responsibility too. It's easy to pray for those we love. Well, it's easy when you realize prayer isn't about long, fancy words or the length of your prayer. Prayer is simply talking to the Father the same way you would talk to a friend. Just tell Him what's in your heart. Sure, He already knows, but He loves for you to tell Him. He wants you to lift up your loved ones and your friends in prayer.

He also wants you to pray for those who persecute you. "But I say unto you, Love your enemies, bless them that curse you, do good to them that hate you and pray for them which despitefully use you and persecute you" (Matthew 5:44 ICB). And He repeats the same instruction again in Luke 6:28, so it must really be important if He says it more than once, right?

Will you begin to pray for others today, if you don't already? Including those who are your enemies? Do it and watch what God does with your prayers!

Today's Prayer

Father,

Remind us to pray for each other, even our enemies. It is easy to pray for those we love, but let us not forget to pray for those who persecute us, as well.

Amen.

Confess your sins to each other and pray for each other. Do this so that God can heal you. When a good man prays, great things happen.

—*James 5:16 (ICB)*

August 12

A New Thing

Remember the theme song to a show that came on years ago, "Sometimes you want to go where everybody knows your name"? That song came to mind as I was reflecting on a trip home this past weekend. It was so nice to be back in a place where I knew people and people knew me. Going to town and seeing people we actually know! It was great! It was familiar. And this morning, in my time with the Father, He spoke to me about the word *familiar*.

So, I looked up the meaning of *familiar*, and guess what it means? (1) Close acquaintance with or knowledge of something; (2) the quality of being well known, recognizability based on long or close association; and (3) relaxed friendliness or intimacy between people. Wow! Then I did some research on what the Scriptures say about familiarity and found a very interesting article where the author made this simple, but thought-provoking, statement: "Familiarity will block your miracle!" Say what? That is so true! Look at Jesus in Matthew 13:54–58. He so wanted to bless His hometown, but people there knew Him too well—or so they thought! They only saw Him as the carpenter's son or Mary's boy, and they even knew His brothers and sisters! So, He didn't get to do many miracles there because of the people's lack of faith. They were too familiar with Him (more on that tomorrow).

And the realization hit: He wanted to do something new, but He had to move me to a new place, where no one knew me. The people here had no knowledge of my past life—the one where I was shy and picked on as a child. He put me in a new place where He could give me new perspective on my own life in Him! A place where He could show me who I truly am, *in Him*!

We will talk more about familiarity tomorrow, if the Lord permits; but for today, think about some things that are very familiar to you. Maybe you need to try looking at them in a different light and see what new thing God may want to show you!

Today's Prayer

Father,

Thank You for creating something new in us! Thank You for the roads in the deserts and for streams of Your living water in our thirsty lands!

Amen.

I am creating something new. There it is! Do you see it? I have put roads in deserts, streams in thirsty lands.

—Isaiah 43:19

August 13

Too Familiar?

Have you ever thought about being too familiar with the Bible? "What is she talking about!" you may be asking yourself. I never really thought about it until yesterday, but it is true. You can become too familiar with the Bible!

For instance, you've probably read the story of Noah and the flood and how God gave the rainbow as a covenant, right? But when was the last time you actually read it for yourself? Have you ever caught the part where God says, "When I bring clouds over the earth, a rainbow appears in the clouds. Then I will remember my agreement." Then, He says it again, "When I see the rainbow in the clouds, I will remember." As many times as I had heard and read (or told) that story, I never caught that until a few years ago. Why would God even say that? He never forgets anything (except our sin when it's covered by the blood of Jesus)! Why would He say the rainbow would be a reminder to Him of His covenant with Noah?

Think back to when you first gave your heart to Jesus. You were reading His Word with such enthusiasm, wanting to learn every little thing you could! You were so eager to soak it all in! Now, as the years have passed, you've become so "familiar" with His Word, you may not even read it much, let alone study in it. That is where the danger comes in! You think you know a passage so well you figure there is no need to actually read it, and you couldn't be any more wrong than that!

God's Word is fresh and alive! Every time you read it, He can show you something new and how it applies to your life! Don't become so "familiar" with His Word you think you don't need to read the same passages you've read a thousand times. Pick one today and ask Him to show you something new in that passage. Then read it again with an open heart to see what God reveals.

Today's Prayer

Father,

Thank You for Your Living Word! May we read and study it today with fresh eyes, a hungering spirit and thirsty souls. As it exposes our innermost thoughts and desires, may we begin to line up with it again.

Amen.

For the word of God is alive and powerful. It is sharper than the sharpest two-edged sword, cutting between soul and spirit, between joint and marrow. It exposes our innermost thoughts and desires.

—Hebrews 4:12 (NLT)

August 14

An Admission of Guilt or True Repentance?

Have you ever been caught doing something you weren't supposed to be doing or saying something you shouldn't say? As soon as you are caught, you start apologizing and trying to excuse your behavior, right?

Why do we do that? I'm just as guilty as the next person. If you start apologizing or trying to excuse whatever it is you were caught doing, then doesn't that tell you it was wrong? So, because you were caught in it, you feel the need to suddenly "make it right"—is that how it is? You offer your apologies or your excuses and expect everything will then be A-OK, am I right?

But what happens when you are no longer with the one(s) who caught you? Do you find yourself doing the same thing again? Using those words you shouldn't be using? Doing that thing you shouldn't be doing? If so, then you weren't really apologizing for it in the first place, right? You weren't really sorry you did it, you were just sorry you got caught!

I wonder how many of us today truly believe in repentance or even know what it means to sincerely repent of something. I once read in the study notes of a Bible that "being sorry for sin is not enough. Repentance demands a change of mind and heart that results in changed behavior."

If you don't change your behavior, if you go back to speaking the way you were speaking or doing what you were doing when the person who caught you is no longer around, then you didn't truly repent, right? How often have I done that? How often have you done that?

And, oh how it hurts the Father's heart when we do! All He wants is for us to admit our sin, admit we didn't obey Him and ask forgiveness in true repentance, which means we change our way of thinking and our behavior! Do you have anything you need to truly repent of today?

Today's Prayer

Father,

Help us repent of our sin and to sincerely change once we do. True repentance does, indeed, demand a change of heart and mind that results in changed behavior!

Amen.

"All you have to do is admit your sin. You turned against the Lord your God. You worshiped the false gods of other nations. You worshiped them under every green tree. You didn't obey me," says the Lord.

—Jeremiah 3:13 (ICB)

August 15

Memorial versus Idol

A memorial is a structure or something similar to remind people of a person or an event. An idol is an image or a representation of a god used as an object of worship, such as a person who is greatly admired or loved.

There are memorials in the Bible. After they had all safely crossed the river, the Lord told Joshua to have one man from each tribe get a stone from the middle of the Jordan, where the priests were standing, and pile them up at the place where they camped that night as a memorial. The memorial was to remind them how the Jordan River stopped flowing when the ark of the Lord's covenant went across.

However, don't let your memorial become an idol. If the memorial you have erected becomes something you worship, then you have crossed the line, and you don't want to go there. Exodus 20:4–5 lists the third commandment:

> *Do not make idols of any kind, whether in the shape of birds or animals or fish. You must never worship or bow down to them, for I, the Lord your God, am a jealous God who will not share your affection with any other god!*

You must keep the memorial in perspective and use it only as a means to remember something God did for you or something He brought you through. You must be especially careful if you have a memorial—whether in your heart or an actual place—to a loved one. No matter how special that loved one was to you while they were on this earth, you cannot allow them to take God's place in your heart. If you do, you are in very dangerous territory, walking on a very slippery slope! God will not be number two to anyone or anything in your life. If He is not number one in your life and in your heart and in your soul, then you need to do a heart check and see what's going on. He never said He wouldn't forgive us. So, search your heart today and see if He really is number one in your life. If you find He's not, ask His forgiveness today and give Him back His rightful place.

Today's Prayer

Father,

You may not have had to rescue us from people, but on the day of our salvation, You rescued us from the slavery of our sin! Let us be careful not to forget You and what You rescued us from!

Amen.

*Be careful not to forget the Lord, who rescued
you from slavery in the land of Egypt.*

—Deuteronomy 6:12 (NLT)

August 16

Details, Details

Some people like to plan things way in advance, others like to plan things more short-term. Either way, most people who like to have a plan also like to have all the details worked out well in advance. Am I right?

So, when life throws you a curveball and messes with all your nice, neat, "tied up with a pretty ribbon" details and plans, it can really throw you for a loop! It can send you into a downward spiral and have you feeling so lost and out of control you don't know what to do!

God spoke to me about details this morning in my prayer time with Him. I was thanking Him for how He is working in someone's life. I told Him it was truly exciting to watch Him work, although it can be nerve-racking for those of us who like to have things planned out and organized well in advance! I went on to say how I'm learning to love just trusting the details to Him because I know when it is what He wants, He will take care of everything! I remember thinking, "Yep! God is in the details all right!" And that's when I felt Him speak so gently to my spirit, "Baby, I'm not *in* the details, *I am* the details!"

Do you feel your life spinning out of control? Are you waiting to hear results of some kind of health test? Are you wondering how you are ever going to make it through the next four years of college? Do you find yourself suddenly alone after being married for more years than you can remember due to a divorce or unexpected death of your spouse?

Remember, God is in control. He isn't *in* the details, He *is* the details. Nothing—I repeat, *nothing*—ever takes Him by surprise. Fall into His arms and just let Him hold you. He will show you His plan when the time is right. He will work out every detail on His time schedule. Not a minute too soon and not a minute late. Would you be willing to set aside your plan with all the neat little details worked out and just begin to trust Him today? I promise He won't disappoint you. He has nothing but the *best* for you. Are you willing to wait for the best?

Today's Prayer

Father,

Thank You for not only being in the details, but for delighting in them, and thank You for directing our steps.

Amen.

The Lord directs the steps of the Godly. He delights in every detail of their lives.

—Psalm 37:23 (NLT)

August 17

Skin–Deep

The world's idea of beauty and God's idea of beauty are two entirely different things. The world says beauty is about outside appearances. God says in 1 Samuel 16:7,

> *But the Lord told him, "Samuel, don't think Eliab is the one just because he's tall and handsome. He isn't the one I've chosen. People judge others by what they look like, but I judge people by what is in their hearts."*

God says your beauty comes from within. He says you are lovely in every way (Song of Solomon 4:7). In Ephesians 2:10, He says, "For we are God's handiwork, created in Christ Jesus to do good works, which God prepared in advance for us to do."

Two days ago, someone sent me a picture of a butterfly sculpture with this quote, "Butterflies can't see their wings. They can't see how truly beautiful they are; but, everyone else can." I looked it up and found Naya Rivera is the one who said that. In fact, she also said this along with it, "People are like that as well." It is so true! You never see yourself as everyone else sees you, but oh how you need to see yourself the way God, your Father, sees you! He created you in your mother's womb, He knit together all your intricate parts and He alone knows all the number of your days!

Maybe you never thought of yourself as beautiful, but may today be the day you change your stinkin' thinkin'. It is time for you to recognize who you are because of Who you belong to, and stop listening to the enemy's lies! The world will tell you it's a cop-out, a way for what they call "ugly" not to feel so bad, but it is *truth* that our beauty comes from inside! Remember what He tells you in Proverbs 31:30, "Charm can be deceiving, and beauty fades away, but a woman who honors the Lord deserves to be praised." Walk in the confidence of who God says you are today! You are *beautiful!*

Today's Prayer

Father,

Thank You for the reminder that our beauty is not on the outside; rather, it comes from within our heart. Please help us to remember this in our daily lives.

Amen.

> *Don't depend on things like fancy hairdos or gold jewelry or*
> *expensive clothes to make you look beautiful. Be beautiful*
> *in your heart by being gentle and quiet. This kind of*
> *beauty will last and God considers it very special.*

> *—1 Peter 3:3–4*

August 18

His Offer of Grace

There's a phrase I heard often as a child and have even used myself many, many times as an adult. However, a while back (like for the last year or so), it hit me in a different way. I'm not sure why, I only know it has nagged at me ever since. I think He's telling me today is the day to dig deeper and explore, so here we go.

There, but for the grace of God, go I. That's the phrase. Now, I know when I hear others say that, and when I said it myself, it was meant in a sympathetic way. But, the thought that went through my head so long ago was, "Really? Are you saying God hasn't, doesn't or wouldn't give grace to the one you are talking about?" What?

In researching this phrase today, I went straight to Google and asked what God's Word says about it. What I found was the verse in 1 Corinthians, shared at the end of this devotion. In reading this verse, it seems to me maybe the phrase we have been using all these years should be worded a little different.

Think about it, who does God offer His grace to? He offers His grace to everyone! Have you forgotten what John 3:16 says? "For God so loved the world that He gave His only begotten Son, that whosoever believeth in Him should not perish, but have everlasting life." Did you catch that word—*whosoever*? That means *anyone*! *Everyone*! Yes! He offers His grace to everyone. It's just that so many won't accept what He has offered, for one reason or another. Personally, I accepted His grace; and because of what He does in and through me, I am what I am today, as Paul said.

So, it's not that God hasn't offered grace to the one you were speaking of, it's just they haven't accepted it yet. Maybe it takes this (whatever caused the phrase to be used) to bring that person to the point of finally accepting the grace offered to them by Him. So, maybe the phrase should be changed a bit to say, "There, but for me accepting the grace of God, go I."

Today's Prayer

Father,

Thank You for offering Your grace to us. Please continue to show us how You wish to use us to help grow Your kingdom!

Amen.

But by the grace of God I am what I am and His grace to me was not without effect. No, I worked harder than all of them—yet not I, but the grace of God that was with me.

—1 Corinthians 15:10 (NIV)

August 19

Expectant Prayers

When you ask for something in prayer, do you expect to receive it? Do you always add, "Your will be done," meaning it sincerely, or are you protecting yourself from disappointment? If whatever you asked for doesn't turn out the way you wanted, you can say, "Well, it wasn't His will for that to happen." It is important to always pray for God's will to be done, but not as a catch-22.

However, if you are staying in His Word and spending quality time with Him, you will be praying and asking in the correct way. If you are not spending time with Him and staying in His Word, you won't know the correct way to pray. James 4:3 tells us, "You ask and do not receive, because you ask wrongly, to spend it on your passions." Selfish prayers are not what God wants to hear, and if you are spending time with Him, in His Word, you are not going to pray selfish prayers.

Mark 11:24 says, "Therefore I tell you, whatever you ask in prayer, believe that you have received it, and it will be yours." And again, in John 16:24, "Until now you have asked nothing in my name. Ask, and you will receive, that your joy may be full." He makes it clear He wants to answer us and give us what we ask for, when we ask in the correct way.

So, if you don't already, you need to begin praying expectant prayers. If you are living in a drought area and you are praying for rain, you need to be carrying an umbrella with you everywhere you go. That way, when—not if—the rain comes, you are prepared!

Are you praying for your marriage to be restored? Start speaking life over it and begin to thank Him, in advance, for it. Are you praying for a wayward child to come home? Have their room prepared and ready for when they walk through that door. Are you ready to begin praying expectant prayers? I challenge you to start today and keep a journal of them so you can log when the answer is manifested.

Today's Prayer

Father,

Help us to stay joined to You and allow Your teachings to become part of us. Then, we can ask whatever we wish, knowing it lines up with Your Word and it will be done for us.

Amen.

If you remain in Me and My words remain in you, ask whatever you wish, and it will be done for you.

—John 15:7 (NIV)

August 20

Shout It Out!

Remember the old Shout commercial? The original one said, "Want a tough stain out? Shout it out!" Do you have something tough in your life right now that you want out? Take a lesson from blind Bartimaeus and shout it out!

Shout it out to Jesus, that is! When you have a need, cry out to the One Who can do something about it! Don't go timidly or meekly into prayer. Shout your prayer—"Jesus, Son Of David, have mercy on me!" Shout it out loud no matter who tells you to be quiet! Everyone was telling Bartimaeus to be quiet, but it only made him shout that much louder!

Back in the days when Bartimaeus lived, blindness was considered a curse from God for sin. Jesus proved this to be wrong when He reached out to heal the blind. Jesus healed quite a few people, most of whom we aren't given their names. This blind beggar, though, did something only a few of those healed by Jesus did—as soon as he received what he had asked for, he *immediately* began to follow Jesus!

Sometimes we are asking for something and wind up getting something else as a bonus! Bartimaeus was blind and wanted his sight to be returned. However, when Jesus healed him, Bartimaeus got more than his natural eyesight restored. When his natural eyesight was restored, he also gained spiritual eyesight! Because of that, he began to follow Jesus immediately!

What else might He want to do in you beyond what you are asking Him for? Are you seeking Him with your whole heart and crying out to Him for what you need? Have you been praying little, quiet, timid prayers almost as if you are afraid to ask because you don't think you deserve an answer? Nothing could be further from the truth! SHOUT out to Him today! This minute! Right now, ask Him, again, to have mercy on you! Then wait and see how He gives you even more than you ever thought to ask for—more than you even realized you needed! And be willing to follow Him, immediately!

Today's Prayer

Father,

Let us not stay quiet when we need a touch from You just because others tell us to stop shouting. Let it only make us shout louder!

Amen.

Many people told the man to stop, but he shouted even louder, "Son of David, have pity on me!"

—Mark 10:48

August 21

Search and Rescue

I read a comment on a Facebook post a few days ago that has been churning inside me ever since. I don't even remember what the post was about or who posted it. I only remember the comment I read, and I don't remember it word for word. I do, however, remember the point they were making.

The comment said something along the lines of "I sometimes feel we lose something when we just read the short devotions others have written. We miss out on the experience the person who wrote it had—the time they put in to search the scriptures etc."

The reason that comment spoke to me? Because, last year at this same time, I couldn't have truly understood what that person meant. This year, after 232 days (today is day 233) of getting up early each morning to pray, search the scriptures and listen for God's voice to give me a devotion, I understand exactly what that person meant! I don't know if I will ever be able to go back to just reading a little devotion each morning. Don't get me wrong—I will go back to reading a devotion book after this year—why would God give them the devotions if He didn't have something He wanted them to share? I simply mean that I will also still listen for Him to give me a personal one each day, as well.

As I was asking what He wanted me to share today, I felt in my spirit it was time to share this. I was going to title it "Search It Out"—as in searching out the scriptures for yourself. However, as I thought that, He changed it to "Search and Rescue." Why? Because, when you search the scriptures for yourself, you will find your rescue for whatever storm you may be in at the moment, or you will discover why you have such peace at the moment. Search the scriptures and let Him rescue you in any way you need to be rescued.

Today's Prayer

Father,

Help each of us search out Your Word for ourselves and receive Your approval. Help us to be good workers with no need for shame, and help us to correctly explain Your word of truth.

Amen.

Work hard so you can present yourself to God and receive
His approval. Be a good worker, one who does not need to be
ashamed and who correctly explains the word of truth.

—2 Timothy 2:15 (NLT)

August 22

Distractions

They're everywhere, they're everywhere! Distractions are one of the finest, most lethal weapons the enemy has at his disposal. First Peter 5:8 tells us that he *is like a roaring lion, sneaking around to find someone to attack*. What better way to attack you than by getting you distracted?

Look at Peter in Matthew 14:28–31. He told Jesus, "Lord, if it's really You, tell me to come to You by walking on water." We all know what happened. Jesus told him to come, and Peter stepped out of the boat and was walking on the water to Jesus. Then he got distracted by the high waves, which terrified him, and he began to sink! The minute Peter took his eyes off Jesus, he began to sink! That's what distractions will do, if you aren't careful!

Are you a people pleaser? I used to be extremely good at it! Not that I pleased everyone—you can't do that—but I sure did everything I could to try to please everyone! I finally realized I was pleasing everyone except the Who that mattered, *Jesus*! We are warned about this in Galatians 1:10, "I am not trying to please people. I want to please God. Do you think I am trying to please people? If I were doing that, I would not be a servant of Christ." Ouch! So, do you still want to be a people pleaser?

What about all the technology we have now at our fingertips? We are talking major distraction now! Now, I'm not saying technology is a bad thing, it's not! I'm just saying you have to be extremely careful, or it can be a bad thing! If it distracts you from spending quality time with the Father, Son and Holy Spirit, then it is controlling you, and you better do a heart check.

So, how 'bout it? Are you ready to ask Him to remove all the distractions from your life so you can get your focus back where it needs to be today? Are you willing to start spending some quality time with Him today to regain your focus?

Today's Prayer

Father,

Please help us keep our focus on You, looking straight ahead and fixing our eyes on what lies before us. Please remove anything from our lives that distracts us from You.

Amen.

Look straight ahead, and fix your eyes on what lies before you.

—Proverbs 4:25 (NLT)

August 23

In Name Only

Have you ever heard of a marriage of convenience? A marriage of convenience is just that—something that is convenient for each person. There is no intimacy involved in a marriage of convenience. It is simply two people who were married, quite possibly, to help each other out. Would you ever want to have a marriage like that?

Why do you think God would want anything different from your relationship with Him? He tells you all throughout His Word how important intimacy is. First, let's clarify one thing. Intimacy is not always something sexual. Intimacy is *a close familiarity or closeness*. It can even be a *private, cozy setting*.

There are many places throughout Scripture where God tells you how He longs for you and longs to have an intimate relationship with you. Look at Jeremiah 24:7, "I will give them a desire to know me and to be my people. They will want me to be their God, and they will turn back to me with all their heart." You can also see it in Matthew 11:25–30 and Revelation 21:2–4 and in the Psalms, chapters 8, 23, 27 and 139!

When you have passionate feelings for someone, don't you want to do any and everything you can to please that person? Don't you want to go out of your way to do whatever you can to be close to that person and be able to spend time together?

That's what God wants! He wants a bride who longs for Him in a passionate way! Have you ever read the book of Solomon? He wants you to be seeking after Him with everything in you! He longs for you to look for ways to spend more time with Him because He longs to spend time with you! Are you making time to be with Him, or did you get saved as a matter of convenience to keep from going to hell? Tough question? Maybe—but only if you don't have the right answer.

Today's Prayer

Father,

May we hunger and thirst after You and pursue that close, intimate relationship You want to have with each of us! May we each love You with all our heart, soul and might! Let us not be satisfied with anything less!

Amen.

You shall love the Lord your God with all your heart
and with all your soul and with all your might.

—Deuteronomy 6:5 (ESV)

August 24

It's Not about You

Do you truly understand that once you come to Christ, you belong to Him, and you no longer get to call the shots? Oh, you can continue to try calling the shots from time to time, but you will soon learn it doesn't go too well when you do.

When you give your life to Christ, you are asking Him to make you more Christlike, and the only way you can do that is with the help of the Holy Spirit living inside you. The Holy Spirit moves in the minute you accept Christ as your Lord and Savior. He is the One Who helps you begin to make Jesus Lord of your life. One way to do that is to spend time with the Father each day.

You need to commit to a certain time each day to spend with Him. You say your day is already so full you just don't have time? No, you have to make time, even if it means getting up a little earlier. What's that? You don't do early? What if Jesus didn't *do* the cross? It's not about you! Even Jesus got up early to spend time with the Father. Mark 1:35 says, "Early the next morning, Jesus woke and left the house while it was still dark. He went to a place to be alone and pray."

"You cannot be my disciple, unless you love me more than you love your father and mother, your wife and children, and your brothers and sisters. You cannot come with me unless you love me more than you love your own life." That is what He tells us in Luke 14:26. Basically, it is not about you anymore. If you truly belong to Him, you will make time for Him.

So, it's not about you, it's all about Him! Are you ready and willing to make sacrifices for Him, or do you just want to stay the same? If you have no desire to change anything, ask Him to put a fire in your soul—one you can't contain or control because, when He puts that fire in your soul, not only will you not be able to contain or control it, you aren't going to want to!

Today's Prayer

Father,

May we learn to kill our selfish feelings and desires and yearn to do what You have called each of us to do.

Amen.

And because we belong to Christ Jesus, we have killed our selfish feelings and desires.

—Galatians 5:24

August 25

The Sinner's Prayer

You have probably always heard, as I have, the only prayer God hears from a sinner is that of repentance. Well, I began to wonder about that and decided I needed to search it out in the scriptures.

There are some scriptures that seem to support that idea. Psalm 66:18 says, "If I regard iniquity in my heart, the Lord will not hear me," and Proverbs 15:29 cites, "The Lord is far from the wicked: but He heareth the prayer of the righteous." And even 1 Peter 3:12 says, "For the eyes of the Lord are over the righteous, and his ears are open unto their prayers: but the face of the Lord is against them that do evil." If you just read those verses on the surface, they certainly seem to support the idea, right?

But, what about Acts 10:30–31, "Cornelius answered: 'Three days ago I was in my house praying at this hour, at three in the afternoon. Suddenly a man in shining clothes stood before me and said, "Cornelius, God has heard your prayer and remembered your gifts to the poor""'? The angel also told Cornelius to send for Peter and ask him to come and visit, and "He will bring you a message through which you and all your household will be saved" (Acts 11:14).

So, you see, Cornelius, although he was a devout man, who feared the God of Israel, was not saved. Yet, God heard his prayer. Therefore, I come to the conclusion, if *any* person is truly seeking after God, yet hasn't surrendered or asked forgiveness for his sin, God can and will hear and answer, and He will even send just the right person(s) to help that individual learn how to be saved.

Yes, all individuals must still accept Jesus Christ of Nazareth as their Savior and ask forgiveness of their sins; it just may not always happen in the order you may have been taught.

Today's Prayer

Father,

Thank You for showing Yourself to all those who earnestly seek You with all their heart.

Amen.

You will seek Me and find Me when you seek Me with all your heart.

—Jeremiah 29:13 (NIV)

August 26

The Forgotten

There are too many people in this world who feel all alone and forgotten. They feel they aren't loved by anyone, and sadly, some feel they don't deserve to be loved by anyone. Some think they have done too many awful, horrible things for anyone, especially God, to be able to love them. Others have just never been shown love or acceptance by anyone, so they feel unworthy of it.

If you are one of those, hear this message today: God *does* love you! He has never left you and will never leave or forget about you. If you think you have made too many bad choices or done too many awful things, try reading His Word. I'm sure you've heard of Paul, the one who God used so mightily. Do you remember, though, that Paul murdered many Christians before his own conversion? And what about David, the man God said was "a man after My own heart"? Do you remember how David slept with another man's wife and then had that man sent to the front of the war zone so he would be killed?

There are so many examples in the Bible of people who God used to do a great work for His kingdom even after they had done horrible, awful things! He never left or forgot them, though. He was always there with them, waiting for them to ask forgiveness so He could wrap them in His arms and love on them. He wants to do the same for you. He is no respecter of persons. The same way He forgave them, He will forgive you. He wants to use you to further His kingdom, if you are willing to go forward and allow Him to work in and through you.

If you aren't one who feels forgotten, are you willing to reach out to one who does? Are you willing to get out of your comfort zone and reach out to the ones who need you to share God's love with them? Will you go and share with them where they are? Are you willing to show them the love of Jesus?

Today's Prayer

Father,

Help us stay strong and brave, not afraid and frightened. Remind us You go with us everywhere we go. Thank You for never leaving us, especially when we feel all alone and forgotten.

Amen.

Be strong and brave. Don't be afraid of them. Don't be frightened. The Lord your God will go with you. He will not leave you or forget you.

—Deuteronomy 31:6 (ICB)

August 27

He Is Good

Everyone knows how easy it is to say "God is good" when things are going well. But, what about when things aren't going so well. What about when you don't know where your next meal is coming from or how you are going to make that next house payment? How easy is it for you to say "God is good" in those times?

The enemy loves to use the hard times, the bad times, the sad times, the difficult times, to try to convince you God isn't with you, that He doesn't care for you and that He is far away from you. That is why it's important to have your own weapons ready before he comes at you with those attacks!

When the enemy comes at you during those hard, bad, sad or difficult times, whispering in your ear, "God isn't with you at all!" you can be ready for him, *if* you have stayed in the Word, as you should. You can fire the arrows of truth at him, and he will have to flee!

What arrows of truth? Isaiah 41:10, where God tells you not to panic and there is no need to fear because He is your God, and He will give you strength, hold you steady and keep a firm grip on you. Then there's Joshua 1:9, where He commands you to be courageous and not be afraid because He is with you wherever you go. He says nearly the same thing in Deuteronomy 31:6, where He tells you to be strong and take courage, to not be intimidated because He is going ahead of you, and He won't let you down, He won't leave you.

There are many verses you can have in your arsenal to combat the lies the enemy throws at you when you are going through difficult times. Be prepared ahead of time, and it will be a great help to you. Remember, if you didn't have bad times, you wouldn't appreciate the good times. Through them all, though, God is good!

Today's Prayer

Father,

Thank You for reminding us You bring good times and hard times. If it weren't for the hard times, we wouldn't know to enjoy the good times. Help us remember to praise You in both!

Amen.

> *When life is good, enjoy it. But when life is hard,*
> *remember: God gives us good times and hard times.*
> *And no one knows what tomorrow will bring.*

> —*Ecclesiastes 7:14 (ICB)*

August 28

Who Will Cry Out?

"The battlefields are strewn about with those who gave their all. They went to fight for freedom; they answered the battle call." Those are the first two lines of a poem the Father gave me about a fallen soldier. But, they also made me think of another battlefield.

The battlefield of life where so many lost souls are wandering aimlessly around. Many of them don't even realize they are lost. They are in a battle they aren't equipped to fight. Who will help them? Who will come to their aid?

Are you burdened for the lost at all? Does your heart hurt or feel so heavy you can hardly stand it when you think of all the people who are lost in this world we live in? God has called us to help them, to go to their aid. How do we do that?

We pray for them. Sometimes we pray for hours on end or, rather, allow the Holy Spirit to pray through us. We don't worry about the time or what's going on anywhere else. We get in our prayer closets, and we pray the glory down! We cry out for those lost souls to come to Jesus from the north, south, east and west! We cry out for those who once knew Him, then turned away, to return to Him.

If we don't cry out for these lost souls, what might happen to them? Do you want that on your hands? He commands us to praise Him and says if we "keep quiet, these stones will start shouting" (Luke 19:40). He also tells us in Ezekiel that if we don't warn them, their blood will be on our hands.

When I tell wicked people they will die because
of their sins, you must warn them to turn from their
sinful ways so they won't be punished. If you refuse,
you are responsible for their death. (Ezekiel 3:18)

Are you ready to start crying out for those lost souls and warning them? I am!

Today's Prayer

Father,

Break our hearts for the lost and let us have such sorrow until we cry out for them!

Amen.

My heart is broken and I am in great sorrow.

—Romans 9:2

August 29

Health Issue or Heart Issue?

My heart has been deeply burdened since a pastor friend told me to pray for him because his schedule has gotten so busy, he doesn't really have alone time with the Lord anymore, and he misses it.

Busyness is probably one of the best used weapons the enemy has in his arsenal. Truly, he could care less how many people you go visit or how many functions you attend "in the name of the Lord" as long as he can keep you so busy you aren't spending quality time with the Father. The enemy knows how important that time is, and he will do everything he can to steal it from you!

Do you ever wonder about all the health issues there are today? Do you think there is any connection between the health issues and where our hearts are? Now, I'm not saying that every person who is sick or has some health issue they're dealing with is not spending enough time with the Father. However, I do firmly believe that He will allow whatever it takes to get your attention, if you are allowing yourself to be kept too busy.

Look at Mary and Martha in Luke 10. Martha is running around like a chicken with its head cut off, being so busy trying to get everything done and wanting things to be perfect while Mary is sitting at the feet of Jesus, just soaking up every minute she can while He is there with them. Martha complains to Jesus about Mary not helping her with the work, and what does Jesus say to her? In today's language, He basically says, "Chill out, Martha! The work will be there when I'm gone. Couldn't you just sit and spend time with Me while I'm here? She has chosen the one thing that is right and important. I will not take it away from her."

Do you have a heart issue today? Are you making the time to spend with Him? If you don't, you just might find yourself in the bed at home or in a hospital where you have nothing but time for Him. What will you choose today?

Today's Prayer

Father,

Thank You for reminding us the only thing that is important is spending time with You. May we always make time and never be too busy to spend quality time with You.

Amen.

Only one thing is important. Mary has chosen the right thing and it will never be taken away from her.

—*Luke 10:42 (ICB)*

August 30

Will You Go?

In Genesis 12, we read where God asked Abram to move away from his country, his people and his father's household; and God didn't even tell him where He was sending him. Yet, Abram went in obedience.

In February 2018, He asked my husband and me to do nearly the same thing. We did have one advantage over Abram—we knew where we were going. Rather, we knew the city where we were going. However, we had no place to stay. We had our own plan, though. Our plan was for me to stay put (I did have a job commitment to finish up, after all), my husband would go to the new place and work, then come home on weekends. We figured, if it didn't work out for him in the new place, he would just come back to stay where we were. God sent us a resounding *no* on our plan. In one day, our house, which had been for sale for nearly eight years with hardly any lookers and absolutely no offers, was sold! They wanted us out in ten days! So, there we sat, scrambling to come up with a place to stay in our new city! Of course, God provided! Then, miraculously, one week after we moved to our new city, He showed us the house that would become our new home.

How did all this happen? How did we become homeowners of a home that, on paper, we shouldn't be able to pay for? How did we move to a place where we didn't know anyone, yet a little over a year later, we have many friends here and a wonderful new church family? How do so many different doors of opportunity for our ministry keep being opened in so many different ways? We both firmly believe it is because we simply said, "Yes, Lord. We will go where You want us to go."

Are you willing to go wherever He wants to send you and do whatever He has for you to do there? He may ask you to go somewhere you don't want to go—away from all that you know and love. Will you go anyway?

Today's Prayer

Father,

Help us get to the place where we are willing to go wherever You may ask us to go and do whatever You ask us to do. May we all say, "Here I am. Send me."

Amen.

After this, I heard the Lord ask, "Is there anyone I can send? Will someone go for us?" "I'll go," I answered. "Send me!"

—Isaiah 6:8

August 31

Where's Your Focus?

As you go through your day, what do you find your mind focused on? Obviously, you likely find it focused on whatever you are doing at the moment. But, what is in the background of your mind? What is lodged deep down in your heart? Do you know?

Imagine yourself walking along, carrying a full-to-the-rim cup or glass of your favorite beverage. You are walking straight ahead without turning to the right or the left, your eyes focused on the drink in your hand, so as not to spill any. Suddenly, someone bumps into you. What spills out of your cup or glass? Your favorite beverage, whether it be coffee or soda or tea or whatever. What you had in the container is what spilled out, right?

As you walk this path called life, Proverbs 4:25–27 says you need to walk with that same focus: Keeping your eyes focused on what is right, looking straight ahead to what is good and always doing what is right. Because, you will inevitably get bumped; and when you get bumped, whatever is inside you—really deep down inside you, in your heart, what you've been focusing on—is what is going to come spilling out. Is Jesus in there, or is it something else? Colossians 3:1 says that if you have been raised with Christ, you need to set your focus on things above, where Christ is seated at the right hand of God.

Most people know the verse Jeremiah 29:11 by heart, and they love to use it a lot! Nothing wrong with that, but do you also know what Jeremiah 29:12–13 says? Those verses say when you call on *His* name and pray to *Him*, He will hear you; and when you seek Him with your *whole* heart, *then* you will find Him. So, if you are focusing on Him and seeking Him with your whole heart, He is what will spill out of you when life bumps into you. Check your heart. Are you ready to get bumped today? If you do, what will spill out?

Today's Prayer

Father,

Help us keep our focus on Your Son, Jesus, which keeps our focus on You. As we do that, we will be better equipped to bring glory, honor and praise to Your name!

Amen.

Therefore, holy brothers, partners in a Heavenly calling, keep your focus on Jesus, the apostle and high priest of our confession.

—Hebrews 3:1 (ISV)

September 1

React or Respond?

Yesterday we talked about our focus, and this goes hand in hand with that subject—are you a reactor or a responder? Do you feel like maybe you are a little of both, depending on the situation at hand? Let's look at the definitions of each:

> A reactor is someone who is driven by beliefs, and other things, of the unconscious mind. A reactor looks at things in the moment and doesn't take into consideration any long-term effects of what they do or say. Being a reactor is more about survival, it's a defense mechanism and, often, is something you regret later.

> A responder, on the other hand, usually takes information from both the conscious mind and the unconscious mind. A responder will take into consideration the well-being of not only themselves, but those around them. A responder weighs the long-term effects and stays in line with his/her core values.

Core values—the fundamental beliefs of a person or organization—and that is what ties yesterday's devotion with today's. If your core values are based on God's Word, it will help you be more of a responder than a reactor.

Imagine what might have happened if Mary had been a reactor instead of a responder, when the angel appeared to her to give her the news she would soon become pregnant by the Holy Spirit. Even after the birth of Jesus, and the shepherds were telling everyone what happened to them, and what the angels had said about this child, Mary didn't react. Instead, "Mary kept all these things in her heart and thought about them often" (Luke 2:19—NLT).

Look at your own life today. If you have always been more of a reactor, as I used to be, ask God to help you become more of a responder. Staying in His Word is a great first step to becoming more of a responder than a reactor. Are you ready to let Him help you make the switch from reactor to responder?

Today's Prayer

Father,
   May we, like Mary, learn to respond to things instead of react. Amen.

Mary responded, "I am the Lord's servant. May everything you have said about me come true." And then the angel left her.

—Luke 1:38 (NLT)

September 2

God Is on Your Side

The Moabites, Ammonites and some of the Meunites had declared war on Jehoshaphat. What did Jehoshaphat do? He stood before the people of Judah and Jerusalem, and he prayed (2 Chronicles 20:1–6)! As he prayed, the spirit of the Lord came upon one of the men (Jahaziel) standing there, and he told them the Lord said do not be afraid! The Lord told them not to be discouraged by the mighty army because the battle was not theirs, it was God's!

Do you know He does the same thing for you today? You may feel you are facing a huge, mighty, powerful enemy, but never forget that God is on your side! He will fight the battle for you, if you will allow Him to do it. Go to Him in prayer and see what He tells you to do. He may tell you to do nothing except stand firm; He may tell you to march forth, as if you are attacking; but, one thing is certain—no matter what He asks you to do—make no mistake about Who is fighting the battle! It isn't you!

Remember what Psalm 118:6 says, "I will not be afraid because the Lord is with me. People can't do anything to me." It's like this sign I've seen before. On it were printed these words:

Speak, Breathe, Repeat: This I know: God is on my side.

He tells you plainly in Psalm 56:9 that on the day you call for help, your enemies will be defeated. He assures you He is on your side.

Exodus 14:14 says, "God will fight the battle for you. And you? You keep your mouths shut" (The Message). He tells us several times in His Word not to be afraid or intimidated but to be courageous and strong! In fact, in Joshua 1:9, He commands us to be strong and courageous: "Have I not *commanded* you? Be strong and courageous." So, today's challenge is simply to be encouraged, knowing God is on your side. Remember to pray and ask Him to take care of whatever you're facing. He will. In fact, He probably already has.

Today's Prayer

Father,

Thank You for reassuring us all we have to do is call on You and You will fight the enemy for us! We have no need to be afraid or let the enemy discourage us! The battle is Yours!

Amen.

Then Jahaziel said: Your Majesty and everyone from Judah and Jerusalem, the Lord says that you don't need to be afraid or let this powerful army discourage you. God will fight on your side!

—2 Chronicles 20:15

September 3

Comfort Zones and Safety Nets

What things do you do a certain way simply because you've always done them that way? Folding clothes, for example—do you fold your towels a certain way simply because it's how you were taught to do it or because it's how your mom (or someone else) always did it? There's really nothing wrong with that; we all do it, right? We tend to be creatures of habit, whether we like to admit it or not.

But what about spiritual things? Are you attending the same church you attended as a child, simply because that's where your family always attended? Nothing wrong with that, *if* it's where God wants you. But, have you asked Him if it's where He wants you?

I shared, a few days ago, about how God opened the door for my husband to minister in the prison he's wanted to minister in since God put him in prison ministry. I also shared that our plan was to stay put and not move until the summer. That way, if it didn't work out the way he hoped, he would just come back and continue ministering in the prison where he was at the time. The problem with that plan? It was *our* plan, *our* way of thinking—we didn't ask God what He wanted! Staying put was our safety net, our comfort zone. So, essentially, if an attack of it not being exactly what he thought it would be came along, he would just fall back into the safety net.

We didn't realize what we thought of as a safety net or comfort zone was actually holding us back from what God wanted to do. So, He had to remove that option from us. We are so glad He did! We see now He couldn't do what He wanted to do without moving us. Is He wanting to move you, literally or figuratively, from where you are today? Are you willing to leave your comfort zone/safety net to be where He wants you to be?

Today's Prayer

Father,

Thank You for reminding us that what we might see as a safety net are actually the things that had us bound. Thank You for leading us far from those things so, when we are attacked, we don't go running back to them. Keep us away from our safety nets, also known as our comfort zones!

Amen.

After the king had finally let the people go, the Lord did not lead them through Philistine territory, though that was the shortest way. God had said, "If they are attacked, they may decide to return to Egypt."

—Exodus 13:17

September 4

No Respect

Continuing our discussion from yesterday, there's another question I felt God was asking—why do you worship the way you do? Not just where do you attend worship, but do you sit there quietly, trying your best not to make a sound? Do you raise your hand(s) or shout *amen* during the service? If so, why do you do those things—or why do you not do those things?

We *must* get back to a place of worship—I'm talking about a heart of worship. We must begin worshiping Him the way the Holy Spirit leads us to worship, no matter how that might be! If the Spirit prompts you to raise your hand(s), do it! If He prompts you to shout hallelujah, shout it! Stop worrying about what anyone else thinks—God will take care of that—you just let the Holy Spirit lead you, and you won't go wrong!

When you enter the building for worship service, to come into God's presence, how do you enter? Are you already wondering what time the service will be over because you need to get home and cook or you want to get home and watch the ball game? What might happen if you entered with a sincere attitude of trembling in His presence? Not trembling out of fear, but out of respect and awe at Who He is! Years ago, there was a comedian who got plenty of laughs telling people, "I get no respect," but it is no laughing matter when you don't respect God. If you have any doubt about that, just read Jeremiah and see what happened to Judah and Israel when they quit respecting God.

Now, you may not literally tremble in His presence; then again, you just might! His presence is so strong and so mighty, if you will allow yourself to be totally open to allowing His presence in, there's no telling what you might feel or do. But, whatever it is, rest assured, from my personal experience, it will be the most wonderful thing you've ever experienced, and you will never want to go back to the way you were before!

Today's Prayer

Father,

May we get to the place where we tremble with respect in Your presence. May we come before You in awe of all that You are!

Amen.

Have you no respect for Me? Why don't you tremble in My Presence? I, the Lord, define the ocean's sandy shoreline as an everlasting boundary that the waters cannot cross. The waves may toss and roar, but they can never pass the boundaries I set.

—Jeremiah 5:22

September 5

Don't Be Afraid

Do you think the people God uses to write devotions are so close to Him they must never have any problems? Nothing could be further from the truth. Just because God has been using me to write these devotions this year, doesn't mean I haven't faced problems. Even worse, some of those problems I brought on myself! What? That's right. I said it, and I meant it.

Some mornings, I truly question why He would ask me to do this—write devotions—when He knows how unqualified and how unworthy I am and how I always seem to make such a mess of things! Then, He uses a morning like this—a morning where I am feeling lower than low because of something I've done that hurt someone very dear to me. He uses a morning like this to remind me that is exactly why He asked me to do this very thing. Because it's not at all about me, it is all about Him and what He wants to accomplish.

How could I share with anyone how loving and forgiving He is if I haven't experienced it for myself? How could I tell you He will take your mess and make a message out of it if He hadn't done it for me? Does it always happen instantly? No. In fact, this is one of those situations where it is going to take time for me to recover, but I know I will because He made sure He led me to the verses this morning to remind me that He is the One Who will fight for me. Even when the enemy He has to fight for me *is* me. That may not make sense to some, but it's true. Sometimes, we are our own worst enemy. Yet, God still fights for us. The same He's done and doing for me, He'll do for you!

It doesn't matter where the attack comes from, it doesn't matter if we brought it on ourselves or not, when we truly turn it all over to Him, and we are sincere in our repentance, He will save us—even from ourselves! I know He's done it for me, and I know He'll do the same for you. Don't be afraid. Be sincere in your repentance and then watch Him work.

Today's Prayer

Father,

Thank You for reminding us not to be afraid because You will save us even from the messes we cause ourselves. When we turn everything over to You and we remain calm, You will fight for us, You will save us!

Amen.

But Moses answered, "Don't be afraid! Stand still and see the Lord save you today. You will never see these Egyptians again after today. You will only need to remain calm. The Lord will fight for you."

—Exodus 14:13–14 (ICB)

September 6

Victory in Honesty

I once had this statement printed on my checks, right above the signature line: "I cannot live in victory if I do not live in honesty"! When you have been dishonest about something, it is very hard to come clean and confess what you've done. However, you can do it.

When you sincerely begin asking the Lord to remove anything in your life that doesn't need to be there, He will answer that prayer! He may not answer in the way you would like, but He *will* answer! He will allow what He knows is necessary for you to get rid of those things, no matter how uncomfortable it makes you. "But we want to do what pleases the Lord and what people think is right" (2 Corinthians 8:21). He does, however, also give you forgiveness of any sin He brings to light, when you ask for it, and He is also right there with you to help you through whatever it is.

Proverbs 24:26 says, "Giving an honest answer is a sign of true friendship," and once you have not been completely honest with a friend or spouse or boyfriend, then you have opened the door to the enemy and invited him in for a feast. You may feel trapped, like you have no way out; but, rest assured, there is most definitely a way out! His name is Jesus Christ of Nazareth! You have to be willing to take the hard step and admit what you did and ask forgiveness, then watch the Father, Jesus and the Holy Spirit go to work!

No, the road won't be easy. It may be long, and you may feel embarrassed, humiliated, ashamed and many other emotions; but, one thing you must remember is this: "You will know the Truth and the Truth will set you free" (John 8:32). As you walk your road toward restoration of your relationship, you can be sure He will be right there with you—even carrying you a few steps when you feel you can't go on any longer!

And don't forget to read on down to verse 36, where He reminds you, "If the Son sets you free, you will be free indeed." Now, go walk in your *victory*!

Today's Prayer

Father,

We are so thankful for Your forgiveness. Thank You for helping us be strong, courageous and truthful so that You may delight in us! Amen.

The Lord detests lying lips, but He delights in those who tell the truth.

—Proverbs 12:22 (NLT)

September 7

Did You Really Lose Them?

Over the last two days, we were made aware of three different deaths in three different families that we know and love. In praying for those families this morning, I found myself saying, "Father, just in the last two days, three sweet friends have lost loved ones," and, immediately, I felt in my spirit, "Lost? Really? Why do you say they are lost?"

Which set me to searching for why it is that we say we *lost* them. Especially Christians, when someone we love dies, whom we know had accepted Jesus Christ as their Savior and was living for Him. When trying to comfort their family members, we say things like "You can rest in the peace of knowing you'll see them again one day. You know where they are."

Hello? If you know where they are, then you didn't lose them, correct? I started my search, as I always do, by asking "what does the Bible say about _____ [and then enter whatever it is I'm searching for]". Sometimes, He shows me exactly what it is I'm searching for, and other days, He points out something a little different. This morning, He used my search to take me to 1 Thessalonians 4:14. In some translations, instead of saying "those who have died," it says "those who have fallen asleep or those who have fallen asleep in Him."

So, in our effort to soften the blow of the reality, we will probably always use euphemisms such as "losing someone" or "they went home" or "they fell asleep" when speaking of someone we love who has died, and that's okay.

But, if someone you love has died—recently or not so recently—and you know beyond the shadow of a doubt they were a child of the King, remind yourself that you didn't lose them at all! You know exactly where they are, and you will get to see them again, either when you die or when Jesus comes back for us all! Isn't that much more comforting than thinking of them as "lost"?

Today's Prayer

Father,

Thank You for reassuring us that when Christians have a loved one who dies, if they knew You, we didn't lose them. We know where they are and can rest in the peace of knowing we will see them again one day.

Amen.

For since we believe that Jesus died and was raised to life again, we also believe that when Jesus returns, God will bring back with Him the believers who have died.

—1 Thessalonians 4:14 (NLT)

September 8

Rest for the Weary

Are you carrying a heavy burden around everywhere you go? Are you still trying to deal with something or figure out how to take care of something that has you weighed down? God never meant for you to carry a heavy burden.

Maybe that heavy burden you're carrying around is caused by sin in your life. I know mine was. When you begin to sincerely pray and ask God to remove anything in you that doesn't need to be there, you better hang on tight to His Word because He will definitely do it!

He may not do it the way you think it should be done, and the way He does it may cause extreme uncomfortableness for you. But, if you truly want Him to cleanse you of all the rotten or rotting things that are in you so you can have the most intimate relationship you've ever experienced in your life, it will be worth anything and everything you have to go through to get there!

He has personally invited you to come clean with Him, to tell Him everything so He can cleanse you. "I, the Lord, invite you to come and talk it over. Your sins are scarlet red, but they will be whiter than snow or wool" (Isaiah 1:18), and again in 1 Peter 5:7, "God cares for you, so turn all your worries over to Him."

Are you ready to be rid of the heavy weight of that burden you are carrying around? Whether it be from sin in your life or just you trying to carry things you were never meant to carry, listen to what He says in John 16:33: "I have told you these things, so that in Me you may have peace. In this world you will have trouble. But take heart! I have overcome the world." He will be your strength (Psalm 73:26), if you let Him; and remember where your help comes from:

"My help comes from the Lord, the Maker of Heaven and earth" (Psalm 121:2). You can be rid of that heavy burden today! Will you give it to Him?

Today's Prayer

Father,

Thank You for carrying our heavy burdens for us. Thank You for reminding us You neither want nor expect us to carry them. Thank You for the sweet rest You give us when we turn everything over to You!

Amen.

If you are tired from carrying heavy burdens,
come to Me and I will give you rest.

—Matthew 11:28

September 9

How Will You Enter?

How do you enter into worship? Not just at church, but anywhere you worship—at home, at work, in the car, etc. I can remember a time when I would start praying—what I called praying anyway—but all I was really doing was giving this long list of wants to the Father. You know, "I want You to…," and on and on I'd go. Can you relate?

However, as we grow in our walk with the Lord, we should come to realize giving Him a long list of wants isn't prayer or worship. Does He want us to ask Him for healing for our loved ones, restoration of relationships and so on? Of course, He does! But first, we should give Him thanks for all He's done and is doing in our lives and praise His name! After we have given thanks, then it is time to make our requests known to Him.

I remember a time when the sanctuary was given much more respect than it is these days. I remember when you could enter a sanctuary, and instead of people gathered around talking about daily life, each individual was already talking with the Father, in their own way. Whether they were doing so quietly or by speaking out, they were entering into worship with Him and preparing for the service to come. These days? You can walk into just about any sanctuary in the United States and, most likely, find people gathered around talking about the previous day's ball games or the weather or anything but the Lord. Everyone is looking at their watches or phones or whatever device they have to see what time it is. Even before the service has started, they are watching for time for it to be over.

How can you truly worship, and how can the Holy Spirit move, if your mind isn't even on the Lord and what He might want to do in, for or through you in that service? Is what you have to do after service truly more important than what He has for you? CHALLENGE: begin entering His presence with the awe and reverence He not only deserves, but demands—whether it be in church, at home or wherever. Are you willing to make a change?

Today's Prayer

Father,

Remind us every time we enter Your gates to do so with thanksgiving and to enter Your courts with praise! Thanking You and praising Your name, Father!

Amen.

Enter His gates with thanksgiving and His courts with
praise; give thanks to Him and praise His name.

—Psalm 100:4–5 (NIV)

September 10

Just One More Thing

A few of you may remember the old detective show *Columbo* and his famous line, "Just one more thing…" God spoke that line to me this morning to share this with you.

That line, "just one more thing"? Not sure it originated with Columbo at all. Just look at our scripture for today. Now, I know, this is the Message translation. The King James and other translations don't word it exactly that way; however, I found it very interesting that God put that line on my mind this morning and then showed me this verse in the Message translation.

I don't believe He did that for no reason. King David is the one talking in 2 Samuel. Look back to verse 18 where he says, "Who am I?" and then, in verse 20, when he says, "What can I possibly say in the face of all this? You know me, Master God, just as I am." Then goes on to say in verse 21, "You've done all this not because of who I am; but, because of Who You are—out of Your very own heart!—but, You've let me in on it."

Today's message from the Lord is so simple and, yet, one that is so hard for many to grasp—it doesn't matter who you are or what you've done or what you've been involved in. There is absolutely, positively nothing—*no thing*—that is so horrible God cannot forgive! King David is a perfect example of that for us all, as well as many others in the Bible. But, when we are truly repentant and change our mind and follow after God with all our heart, He loves to show up and show out in bold, unthinkable ways! Simply because He loves you with an unconditional love, the way no other can!

Be encouraged today and rest in His love for you. Oh—and, just one more thing…pass it along to someone else.

Today's Prayer

Father,

In the words of King David, just one more thing—bless our families and keep Your eye on them always! May Your blessing be on our families permanently!

Amen.

And now, Master God, being the God You are, speaking sure words as You do and having just said this wonderful thing to me, please, just one more thing: Bless my family; keep Your eye on them always. You've already as much as said that You would, Master God! Oh, may Your blessing be on my family permanently!

—2 Samuel 7:28–29

September 11

Does All Mean All or Not?

Sin entered the world through Adam, and since then, every person born is born into sin. We don't like to think of that, but it's truth. Sin comes in many different forms—anger, lying, unforgiveness, gluttony, suicide and on and on—but it's all sin.

When sin came into the world, our fellowship with God was broken. There was no way we would ever be able to pay the price required to get that fellowship back again. It would require the blood of one perfect, without blemish or spot; and the only One who could fulfill that requirement would be Jesus Christ, Son of God. He came to pay the price we could never pay.

He willingly came to earth as a baby, grew into a man and showed us the way. His blood has redeemed us (Ephesians 1:7). Every person who confesses that Jesus is Lord and believes in their heart God raised Him from death will be saved (Romans 10:9).

Once you do that, your sin is forgiven—*all* your sin, not just one or two sins or some sins, *all* your sin is forgiven! Past, present and future sin—forgiven! Does that mean you never have to ask forgiveness again? No! He wants you to ask forgiveness on a continual basis, mostly because He wants to know you recognize it as sin. He has already forgiven you, but as your Father, He wants you to ask because it still grieves Him when you sin. He doesn't disown you, He still loves you, but sin breaks the fellowship you have with Him and the fellowship He has with you.

So, if you get angry with someone or you lie about something or eat too much at the buffet, and you are in an accident, or you simply die before you have a chance to ask His forgiveness, does that mean you won't go to Heaven? Of course not! Your sin was already forgiven! So, if someone has been fooled by the enemy into thinking the only solution to their problem is suicide, and they complete it, does that mean they won't go to Heaven? Well—I ask you, does His Word say *all* sin is forgiven or not?

Today's Prayer

Father,
Thank You for forgiveness of *all* our sin!
Amen.

But if we walk in the light, as He is in the light, we have fellowship one with another and the blood of Jesus Christ, His Son cleanseth us from all sin.

—1 John 1:7 (KJV)

September 12

An Offering

As I was writing in my prayer journal this morning, I felt in my spirit He was telling me, "*This* is today's devotion. Share this." So, may my prayer be your prayer today.

Father,

Thank You so much for Your forgiveness, Your wonderful mercy and grace! The blessing of another morning and pure joy found only in You! The Holy Trinity—God the Father, God the Son and God the Holy Spirit! How much more of a blessing does anyone need? Yet You continue to pour out more and more simply by waking me in the morning, spending this special time with me and inviting me to join You for the rest of the day and join in what You're doing. What honor You bestow upon me by including me, when You don't need me at all! You simply give me the chance, and it is mine to take—or not—but I absolutely cannot imagine not taking it! How much I would miss if I didn't join You!

Father, in the name of Jesus Christ of Nazareth, help me to always join You and Your plan, instead of asking You to join me in my plan! Your plans and Your ways are oh so much better than mine (Isaiah 55:8–9)!

What better way to say "thank You" than to live my life as an offering to You (Romans 12:1)? You are flooding me with such a thankful, special peace this morning that I truly can't comprehend, and yet I know it's because of You! You are so good to me! It doesn't matter how badly I mess up, the very second I turn around, change my mind (repent) and ask Your forgiveness—You give it! You not only give it, You begin to pour such wonderful blessings on me! Not material blessings, blessings that are much more precious than that—

the blessing of Your presence, Your peace, joining You in Your plan and many others that aren't tangible but are oh so precious—like the blessing of others who have gone through similar experiences and can now come alongside and help me learn a better way, as they did. You just continue to pour into me, over me and all around me; and I simply ask, in the name of Jesus Christ of Nazareth, for You to help me live my life as an offering to You!

Today's Prayer

Father,
Thank You for helping us live our lives as an offering to You! Amen.

Therefore, I urge you, brothers and sisters, in view of God's mercy, to offer your bodies as a living sacrifice, holy and pleasing to God—this is your true and proper worship.

—Romans 12:1 (NIV)

September 13

The First Step

From the time a baby is born, it seems, everyone is waiting for him/
her to take those first steps. Sometimes, people even want to rush
them right past crawling into walking, encouraging them to take that
first step!

You know, it's not just true for babies—taking the first step in
anything is something that's hard to do! Especially when it comes to
taking that first step toward accepting Jesus Christ as your personal
Savior!

For some, it's a matter of coming to terms with the fact that
you are not in charge of your life, and that is a hard pill for you to
swallow! You like to think you are in charge of your own life, that
you make your own decisions, go where you want to go, do what you
want to do so forth. In reality, though, you know that isn't true.

It's also hard to take the first step in asking forgiveness because
that first step is admitting you did something wrong! You may argue
with God about it and try to tell Him all the reasons it is okay that
you did what you did. But, once you take that first step and admit
your sin, it gets so much easier after that. The very minute you do,
though, He will take over for you! He will forgive you, and He will
begin to work in your life the way He has truly wanted for so long!

When you are faced with a new direction in your life, taking the
first step toward that new direction—be it a job, a marriage, whatever—can be quite hard too. You don't know what's ahead, you don't
know what to expect.

But, when you have taken the absolutely most important ever
first step—the one to accept Christ as your personal Savior—all the
other first steps are so much easier! No, not necessarily easy, just eas-

ier! Easier because you know Who orders your steps (Psalm 37:23), and you know you can trust Him to guide you. He always wants you to be willing to take the first step in every journey, and that first step is trusting Him. Are you ready to take that first step today?

Today's Prayer

Father,

Thank You for helping us take our first steps by trusting You and knowing that You have already gone before us.

Amen.

We can make our plans; but, the Lord determines our steps.

—Proverbs 16:9 (NLT)

September 14

Prepare Yourself

"Prepare yourself." That's the text my husband sent me at eleven twenty-four the morning of September 13, 2019. I replied to him, "For what?" and he answered, "Not sure." Although he kind of knew what *he* was talking about, even he had no idea those words had a meaning far beyond what he thought!

Around eleven that night, those words were already in the back of my mind when my husband woke me up, saying, "Help me, baby." He was so hot I could barely stand to touch him, and he quickly began talking in a way that I knew something was terribly wrong—or definitely not right anyway.

He was, obviously, running a very high fever, which, for lack of a better way to put it, had him hallucinating. He was talking about people in the room (who weren't there) and kept saying he needed to go outside. "If I could just get outside, everything will be okay. They like me out there."

I didn't know how to help him. I finally got in touch with some wonderful friends from our church who immediately came to our house, helped me get my husband in the car and get him to the local emergency room. These same friends stayed with us the entire night, and the husband later drove me to the hospital they transferred my husband to, which was forty-five minutes away, and stayed the rest of the night with us there!

I tell you all this to simply share what I feel God wants me to pass on to others: *be prepared*! During our conversation, I had also sent a text that said, "Well, I'm definitely prayed up, and I don't know how else to be prepared, so I guess I'm good, right?" and "Yep! I'm as prepared as I can be for whatever He has next." I had no clue what was coming, but I had recently confessed some things I knew I needed to confess, and I firmly believe it was because of that confession God was able to have me prepared and ready for the events of last night. Are you prepared? Are you prayed up? Are you ready for what might come next, whether it's good or bad? You can be—just *pray*!

Today's Prayer

Father,

Thank You for giving us all we need to always be prepared for whatever You have in store for us and for whatever the enemy tries to throw at us.

Amen.

Watch out and keep praying that you can escape all that is going to happen and that the Son of Man will be pleased with you.

—Luke 21:36

September 15

Joy Comes in the Morning

Due to the events of yesterday (late Friday night into yesterday), our sweet daughter, wonderful son-in-love and precious granddaughter spent the night with me last night. Our granddaughter just turned one last month. Hearing her sweet precious voice in the next room this morning was such a welcome reminder of that verse in Psalm 30.

I've shared with y'all before how I get up extra early each morning to have my special time with the Father. Obviously, that time didn't happen yesterday; and this morning, it is much later. They (daughter and family) have left to go visit a friend here in town for a few minutes, but will be back shortly. I think they mostly wanted me to have this quiet time.

Father spoke to me, though, even before they left, and I agree with Him. It's true my time this morning wasn't as quiet as normal, but oh how precious it was to hear that baby's excited giggles and watch her loving all over her daddy and mommy—and she even had some for Grammy too!

Friday night (into the early hours of Saturday morning and off and on all day Saturday) was a time of weeping, but this morning, He reminded me of Psalm 30 and the chorus to a song written by Bill and Gloria Gaither called "Joy Comes in the Morning." The chorus goes like this:

> Hold on my child, joy comes in the morning.
> Weeping only last for the night.
> Hold on my child,
> Joy comes in the morning.

The darkest hour means dawn is just in sight.

Friday night and Saturday were dark hours. Watching my husband in such pain and misery was awful. We never like to see our loved ones hurting, do we? But, through it all, as much as I wished my mom could have been there with me, as much as I felt so alone at different times during the day, as much as I hurt watching my husband suffering the way he was, I trusted God had a plan and all would be well, if I could just make it 'til the morning. And I did. And it is. All is well with my soul. Is it well with your soul? Are you ready for your joy in the morning? Stay close to Him, and He'll stay close to you!

Today's Prayer

Father,

Thank You for the rainbow after the rain, the testimony after the test and for joy in the morning after a night of weeping!

Amen.

Weeping may last through the night, but joy comes with the morning.

—Psalm 30:5 (NLT)

September 16

The Unknown

There is probably nothing more frustrating than being sick and not knowing why you are sick. When you know why you are sick, you can treat what is causing the sickness so you can get better. When you don't know what is making you sick, you don't know how to treat it, and it can be extremely frustrating.

There are many other variables in life too. Many other things that are unknown to us. We (humans) like to think we are in control, in charge and that we have it all together. The reality is, we (humans) are absolutely not in control or in charge, and we will never have it all together.

The good news—or great news—is that you can know the One Who *is* in charge and Who *does* have it all together, if you want to know Him. There is nothing—*nothing*—that is unknown to Him. He sees the big picture when all you see is what is right in front of you. He knows how all things are going to work together for His good, and He knows what is best for you in every situation.

He tells us in His Word, "Don't panic. I'm with you. There's no need to fear for I'm your God. I'll give you strength. I'll help you. I'll hold you steady, keep a firm grip on you" (Isaiah 41:10, the Message).

The enemy loves to throw things at you and have you wondering, where in the world did this come from? What's going on? Why is this happening? But, if you will stay in the Word of God and lean on Him and trust in Him, you will realize you don't have to be afraid or fear the unknown. All you have to do is remember to trust in Him and let Him have all your questions. He may not give you an answer immediately or even at all, but you can rest assured nothing comes against you that didn't have to pass through His hands first, if you are His child. Keep your focus on Him, no matter what fear you are facing, and He will give you strength you never knew you had, and He will give you a peace you can't explain.

Today's Prayer

Father,

Thank You for giving us the spirit of power, love and a sound mind. Thank You that we can put our trust in You and not fear the unknown.

Amen.

For God hath not given us the spirit of fear; but, of power and of love and of a sound mind.

—2 Timothy 1:7 (KJV)

September 17

LOL

In a time where we are connected with many people at once via social media like Facebook, Instagram, Twitter and many other platforms, some of us tend to hide behind the screen we are using. Instead of being honest with others about what they are going through, they post things that make them appear happy and carefree all the time.

We live in a very broken world where we think we are supposed to be brave all the time, showing our strength and not our weakness. If you show your weakness, you stand the risk of being ostracized—shut out or excluded. Sadly, this is even true among believers—the very ones you should be able to talk with openly and honestly and expect to be treated with love in return.

Why, then, does it seem believers are the very ones who tend to shun those who mess up or share their vulnerability instead of loving on them, praying for them and lifting them up to the Father, especially when it is someone who lived a rough life before coming to the Lord.

It's time we started living the way He showed us to live (Colossians 3:9). Start loving each other so we know it is okay to share when we mess up and know, instead of being judged, we will be prayed for.

Just because you see someone post *LOL* at the end of their post or insert a ton of crying laughing faces at the end of their comment, doesn't mean they aren't hurting inside. That hurt may not even be the result of sin; it could be the result of feeling all alone with no one to talk to for understanding.

Think about it, have you ever posted an *LOL* or a crying laughing smiley face when you were actually crying your eyes out behind that screen? What might happen if we could all start being honest with each other? What might happen if we begin to reach out in love and support for each other? Why don't we try it?

Today's Prayer

Father,

Thank You that we can confess our sins to each other and know we have others praying for us as we pray for them. Thank You for Your healing and for making great things happen when we pray.

Amen.

Confess your sins to each other and pray for each other. Do this so that God can heal you. When a good man prays, great things happen.

—James 5:16 (ICB)

September 18

Perfection

Do you know a perfectionist? Are you a perfectionist? What is a perfectionist? A perfectionist is someone who refuses to accept any standard short of perfection. Perfectionism can be a huge weight to carry around, and it is one God never intended for us to carry. None of us are perfect; in fact, we are far from it!

Why, then, do we expect others around us to be perfect? For instance, when you go out to eat, do you expect everything to be perfect—from the service to the food? Now, it's true you should expect to receive your food the way you ordered it. But, do you expect your server to be right there at your table the minute you need something? Do you not take into consideration what that server might be going through, at work or at home, that could be affecting their performance? Do you ever offer to pray with or for your server, instead of speaking badly about them?

Have you ever found yourself a patient in a hospital? Let's be honest, when you don't feel well, and especially when you are sick enough to be admitted to a hospital, you are certainly not at your best—can I get a witness? However, does that mean you, suddenly, have the freedom to treat people any way you want, just because you aren't feeling your best? Absolutely not!

You should always be so full of Jesus that any time life bumps into you, He is what spills out. Instead of concentrating on the bad things that happen or things that just haven't gone your way, why not try praying about it instead? Instead of bad-mouthing the one who is serving you, say a prayer for them. When you are feeling bad and someone is trying to make your life as comfortable as possible, say a prayer for them. When you concentrate on others and put them before yourself and your needs, you get a huge blessing in return, and nothing is better than knowing you prayed for someone. Your prayer could be the very thing that works a miracle in someone else's life!

Today's Prayer

Father,

Thank You that, while You want us to strive for perfection, You don't expect us to be perfect. Thank You for Your Son, Who always does the right thing and speaks to You for us.

Amen.

> *My children, I am writing this so that you won't sin.*
> *But if you do sin, Jesus Christ always does the right*
> *thing, and He will speak to the Father for us.*

> *—1 John 2:1*

September 19

Recognize and Visualize

Six years ago, I was texting with a friend who was going through a tough time, being attacked by the enemy. I was simply trying to encourage her in her walk and remind her the attack wouldn't last forever. Then, I found myself texting her something I had not even thought of before!

Proof that God will give you words of wisdom to pass on to others when you don't even realize it! I'm sure I had been reminding her of who God says she is in Him—an overcomer, a child of God, a warrior, etc. Then I typed these words: "No matter what you do or don't do, the enemy is always going to attack it—recognize (where it's coming from) and then visualize (see yourself through your Father's eyes)."

Recognize—the enemy is always prowling around seeking someone to destroy. If you don't keep your armor on, he can find a way to get to you! He will find your weak spot and go for it! It is imperative that you learn to recognize his attacks so you will realize how to fight back. How do you fight back? You fight back by learning to

Visualize—see yourself the way the Father sees you. In order to do that, you will need to search the Scriptures. Write them out, if you need to, and place them all around your house as constant reminders! You are a child of God (John 1:12); you are a friend of Jesus (John 15:15); you are justified and redeemed (Romans 3:24); you are accepted (Romans 15:7); you are no longer a slave (Galatians 4:7); you are set free (Galatians 5:1); you are chosen, holy and blameless before God (Ephesians 1:4); you are an overcomer (Revelation 12:11). There are many other scriptures that tell you who God says you are! Search them out and keep them close to you.

The next time the enemy launches an attack on you, take a minute to stop. Remember to *recognize* where the attack is coming from and *visualize* yourself through the Father's eyes.

Today's Prayer

Father,

Thank You for reminding us who You say we are. Help us learn to recognize the attacks of the enemy and then visualize ourselves through Your eyes.

Amen.

Be on your guard and stay awake. Your enemy, the devil, is like a roaring lion, sneaking around to find someone to attack.

—1 Peter 5:8

September 20

If You Can't Say Something Nice...

I don't know about you, but I can remember being taught, as a young child growing up, "If you can't say something nice about someone, don't say anything at all." Sound familiar? I thought it might. It's the way things were back in the day. Children were taught manners by their parents. We were taught to respect our elders and "watch what you say, young lady [or young man, as the case might be]."

I believe, for the most part, many of you in my age group (sixties) were brought up that way. It's simply the way things were back then. Whether you came from a Christian family or not, teaching your children good manners and how to treat others with courtesy and respect was the thing to do. It was how we were taught. I never realized that not only should that be true of how you treat others, it should also be true of how you treat yourself. Have you ever thought about it that way?

Father showed me this verse (Ephesians 4:29) yesterday, and I felt Him speak to me, "There's a devotion I want you to write." I thought I knew how it would go. Given the world we live in now where, it seems, everyone is all about themselves, I figured He wanted to remind us how we need to treat others and how we need to talk about others—lifting them up and encouraging them, rather than tearing them down.

That wasn't the case at all. Yes, it's true, we do need to make sure when we speak of others that it is helpful for building them up and benefiting those who are listening; however, He reminded me we need to make sure we do the same thing when we are talking to ourselves about ourselves. Stop talking trash to yourself about who you are. Speak only what is helpful for building yourself up, according to your needs, that it may benefit the one listening—*you*! So, today, remember to talk to yourself the way you should talk to others: with wholesome, encouraging talk to build up and not tear down.

Today's Prayer

Father,

Thank You for the new perspective on this verse. May we learn to apply this not only when we speak of others, but also when we speak of ourselves.

Amen.

Do not let any unwholesome talk come out of your mouths;
but, only what is helpful for building others up according
to their needs, that it may benefit those who listen.

—Ephesians 4:29 (NIV)

September 21

Last Minute or Right on Time?

This morning was one of those mornings. I sat and I listened and I listened and I listened some more. I couldn't hear anything! I tried writing something, a couple of different things, to be honest. Yet, even though He had given me ideas about them, I just couldn't make it work.

So, I stopped. I prayed again, "Okay, Father, You don't seem to have a devotion for me today—or at least right now anyway. I am going to shut down the computer and go back to bed and wait for You to give it to me later in the day, when You are ready." I went back to bed, knowing I would be watching my granddaughter, who recently turned one, for most of the day.

A little after nine last night, my husband and I were getting ready to turn in for the night, and I remembered a devotion had never been given to me. So, I whispered a little prayer, "Father, if You want to give me a devotion today, you will have to wake me up after I go to bed."

I woke up, wide awake, looked at my phone, and it was 11:34 p.m.! He spoke the devotion to me in one sentence. "Sometimes, what may seem like the last minute to you is right on time for Me."

Are you struggling with something in your life today? Are you going through a battle of any kind? Have you prayed and prayed and feel like you are getting absolutely no answers? Do you feel like your prayers are hitting the ceiling and falling down to the floor?

Don't give up! Don't lose hope! While it may seem that way to you, those are only lies from the enemy! You *will* regain your strength after that health setback, you *will* see the Father come through for you, your prayers *are* going through to His throne room; whatever you are struggling with, the struggle *will* come to an end! You just have to remember: what might seem like the last minute to you, is actually right on time for God! So, go ahead and go on to sleep. Get the rest He wants to give you—because He's got this!

Today's Prayer

Father,

Thank You that Your timing is not our timing. Whether Your answer or You making Your presence known is a day or a thousand years, we know You are always right on time!

Amen.

Dear friends, don't forget that for the Lord one day is the same as a thousand years and a thousand years is the same as one day.

—2 Peter 3:8

September 22

Where Do You Live?

This seems to be something Father keeps talking to us about this year—this place we call our comfort zone. He is making it very clear we don't need to live there, but why?

Why is it so wrong to stay where you are comfortable? Why is it so wrong to stay where you know what's going on and you know what to expect at any given moment? Why is it wrong to want to live there?

Have you ever wondered why God doesn't want you living in your comfort zone? How can you grow if you are comfortable where you are? What about the mighty, redwood trees in California? What if they grew as large as an oak tree and said, "Okay, I'm good here. No need to grow anymore"? They would miss out on what they were called to be—a mighty, towering redwood!

It's the same for you. If you continue to live in the place where you are comfortable, you miss out on what God has called you to be and/or to do. You are called to be a mighty warrior in His army! He may want you to be a warrior on the front lines, or He may want to use you more behind the scenes, but whichever it is, He wants to use you.

He wants to do a new thing, and He wants you to be part of it. He might want to use you to make a road in the desert or a river in the dry land of someone else's life. You may have gone through that tough time so you would be able to help someone else get through the same thing! But, if you stay in that awful place called the comfort zone, you most likely will miss your chance.

Wouldn't you rather allow Him to grow and stretch you so you can see how wonderful it is to live outside your comfort zone?

Nothing can grow there, especially not you. If you stay there, you run the risk of withering and dying there! Yes, it can be a little—okay, sometimes a lot—scary, but it's much better than the alternative! You may even find you like living on the outside! His challenge to you today: are you willing to step out and see what happens?

Today's Prayer

Father,

Thank You for the new thing You are doing. Help us be ready and willing to come alongside You and join in!

Amen.

> *Look at the new thing I am going to do. It is already*
> *happening. Don't you see it? I will make a road in*
> *the desert. I will make rivers in the dry land.*

> —*Isaiah 43:19 (ICB)*

September 23

Light at the End of the Tunnel

Today's devotion is extra special because of how God chose to give it to me. He sent it through my daughter. She sent me a text yesterday telling me she felt led to share what she had said to a friend because "God may use it for a devotion!"

She and her friend were having a discussion, and her friend asked, "Just where is the light at the end of the tunnel?" I will share my daughter's response a little later. First, I'd like to share what I found in my research this morning to see if there was anything in God's Word about a "light at the end of the tunnel."

One article stated, "The light at the end of the tunnel is no illusion, the tunnel is." It talked about the tunnel being an illusion of separation, of being alone, being lost. In essence, you have to choose whether you will focus on the darkness of the tunnel or take positive steps to focus on the Light!

When you're the one in the tunnel, though, it can be hard. The enemy comes at you from all directions and does his best to make you think there is no hope, but the Light—the Light is still there, if you're a child of God. Keep your focus on the Light because the Light is Jesus! (See John 8:12 below.)

Now, on to my daughter's reply to her friend: "It's called Heaven, honey, and until we get there, we're gonna have trials constantly, but we know Who has our back until we make it, even if life isn't always easy!" My daughter then told me, "I know it came from God because I've *never* thought about it until I said it, and then I thought, 'Well, dang! I get it!'"

Heaven is the ultimate light at the end of the tunnel, but Jesus is the Light to see you through on this earth! Do *you* get it? Do you see that He is the One Who will guide you through any dark space you find yourself in, whether it be a dark space of your own making or just due to life events beyond your control? Will you choose to focus on the Light today instead of the tunnel? Will you choose to not only trust Him but also to trust His timing?

Today's Prayer

Father,

Thank You for being our light! Thank You that we don't have to walk in the dark when we have the Light that gives life!

Amen.

Once again Jesus spoke to the people. This time He said, "I am the light for the world! Follow Me and you won't be walking in the dark. You will have the light that gives life."

—John 8:12

September 24

The Contented Life

As I was writing in my prayer journal this morning, with my cat laying on top of my left arm (to keep him from being on top of my journal), the Lord spoke to me through my cat's purring. I felt Him ask me, "Are you as content as he is? Are any of My people truly content? Do any of you really understand what it means to be content?"

What does *contentment* mean? According to the Cambridge English dictionary, the meaning of *contentment* is "happiness and satisfaction, often because you have everything you need." I believe that is an accurate description of contentment for a Christian too. If you are a child of God, you can be content knowing that He will supply your every need (Philippians 4:19).

Even the *Cambridge Dictionary* didn't say "because you have everything you *want*"—it said "everything you *need*." Do you know how to be content no matter what circumstances you are facing? Did you know the Amplified Bible describes being content as "satisfied to the point where you are not disturbed or disquieted"? That doesn't necessarily mean you don't want things to change. It simply means that you are okay with where God has you at the moment, until He brings the change.

It means, no matter what life throws at you, you know God is holding you in the palm of His hand, and He is going to protect you and provide for you everything you need to make it through. It doesn't mean you never get caught off guard or blindsided by something you didn't see coming.

Sometimes, life's circumstances might knock you down for a second and knock the wind out of you. But, when you remember Who you belong to and Who is fighting your battles for you and you remember that *nothing* takes Him by surprise because it had to pass through Him first, then you can get back up and face whatever it is that has come against you. "Those who respect the Lord will live and be content, unbothered by trouble" (Proverbs 19:23 ICB). So, how 'bout it? Are you willing to give living a contented life a try?

Today's Prayer

Father,

Thank You for helping us learn to be content with whatever we have and in whatever circumstances we find ourselves.

Amen.

Not that I was ever in need, for I have learned how to be content with whatever I have.

—Philippians 4:11 (NLT)

September 25

Feelings

Emotions, feelings, can be such fickle things. We can be over-the-moon excited about something one minute and be all down in the dumps the next. Am I speaking truth here? You know I am.

Ecclesiastes 3:4 tells us, "There is a time to cry and a time to laugh. There is a time to be sad and a time to dance." We shouldn't be ashamed of our emotions or feelings. God gave them to us. He doesn't want us to deny them.

However, He also gives us further instruction on how to deal with them. Sometimes, life just comes at us faster than we know what to do with it, and we find ourselves stressed or trying to figure it all out. He tells us in Philippians 4:6–7 not to be anxious about anything and to give every situation to Him in prayer with thanksgiving. When we do this, He will give us peace that no one understands. Proverbs 3:5 says, "Trust in the Lord with all your heart and lean not on your own understanding"—because our understanding is so very limited!

He even tells us, in Romans 12:15, how we can handle other people's emotions: "When others are happy, be happy with them, and when they are sad, be sad."

One thing we know for sure, and He reminds us in Hebrews 10:23, "Let us hold fast the profession of our faith without wavering; (for He is faithful that promised)." That verse, to me, speaks to how the enemy will try to make us doubt our salvation from time to time. We must hold fast to what we know to be true during those times, and the truth is it doesn't matter how we feel, it matters what we know He has told us! And He told us in John 8:31–32, "If you keep on obeying what I have said, you truly are My disciples. You will know the truth and the truth will set you free."

So, no matter what you are feeling today, remember God is with you through it all—the good, the bad, the happy, the sad—and He will see you through.

Today's Prayer

Father,

Thank You that we don't have to listen to our heart or what we might be feeling at the moment. Thank You that we don't have to understand it, we need only give it all to You.

Amen.

The heart is deceitful above all things and
beyond cure. Who can understand it?

—Jeremiah 17:9 (NIV)

September 26

Join the Living

It's amazing how you can feel so strongly about something, and then, one day, God uses a song to give you that "aha!" moment about it. I want to share one of those aha moments of mine with you today.

I have never cared for any of the movies or television shows about zombies or the walking dead or any other such form of those things that seem to be everywhere these days. It always struck me as going against everything God's Word teaches Christians.

If you are a blood-bought, born-again child of God, why in the world would you be interested in watching anything about darkness and death? It just seems that it should go against everything in your Spirit-filled nature to be interested in such darkness and dark activities.

Then, I heard this song playing on the radio. I've heard it several times before and never really thought much about it. The radio in the car stays on a Christian radio station, so it's not like I have to be listening that close to make sure what's playing is appropriate, right?

But, as I found myself listening to the words, I felt God speak clearly to my heart, "Yes, there really is such a thing as the walking dead." He reminded me that it's in His Word. I had never even thought about it that way before! The song was Jeremy Camp's "Dead Man Walking," and while I couldn't quite understand all the lyrics as the song was playing, I looked them up later and found them to be very accurate! It's so true!

Until we come to Christ, we are the walking dead—dead in our transgressions and sin. True, not like the shows and movies make it out to be, but I still found it interesting that I never really thought of it that way before. Just because you're reading a devotion doesn't mean you've given your life to Christ yet. Are you still a dead man (woman) walking? If so, would you consider giving your life to Him now, right where you are, to join the living?

Today's Prayer

Father,

Thank You for the new life we have in You through Christ when You forgive all our sins.

Amen.

You were dead, because you were sinful and were not God's people. But God let Christ make you alive, when He forgave all our sins.

—Colossians 2:13

September 27

A New Understanding

As I began writing today's scripture from the daily scripture writing plan, I heard them in a way I've never heard them before. These are verses that most everyone, including me, have memorized at one time or another and can usually quote at any given moment.

The scripture is from Proverbs 3:5–6, and if you've been a Christian very long, you probably know it well: "Trust in the Lord with all thine heart and lean not unto thine own understanding. In all thy ways acknowledge Him, and He shall direct thy paths." Put *all* your trust in the Lord, right? And lean not on your own understanding. Does it really get any plainer than that?

Yes, it does. Though I thought I knew what it meant, it suddenly seemed much clearer to me this morning as I wrote, from the Contemporary English Version (CEV): "Trust the Lord and not your own judgment." For whatever reason, when I wrote (and read) it that way, it was like it just jumped out at me! I truly never thought of my *own understanding* as my *own judgment*. Yet, it is very clear to me now! If I am using my own judgment for anything, I better take a step back, do some more praying and reassess my plans to make sure they are, indeed, His plans! Because the only way He can clear the road for me to follow is if I am letting Him lead me and not trying to take the lead myself.

Have you ever read a verse in a different version than what you're used to and have it suddenly become even clearer in your heart and your mind? Has He ever shown you something brand-new that way? If you've been stuck reading the same translation all the time lately, try reading from a different one today and see what He might show you. Yes, you do need to be careful about the translation you choose, but there are a lot of good ones to choose from, too. Just pray and ask Him to lead you to the translation He wants you to read. He will, and He will clear the road of understanding for you too.

Today's Prayer

Father,

Thank You for a fresh, new look at this verse and reminding us, in very easy-to-understand English, not to trust our own judgment, but to let You lead us because You will clear the road for us when we follow You.

Amen.

With all your heart you must trust the Lord and
not your own judgment. Always let Him lead you
and He will clear the road for you to follow.

—Proverbs 3:5–6

September 28

All for One

This may wind up being the shortest devotion of the year, or it may not—either way, it's what He wants shared, so here it is.

Romans 8:26 (NLT) tells us, "And the Holy Spirit helps us in our weakness. For example, we don't know what God wants us to pray for. But the Holy Spirit prays for us with groanings that cannot be expressed in words." I know that to be true, as I have personally experienced it. However, I am also beginning to see that, sometimes, He also gives us the words when we don't expect it.

For instance, this morning, as I was writing in my prayer journal, I began to write things I hadn't even thought about and was surprised to find myself writing. It simply amazes me what He can do when we allow Him to do it.

Forget, for a minute, that He sent His Son for all, and think about this: God, not only were You willing to send Your Son, but Your Son, Jesus, was willing to leave His place in Your kingdom, come to this earth, as a newborn baby and grow up showing me there is a better way! Not only was He willing to live His life showing me, He was willing to give His life in order for me to have eternal life with You, Him and the Holy Spirit in Heaven. Thank You for the Holy Spirit, the Comforter, being willing to come and live in me to enable and help me live the life You would have me live!

When I finished writing that in my prayer journal this morning, I sat in awe at what He'd done and what He'd shown me, and immediately I knew in my spirit it was what He wanted to share in the devotion this morning. Then, He confirmed it through the scripture writing for this morning. The passage to write this morning was Psalm 27:1–5. The whole passage spoke to me, but as I was writing verse 4, I knew that was the scripture to go with today's devotion. What has He spoken to you this morning as you read this devotion? Did He remind you He would have done all this for the sake of one, even and especially if you were that one? Yes, He loves you that much!

Today's Prayer

Father,

Thank You for allowing us to live in Your house every day of our lives, if we so choose. Thank You for showing us how wonderful You are and allowing us to pray in Your temple.

Amen.

I ask only one thing, Lord: Let me live in Your house every day of my life to see how wonderful You are and to pray in Your temple.

—Psalm 27:4

September 29

The Five *W*s and an *H* of Forgiveness

Who? Colossians 3:13 gives a quick, good answer for that one: "Put up with each other and forgive *anyone who does you wrong*, just as Christ has forgiven you." The italicized words are strictly for emphasis on the answer.

What? Micah 7:18 makes it clear: "Our God, no one is like You. We are all that is left of Your chosen people and You *freely forgive* our *sin and guilt*. You don't stay angry forever; You're glad to have pity and pleased to be merciful."

When? Luke 23:34: "Jesus said, 'Father, forgive them, for *they don't know what they are doing.*' And the soldiers gambled for His clothes by throwing dice." Before they even ask for your forgiveness, give it to them. The same way He forgave you, through Christ, Who died while you were yet in sin.

Where? Wherever you are, even if you are praying, according to Mark 11:25, "But *when you are praying*, first forgive anyone you are holding a grudge against, so that your Father in Heaven will forgive your sins, too."

Why? Matthew 6:14: "Yes, *if you forgive others* for the things they do wrong, *then your Father in Heaven will also forgive you* for the things you do wrong."

How many times? Luke 17:4 tells us, "Even if that person wrongs you seven times a day and *each time* turns again and *asks forgiveness*, you must forgive."

There's lots of talk about forgiveness. Hopefully, this helps you understand it in a new way. When He instructs you to do something, He will always answer the "five *W*s and an *H*" question, if you are willing to search for them. All you have to do is ask Him to guide you, and He will. Today, the when answer got my attention the most. Realizing I should be prepared and ready to forgive anyone before they even do anything to me, or before they even ask for my forgiveness, was an eye-opener. Did one stand out to you? What will you do with it?

Today's Prayer

Father,

Thank You for Your forgiveness while we were yet sinners. May we be kind and merciful and forgive others the same way You forgave us.

Amen.

Instead, be kind and merciful, and forgive others,
just as God forgave you because of Christ.

—Ephesians 4:32

September 30

Decisions, Decisions

What do you have going on in your life at this time? Are you newly married? Newly engaged? New parent? New home? Maybe it's not a time of new anything in your life. Maybe you are simply in a season of having to make some hard decisions.

Sometimes the decisions you have to make aren't made clear. It may not even be a decision that has a right or wrong choice. After all, those kinds of decisions really shouldn't be that hard, right? Well, true, it is sometimes hard to make the decision to do the right thing, but hopefully, you do it anyway.

However, sometimes it's simply a case of having to choose what is best. What is best for you, your family, etc. Those are probably the hardest decisions you have to make sometimes. Trying to decide not what is the *right* thing but what is the *best* thing?

Having to make a decision of what would be the best thing instead of what is the right thing is no fun! It may even be the hardest part of being an adult. As children, it was so much easier when everyone just made decisions for you, right? You've surely seen the memes on some form of social media that say something like, "Please don't make me adult today" or "That horrifying moment when you're looking for an adult and you realize you are an adult, so you start looking for an adultier adult" and so on.

Did you know you have the best adult ever to call on? Someone much more "adultier" than yourself? You do! All you have to do is call on Him. Ask God to clearly show you the decision that will be best for you, and He will. He will give you such a peace that it will surprise you!

So, when you have any kind of decision to make—especially one where there is no right or wrong, only what's best—be sure to ask Him for help. He will make it clear to you by giving you that peace only He can give. Try it today!

Today's Prayer

Father,

Thank You for giving us peace and clarity in our situations. Thank You for being the peace and calm, no matter what we are facing.

Amen.

For God is not the author of confusion, but of
peace, as in all churches of the saints.

—*1 Corinthians 14:33 (KJV)*

October 1

Misfits

You've heard the song "We're a Couple of Misfits," from *Rudolph the Red-Nosed Reindeer*, but have you heard the song performed by Casting Crowns called "Nobody"? It surely brings things into perspective. If you haven't yet heard it, I highly recommend you find it on YouTube and give it a listen.

Were you a misfit when you were younger? I definitely was—especially beginning in fifth grade! We had moved again, and I began attending a small school where if you didn't have a certain last name or you hadn't been there since first grade (there was no public kindergarten in those years), you were considered a nobody and were treated that way.

That's something that, unfortunately, can follow you all the way into your adult years and wreak havoc there too. I believe that's why this song got my attention so fully. I have dubbed it the theme song for my life! Because it puts into words what God has been showing me over the last few years—that I am exactly the kind of person He wants to use, and the best news of all? He wants to use *you* too!

No matter how unworthy you feel, no matter how mistreated you may have been, no matter what! You are exactly the person God can use to show others the way! Do you realize the Bible is full of what we call misfits? Moses, David, the apostles. And have you ever thought about Who the biggest misfit is in the Bible? Jesus! Think about it: everyone was expecting a king to come in grandeur and prestige! Yet, Jesus came as a baby in a manger, and He never did what the people expected Him to do. In fact, He usually did the opposite!

So, you see, even if you do consider yourself a misfit, you are in great company! Do you realize now that, no matter what, God can use you and you do have a purpose? Ask Him to use you daily; He will!

Today's Prayer

Father,

Thank You not only for loving those of us who feel like misfits but also for using us to further Your kingdom. Thank You that we are weak, whether in reality or in our minds, for it is in our weaknesses, You make us strong!

Amen.

Yes, I am glad to be weak or insulted or mistreated or to have troubles and sufferings, if it is for Christ. Because when I am weak, I am strong.

—2 Corinthians 12:10

October 2

Shake the Dust—or Not

We had some dear, sweet friends come to visit last night, and we found out the wife had been spoken to really harshly, earlier in the day, by some "religious" ladies. My response to hearing this was: "How could they talk to you like that? I can't believe they would actually say that directly to you!"

The Lord immediately answered me, "Why does that surprise you? Do you not remember how the 'religious' leaders treated Me? Why would you expect anything different for yourself or anyone else?" Then, the scripture writing this morning was 2 Corinthians 4:7–9: "We are like clay jars in which this treasure is stored. The real power comes from God and not from us. We often suffer, but we are never crushed. Even when we don't know what to do, we never give up. In times of trouble, God is with us, and when we are knocked down, we get up again." And I thought, *Yes! She needs to get back in there!*

He also reminded me about His meeting with the woman at the well. What if He had spoken to her the way those ladies yesterday spoke to my friend, instead of the way He did? He also reminded me of when He was sending out the disciples and giving them their instructions. He told them, basically, if they weren't welcome, to shake the dust from their feet at them and move on. That's when I realized I was trying to get an answer not meant for me.

How do you know when you should stay and stand your ground or move on? You have to pray. Because every situation calls for different responses. If you aren't in constant communion with the Father, you will be tossed around like the waves in the ocean. But, if you stick close to Him and talk with Him regularly, He will make your answer clear to you. Because He is the only One Who knows what He has planned for you. You have to be in communion with Him in order to discern what He is telling you. You can't rely on what anyone else might tell you—even though they mean well. And, what He might have someone else do in the same situation could be different than what He asks you to do. Yes, He may want to use you to speak to someone or their situation; just be very sure you share only what He would have you share.

Today's Prayer

Father,

Thank You for allowing us to come, individually, to You for the answers You have for us.

Amen.

I pray to you, God, because You will help
me. Listen and answer my prayer!

—Psalm 17:6

October 3

Impersonator or Imitator?

Do you know the difference between impersonating someone and imitating someone? Some people think it's the same thing, but it's not. To impersonate someone, you actually have to pretend to be that person. When you imitate someone, you try to model your life so it is a mirror image of theirs, a reflection of the person themselves.

God wants us to be imitators, not impersonators. He doesn't want us going around trying to *be* Him; He wants us to be *like* Him. The problem is, there are too many in this world today who want to impersonate Him. They want everyone to think they are God; and that, my friend, is so dangerous. The ones who want to impersonate Him have no idea of the danger they place themselves in—or maybe they do, and they just don't care.

What about you? Do you want to impersonate God, or would you rather imitate Him? Maybe you never really thought about it before. I know I hadn't until this morning when I heard Him speak to me about it. To be honest, I first thought He was speaking to me about being an impersonator; then, I realized I was getting the word wrong. He was saying *imitator*, but it led me to look up the definition of both, and that's when I realized what He was telling me.

If you are trying to impersonate Him, you need to stop! Your sin keeps you from even coming close to being God. It screams louder than you could ever talk and reveals your true character to everyone.

However, you can follow Christ's example and live a life filled with love. Love for all—not just those who are easy to love, but also the ones that are hard to love. Like the beggars on the street, that person who cut you off in traffic, the coworker who stole your idea and got a promotion and so on. You get the idea. Are you willing to be an imitator today and every day?

Today's Prayer

Father,

Thank You for showing us we need to be imitators of You, not impersonators. May we live a life filled with love for others as He did. May our lives, offered daily as a living sacrifice, be a pleasing aroma to You.

Amen.

Imitate God, therefore, in everything you do, because you are His dear children. Live a life filled with love, following the example of Christ. He loved us and offered Himself as a sacrifice for us, a pleasing aroma to God.

—*Ephesians 5:1–2 (NLT)*

October 4

Who Cares for You?

Have you ever been a caregiver for someone? My sister was a caregiver for her husband. My mother was a caregiver for my dad, though not in the traditional way some might think. My dad wasn't confined to anything. I guess maybe Mom was more of an emotional caregiver than a physical caregiver. Both, however, require much sacrifice.

I saw my sister sacrifice many things when she was a caregiver for her husband. They were only married for five years, and only about the first two were "quality" years, by most people's definition of *quality*. My sister would probably disagree with those people though.

Some people are caregivers by profession, others are caregivers because life happens and you have to do what you have to do. No matter how anyone steps into the role of caregiver, it is a hard role to step into, whether it is for a short time or a long time.

Most caregivers will tell you they wouldn't change a thing either. Not to say they wouldn't love to see the one they are caring for get better and no longer need the special care, but given the situation, they are happy to be caring for their loved one. Not so much because "it's the right thing to do" but because they want to be there for the one they love.

But, even a caregiver needs care. They can get worn down and need to be lifted up. Who cares for the caregiver? When is it their turn to have someone take care of them?

All the caregiver has to do is lean on and lean into the arms of the Father. He cares for each of us, caregivers or not, like no other can. He, alone, gives us the Holy Spirit to comfort us as no other can. He is the breath of life, the giver of hope, and He is the absolute best caregiver anyone could ever ask for!

So, for the caregiver or anyone else asking the question, "When is it going to be time for someone to care of me?" Your time is now, if you only ask. The Father is ready and waiting to care for you. Will you allow Him to do so?

Today's Prayer

Father,

Thank You for caring for each one of us. Help us turn all our worries over to You and leave them there.

Amen.

God cares for you, so turn all your worries over to Him.

—1 Peter 5:7

October 5

Who Believes in You?

Quite possibly, the first person(s) you thought of when asked the question "Who believes in you?" was your parents. More specifically, even, you probably thought of your mom. Moms are very special people who have been given special gifts of nurturing and caring for another person, sometimes even before they care for themselves.

Or maybe you thought of your spouse or a really good friend, your bestie, or maybe you were even sitting there thinking, "Wow! I don't know of anyone who believes in me!" Yes, believe it or not, there are some who think no one believes in them. That is such a sad place to be in.

Worry no more about that, though, because there is good news! Did you know that God believes in you? Did you know He believes in you even if you aren't…"saved"? Gasp! It's true! If you are saved, He still believed in you even before you were! Mind-boggling, isn't it? But true. He believed—by giving you free will and the opportunity to choose whether or not you believe in, love and serve Him—you would choose Him!

Why would He have created us in His image and entrusted everything His hands made to us if He didn't believe in us—in you— to take care of it? Why would He invite you to take part in what He is doing here if He didn't believe in you? Do you really think He needs you to do anything? Of course, He doesn't! He even tells you in His Word that He can use the rocks to cry out for Him, if He so chooses (Luke 19:40), but He believes in you!

God used one of my Facebook memories to give me this devotion. The memory was a quote, but the author is unknown to me. It said, "He lived like he believed in God; but, more than that, he lived like God believed in him." Now, maybe today's devotion was nothing new to you. So, now the question is, will you live like God believes in you?

Today's Prayer

Father,

Thank You for showing us You believe in us! You truly did crown us with glory and honor and let us rule what You have made. You would never have done such a thing if You didn't believe in us, and we thank You.

Amen.

You made us a little lower than You Yourself and You have crowned us with glory and honor. You let us rule everything Your hands have made. And You put all of it under our power.

—Psalm 8:5–6

October 6

No Rock's Gonna Cry Out for Me

God did something for me last night He's never done before—at least not that I remember, and I'm fairly certain I'd remember if this had ever happened. He gave me a message in a dream! Of course, I didn't realize it until I woke up this morning and was having my quiet time with Him.

During our time, He reminded me of the dream I had last night, and at first, I didn't think much about it. Then, I realized what He was telling me about it, and I got so excited I could hardly stand it!

My dream: I was in church somewhere, and I was standing there (during the singing part) thinking, "I don't want to offend anyone, but I want to worship how the Holy Spirit leads me. If He tells me to raise my hands, I want to raise my hands." Then, I decided I'd close my eyes and do what the Spirit told me to do. At one point, I remember opening my eyes and seeing that several others had their hands raised in worship also!

What He spoke to me about the dream: I wonder how My people, in churches everywhere, would worship Me if they knew nobody was watching!

Wow! That just set my soul on fire! It's so true! Personally, I've had more than one person say to me, "Sometimes, I feel like I want to raise my hands in church, but I don't want anyone to think I'm just trying to draw attention to myself, so I don't do it."

It's time to stop worrying about what other people think! What does God think? He says if we don't cry out, the rocks will (Luke 19:40)! Yes, that scripture was just mentioned yesterday. This makes twice—better listen!

A majority of preachers today, at the end of their service, will say, "All heads bowed, every eye closed, no one looking around..." I'm thinking, what would happen if they said it at the *beginning* of the service? How would *you* worship if you knew nobody would see you? Will you worship like that next time—no matter where you are? God will see, and He knows your heart.

Today's Prayer

Father,
Thank You for giving us freedom in the spirit. May we learn how to use this freedom in our worship of You.
Amen.

Now the Lord is the Spirit and where the Spirit
of the Lord is, there is freedom.

—2 Corinthians 13:7 (NIV)

October 7

Death Threatening

Well, you've probably never heard that term before, right? I never had until God spoke to me this past Sunday morning during the message. The preacher was telling about a time when he decided he was going up in the attic to fix their air conditioner. To make a long story short, he wound up having 240 volts of electricity going through him instead.

He shared that story because he was talking about impartation. He was saying that, as Christians, we spend time in prayer, alone with God, to receive what He would have us to impart to others. Speaking of the incident in the attic, he said, "It's no different than when that electricity was being imparted through me," and when he said it, God used the Holy Spirit to speak to me, "Oh yes, it is different!" And that's when He spoke to me, "The impartation of that 240 volts was life-threatening, but the impartation of Jesus is death threatening because when Jesus imparts something, He imparts life, not death!"

Simply put, when God gives you something, He wants you to share with someone. You can be rest assured it is something that will "build up" the other person and not tear them down. Do you understand? If you find you are about to "impart" something to someone else, please make sure you are hearing straight from Him. Be sure it is going to build them up and not tear them down; you want to be sure you are speaking life and not death.

The power we receive from God is so powerful that it puts death (the enemy) in its place; it is "death threatening." You have the choice to speak life or death (Proverbs 18:21) every day. The only question that remains is which one will you choose? Will you be life-threatening or death threatening?

Today's Prayer

Father,

Thank You for reminding us You have put in us the same power that raised Jesus from the dead! Amen.

I want you to know about the great and mighty power that God has for us followers. It is the same wonderful power He used when He raised Christ from death and let Him sit at His right side in Heaven.

—Ephesians 1:19–20

October 8

Right or Left?

So many things in our everyday lives have a much deeper spiritual meaning than we realize. Even something as simple as the words *left* and *right*. As I was searching through Scripture yesterday, asking the Father to show me the one He would have me use for the devotion, He pointed out something else.

As I read Ephesians 1:20, He took my eyes to the footnote for that verse, and I read, "*1.20* right side: The place of power and honor." As I read that, the next thought that went immediately through my mind was, "That is why the groom stands on the right side in a wedding. Because the husband is the one who is supposed to have the place of power and honor." Not power in the sense that he controls everything, but that as Christ is the head of and leads the church, so the husband is to be the head of and lead the marriage.

Then, He got me to thinking about left and right and the significance of both in the Bible, so I started looking into that. Wow! There is so much more to His Word than I realize! So much more I need to study and learn. I knew there was mention of things about left and right in the Bible, but I never knew how much!

Not only does it help spiritually, it also helps us understand our own language even better. Especially how we talk about choosing the right things over the wrong (or left) things. His Word tells us, in Matthew 25:32–33, He will gather all nations unto Him, and He will separate them as a shepherd separates the sheep from the goats. He will put the sheep on His right and the goats on the left.

Do you ever think about things like this? Did you know something as simple as right and left could have such a deeper meaning?

Do you want to be right, or do you want to be left? Do you see the significance in that question?

Today's Prayer

Father,

Thank You for reminding us that even something as simple as right and left have deep meaning in Your Word. May we have the heart of the wise and be inclined to the right and not the heart of a fool.

Amen.

The heart of the wise inclines to the right; but,
the heart of a fool inclines to the left.

—*Ecclesiastes 10:2 (NIV)*

October 9

He Is When We're Not

Today's devotion comes from a friend's Facebook post from six years ago. Seeing her post, I felt the Father say, "Share how you know these things."

Even on days when we doubt, He is still the truth (John 14:6). When that doctor gives you a report of his facts, Jesus is still truth. When the loved one you're praying for continues living a life far apart from the way they were taught, Jesus is still truth.

You are who He says you are, not who you say you are! He says you are loved (John 3:16), He says you are worthy (Zephaniah 3:17), He says you have purpose (Jeremiah 29:11) and He says you are His (1 John 3:1)!

He is always faithful, even when you are not (2 Timothy 2:13). No matter how many times you feel you let Him down, He remains faithful. You can't let God down, because you were never holding Him up.

When you are weak, He is strong (2 Corinthians 12:9–10). Like the old poem states, when you see only one set of footprints, it is because those are the times He carried you.

No matter how far away you may wander from Him, He is there, waiting for you to return (Luke 15:20). You can never go so far that He won't welcome you back.

You can ask for and receive forgiveness, no matter how many times you mess up in a day (Hebrews 10:10) because His mercies are new every morning (Lamentations 3:22–23).

So, as my friend said in her post, I am "so thankful for Him, especially when I am me." Are you thankful for Him today—simply for being Him when you are you? Will you go and encourage someone else with this word today?

Today's Prayer

Father,

Thank You that even though sometimes we don't know what You are doing, we will understand later. Thank You for Who You are and who we are in You. Thank You for Your faithfulness, Your truth, Your strength and Your forgiveness.

Amen.

Jesus answered, "You don't really know what I am doing, but later you will understand."

—John 13:7

October 10

Hide and Seek

What games did you play as a child? I don't remember much about my childhood days or games we played, but there is one day that has stuck with me for many, many years, and it involved a game of hide-and-seek.

I remember a certain game of hide-and-seek with my siblings, and if I remember correctly, I was the one doing the seeking of the other three. I found my older sister and my younger brother but could not find my older brother anywhere I looked! I finally gave up, and I went all through the house saying that "I give up! We're not playing anymore. You can come out now." A little later, my sister and I were in our bedroom, listening to records (you know, those really big CDs), and the record player was beside the upright piano, across the room from the end of our bed. The records had finished playing on one side, so I was going to the record player to turn them over so the other side could play; and just as I got to the record player, my older brother jumped out from behind the piano and scared me! I literally jumped from where I was back onto the bed (most likely without touching the floor—not that it was that far) and screamed so loud our parents came running in the room to see what was going on. My brother probably thought it was hilarious until he got in big trouble for doing it! He had been there the whole, entire time, and we never knew it. Obviously, I had not looked everywhere as I thought I had. He had chosen a really good hiding spot.

Aren't you glad our Heavenly Father isn't like that? He doesn't want to jump out and scare you. He wants you to find Him, but you can't search for Him with your eyes, and you will never find Him by praying one- or two-sentence, superficial prayers and going on your way.

To find Him, you need only to dig into His Word and pray heartfelt, genuine prayers. Get on your face (literally or figuratively) in prayer, and you will find Him. Have you been superficially searching for Him? He wants only for you to search with all your heart. Are you ready to do that? He's waiting to meet you there. Will you go search for Him now, with all your heart?

Today's Prayer

Father,

Thank You for not hiding from us. You are always right there, available for all. We simply have to open our hearts to see You.

Amen.

And you will seek Me and find Me, when you search for Me with all your heart.

—Jeremiah 29:13

October 11

Traditions

Traditions have their place. It's nice and somewhat comforting, if you have certain family traditions you follow at certain times of the year—like Thanksgiving, Christmas, New Year's, birthdays, etc. There is a time and place for traditions in our lives.

But, what about a tradition of religion? Is that something that can truly be passed down from generation to generation? I don't think so. First of all, religion can take you straight to hell, tradition or not. You must have a personal relationship with the Lord, if you want to grow closer to Him and let Him grow you in ways you never imagined!

My husband told me about a dream, or maybe it was a vision the Lord gave Him. This happened a while back, and it is very sobering. He said He saw God walking through hell, weeping over all the people there because they were stuck in their traditions and letting other people tell them how they should worship.

It is the responsibility of each of us to study His Word and know for ourselves what He teaches us there. We also have responsibility to share with others that they can't get to Heaven by living in their tradition. Doing or teaching things because it's the way Mom and Dad and Grandma and Granddad and brother and sister and on and on always did it or taught it. Get in the Word and find out for yourself what He wants to teach you.

Yes, traditions have their place, but your relationship with God isn't a place for tradition. Believing something because of the tradition of how it was always taught to you isn't a good idea. Do you get in His Word and search out answers for yourself, or do you rely on someone else to tell you what's in the Bible?

Today's Prayer

Father,

Please help us not live by our traditions but by Your Word. May each of us deepen our personal relationship with You through prayer and studying Your Word on our own.

Amen.

And so you cancel the word of God in order to hand down your own tradition. And this is only one example among many others.

—Mark 7:13 (NLT)

October 12

Always There

No matter what you might be facing today, do you realize Jesus is right there with you? No matter where you have to go, not only has He already gone before you, but He is right there with you as you go through it.

In seeking His leading this morning for the devotion, I felt prompted to get out a study book from a Bible study I went through thirteen years ago. It was a study in Revelation by Anne Graham Lotz. The title of it is *The Vision of His Glory: Finding Hope through the Revelation of Jesus Christ*.

This study will always hold a special place in my heart because the Lord used it to get through to me on a personal level. Even though I got saved as a teenager, it was during this study that I began to develop a personal relationship with Him. He began to teach me so much through His Word, using this study as a guide.

Suddenly, being His child became so much more than following a list of rules. He began to show and teach me things I had never been aware of before. He showed me He truly holds everything in His hands. There is nothing that happens in my—or your—life that didn't have to pass through Him first.

We often hear it said, "He won't put more on you than you can handle." I've been guilty of saying it myself in the past. But, I have learned how wrong that is. If you could handle everything that came your way, why would you need to call on Him? He most assuredly will give you more than you can handle on your own, but not more than you can handle with His help!

No matter what things might look like right now—good or bad—He is still right there with you. He already has it handled. Will you trust Him with it?

Today's Prayer

Father,

Thank You for assuring us You are always there as the mighty Son of Man with Your wisdom and divine nature. Thank You for holding everything in Your hands.

Amen.

There with the lampstands was someone who seemed to be the Son of Man. He was wearing a robe that reached down to His feet and a gold cloth was wrapped around His chest. His head and His hair were white as wool or snow and His eyes looked like flames of fire. His feet were glowing like bronze being heated in a furnace and His voice sounded like the roar of a waterfall.

—Revelation 1:13–15

October 13

Too Heavy

Have you ever tried to carry something you weren't equipped to carry or move something you should never attempt to move or do something you were never meant to do? Man or woman, makes no difference. We all have limitations.

Let's face it, sometimes we all carry things that are way too heavy for us and that God never intended for us to carry. What burden are you carrying today that God has asked you to give to Him in exchange for the light load He has for you? Are you carrying the burden of lost loved ones on your own? He doesn't want you to carry those kinds of burdens. He wants you to give those lost loved ones to Him in prayer and leave them there.

Are you burdened down by carrying the load of your past and the things you did before you came to know the Lord? He never intended for you to keep carrying that load. He took it from you the day you gave your life to Him. Stop beating yourself up, and give that heavy burden back to Him.

Are you beating yourself up over mistakes you've made since coming to Him? Do you think you are supposed to be perfect since you are a Christian now? He never tells us anywhere in His Word that He expects us to be perfect. That's way too big a load for you to carry. Only one man was perfect, and we crucified Him.

Take another look in the Word. God called David "a man after My own heart," yet David had a man killed because he (David) wanted his wife and had an affair with her. You will still make mistakes after becoming a Christian, but you ask His forgiveness; and if it involves anyone else, you ask their forgiveness, and you move on. He doesn't expect perfection, He expects obedience out of a place of love, not demand. Will you give your heavy burden to Him today? And, if you pick it back up later, will you give it to Him again?

Today's Prayer

Father,

Thank You for allowing us to lay our heavy burdens at Your feet and take on the light load You give us. Forgive us when we pick the heavy load back up, and help us remember to give it back to You.

Amen.

Come to Me, all of you who are tired and have heavy loads. I will give you rest. Accept My work and learn from Me. I am gentle and humble in spirit. And you will find rest for your souls. The work that I ask you to accept is easy. The load I give you to carry is not heavy.

—Matthew 11:28–30 (ICB)

October 14

Negative into Positive

Are you old enough to remember when that word was being used, usually accompanied with an attitude and an eye roll, in a negative context? I remember it, and I did not like it.

However, I remember coming across this verse during that time, and I have no doubt the reason it stuck with me the way it did is because it was a way to turn the word *whatever* into something good instead of something bad or annoying.

During that time, one of my responsibilities (at the church we were attending) was to put something on the bulletin board located in the entryway to the sanctuary. I put the word *whatever* in huge letters in the center of the bulletin board. Then, all around it, placed the words *true, noble, right, pure, lovely, admirable, excellent* and *praiseworthy*. And, underneath, were the words "think about such things" and the scripture reference.

It seemed to make an impact on everyone who saw it. This is one of the first times I remember God showing me how to take something the enemy meant to use for bad, disrespect or whatever you'd like to call it, and turn it into something to be used for His glory!

A word the enemy tried to use to make something ugly out of, God used to help me remember a verse from His Word; and because of the bulletin board He nudged me to create, it helped others recall that verse every time they heard the word *whatever*.

You see, God can take anything the enemy wants to use for negative and turn it into something positive, if you allow Him to. Whether it be a word, a deed or anything else. Ask Him to show you a way to turn a negative into a positive, and watch what He will do for you! Are you ready for it?

Today's Prayer

Father,

Without the attitude or the eye roll, we ask You to help us think about whatever things are true, noble, right, pure, lovely and admirable. Help us keep our minds on those things that are excellent or praiseworthy.

Amen.

Finally, brothers and sisters, whatever is true, whatever is noble, whatever is right, whatever is pure, whatever is lovely, whatever is admirable—if anything is excellent or praiseworthy—think about such things.

—Philippians 4:8 (NIV)

October 15

A Simple Solution

Have you ever had a problem with anything and you just could not seem to find the solution to it? No matter what you tried, no matter what you did, you just couldn't seem to fix it?

A few months back, we bought a new printer. We still have the old one to use for scanning and printing everyday things. It still works, just doesn't have the quality print it once did.

The new printer is great, though, and it prints good quality items we need for my husband's ministry and my home business. However, the first time I tried to print labels with it, it kept telling me to insert the CD/DVD tray. Even though I chose the setting for rear paper feed, it kept giving me this message, and for the life of me, I could not figure out why! I tried everything I knew to try and, honestly, was becoming quite frustrated with it. Labels are one of the main things we need to print in good quality, and I couldn't print them!

Finally, I realized I had exhausted all avenues of everything I knew to possibly try to correct the problem. So, I got desperate. I located a phone number to call for technical help. The voice on the other end of the phone told me I needed to go into my program settings (Word), click Page Setup, click on the Paper tab and change the default to Rear Paper Feed instead of CD/DVD Tray. I tried it this morning, and what do you know, it worked like a charm!

Do you find you come at life the same way? So many times, when you face difficulties, do you find you try and try to figure out the solution on your own? You try this thing and that thing, and when those don't work, you try the other thing? You do this until, finally, in your exhaustion, you give up! And, that is when you realize there is a simple solution. Ask the Father for help. He has the solution to anything and everything you face; He's just waiting for you to ask Him for help.

So, that problem you've been trying to fix? He's waiting patiently for you to ask Him about it. Will you call on Him today? He has the solution you need.

Today's Prayer

Father,

Thank You for giving us the answers when we ask, seeking You with our whole hearts and knocking so You can open the door of knowledge.

Amen.

Ask and it will be given to you; seek and you will find;
knock and the door will be opened to you.

—Matthew 7:7 (NIV)

October 16

The Secret Life

Recently, some things have happened that had me in much conversation with Him about how we should help others. I've always been taught and understood the concept of giving in secret. That way, your reward comes from God and not man.

When a popular radio station began a promotion of *encouragement* month, my first reaction was "How nice!" Then, as I began to listen, they were asking their listeners to encourage others, which was great, but then they were asking them to call in and tell what they did to encourage someone. Now, I sort of understood where they were coming from, but at the same time, it just bothered me.

Then, there was a personal experience of wanting to do something for others as quietly as possible, yet another wanted to do this and have the newspaper there and let them get a picture for their scrapbook and so on. That also bothered me.

And so, the conversations with Father began. When I have a hard decision to make, one way I have learned to know for sure when I am hearing the answer from the Father is when I have peace about my decision. He is not the author of confusion (1 Corinthians 14:33).

He clearly tells us in His Word, Matthew 6:1–4, how it should be done. After reading those verses, the peace, which can only come from Him, returned. So, things will proceed as originally planned, and the rest is up to Him.

When you do something for others, do you want everyone to know about it? Is that your inspiration for doing it? If you receive your praise from man, that is all you will receive. Be honest, would you rather receive your reward from man instead of your Heavenly

Father? Which reward do you think would be best for you? Remember, He knows your heart, and it's what you have in there that matters.

Today's Prayer

Father,

Thank You for teaching us to do things from our heart to help others and not for recognition. Your rewards are so much greater than any reward man could give.

Amen.

Give your gifts in private and your Father,
Who sees everything, will reward you.

—Matthew 6:4 (NLT)

October 17

A Time for Reflection

Some days you just need to stop and reflect on things. Why are you doing the things you're doing? What is the meaning of it for you, personally? Today is a good day to stop and spend some time asking yourself why your quiet time is important to you.

Why do you carve out the time slot to spend quality time with the Father? Is it a sense of responsibility? Is it something you feel you are supposed to do? Do you do it from a sense of obligation, or do you look forward to it every day?

Let me share with you some of my own reflections. This time is important to me because I crave to meet with Him; learn from Him; be refreshed, steadied and reoriented by Him—by drawing near to Him through His Word and His spirit.

It is important to me to meet with Him every morning to be able to make it through the day. It is a time for me to remember and to thank Him for all He's done, is doing and will do in and through my life. This time is to help me stay steady, calm and connected to Him.

It wasn't always that way. For years I had what I called a quiet time because I thought He would be disappointed in me if I didn't. I thought it was something I was *supposed* to do. It was a legalistic ritual, and it didn't always happen.

Would you do something for yourself today? If you've been trying to have a quiet time with Him out of a sense of obligation, stop. He isn't interested in your legalism. Take it from one who knows; He wants a relationship with you. He wants you to spend time with Him because you want to get to know Him better and you want to be with Him. So, your challenge today is to take some time to think about why your quiet time is important to *you*. When you have, it doesn't matter. Where you have, it doesn't matter. *Why* you have it and the attitude of your heart—that is what matters.

Today's Prayer

Father,

May each person reading this devotion long to have time with You to strengthen the relationship and not because they feel obligated. Reveal to them why this time is important to them, as You did for me.

Amen.

But seek ye first the kingdom of God and His righteousness;
and all these things shall be added unto you.

—Matthew 6:33 (KJV)

October 18

Before the Storm

There's a popular song, "Praise You in the Storm," that speaks of praising Him, even when we're in the middle of a storm. Do you find it that easy, though, to truly praise Him when you find yourself in the middle of a storm? Sometimes, we make choices that put us in the middle of a storm, but other times, storms just come, and sometimes they come without warning! And when they do, is your first reaction to praise Him? Probably not.

How do you get to that place of praising in the storm then? You can't wait until the storm hits; you better be prepared ahead of time. How can you prepare for something you don't know is coming? You develop that relationship with the Father, the Son and the Holy Spirit. You do that by spending time in the Word and spending time in prayer. You prepare by living every day in His presence. That is the only way you will be ready when the storm hits.

True, that first gust of wind might knock you off your feet for a minute because it hits you by surprise, but then you quickly regain your footing, you dig in your heels and you begin to praise Him for what He is going to do through this storm. You call on your inner circle, those you know you can trust, to help you by keeping you lifted up in prayer. The same way Aaron and Hur kept Moses's arms lifted in the battle, your inner circle will keep you lifted up.

Your storm may blow through in a short time, or it may be one that decides to stall and hang around a while; either way, you will make it through, if you remember to trust Him and remain brave and strong! Another song comes to mind: "You may feel like everything's falling apart when really everything is just falling into place." Stay true to Him, and even when you slip, it's okay. He's still holding on to you. He won't let you go. He will not fail you. You are His child, and He will protect you. He will protect you even if the storm is a result of choices you made. How much more, then, will He protect you when the storm is not one of your own making? Will you decide today, before the storm hits, that you will praise Him in the middle of it?

Today's Prayer

Father,
Thank You for reminding us to trust You, no matter what. Help us to remain brave and strong and to trust in You!
Amen.

Trust the Lord! Be brave and strong and trust the Lord.

—Psalm 27:14

October 19

The Devil's Game

Have you ever played the what-if game? There are many variations of this game out there, but I'm actually thinking more about the game the enemy loves to play with your mind—especially when you are in the middle of one of those storms we talked about yesterday.

The enemy loves to get you to engage in a game of "What if" with him because he knows, if he can get you playing that game, he can sneak his fear into your very core! How do you not engage with him in that game? It's so easy to join in and allow him to control your thought process. How do you resist?

The only way to not engage in his what-if game is to combat it with the Word of God! Another reason you can't wait 'til you're in the middle of a storm to try to prepare for it. You need to have those scriptures in your heart. You don't even necessarily have to be able to quote them from memory these days; if you simply know enough to put a few key words in Google, you can find them in a matter of seconds.

You also need to be prayed up, as the saying goes. If you are in constant communication with the Father, He will put the scriptures in front of you exactly when you need them. He's done it for me so many times!

Then, if you really want to defeat the enemy at his own what-if game, turn it around on him! Instead of following his lead and thinking about all the things that could go wrong, "if this" or "if that," start asking, instead, "What if God is allowing me to go through this to make me stronger?" "What if God has allowed this storm because He knows I know I can trust Him to get me through it?"

If you are His child and in the middle of a storm, He *will* see you through. So, every time the enemy throws a "What if" at you, throw it off with scripture or throw it right back at him with a better "What if" from God's view.

Today's Prayer

Father,

Thank You for Your protection when the enemy attacks us. Thank You for giving us peace in place of fear. Thank You for helping us disengage from the enemy's what-if mind game and trusting only in You.

Amen.

Brutal people may attack and try to kill me; but, they will stumble. Fierce enemies may attack; but, they will fall. Armies may surround me; but, I won't be afraid; war may break out; but, I will trust You.

—Psalm 27:2–3

October 20

Family Reunion

Do you come from a family that has big (or small) family reunions ever so often? Maybe yearly or every few years? I don't. I do remember once, as a very young child, my dad's side of the family decided they wanted to have a family reunion. We all went and gathered at a park and visited and had a good time. They decided they wanted to do this yearly, and they did, for the next couple of years—two or three, maybe, then they just stopped.

My husband and I attended the Celebration of Life service yesterday for a very dear friend of ours who moved to Heaven September 24. As I've shared before, we moved away from our town about a year and a half ago, and it was good to be back and see some of our dear friends again, even though it was due to our friend being promoted. That is only sad because we will miss our friend, but we know we will see him again one day.

As I was seeing different ones that I knew come in, I began to be amazed at some of the people I saw there. People I would have never imagined seeing, yet they also knew our friend and loved him. As I was sitting there, during the service, I began to think about how wonderful it was—seeing all these friends I hadn't seen in so long— and I started thinking about how it will be when we get to Heaven!

Talk about a family reunion! The way I understand it, we will not only see our loved ones again, but when we see people who lived ages before us—like Moses, Elijah, David, Paul and so on—we will know who they are! The same way Peter, James and John recognized Moses and Elijah when they saw them (Matthew 17:3–4)!

That is one family reunion I don't want to miss! How about you? Are you ready for the biggest family reunion celebration of all time? If not, you can be. You know what you need to do—accept Jesus as your personal Savior, ask Him to forgive your sins, and He will wash you white as snow! Are you ready?

Today's Prayer

Father,

Thank You for giving us a glimpse of what it will be like when Jesus comes to take us home to You. What a great family reunion that will be!

Amen.

And I tell you this, that many Gentiles will come from all over the world—from east and west—and sit down with Abraham, Isaac and Jacob at the feast in the Kingdom of Heaven.

—Matthew 8:11 (NLT)

October 21

Our Plans—His Plans

We had our plan: We would stay where we were, and he would go and spend a couple days each week at his new job, then come home. Then, we would see if it worked out, and if it did, we would move in the summer.

He had His plan: He sold our house a few weeks later, leaving us no choice but to move to the city where his new placement was located.

We had our plan: We were going to come and share in the Celebration of Life service for our sweet friend, stay the night and go to church Sunday morning, then go back home.

He had His plan: Hubby woke up sick Sunday morning, got progressively worse instead of better, and we started the afternoon in Urgent Care, who punted him to the ER, where they could do a better blood workup. We wound up being there until 7:00 p.m. So, we spent another night here and will head home later this morning.

You may not understand God's plan sometimes; we don't yet understand why He wanted us to stay here an extra night. We may never know, and if we don't, we're okay with that. We know He had a reason for it, and that is all that matters.

Do you get really upset when things don't go according to your plans? Does it really throw you for a loop, as the saying goes? Do you get frustrated and aggravated when something interrupts your day? Do you ever stop to think those interruptions just might be God's divine intervention? Do you ever think maybe, just maybe, He is protecting you from something worse? The next time something doesn't go according to your plan, remember: it is good for you to make your plans, but the truly important thing is to write those plans in pencil and give God the eraser! Then, instead of getting angry or upset, choose to trust Him and His plan. His plan is always the best plan!

Today's Prayer

Father,

Thank You for reminding us we don't know what tomorrow or even the next minute holds. While we make our plans, remind us to stay flexible and open and, ultimately, to trust Your plan.

Amen.

What do you know about tomorrow? How can you be so sure about your life? It is nothing more than mist that appears for only a little while before it disappears.

—James 4:14

October 22

Set a Fire

What does it mean to be on fire for the Lord? I believe I've been shown something a little different this morning—a new way to look at it.

In the past, being a lukewarm Christian, to me, meant someone who went to church when they felt like it, didn't necessarily read their Bible every day and so on. Being on fire—well, that was a different story altogether. Someone on fire for the Lord was always in church, always reading their Bible, doing things for others and on and on. You get the idea.

The problem with that thought process? Maybe it's the fact that it goes from one extreme to the other, I really don't know. But, He gave me a revelation this morning. The truth is, I have been lukewarm lately! Yes! Because, instead of giving up some things to pursue what He wants for me, I tried to compromise and fit it all in.

As long as I was getting up in the morning and having my time with Him, having devotions and prayer time with my husband, tithing and going to church—surely all those things meant I was *on fire* for Him, right? So, it was okay for me to not do anymore, right? It was okay to come home from work and just plop on the couch and mindlessly watch old television shows until time for bed, right? Wrong! The reason it was (is) wrong for me to do that is because I knew He was asking me to do something else.

Anytime we refuse to do what the Lord is asking us to do, how can we say we are on fire for Him? He has gotten my full attention now, and I am waiting to see what He has next. I have been sensing a shifting of sorts, lately, a change of some kind. For now, it's time to stand still and see what He does.

What is He asking you to do? Are you paying attention to Him? If you're His child and you're not paying attention, He will get it—one way or another. Maybe He is using today's devotion as a gentle nudge—will you listen and make necessary changes, or will He have to do something more drastic?

Today's Prayer

Father,

We have no excuse for not doing what You tell us to do. Please forgive us for our time of being lukewarm, and set a fire down deep in us that is unquenchable.

Amen.

Why do you keep on saying that I am your Lord,
when you refuse to do what I say?

—Luke 6:46

October 23

No Matter What

How often have you said the words "no matter what"? When you have said them, were you truly taking into consideration what it might mean? What about when it comes to serving God? Living for Jesus? Allowing the Holy Spirit to lead you? Are you willing to do all those things, no matter what?

Would you be willing to move out of your comfort zone? Suppose you aren't comfortable speaking in front of others; if God called you to share your testimony in front of different groups of people, would you be willing to give it a try? Would you trust Him enough?

Suppose He called you to be a missionary, whether it be a home or foreign missionary; would you be willing to serve Him that way? Would you be willing to move far away, where the conditions would not be what you are used to living in at this moment?

When you say, "I'm Yours, Lord. I will serve You no matter what," are you sincere in what you say? Suppose all He asks you to do is serve Him right in your church's neighborhood? Would you be willing to go outside the walls of your church to reach them?

Should you find yourself in the middle of a battle raging all around you, and you find you are asking, "Where did this come from? I wasn't expecting this. I didn't do anything to cause this." When you realize that battle could be one of your "no matter what's," are you willing to go through it and still give Him the glory, praise and honor?

Face it, sometimes—maybe even most times—life is hard. Once we brought sin into this world, everything changed. It won't be perfect again until we are in Heaven with Him. Jesus went through pain and agony when He lived on this earth as a man. Why should you expect anything different? Anything He asks you to do or go through, He will give you everything you need to do it. Now, are you willing to say, "Lord, I will serve You, no matter what," knowing He will take care of you every step along the way?

Today's Prayer

Father,

We will praise You, no matter what happens! We will constantly speak of Your glory and grace!

Amen.

I will praise the Lord no matter what happens. I will constantly speak of His glories and grace.

—Psalm 34:1 (TLB)

October 24

The Wind Is Blowing

Do you feel that? Something stirring in your heart? What is it? What's going on? You find yourself volunteering for things you never imagined you would volunteer to do. You find yourself thinking in ways you never thought before. Could it be the gentle breeze of the Holy Spirit blowing you in a new direction? Easing you into the next step the Father has for you?

Are you finding some things, way outside your comfort zone, that seem to suddenly pique your interest instead of scaring you? Wait, whoa! What's that? Why would you suddenly be thinking of doing something you never had any interest in doing before?

That's what happens when you truly surrender to God's will and you ask Him to use you in whatever way He wants to use you. Once you do that, you have given Him permission to do what He's had in mind for you since before you were born!

Both my husband and I have done this recently. We said, "We want what You want, Lord. Prepare us for it and help us walk in it, whatever *it* is." We have both felt a sense of something happening for a while now—the wind (Holy Spirit) is blowing in a new direction; a shift is taking place in our hearts, in our thoughts, in our lives (both individually and together); and we are excited to see what He has next for us.

What about you? Do you feel the wind blowing you in a new or different direction? Are you willing to give Him permission to use you any way He would like? He had a purpose in creating you; are you willing to surrender to Him and find out what that purpose might be? It might not be easy, and you may have to go through a battle or two along the way—are you willing to do it anyway?

Today's Prayer

Father,

Thank You for the wind of Your Holy Spirit, blowing us in the direction You would have us go. Help us not fight against the wind but to go with it into places we never could have imagined!

Amen.

The wind blows where it wishes and you hear the sound of it, but cannot tell where it comes from and where it goes. So is everyone who is born of the Spirit.

—John 3:8 (NKJV)

October 25

Your Defender

You can sit around and say you trust the Lord all day long, but do you really? Do you trust Him when it seems everything is going south, as the saying goes? Do you trust Him when you get the report from the doctor that wasn't exactly what you wanted to hear?

When it seems the enemy is coming against you from every direction, do you trust the Lord to fight for you? Or are you trying to figure everything out for yourself? Do you try to fight your own battles in your own strength, or do you remember He said He would fight for you?

He is your defender! The same way He fought for Joshua in Zechariah 3:1–5, He wants to and will fight for you! He will fight for you even if you don't trust Him, because it never was about you anyway!

But, oh how much more wonderful it is when you do trust Him! You don't have any stress. You don't have any worry. You have the peace of knowing Who is fighting for you, and you don't have to lift a finger!

My husband and I are currently in the middle of a battle like we've never seen before. It truly came out of nowhere and blindsided us. I share that with you so you know I'm not just glibly saying these things. Someone told my husband today, "Just go on with life and try not to even think about what's going on," and my immediate thought was, "That's easy for you to say because you're not the one going through it!" Not long after, Father had the Holy Spirit convict me of what I'd said. I felt Him asking me, "So, do you really trust Me or not?" Ouch! That one hurt.

I decided right then I'm not letting the enemy have one more second! I will praise the Lord and call on Him, for I know He is our defender, our strong tower! I will choose to run to Him and praise! Will you do the same with whatever you may be facing? Will you choose to believe His report over the doctor's report? Will you let Him be your defender today in your situation?

Today's Prayer

Father,

Thank You for being our protector and strong fortress. Thank You for protecting us like a shield, defending us and keeping us safe. Amen.

The Lord is my Protector; He is my Strong Fortress. My God is my Protection and, with Him, I am safe. He protects me like a shield; He defends me and keeps me safe.

—Psalm 18:2 (GNT)

October 26

En Garde

According to the *Cambridge Dictionary*, to be on your guard means "to be careful to avoid being tricked or getting into a dangerous situation." As Christians, we definitely need to be on our guard. First Peter 5:8 tells us, "Be on your guard and stay awake. Your enemy, the devil, is like a roaring lion, sneaking around to find someone to attack."

Don't be fooled by the "roaring lion" reference. It doesn't mean you will hear him coming. On the contrary, more often than not, you will never know what hit you! To be on your guard doesn't mean you won't be tricked or find yourself in a dangerous situation. It does mean, however, you will have a much better defense against these things.

In a fencing match, the judge will say, "En garde!" (On guard), which tells the fencers they should get into position. When the Lord says you need to be on guard, it simply means you need to be sure you go through this life ready for anything you might face.

How do you get ready? How do you live on guard? You stay in His Word, you stay in communication with Him through prayer—not just talking to Him and asking for things but also listening to see what He wants to say to you—surround yourself with people who do the same, people who will hold up your arms for you when you become battle-weary.

Being courageous doesn't mean you don't get weak or battle-weary. It means, no matter how battle-weary you may get, you know Who is fighting the battle for/with you, and you know He will be victorious! As you stand firm in your faith and do everything in love, you will see Him work. You may not realize it when He first starts working; He may do things behind the scenes that you can't see, but you will know He is working. You will have that peace that others don't understand. They will wonder why you aren't fighting back and trying to defend yourself. You just keep staying on guard, standing firm, being courageous and strong, doing everything in love and watch Him win.

Today's Prayer

Father,

Thank You for helping us be on guard, stand firm in our faith, be courageous and strong and to do everything in love.

Amen.

Be on your guard; stand firm in the faith; be men
of courage; be strong. Do everything in love.

—1 Corinthians 16:13–14 (NIV)

October 27

On the Throne

Who is sitting on your throne? As a child of God, He is the One that must be sitting on your throne. You are redeemed by the blood of the Lamb. The Holy Spirit drew you to Jesus, and you must respect God's magnificence and holiness by letting Him shine through your life. You should live in a way that your very life is guarding His throne.

You must not let anything interrupt your worship of Christ. He deserves and expects you to give Him glory, honor, and thanks at all times in all things—the good times and the bad times. Your life should worship and bring honor to Him as you praise Him continually.

Having the knowledge that Jesus exists must make a difference in your daily life, but you can't do it in your own power. He is the only One that can accomplish anything! You must remember that without Him, you are not worthy and are unable to do anything. He is the One with all the power. You need to live in His strength and power. You must relinquish everything to Him and give Him praise and worship.

He is worthy of your praise simply because He created you. Thank Him daily for your salvation. He is the One worthy of your glory and honor and worthy of being on the throne of your life. He must be Lord of all in your life, or He won't be Lord at all! He is always in control.

Read His Word so you will be able to listen to the Holy Spirit, and let God's glory shine through you. Become more aware of who is on your throne and, if it is anyone or anything besides Him, make the necessary changes. Spend more time in worship and less time on social media or whatever you spend time on. Let go of everything, including your finances, and trust Him, giving Him all the praise. Remember: your joy comes from Him, and nothing can take it away! So who is on your throne? Do you need to make a change?

Today's Prayer

Father,

Help us to live in a way that we are "guarding" Your throne by leading others in worship and proclaiming Your holiness. Amen.

Each of the four living creatures had six wings and was covered with eyes all around, even under its wings. Day and night, they never stop saying: "'Holy, holy, holy is the Lord God Almighty,' Who was and is and is to come."

—Revelation 4:8 (NIV)

October 28

Eyes of Faith

"Thank You for each one's day of salvation that is on the horizon—so close I can see it with my eyes of faith!" That is what I found myself writing in my prayer journal this morning. "Eyes of faith"—hmmm, never thought of that before, not sure why or how I found myself writing it, but I did and immediately sensed that was what He wanted to share with me this morning.

How do you look at things that happen in your life? Do you view them through the lens of faith and ask God what He wants to show you? Or do you find yourself asking Him why is this happening to you?

When you pray for others, whether it be for healing, salvation, their marriage, their parents, their children or anything else, do you pray believing God is going to answer your prayer? Do you tend to rely, a little too heavily, on the crutch of "if it be Your will, Lord"? I know that is something I have battled before, and still do, if I'm not careful. Yes, of course, we always pray for His will to be done. However, He tells us in Isaiah 53:5 that "by His stripes we are healed." So, we know it is His will for us to be healed. How He chooses to perform that healing is up to Him. When it comes to salvation or someone's marriage, we also know it is His will that all be saved, and we know He wants marriages to last, so you can confidently pray for these things, knowing You are praying in His will, and leave the results up to Him. You also have to remember He is a gentleman and will not override man's free will.

No matter what situation you find yourself in or you see others in, it is definitely important how you view these things. Do you pray and trust and do your best to see things with eyes of faith, or do you constantly find yourself doubting? You know where the doubt comes from—the enemy—so, decide today to kick him to the curb and begin praying with boldness, using your eyes of faith to see it all coming to fruition! Are you ready? Do you have those eyes of faith open now?

Today's Prayer

Father,

Thank You for giving us eyes of faith to see the many things You are doing and to help us through each day.

Amen.

Jesus replied, "Why do you say 'if you can'? Anything is possible for someone who has faith!"

—Mark 9:23

October 29

Burdened

How many of you are burdened today? What are you burdened about? Is your burden for yourself or someone else? Why all the questions this morning? Because I find myself to have a very heavy heart this morning. It actually started last night as I was reading some friends' posts on Facebook.

My burden is for the lost. Those who don't know Jesus as their personal Savior. I shared a few days ago about feeling a shift in my heart and thoughts, and I believe He is showing me that at least part of this shift is a heavy burden for those who don't yet know Him. He is bringing me to the place where winning the lost for Him is becoming more important than anything else I do.

This is new to me—in the sense I've never felt it this strong before. In April this year, I began praying for two particular individuals God put on my heart. I am praying every day and thanking Him, in advance, for their salvation. Perhaps, He used this to grow my awareness of the lost.

You've probably heard it your entire life—time is getting short! I believe that has probably been said since the time Jesus returned to Heaven. Just imagine, though, how much shorter it is now! All you have to do is read your Bible and look at the awful mess around us, even just here in the USA, and you can't deny it!

James 5:20 tells us: "You can be sure that whoever brings the sinner back from wandering will save that person from death and bring about the forgiveness of many sins." Matthew 28:19–20 tells us to go! Your mission field is wherever He has you—work, grocery store, anywhere! How do we do this? How do we make disciples? Perhaps we will discuss that tomorrow. Today, just focus on loving one another and giving grace to each other. That's a good place to start!

Today's Prayer

Father,

Please help us never deny You before men. Help us grab hold of the courage and boldness You have already given us. May You so shine through us that others see only You and want what we have.

Amen.

But he who denies Me before men will be
denied before the angels of God.

—Luke 12:9 (NKJV)

October 30

Go!

Yesterday we discussed having a burden for the lost and how God has called each of us to our own mission field. I shared how we are all to go and make disciples whether our mission field is at our workplace, at home, in the grocery store, wherever. Your mission field is everywhere and anywhere God has placed you at each moment.

So, how do you make disciples? How do you tell others what Jesus, Son of God, did for them? Do you know you are always witnessing, like twenty-four hours a day, seven days a week? Your life is a huge witness! Now, it can be a good witness or a bad witness; but it is always a witness. Especially when you are a Christian—or someone who says you are. When others know you claim to be a Christian, they are watching everything you do. How you handle things, how you react to things, whether good or bad. No, you aren't perfect if you are a Christian, you are simply forgiven! You need to let others know that also.

A great way to be a good witness is simply to love others right where they are. I'm not saying you condone their sin, but you show them love and mercy and grace, the same way God shows these things to you. You develop a relationship of genuine love, concern and trust with them first. You may never even have to mention Jesus, if you model Him for them instead. When you do that, they will ask you questions.

They will want to know why you care about them, why do you love them, why are you so gracious to them? That is when you can share about Jesus and what He did for you and how He can and wants to do the same for them. Will you allow God to give you a pliable heart instead of a judgmental heart? Will you allow Him to use

you to reach the ones that others consider unreachable or unlovable?
Are you willing to go and make disciples by sharing His love?

Today's Prayer

Father,

May we take the courage and boldness You have already given us and go tell others about You and what Your Son did for all of us that they may become Your disciples and be baptized in the name of the Father, Son and Holy Spirit.

Amen.

Therefore, go and make disciples of all peoples, baptizing them in the Name of the Father and the Son and the Holy Spirit.

—Matthew 28:19 (NLT)

October 31

What's in Your Toolbox?

Everyone needs a basic toolbox, right? You know, hammer, screwdrivers, pliers, etc. Items to help you with basic home care and/or repairs. But, did you know it is also important to have a spiritual toolbox?

You need to be able to be strong and immovable in the Lord. How do you do that? You need to learn how to encourage yourself in the Lord! There may be situations that come up where you don't have anyone else around to encourage you, like when you're home alone and everyone else is working, but you are struggling to make it through the day.

You need a spiritual toolbox to help you with soul care and/or repair. You need a spiritual toolbox full of items to encourage you when you need it. What items do you need in your spiritual toolbox? You are the only one who knows the specific answer to that question. However, here are some ideas that might help.

It can actually be summed up in one sentence: Anything that motivates you should be in your toolbox. A favorite song, a good sermon, a scripture passage or passages, a letter or note of encouragement that you may have received from someone. Anything to remind you of these important facts:

You have to keep growing. Maybe what you're going through is to help Him grow you. Don't stop caring—about others or yourself. Keep pressing forward. Don't stop listening for His voice. Don't get distracted from what He has called you to do. Don't become complacent and think there is nothing more you can do.

If you are still breathing, He still has work for you to do. So, get your spiritual toolbox ready and keep it where you will have easy access to it when you need it. What will you put in your spiritual toolbox? Will you start preparing it today so you'll have it when you need it?

Today's Prayer

Father,

Thank You for reminding us we can stand strong and encourage ourselves, when needed. Thank You for reminding us to work enthusiastically for You, because nothing we do for You is useless.

Amen.

So, dear brothers and sisters, be strong and immovable.
Always work enthusiastically for the Lord, for you know
that nothing you do for the Lord is ever useless.

—*1 Corinthians 15:58 (NLT)*

November 1

Too Familiar?

The old saying is, "You can't teach an old dog new tricks," and that may or may not be true. What I do know to be true, however, is no matter how old a person may be, that person can still learn new things.

Sometimes, people reach an age where they may think they finally "know it all" and they couldn't possibly learn anything new. Nothing could be further from the truth, though. Example? Despite turning sixty this past July, I only learned how to create an actual budget about a week and a half ago! All my life I was taught, pay your bills first, and then, if there's anything left over, you can buy groceries or do what you want. While not entirely accurate, at least it gave me a good foundation for learning how to do a budget when the time finally arrived. But, I had to be willing to be taught, then take what I was taught and actually apply it. It got me to thinking...

Have you been a Christian so long you feel like you've got it down pat? Do you think there's nothing more you could possibly learn from God that you haven't already? Are you ready to be challenged? No matter how long you have been a Christian, you will never learn it all! His Word is alive, which means you could read a scripture today that doesn't impact you at all, come back a few weeks—or even days—later, though, and it just might be the very thing you need to help you get through whatever it is you find yourself facing that day!

The same way learning how to budget is challenging, learning to keep growing in your Christian walk is also challenging. If you have a good, solid foundation first, however, it won't be so bad. It may take up a lot of your time at first, but the more you put into it, the more you get out of it. Are you ready to learn something new today? Are you willing to put in the time in prayer and searching His Word to see what He might want to say to you today? Are you willing to take the first step? He will meet you there, and He will be with you every step along the way. Go for it! Learn a new thing and see what He does!

Today's Prayer

Father,

Thank You for showing us we are never too old or too young to learn. Help each of us be open to You teaching us new things.

Amen.

The mind of a smart person is ready to get knowledge.
The wise person listens to learn more.

—Proverbs 18:15 (ICB)

November 2

Focus

My husband and I have been watching/listening to Steven Furtick's message, "When the Battle Chooses You," quite a lot the last few weeks; but last night, the Lord reminded me of something I hadn't thought about the other times we'd watched. At one point in the message, he is talking about how our focus should be on worship, and God spoke to my spirit, "Like the acrostic I gave you a few years ago about what to focus on." I know He reminded me so I could share with you the new thing He showed me last night.

Years ago, I was trying really hard to lose some weight, and He gave me the acrostic "*f*east *o*n *C*hrist's *u*nlimited *s*upply" to help me. It was to remind me that when I thought I wanted something to eat, to go read—to feast on—His Word instead. Then, when I finished, if I was still wanting something because I was truly hungry, go get something to eat.

Last night, as we were listening to the message, He spoke to me that I needed to do the same thing with this battle we are in—when fear, doubt and anxiety try to creep in, I need to go immediately to the Word of God and *feast*! When I do that, fear, doubt and anxiety have no choice but to leave!

Even though He gave me that acrostic years ago, I never realized it's in His Word until today. I kept looking for verses about keeping our focus on Him, but every verse I found just didn't seem quite right. Then I changed the search to scripture about Christ's unlimited supply, and this was the very first one to pop up. As soon as I read it, I heard in my spirit, "That's it!"

No matter what you are battling—losing weight, bad health, troubled relationships, new-mommy stress, new-marriage stress, divorce, single-mommy stress, death—anything! If you will keep your FOCUS on Him, He will see you through. He has unlimited resources, and He is the only One Who can empower you, through His Holy Spirit, with the strength you need to make it through. Are you ready to keep your FOCUS and *feast on* Christ's *unlimited supply* today?

Today's Prayer

Father,

Thank You for Your unlimited resources and for empowering us with inner strength through Your Holy Spirit.

Amen.

I pray that from His glorious, unlimited resources He will empower you with inner strength through His Spirit.

—Ephesians 3:16 (NLT)

November 3

Family

Search the definition of *family*, and you find (1) "a group consisting of parents and children living together in a household" and (2) "all the descendants of a common ancestor." Before I searched the definition of *family*, I searched for scripture on the Trinity, and I was amazed at what I found! As I began to read the scriptures, the Holy Spirit took over and was ministering to me the importance of this subject. I'm praying as I type this, asking Him to help me get down the words, the thoughts, He wants to share. This one is too important; I don't want to mess it up.

Our earthly families are important—a mother, a father and children—but, so many don't have the luxury of a good family. Some couples aren't able to have children, some couples have children and don't care for them or each other the way they should. It may lead a lot of people to believe family can't be that important. If it were, why would God allow such things to be? He didn't allow it. We did, when we brought sin into the world. All these other things are the consequences of that action.

If you have the luxury of being part of a good, loving family where you all love and care for each other, are there for each other through good and bad, be thankful for your blessing. If you don't have that, ask God to help you forgive anything you need to forgive and move on with Him. Leave it in His hands and let Him do what He will with it. He may restore it, He may use you to bring other family members into His family, the family of God, or He may move you out of what you don't need to be in. Once you are His, however, you are part of the most important family of all—His family!

Yes, there are Christians who will let you down the same way your blood family might. Christians aren't perfect, just forgiven. But you can be part of God's family: Father, Son and Holy Spirit. If you aren't already part of His family, would you like to be? Just ask Him to forgive your sins, and He will cleanse you, and you will be part of the best "blood" family, forever!

Today's Prayer

Father,

Thank You for showing us from the beginning that family is important to You. Our earthly families are important, but not as important as the family of Father, Son and Holy Spirit.

Amen.

In Whom (Jesus) you also are being built together
for a dwelling place of God in the Spirit.

—Ephesians 2:22 (NKJV)

November 4

Dead or Alive

Yesterday, I found myself singing along with a song on the radio. Not unusual, I do that all the time. But, this time, this song was different. This time, I felt the Lord speaking to me through the Holy Spirit. It was like He was saying, "Listen! Do you even hear what you are singing?" I felt compelled to look up the scripture the song was based on.

It was in Ezekiel 37:1–14, and as I read it, He began speaking so many things to me! Do you know the scripture? Are you familiar with it at all? Yesterday, I wasn't; today, I am.

Let's take a look at verses 9–10:

> *Then He said to me, "Prophesy to the breath; prophesy, son of man, and say to it, 'This is what the Sovereign Lord says: Come, breath, from the four winds and breathe into these slain, that they may live.'" So, I prophesied as He commanded me and breath entered them; they came to life and stood up on their feet—a vast army.*

A while back, I felt something in my spirit about calling from the north, south, east and west and thought maybe He was saying He was going to be calling people back that had left, moved away for some reason. Then yesterday, as I read verses 9 and 10, I felt Him saying, "This!" Maybe, what He was trying to tell me weeks ago was that He wants to breathe new life into what's already here!

Have you felt more dead than alive lately, spiritually speaking? Do you feel like you are just dead, dry bones? God hasn't left you or forgotten you! Let His spirit breathe new life into you today.

Do you find yourself in a valley? Do you feel lost or alone? Do you feel like you have no life left in you? Then, my friend, you need to read this passage of scripture! Read this passage and ask yourself, "If He can make an army out of dead, dry bones, what can He do in my situation? What can't He do?" Are you ready to let Him take you from being spiritually dead to being alive?

Today's Prayer

Father,

Thank You for allowing Your spirit to breathe life into dead, dry bones and make them live again!

Amen.

My Spirit will give you breath and you will live again.
I will bring you home, and you will know that I have
kept my promise. I, the Lord, have spoken.

—Ezekiel 37:14

November 5

Break My Heart

Yes, my heart is breaking this morning—so much that it was hard to write in my prayer journal! My heart is breaking because I have to say goodbye to my sweet, sweet Patches when the vet's office opens. Patches didn't ask to be brought into my world, my life, all those years ago—fifteen to be exact. He was a sweet, carefree little kitten living next to my mom's house in a vacant lot. I got to know him after Hurricane Ivan swept through our little town, devastating it and knocking out the power for a couple of weeks. Due to no power, Mom and I found ourselves sitting outside a lot because the heat of the day was unbearable inside the house. During those times outside, the kittens from next door would venture over, and some were brave enough to get close to us and let us love on them. Yep, Patches was one of those kittens. That was in September, and in December, I took him to live with me.

He has been with me a long time, and he has helped me through many rough times in my life. He has always been a very loving cat. He loves to be held and be loved on. Lately, though, he hasn't been in the best of health and has taken to staying mostly in one room, making the most pitiful, crying sounds that breaks my heart! So, I know it is time to say goodbye to him because he no longer has quality of life, and it would be selfish of me to keep him around.

Why have I shared that with you this morning? Because I had to share that to share what God taught me in all my hurting and crying this morning. From my prayer journal:

> *Maybe that's what You want to teach me*
> *through this whole ordeal—that my heart should*

be breaking and hurting for the lost souls even more than it is this morning with what I'm facing. There are so many lost souls out there, Father, who have no one praying for them! Let me be the one who prays for them, Father! Let my heart break for them the way Yours does. I may not know their names, but You do! You knew them before You created them, the same way You did me!

If you belong to Him, would you be willing to ask Him to break your heart for the lost souls? You don't have to know their names, He does. Will you pray for them anyway?

Today's Prayer

Father,

Thank You for loving us enough to teach us the hard lessons and for giving us new life!

Amen.

You made me suffer a lot, but You will bring me back from this deep pit and give me new life.

—*Psalm 71:20*

November 6

Safely Through

Has your heart ever felt so broken you didn't think the pieces would ever be put back together again? What do you do during times like that? Who do you call on for help? That might depend on why your heart is broken, am I right?

If your best friend has betrayed you and that's why your heart is so broken, you can't call on your best friend for comfort, right? Unless your best friend is Jesus. Do you ever feel Jesus has betrayed you for some reason? He would never actually betray you, but, sometimes, you may feel as though He has.

Has He ever taken you somewhere you didn't want to go? When He asks you to do the hard things, are you willing to do them just because you know He would never lead you wrong?

Did He ever give you something as a way of showing you He does care about you and what you are going through, then He takes that something away?

When you asked Him to forgive your sins and cleanse your heart and you accepted Him as your Savior, did you expect things to suddenly all be okay? Wouldn't it be great if it worked that way? Do you know how many lost souls would be saved if that were the case? But, it's not, is it?

Sometimes, your best friend has to tell you the hard things—things you don't want to hear about yourself or others. Would they be your best friend if you couldn't trust them to be honest with you? It's the same with Jesus.

Sometimes, He needs you to go where you don't want to go so He can show you the wonderful things, like new friends, He has there for you. Sometimes, He isn't really taking away something He gave you; He wants you to be thankful for the time you had with what He gave.

Just because you surrender your life to Him doesn't mean it will be all peaches and cream from then on. In fact, most likely, the opposite is true. But, when you pray for help, you can be sure He will answer, and He will see you safely through whatever it is that is troubling you!

Today's Prayer

Father,

Thank You for listening to us when we pray for help, and thank You for being our rescuer.

Amen.

When His people pray for help, He listens and
rescues them from their troubles.

—Psalm 34:17

November 7

Speak the Language

That's how it is when you speak unknown languages. If no one can understand what you are talking about, you will only be talking to the wind. There are many different languages in this world, and all of them make sense. But if I don't understand the language that someone is using, we will be like foreigners to each other.

That is straight from God's Word in 1 Corinthians 14:9–11.

What if "speaking their language" means something totally different? What if "speaking their language" means a cultural thing or a generational thing? Are you willing to learn, anyway, if it means you can witness to someone? If you want to win others for the Lord, to add to the family of God, then you must be able to speak their language, whatever that might mean.

It doesn't mean going against God's Word or condoning anyone's sin. It simply means to meet them where they understand you. It isn't your job to judge them, it is your job to love them and witness to them. Witnessing doesn't mean you have to use words. Sometimes, it means taking action—helping someone with a project to benefit them, asking nothing in return. When you help someone who isn't a believer, they don't understand it. They may question you as to why you are helping them when you don't agree with their beliefs or their lifestyle, and that gives you the opportunity to say, "I just want to love you the way Jesus loves you," and leave it alone—unless they ask more questions, which they just might. If they do, then you can answer their questions and tell them how Jesus has helped you many times and what He has done for you.

What steps will you take today to learn how to speak someone else's language? Will you allow God to use you in this way, even if it means you might have to get out of your comfort zone? Are you willing to be the one God uses to reach those who some consider "unreachable"?

Today's Prayer

Father,

Help us learn to speak languages that are different. Thank You for reminding us we need to convey Your truth with knowledge to others.

Amen.

Brothers, will it help you if I come to you speaking in different languages? No! It will help you only if I bring you a new truth or some knowledge, or some prophecy, or some teaching.

—1 Corinthians 14:6

November 8

Nobody Did It

Did you grow up with siblings? Maybe you are an only child, and you didn't have any brothers or sisters, but did you have pets? I was blessed to grow up with two brothers and a sister, although I didn't count it so much "blessed" during our growing-up years.

Apparently, we had a fifth sibling: the one that was always getting into trouble! His name was Nobody. Did you grow up with Nobody? I can remember our mom asking who did something, and each of us four kids would say, "I didn't do it" or "I don't know what happened." Mom was always saying, "Well, I guess Nobody did it again!"

Today, the Lord reminded me of a story I heard several years ago about four people: Everybody, Somebody, Anybody and Nobody. Have you ever heard the story? Something important needed to be done. Everybody thought Somebody would do it, Anybody could have done it, but Nobody did it! It makes me wonder if that's where they got the idea for the song "Nobody."

Can you even imagine all the things God wants to accomplish, realizing He could do it all on His own? He doesn't need our help; He simply wants us to join Him in what He's doing and be a part of it with Him! Isn't it wonderful how He loves to use the ones considered a Nobody by the world's standard?

He has plenty of things He wants Everybody to do! Somebody could choose to do them, and Anybody is welcome to join in, but as usual, Nobody is the one who winds up doing it! I wonder which person you are today? Are you Everybody? Are you Somebody? Are you Anybody? Or are you the Nobody He can count on to join with

Him and get it done? Which one would you like to be? Will they be talking about you when they say, "Nobody did it!"

Today's Prayer

Father,

Thank You for using those of us who feel so unqualified and unworthy to help further Your kingdom. Thank You for reminding us today that You will always be with us when You call us to do something for You.

Amen.

But Moses said, "Who am I to go to the king and lead your people out of Egypt?" God replied, "I will be with you. And you will know that I am the one who sent you, when you worship Me on this mountain after you have led My people out of Egypt."

—Exodus 3:11–12

November 9

Come on Home

A great man of God was welcomed to his eternal home in Heaven yesterday morning around eight twenty-five. I only knew this man for six short years, but what an impact he had on my life in that short time! I believe he was ninety-three years young, but if that's not correct, it is close. He lived a long life. A lot of people would probably say he lived a good, long life, but I imagine Uncle Jr. would probably say, "Well, the last fifty-one years were good, anyway." I say that because of his testimony.

Apparently, he lived a pretty rough life before he met Jesus on July 18, 1968. But, after giving his life to Jesus, he had some good years, indeed. He was a member of a quartet that went, probably, a little bit of everywhere sharing Jesus through music. In fact, he is probably known most for singing his testimony in "The Apple Tree Song." Thanks to him giving us a CD, I was able to listen to him sing that song this morning, and it touched me in a special way!

Hearing him sing about being welcomed home after he had been away for so long made me think of how welcomed he was yesterday as he entered the gates of Heaven! What rejoicing there was, I'm sure! While we, who are left here, are sad because we miss him so much already. There is a way we can see him again, though.

We were told, however, that before Uncle Jr. left us yesterday morning, he had the opportunity (the day before, I think) to speak with each of his children, individually. He asked them would he get to see them in Heaven one day.

What would your answer be? Will you get to see your loved ones again in Heaven one day? Have you accepted Christ as your personal Savior and asked Him to forgive your sins? If you haven't, will you do it today? Do you know that is the only way you'll be able to hear Him one day say, "Come on home"?

Today's Prayer

Father,

Thank You for welcoming us into Your family no matter how far away we may have roamed. And, today, Father, I want to personally thank You for welcoming Uncle Jr. to his eternal home with You yesterday morning.

Amen.

So he returned home to his father. And while he was still a long way off, his father saw him coming. Filled with love and compassion, he ran to his son, embraced him and kissed him.

—Luke 15:20 (NLT)

November 10

Preapproved

How many offers do you receive in the mail saying you are "preapproved"? Sometimes, we receive two or three the same day! They immediately go in the trash, but this morning, as I was throwing yet another one away, I had a thought I'd never had before when I saw the word *preapproved.*

I suddenly felt in my spirit, "Yes! I was preapproved! So is everyone else in this world!" You were preapproved by Jesus when He died on the cross! Does that mean you don't have to do anything else? Of course not!

When you receive those "preapproved" offers in the mail, you still have to give them more information, correct? In fact, if you open it and read the letter, you will see words like, "You've already been preapproved. Act now!" and "If you apply and are approved"—so, you aren't actually approved, you are, as clearly stated, "preapproved."

Jesus's death on the cross preapproved you for Heaven. But, you still have to accept Him as your personal Savior. You have to ask Him to forgive your sins and invite Him into your heart. When you do that, then you are approved! It doesn't matter where you were before or what you have done before. Once you come to Him, in full confession and true repentance, you are approved!

Another thing that caught my eye on this "preapproved" offer? *Time-sensitive!* You only have a certain amount of time to respond to the offer. If you don't respond in that time frame, the offer is null and void—no longer any good.

That is also true of the offer from Jesus. While you may not like to think about it, you only have a certain amount of time to respond to His offer of eternal life with Him in Heaven. Unlike the offers you receive in the mail that have a written, definite expiration date, you don't know how long you have to respond to Christ's offer. He is the only One Who knows your expiration date.

Therefore, don't take a lot of time trying to make up your mind. Don't wait too long to make the best decision of your entire life! If you have already accepted His offer, great! If not, why not do it today? He's waiting for you.

Today's Prayer

Father,

Thank You for treating us better than we deserve and for accepting us because of Christ Jesus and setting us free from our sins. Amen.

But God treats us much better than we deserve and because of Christ Jesus, He freely accepts us and sets us free from our sins.

—Romans 3:24

November 11

Reminiscing

Sitting at the kitchen table, listening to my husband and his cousin talk about the bygone days, days of their youth, growing up near each other and the mischief they used to get into—it started me thinking about something else.

One thing you tend to do when you lose a family member is begin to reminisce. You begin to talk about all the wild and crazy times, and you laugh at things now that when they actually happened, you weren't laughing at all! Isn't it funny how time turns things around like that?

It started me thinking about the conversations we might have with the Father, Jesus and the Holy Spirit one day. Yes, I realize, once we are in Heaven, we will be busy worshiping and praising; but just for a moment, let your imagination take over.

Can you, for just a minute, imagine sitting around the table with the Trinity and talking about bygone days? Can you imagine saying something like, "Father, remember the time You allowed me to have what I was asking for and what a fiasco it turned out to be? And how You had to have the Holy Spirit eventually guide me out of the mess I had created because I didn't realize I didn't need what I was asking for?"

Can you think of a particularly hard struggle you had with something and imagine yourself saying, at that table in Heaven, "Father, remember the time I was having that hard struggle with _____ [you name whatever it was], and You had the Holy Spirit give Your unexplainable peace to me?" "Father, remember the day I was ready to accept Jesus Christ as my personal Lord and Savior?"

Now, these kinds of conversations will most likely never take place, but what if they could? Would you get to have a conversation like that around the table with God, the Father; Your Lord, Jesus Christ, God's Son; and Your Comforter, the Holy Spirit? Do you know Him? Have you given your life to Him? Why or why not?

Today's Prayer

Father,

Thank You for preparing a place where we can be with You forever. What a grand time it will be!

Amen.

After I go and prepare a place for you, I will come back. Then I will take you to be with Me so that you may be where I am.

—John 14:3 (ICB)

November 12

Clear the Land

Yesterday, I heard something I thought was going to be spiritual—turned out to be a commercial. But, God used it to speak to my heart. I wrote it down so I wouldn't forget: "Before building can begin, the land must be cleared."

How true and logical that is. If you buy a piece of land, full of trees and covered in weeds and bramble, you can't just start building on it. You have to clear it first, *then* you can begin to build.

Don't you know it's the same way in your Christian walk? You can't begin to build your faith or your Christian life until some clearing out is done first. Clearing out your heart is absolutely the first step when you start your journey with Jesus.

It's not something you can do on your own. In fact, I would venture to say it isn't really something you can do at all. The biggest part you can play in the clearing is to give Jesus permission to move in and start doing it for you.

Let Him tell you the things that need to go. Only you and He know what's in your heart; therefore, you can't listen to what anyone else says. You can only listen to Him and trust Him to know what's best for you.

Other people, your Christian brothers and sisters, may give you advice about how to "clear the land that is your heart"—it's okay to listen to them. The Lord may use some of them to speak to you about something. But, before you do anything, take it to the Lord first! Let Him be the One Who has the final say in what needs to be cleared out. He may find some good trees in there that He wants you to keep. He may find some pretty flowers among the weeds and the bramble. Once He gets the land of your heart cleared out, though, get ready! He will begin to build your Christian life by building your faith and your trust in Him. It won't always be easy, but He'll be there with you and for you, and He will see you through each and every process.

Are you ready to let Him clear the land of your heart and start building?

Today's Prayer

Father,

Cleanse us from our guilt and purify us from our sin. In so doing, You are clearing the land before You start building our faith and our Christian lives.

Amen.

Wash me clean from my guilt. Purify me from my sin.

—Psalm 51:2 (NLT)

November 13

The Power

Music has been part of my life as long as I can remember. The words in a song will sometimes minister to me more than hearing a spoken message. Lately, Father has made me even more keenly aware of the words in different songs. As if He is asking, "Do you really know what you are saying when you sing this? Are you paying attention?"

Confession: A lot of times, the answer to both those questions is *no*. Sadly—full confession here—most of the time, I would find myself just singing along with the song and not really paying a lot of attention to what I was saying/singing.

This happened again yesterday while hubby and I were travelling back home. This song started playing on the radio; and I, as usual, began singing along. Suddenly, Father made me very aware of the words, and I just stopped and began to cry as I realized what they were.

It suddenly hit me, and I thought, "If we—I—could truly grasp what these words were saying, I could/would live a much different life!" The song was "Same Power" by Jeremy Camp, and it is based on Romans 8:11, where it talks about the power that raised Christ from the dead being in us.

If I—if you could truly grasp what the Father is telling us here, we would definitely live different lives. Maybe it's just me. Maybe you have grasped what He is telling you here. Maybe you are already living and working in that power. If so, kudos to you! I want to live and work there, and I'm asking Him to help me be able to do so.

It's not saying you have power and can go do any- and everything you want. It's not you that has the power, it is God; but, He has placed this power in you, through Christ! If you submit to Him, He will allow you to operate in His power, and you will do even greater things than Christ did (John 14:12)!

Today's Prayer

Father,

Thank You for speaking to us about the power You have placed in us. It isn't us, it isn't our power; rather, it is Your power *in* us, and if we will truly trust in You, You can do great things through us in Your power!

Amen.

The Spirit of God, who raised Jesus from the dead, lives in you. And just as God raised Christ Jesus from the dead, he will give life to your mortal bodies by this same Spirit living within you.

—Romans 8:11 (NLT)

November 14

My Way

Are you old enough to remember a song that talked about doing things "my way"? Do you think you are doing things your way today? Do you want to?

I remember singing along with that song and really liking it. However, looking at the lyrics today, it makes me cringe. Perhaps, because now, having grown in my relationship with the Lord, it is easy to see how every line in this song goes against everything Jesus not only taught but also showed us.

The same way that Christ was here to do His Father's will, we are to do the same. We don't plan our course—not if we belong to Him. Look what it says in Psalm 37:23, "The steps of a good man are ordered by the Lord, And He delights in his way." That tells us the Lord is the One Who orders our steps, if we belong to Him.

Do you think you are so good at planning your entire life? Do you get mad, angry or upset when things don't go your way? If you love the Lord with all your heart, mind and soul (Matthew 22:37), then you should be glad you don't have to worry about planning your life. After all, don't you find comfort in knowing your steps are planned (ordered) by the One Who sees not only today, but yesterday and tomorrow too? He sees the big picture, while all you can see is what is right in front of you.

Jesus knew He was here to do His Father's will and not what He wanted or would like to do. He knew He was here not only to teach us how we should live, but also to show us how. He knew He was born to die for our sins, to make a way for us to be with Him and the Father and the Holy Spirit in Heaven; yet, He still prayed in the garden, "My Father, if it is possible, don't make Me suffer by having Me drink from this cup. But do what You want and not what I want."

Aren't you glad you can trust Him to do what is best for you? He will never lead you in the wrong direction, and if you make a wrong turn on your own, He will lovingly guide you back to the right path, if you only ask. Life goes much better when you do things His way instead of your way.

Today's Prayer

Father,

Thank You for reminding us we are here to do Your will and not just what we want to do. Help us to live this way.

Amen.

I came down from Heaven to do what God wants Me to do. I did not come to do what I want to do.

—John 6:38 (ICB)

November 15

The Victory Walk

Have you ever found yourself in the middle of a battle you did not choose? In other words, you didn't do anything wrong, yet you find yourself in the middle of what seems like full-on war?

We just talked about this not long ago. When God allows a battle you did not choose, He will fight it for you, and you don't have to do anything but face it, remember?

Do you find that hard to do—trust Him with the battle? In our human weakness, that is understandable. It's easy for us to *say* we trust Him with it, it is quite another to actually put that trust into action.

Trust is an action? Absolutely! If you trust someone or something, your actions will show it and will prove that trust. For instance, you act on your trust every time you sit on a couch or a stool or a chair or anything. You trust the object you are going to sit on will support you, and you show that trust by sitting on the object. Makes sense, right?

Do you trust God the same way? When you find yourself surrounded by enemies and you ask Him to help you and you trust He is going to fight the battle for you, do your actions prove out that trust?

Do you walk in victory, or do you still walk around worrying about what might happen if...? You know, letting the enemy pull you into his game of "What if," which we also talked about earlier.

Find comfort in today's verse. Let it really sink in. It says that *on the day* you call for help—not tomorrow or the next day, the very day! The very minute you call on Him, it is done! Now, start walking in that victory! Hold your head high and let everyone know, that no matter what happens, you know God has already defeated your enemy! Let others *see* you walking in that victory, not being pulled into the enemy's what-if game! WALK THE VICTORY WALK!

Today's Prayer

Father,

Thank You for reminding us our enemies are defeated the very day, the very minute, we call on You for help! Thank You for being on our side and fighting for us, whether we chose the battle or not! Amen.

On the day I call for help, my enemies will be defeated. I know that God is on my side.

—*Psalm 56:9 (ICB)*

November 16

Are You Mad?

We've been talking about battles that choose us, even though we did nothing to cause it. We've talked about how those are the battles we know, beyond the shadow of a doubt, God will fight for us, if we allow Him to do so. But one thing we haven't discussed is how those battles might make us feel. It is highly possible it just might make us feel mad or angry. Do you think it's okay to be mad at God? Do you sometimes feel anger toward Him, but because you are a Christian, you try to hide it or cover it up or stuff it down inside yourself?

Why—or how—did we get to the place where we think it is wrong to be angry at God? If you read the Bible, you see several people who not only got angry or mad at God, they voiced their anger as well. David showed his anger many times. Even Jesus, God's own Son, cried out, "My God, My God, why have You forsaken Me?" (Matthew 27:46).

Do you think God can't handle your anger? Let me assure you, He can. He is a big God! Not only can He handle it, He already knows about it anyway. So, when you don't voice it to Him, you are lying to Him. Don't you think it would be better to voice it? Just cry out to Him and tell Him how mad you are and why. He can handle it. No, He may not instantly make your circumstances go away, but you will get closer to Him because you will have removed that wall you put up. It is more important to be honest with Him than to try to cover up or stuff your true feelings. As stated before, He already knows anyway!

When you start crying out to Him and telling Him exactly how you feel, you are letting go of the anger. You are not allowing it to stay inside you where it can grow and get worse. Giving it to God is the best way to deal with it and start the healing process. So, if you are angry or mad at God today, will you just start telling Him right now? He can handle it, and you will begin to feel better. Don't know how to start? Read some of the psalms—Psalm 22:1–2, Psalm 55:2 and Psalm 44:23–24, just to name a few. He's waiting for you. Are you ready to start the healing process?

Today's Prayer

Father,

Thank You for allowing us to share everything with You, including our anger from time to time. Thank You for taking care of us and always being there for us. We know You will never let us down.

Amen.

Give your worries to the Lord. He will take care of
you. He will never let good people down.

—Psalm 55:22 (ICB)

November 17

Before You Were Born

You made all the delicate, inner parts of my body and knit me together in my mother's womb. Thank You for making me so wonderfully complex! Your workmanship is marvelous—how well I know it. You watched me as I was being formed in utter seclusion, as I was woven together in the dark of the womb. You saw me before I was born. Every day of my life was recorded in Your book. Every moment was laid out before a single day had passed. (Psalm 139:13–16 NLT)

Is that hard for you to comprehend? In your mind, is that something that's nearly impossible to even imagine? Yet, it's true, and you know it's true because it is in God's Word.

Well, today I want to tell you something else that is in God's Word, and if the verses above nearly blow your mind, you will be blown away for sure by this little bit of information. This is something that was brought to my attention a couple of weeks ago in a Wednesday night Bible study.

As you learn God loved you before He created you in your mother's womb, try to imagine the fact that He loved you even before He created the world! Say whaaaat? Yes! It is true, as evidenced by today's scripture! In fact, back up one verse, and read what it says in verse 3: "All praise to God, the Father of our Lord Jesus Christ, who has blessed us with every spiritual blessing in the heavenly realms because we are united with Christ."

So, He not only loved you before He even created the world, He blessed you with every spiritual blessing in the heavenly realms! What a difference this will make in your life, if you will meditate on it and let it begin to sink in! What *Godfidence* you could walk in if you will let this realization permeate your being! He loved you *and* blessed you with every spiritual blessing *before* He created the world! It's true. His Word says it. Will you receive it today?

Today's Prayer

Father,

It is so hard for us to comprehend how You loved and chose us in Christ before You even created the world! It's hard enough to imagine You loving us before we were in our mother's womb, yet both these statements are true. All we can do is say "thank You."

Amen.

Even before He made the world, God loved us and chose us in Christ to be holy and without fault in His eyes.

—Ephesians 1:4 (NLT)

November 18

Another Chance

If you are reading this, it means God woke you up this morning. He continued to breathe life into you throughout the night and allowed you to see another day. What will you do with this day? Do you realize what a gift He has given you by waking you this morning?

You have another fresh, clean start. Another chance to get it right. Another day to allow Him to use you to shine His light on someone who may be in a dark place.

Another chance to make good choices, Godly choices. Another day to choose to serve Him by serving others. Another chance to be either a planter, a waterer, a fertilizer or a harvester or maybe even all those things at different times during the day with different seeds. (Tomorrow, we will talk more about those things.) Ask Him to use you in whichever capacity He needs you and to help you be whichever one it is.

He has given you a very special gift by giving you another day. Ask Him to give you an awareness for the divine appointments He has for you today. When you think you are being interrupted by someone or something, take a moment to stop and think. Maybe this is not an interruption at all, but, instead, a divine appointment.

Arise, shine; For your light has come! And the glory of the Lord is risen upon you. (Isaiah 60:1 NKJV)

Did you know the glory of the Lord rose upon you this morning? This is the day the Lord made, let us rejoice and be glad in it

(Psalm 118:24)! Will you bless Him every day and praise His name forever and ever (Psalm 145:2)?

When you choose to look at every day as another chance for all these things, you will begin to see things differently. You may even begin to think different, and after all, thinking different is what it takes to live different. Are you glad this morning for another chance today?

Today's Prayer

Father,

Thank You for daily renewal of our inward man. A new chance to make right choices and let Your light shine through us!

Amen.

Therefore, we do not lose heart. Even though our outward man is perishing, yet the inward man is being renewed day by day.

—2 Corinthians 4:16 (NKJV)

November 19

All about the Harvest

What does it mean to be a planter? It simply means you could be the one God chooses to plant the seed of salvation in another person. You may talk to them about what Christ has done for you and how God moves in your life, and you may even share scripture with this person. Even if they don't accept Christ as their Savior when you share these things, you have planted the seed. You were a planter.

What is a waterer? You could be the one God uses to water the seed that was planted by someone else. There are a number of different ways He could do this. You might share with that person things God has done for you in your life, share some more scripture, or they may simply see the way you live your everyday life, and it causes them to think they want the same thing. In doing any of these things, you have just watered the seed that was planted earlier.

But, seriously, a fertilizer? Yes, you could be the fertilizer God uses to germinate the seed and help it grow. You could help it grow because this person now sees yet another example of how God works in people's lives.

Finally, we come to the harvester. You know God is the harvester. He is the only One Who can do the harvesting; however, He just might choose you to be the one who is with this person when that previously planted, watered and fertilized seed is ready to harvest. While you aren't the one responsible for the harvest, it is wonderful to share in it when it happens!

It is possible God may use you to be all these things in one day to different people. The important thing is for you to remain obedient to Him and do whatever He asks you to do, whether it be to plant, water, fertilize or witness the harvest. Are you willing to do/be any or all of these things for Him?

Today's Prayer

Father,

Thank You for reminding us that each job is important, and it doesn't matter if we plant, water, fertilize or see the harvest. It only matters that we are obedient to do what You ask us to do.

Amen.

I planted the seeds, Apollos watered them, but God made them sprout and grow. What matters isn't those who planted or watered, but God Who made the plants grow. The one who plants is just as important as the one who waters. And each one will be rewarded for what they do.

—1 Corinthians 3:6–8

November 20

Needle and Thread

One thing I am not is a seamstress. I never had any interest in learning to sew because I watched my mother have so many headaches from sewing. My mother may not have been a seamstress either, but she could sew well enough to make our clothes for us when we were growing up.

I learned a few things about sewing—very few! I learned how to sew a hem, how to sew on a button and how to make small, minor repairs to seams that became "unsewed," as I called it!

Did you know there is one very interesting fact about sewing that a lot of people don't even pay attention to? I'm not sure why they don't, but they just don't even seem to think about it! Would you like to know the interesting fact I'm talking about?

No matter who is sewing, no matter what they are creating, this one thing is true of every single person who sews anything—by machine or by hand! There is no getting around it; this must happen for anything to be sewn, knitted or even crocheted: the thread must follow the needle! Without the needle guiding it, the thread would just lie there and be of no use whatsoever. But when the thread is in the needle, it follows the needle wherever it goes!

Think of it this way: The needle represents the Father, and the thread represents you. When you give your life to Him, you need to be willing to follow wherever He leads you—even somewhere you may think you don't want to go. If the thread doesn't follow the needle, it can get all knotted up and tangled and be in a big mess! The most wonderful news, though, is that even if you do mess up by not following Him, He will lovingly untangle the knots and straighten out the mess and continue to create something beautiful with the thread! Are you willing to be the thread? Would you pray, "Father, You be the needle, and I will be the thread following wherever You lead. Amen."

Today's Prayer

Father,

Thank You that we can know Your voice by reading Your Word. Help us listen closely and follow Your voice. Help us to be the thread in Your needle, following wherever You lead.

Amen.

When he has led out all of his sheep, he walks in front of them and they follow, because they know his voice.

—John 10:4

November 21

Developing Discernment

Today's devotion certainly fits in this book, *Challenging Encouragement*. God has been encouraging me through it this morning, yet as encouraging as it is, it is also challenging. It is a hard one to hear, even harder to write, and it will probably not be easy for you to read.

For quite a while I have been praying for discernment, and I know He has been giving it to me. (Now, I'm asking Him to continue developing it—you'll understand in a minute.) While it is something every Christian should have (see 1 Thessalonians 5:20–22), it carries a responsibility along with it. A responsibility to speak up when you hear false teachings etc.

A lot of Christians today—and non-Christians, for that matter—use the scripture in Matthew 7:1 the wrong way. This verse is talking about hypocritical judging of others and judging what their thoughts or motives are. Christians, however, are responsible for judging what others teach in Jesus's name. If you are a Christian and you aren't able to discern when someone is teaching something false, you will be easily fooled by the false prophets and messiahs that are here, and you run the risk of being fooled by the antichrist, as well (2 Thessalonians 2:3–4). Don't leave your Bible on a shelf during the week—read it for yourself! Reading His Word for yourself is the only way you will be able to discern false teaching from anyone!

Keep your spiritual eyes and ears open at all times, and you will begin to get better and better at just knowing in your knower when something is real and when it isn't. Oh my! God just dropped this little tidbit in my ear—we don't even have to ask for discernment! He gave it to us when we accepted Christ as our Savior. We just need to ask Him to help us develop it!

Don't be one who refuses to love the truth, leaving yourself open to the enemy and his wily ways! Be encouraged in knowing you will recognize his evil schemes, if you love the Lord and let His Word get inside you!

Today's Prayer

Father,

Please develop, in each of us, our spirit of discernment so we may know the false messiahs and prophets and not be fooled by them or their seemingly great miracles and signs.

Amen.

False messiahs and false prophets will come and work great miracles and signs. They will even try to fool God's chosen ones.

—Matthew 24:24

November 22

No Doubt

Years ago I wrote this phrase, "If you walk with Mr. Doubt, you will be left out!" in the front cover of one of my Bibles. I wish I had written who I heard say it, but I didn't. It is so true, though! Doubt is another huge tool the enemy uses to stop us from receiving what is rightfully ours as children of the Most High God.

When you pray, do you pray honestly believing you will receive, and are you ready to receive what you are praying for? Or, do you continue to doubt? Just like the people who were gathered at the home of Mary, the mother of John, to pray for Peter's release from prison. While they were praying for his release, he knocked on the outer door, and a servant girl went to answer it. She recognized Peter's voice and was so excited she ran back to tell everyone and didn't open the door for him! She ran and told them all, "Peter is at the door!"

But, did they get as excited as she was and run to the door to let him in? No! They told her she must be out of her mind, yet she kept insisting, and they told her it must be his angel. All the while, Peter kept knocking, and when they finally opened the door and saw him, they were absolutely amazed!

Why were they so amazed? Hadn't they been praying for his release? If they were praying, truly believing they would receive what they were praying for, wouldn't they have been excited to hear he was at the door?

So, you see, doubt isn't something new. The enemy has used doubt for a very long time, and he uses it a lot because it is so effective for him! Imagine what could/would happen if you could get to the place where you no longer doubted? You simply take God at His Word, believing you will receive what He has for you? Oh, I confess.

I'm certainly not there yet either, but I am becoming more and more aware of when I am doubting, and I am striving toward getting rid of it. Would you join me on that journey of removing doubt? If you will, ask God to help you become more aware of when you are doubting. He will, and you will be amazed at the things that begin to happen!

Today's Prayer

Father,

Please help us be ready to accept the miracles You send our way and not to doubt.

Amen.

"You are crazy!" everyone told her. But she kept saying that it was Peter. Then they said, "It must be his angel."

—Acts 12:15

November 23

Just Wait

As I sat here this morning, reading scripture after scripture to try to hear what God was wanting to share with me this morning, I got nothing! I thought, "Okay, Father. I guess You are going to give it to me later in the day, as You do sometimes." All I kept hearing was "Just wait."

So, I thought I was listening to Him by going back to bed for a little while and waiting 'til later in the day for the word He wanted to speak to me. As soon as I got in bed, I realized He *was* giving me what He wanted to share with me.

Have you ever been one to pray for patience? Have you ever prayed, "Lord, give me patience, but hurry!"? If so, I'm sure you found out what happens when you pray for patience, right? You get to go through all kinds of trials to help you get that patience you prayed for! I always say, "I learned a long time ago not to pray for patience, and I'm certainly not going to pray for anyone else to have patience!" But, you know what He told me this morning? He has given me patience. I am much better about being patient in some situations than I used to be. So, I'm glad I asked for it because, in looking back, I can see how He has done a work in me. Oh, I've certainly not arrived yet, especially in the patience department, but I can see the huge work He has done.

Just like this morning, I was willing to be patient and wait for Him to share with me later in the day, and then I realized He was giving me the devotion all along! He was saying, "Just wait"! He wants you to know you need to wait on Him. There are many verses that talk about waiting: Lamentations 3:25, Psalm 27:14, Psalm 37:4, Psalm 37:7, Psalm 40:1 and Psalm 130:5, just to name a few.

Have you been praying and seeking Him for an answer to something? Be assured, He has heard you, and He has an answer on the way. If you will continue to pray and trust Him, He will reveal it to you when the time comes. It may seem last minute to you, but He will never let you down!

Today's Prayer

Father,

Thank You for reminding us to wait on You. We can trust You hear our every prayer, and we can trust You to answer.

Amen.

Therefore, I will look to the Lord; I will wait for the God of my salvation; My God will hear me.

—Micah 7:7 (NKJV)

November 24

To Whom Should We Pray?

Do you ever get confused about Who you should be praying to? I'm not talking about praying to any false god, I'm talking about the Trinity: God the Father, God the Son and God the Holy Spirit. Am I the only one who ever got confused on all that? I'm thinking not, or Father wouldn't have given me this message for today.

You all know I write in my prayer journal every morning. I always start by saying, "Good morning, Father! Thank You for waking me this morning." So, yes, I generally am praying to the Father. I've always felt this was okay because I have accepted Jesus as my Savior, and I am covered by His blood. He died so I could have access to the Father. Ephesians 2:18 tells us, "And because of Christ, all of us can come to the Father by the same Spirit."

Then there are some days when I question—what about the Son and the Holy Spirit? Am I leaving them out of the equation? I do know they are the Trinity, the Three in One, so why do I feel I'm wrong some mornings—or any other time of day that I find myself praying. Actually, other times during the day, I do find myself calling on Jesus or the Holy Spirit.

I felt Father whisper in my ear this morning to "search the scripture about it and share what you find," so I did. Here's what I found: God the Father designed the plan (see Galatians 4:4–5). He was the planner. Jesus the Son carried out the plan (see John 6:37–38). He was the means. The Holy Spirit was the applier (see John 14:26, John 16:8 and Romans 1:19–20). He is the One that convicts you of your sin, and when you accept Jesus as your Savior, He transforms your life and heart. He also prays for you when you don't know what to pray.

So, you see, it doesn't really matter because when you pray to One, you are praying to all three. You can pray to the Father through the Son by the power of the Holy Spirit. The important thing is to pray! And remember to listen too.

Today's Prayer

Father,

Son and Holy Spirit: we are so blessed to have Three in One, the Triune God, One God, yet three. Thankful we can pray to the Father through the Son by the power of the Holy Spirit.

Amen.

For there are three that bear witness in Heaven: the Father, the Word and the Holy Spirit; and these three are One.

—1 John 5:7 (NKJV)

November 25

Army of Angels

Did you know you have an entire army of angels just waiting to fight for you? Did you also know they can't do anything until you give them permission? How do you give them permission to help you? Let's explore that today.

God tells us in His Word that He has assigned angels to help you, to keep charge over you (Psalm 91:11–12). But, before the angels can do anything, you must give them permission. They can only do their job when you release them to do it. How do you release them?

Angels obey God's Word; when they hear His Word, they obey. Psalm 103:20 (ICB) says, "You who are His angels, praise the Lord. You are the mighty warriors who do what He says. Listen to what He says." So, you release them to work (give them permission) when you speak His Word.

If you are speaking anything besides His Word, the angels are helpless to help you. So, if you are always talking about how you're in so much pain or how you're in so much debt, those things will continue to be true. However, if you will command your angels by speaking God's Word to them, then they can go to work to change things. You are putting your faith into action when you do this!

But, they won't do anything—they can't do anything—until you call for them! Remember what Jesus said in Matthew 26:53? "Don't you know that I could ask my Father and right away He would send Me more than twelve armies of angels?"

You have God's Word, and God's Word is alive, which means it has the same power coming out of your mouth as it did when it came out of Jesus's mouth. It's not you that has the power, it is God's Word, and His angels obey His Word! If you haven't already, start putting them to work for you today!

Today's Prayer

Father,

Thank You for giving us angels to protect us wherever we go. Thank You for them carrying us in their arms and not letting us hurt our feet on the stones.

Amen.

God will command His angels to protect you wherever you go. They will carry you in their arms, and you won't hurt your feet on the stones.

—Psalm 91:11–12

November 26

Quickly and Completely

Have you ever read or written out a scripture passage and all of a sudden you see something you never saw before? Sometimes, reading or writing scripture in different translations will help you do this. A while back, it happened to me as I was writing out Colossians 3:13 in the Message translation.

> *Be even-tempered, content with second place,*
> *quick to forgive an offense. Forgive as quickly and*
> *completely as the Master forgave you.*

Two words in that translation really jumped out at me. Do you see them? Did the same two jump out at you? The words? *Quickly* and *completely.*

Have you ever been so angry you thought you would never forgive someone for what they did? I'm talking about "chew up nails and spit them out" angry at someone. Or maybe you thought to yourself, as I have on a few occasions, "Oh, I'll forgive that person, eventually, but, it's going to take some time. They just need to keep their distance from me in the meantime."

Ouch! Do you see why that thought—or sentiment—is not okay with God? How many times do we disappoint Him in one day? How would you feel if God told you that when you went to Him asking for forgiveness? He never does that to us. He is always waiting, ready, not only to forgive us but also to completely forgive, not holding anything back! So, you not only need to forgive quickly, you need to forgive completely!

This scripture really stepped on my toes a lot! Did it step on yours? Read this scripture several times throughout the day. Think on it, let it get down in your innermost being. Will you let it begin to change the way you think?

Today's Prayer

Father,

Help us remember to forgive others quickly and completely, the same way You forgive us when we do wrong. Help us learn to love others as You love us—unconditionally.

Amen.

> *Be even-tempered, content with second place, quick to forgive an offense. Forgive as quickly and completely as the Master forgave you. And regardless of what else you put on, wear love. It's your basic, all-purpose garment. Never be without it.*

> —*Colossians 3:13 (MSG)*

November 27

Excitement Is Building

You have doubtless heard it many times before: You cannot go on your feelings! Your feelings will lie to you in a heartbeat! Your feelings are a tool the enemy loves to use to get inside your head and mess with your mind!

In my quiet time this morning with the Father, I was finding it hard to keep my focus on Him. I was beginning to think, "Why am I having such a hard time this morning? Maybe I'm just not sincere enough, or maybe I just don't really know how to do this." I never even asked Him to help me. I didn't have to because, before I knew it, He took over without me even realizing it! Just as I began to have those feelings of inadequacy, I stopped and began to think about all the amazing things He has waiting for me and my husband. We are in the middle of a battle that chose us, so we are doing our best to stay out of it and let the Lord fight it for us. But, this morning, as I began to ponder all the amazing things He has in store for us—for our ministry—I began to feel the excitement building! Why? I have no idea what God has in store for us, but I know He gives good gifts to His children (Matthew 7:11)!

As I began to ponder on Him and how amazing He is, He immediately responded by filling me to overflowing, and I didn't even have to ask! Yes, serving the Lord can be scary sometimes when the battles come, and you have no idea what's going on or why He allowed it, but the upside is this: when you are serving the Lord, you know, beyond the shadow of a doubt, that He is in control, and He will take care of everything in His way and in His time! You only need to trust Him completely, sit back and ponder on His Word; remember all the things He has done for you before and how He has never let you down—not even once! Will you take some time to ponder His goodness today? No matter how tough things may seem, just remember He has never left you, and He never will (Deuteronomy 31:6).

Today's Prayer

Father,
Help us slow down as we spend time with You. Whether it be in prayer, reading Your Word or in a group with others. May we, as Mary did, take time to be quiet and ponder in our hearts what You have said to us.
Amen.

But Mary kept all these things and pondered them in her heart.

—Luke 2:19 (NKJV)

November 28

Overflow

Maybe it's not Thanksgiving Day when you read this, but every day is a great day for giving thanks! The Lord knows my mind has been a whirlwind of thoughts this week, and I believe He wants me to share them here today.

Thanksgiving Day has been different for our family for the last few years. Even before my mom moved to Heaven last year, it had been a long time since we all gathered at her house to celebrate the day and be together as a family. We had begun gathering at different places the last few years—my sister's a few times, and one of my brothers' at other times. So, it isn't just because our mom is no longer here that Thanksgiving is different. Last year and this year, though, have been very different for me, as my husband and I moved too far away to just run over to someone's house for dinner and come back home. Am I complaining? No, just stating it like it is. The flip side to that is we are much closer to my daughter and her family now, so they will join us today.

Our table may not be overflowing with so much food you can't sample it all, but there will be plenty to eat and leftovers, I'm sure. One thing our table will be overflowing with is love and thankfulness—not just because it is a special day set aside for giving thanks, but because we are thankful for every day God gives us. Yes, we are even thankful for these hard, difficult, "don't understand why we're having to go through this" times because we know God is in control, and He will always be victorious!

Are you thankful when you face trying times? Are you thankful when things don't go exactly the way you planned or wanted? Do you give thanks in all things the way 1 Thessalonians 5:18 instructs us all to do? Is it easy to be thankful in all things? Of course not, but we must learn how. When you learn how to be thankful, even in the bad or sad times, you begin to understand the fullness of God's grace and mercy. You learn you can trust Him with any- and everything, knowing He has only the absolute best for you! Are you ready for God's best? Will you thank Him for it today, even if you don't understand it?

Today's Prayer

Father,

We have so much to thank You for, but today we want to praise You, simply because You are so good to us and You never fail us.

Amen.

Praise the Lord because He is good to us and His love never fails.

—1 Chronicles 16:34

November 29

Keep It in Perspective

If you live in the South, you know that football is something most people here live and breathe. There are many who won't plan anything that would interfere with their favorite team's football game.

There's a day in November known as Rivalry Saturday in football. It's the day all the major rivalry teams play against each other. Everyone will be posting on Facebook for their team and wondering who will get bragging rights for another year. This brings a thought to my mind about the *real* rivalry. What a difference could be made for an *everlasting, eternal* victory for God's kingdom if they would put as much thought and effort into which "team" they want to be on for that rivalry. You know the rivalry I mean—Jesus versus satan—I mean, we already *know* who the victory goes to, so are we working as hard at winning people over to Him as we are at winning people over to "our" football team?

Don't misunderstand—there's nothing wrong with having some good, clean fun on Rivalry Saturday, and nothing wrong with some good-natured, *fun* ribbing of each other; as long as you keep it in perspective—it's good to be able to have fun and enjoy this day once a year. I'm just saying, don't get so caught up in *temporary* victories that you forget to be fighting for the *eternal victory* that can belong to *everyone!* And the way you respond/react to your team's winning or losing on Rivalry Saturday *can* say a *lot* about the team you're on for eternity. If your team loses, do you get all bent out of shape and get ugly with others? If your team wins, do you mercilessly rub it in the face of the ones who lost? Or do you just say, "Oh well, we'll try again next year"?

Sooooooooo—War Eagle! Roll Tide! Go, 'Noles! Get 'em, Gators!—I don't even begin to know all the rivalry teams that will be playing, but I can say with great confidence, "Gooooo, team Jesus!"

Today's Prayer

Father,

Thank You for allowing us to have fun with our sports teams, but remind us to be even more emphatic and enthusiastic about winning people over to Your team!

Amen.

Do nothing from rivalry or conceit, but in humility count others more significant than yourselves. Let each of you look not only to his own interests, but also to the interests of others.

—Philippians 2:3–4 (ESV)

November 30

Far from Perfect

One thing I've been guilty of in the past is reading a devotional and thinking to myself, "Man! I wish I had it together like the person that wrote this." How silly of me to think that! Just because God chooses to send a message through someone doesn't mean that person has it all together! In fact, He probably uses the ones who are least likely to have it all together. Can I get an Amen on that?

As I've said before, I don't know if He will ever choose to have the devotions He's given me this year put in a book or not; and if He does, all glory, praise and honor to Him and Him alone! I could never give to anyone what He has given to me in writing them this year. So much more than words on a paper. He has used this journey to grow me in ways I never could have imagined, and He has taught me so much! Remember, when you read one of these devotions, He taught me before He allowed me to share it. Many scriptures were read and prayers prayed before a single word was penned.

Today is another prime example. He delivered a lifelong sermon to me in one little verse this morning. It was the first verse of my scripture writing plan, and it is the one I have shared at the end of this devotion. This is a battle I fight daily, almost minute to minute! Using my time wisely—most days, I know I don't. This is something He has been dealing with me about lately, and I am trying to be more conscious of how I'm doing. For a few days, I did great, and then I hit that snag again—being tired when I get home from work, and instead of getting busy doing what I know I should be doing, instead, I to sit on the couch and do nothing. So, you can pray for me in this area of my life.

What about you? Do you use your time wisely? Maybe you struggle with something else that is just as big an obstacle for you as time management seems to be for me. If we will just sincerely ask Him to continue to help us, I know He will. I also know, however, that if we are sincere, we will realize we must also do our part in the process. He won't just hand it to us. My spirit is willing, but my flesh is weak (Matthew 26:41). So, pray for me, and I'll pray for you.

Today's Prayer

Father,

While we make our plans, we understand You are the one that determines our steps. Please teach us to use our time wisely.

Amen.

Teach us to use wisely all the time we have.

—*Psalm 90:12*

December 1

After the Yes

Sitting here this morning, during my prayer time, I began to think of the many different situations my husband and I have been hit with over the last couple of months, and I couldn't help but *praise* the Lord for what He has done in me—even since the beginning of this year.

It began to dawn on me that all I have to do is give Him permission, by saying "Yes, Lord," and He will work in me the changes that need to take place—in my thinking and in my doing. What an awesome, mighty God He is!

Do you find it interesting that you can hear a sermon preached about something, and then, a few weeks later, God really drives it home to you? I find it happening to me a lot lately. For instance, after I wrote the above paragraph in my prayer journal this morning, I remembered hearing a sermon preached a few weeks ago about saying yes to God. I never connected that sermon to what I have been doing this year, until God pointed it out to me this morning! Oh! So, that's what the preacher was talking about!

You can truly tell if you are saying "Yes, Lord" when trials hit. How you handle those trials lets you know if you are allowing Him to make changes in you so that you fully depend on Him and don't get upset or overwrought when the enemy shoots his darts. When our plumbing backed up in a huge way yesterday, I was truly surprised at how I handled it. I know it is only because of the changes I have allowed Him to make in me that I didn't get overwrought. Was I happy about the problem? Of course not! Did I want to just sit and cry? You bet I did! And, I did, for about thirty seconds. Then, I remembered this is God's house and His plumbing, and He will get it corrected at minimal cost to us.

After you say yes to God, He is free to make the same changes in you. He will completely turn around your whole way of thinking, if you let Him. Will you?

Today's Prayer

Father,

Search our hearts, test us and know our anxious thoughts. Show each of us anything in us that is offensive to You and help us get rid of it as You lead us along the path of everlasting life.

Amen.

Search me, O God, and know my heart; test me and know my anxious thoughts. Point out anything in me that offends You and lead me along the path of everlasting life.

—Psalm 139:23–24 (NLT)

December 2

Fight the Good Fight

We (USA) are so far away from the Christian morals our country was founded on that it can be very scary sometimes. He tells us in His Word, though, that it would come to this (Matthew 10:21–23), so why are we surprised?

If you are one of the lost ones who hasn't given your heart to Jesus yet, today's scripture doesn't exactly make you want to raise your hand and say, "Oh! I want to be part of this!" does it?

As a Christian, however, it should give you great hope! Throughout your Christian walk, you have undoubtedly faced many obstacles. But, you also know, when you are facing those obstacles, God is right there with you. He gave you the Holy Spirit to help you, to be your comforter and to intercede for you in prayer, when you don't have a clue what to pray for or even how to pray!

When you face opposition, do not be afraid. Jesus faced opposition when He walked this earth as a man. Why would you think it would be any different or better for you? No matter what opposition you might face, there is one thing you will never have to face, and that is eternal death. Jesus died on the cross so you would have the opportunity for eternal life with Him (John 3:16).

True, He never promised it would be easy, but He did promise He would always be with you and never leave you (Deuteronomy 31:6)! He gives you the armor and the weapons you need. If you haven't already, will you join His army today and fight the good fight (2 Timothy 4:7)?

Today's Prayer

Father,

Give us the strength we need in these last days to stand strong in You. Help us be ever watchful and know when to speak, waiting for the Spirit to give us the words to say.

Amen.

I am sending you like lambs into a pack of wolves. So be as wise as snakes and as innocent as doves. Watch out for people who will take you to court and have you beaten in their meeting places. Because of Me, you will be dragged before rulers and kings to tell them and the Gentiles about your faith. But when someone arrests you, don't worry about what you will say or how you will say it. At that time, you will be given the words to say. But you will not really be the one speaking. The Spirit from your Father will tell you what to say.

—Matthew 10:16–20

December 3

You Deserve It

It probably goes back further than you could even imagine—all the commercials with companies trying to play on your *ego* to get you to buy or try their product because *you deserve it!*

Dictionary.com defines the word *deserve* as "to merit, be qualified for, or have a claim to (reward, assistance, punishment, etc.) because of actions, qualities, or situation." The world certainly tries hard to get you to believe you deserve the best, you deserve to treat yourself to whatever it is they are trying to sell; and many times, apparently, it works.

Where would you be if you got what you truly deserved? Think about how many times a day you sin, in some fashion. We all do it—we all sin every day! Not one of us is perfect! So, does God give us what we deserve?

Psalm 103:11–14 says, "How great is God's love for all who worship Him? Greater than the distance between Heaven and earth! How far has the Lord taken our sins from us? Farther than the distance from east to west! Just as parents are kind to their children, the Lord is kind to all who worship Him, because He knows we are made of dust." He knows we are nothing without Him, and He chooses to love us anyway! He knows we don't *deserve* to live with Him in Heaven, but He offers it to us anyway!

Yes, He wants you to love yourself. He doesn't, however, want you to love yourself in a prideful, egotistical way. He doesn't want you to put yourself first; He wants you to put others ahead of yourself. You just might be surprised if you begin to love in this way—putting others first.

Start paying attention to the commercials, and every time you see one—or hear one—that says *you deserve it,* let it be a reminder to you to stop and thank Him for *not* giving you what you deserve, but for giving you His mercy and grace!

Today's Prayer

Father,

Thank You for not giving us what we *deserve.* Thank You for giving us, instead, unlimited mercy and grace and forgiveness.
Amen.

The Lord is merciful! He is kind and patient and His love never fails. The Lord won't always be angry and point out our sins; He doesn't punish us as our sins deserve.

—Psalm 103:8–10

December 4

From Hopeless to an Eternal Home

We have been watching the show *Lucky Dog* for a couple of years now. Every time it comes on, the mission statement is proclaimed, which means we have heard it many times over: "From hopeless to a home. That's my mission, one dog at a time." This show is about a man who rescues dogs from shelters, takes them in, trains them and finds them a forever home.

A few weeks back, the show was coming on, and as I heard the statement being made, I felt a quickening in my spirit and thought, "That is exactly what our (Christians) mission statement should be—not about dogs, but about people: 'From hopeless to an *eternal home*! That's our mission, one person at a time.'"

Do you ever get bogged down in wondering what you could do to reach people for the Lord? Do you start thinking, "What can I do? I'm only one person, and I'm no Billy Graham"? God didn't create you to be Billy Graham. He created you to be you! He needs you to reach the people He puts in your path. What might happen if you stopped trying to figure out how you could reach many people and decided to focus on one at a time? Your impact could be huge!

Can you imagine what would begin to happen if you took in just one person? Not literally, but in your heart. What if you took that one person and prayed for them, talked with them and encouraged them? What if you shared the hope you have in Christ Jesus with just that one person, and they accepted Christ as their Savior? What a wonderful, glorious day that would be!

Are you willing to keep your eyes and heart open for the person the Father puts in your path for you to share with? Are you willing to help someone go from being hopeless to having the assurance of an eternal home in Heaven? It's not hard. All you have to do is share your story, in your words. God will do the rest.

Today's Prayer

Father,

Thank You for the hope we have because of Your Son, Jesus Christ of Nazareth. Help us share this hope, one person at a time, that more may come to know You.

Amen.

Honor Christ and let Him be the Lord of your life. Always be ready to give an answer when someone asks you about your hope.

—1 Peter 3:15

December 5

Instruct Each Other

Do you want to know a secret that isn't a secret? God loves you and has chosen you as His own (Colossians 3:12)! How is something a secret that isn't a secret? Well, when something is right in front of you, made available to you, but you just can't believe it.

So many times, that's how it is with Christians. You know Jesus died for your sins, and you accepted that when you asked Him to come into your heart and live and to forgive all your sin. But some of you have a hard time accepting what comes with your acceptance. You just can't quite seem to grasp the idea that God would want to use you to teach and instruct anyone else—especially those who are closest to you and know all your little faults and quirks.

The truth of the matter is this: God wants you to live in harmony (in peace) with everyone. You want to say, "That is impossible," but the hard reality is found in Colossians 1:15, where it says "you are a part of the body of Christ and you were chosen to live together in peace." If He tells us, through His Word, to do something, it is easy for us to do. No, we can't do it in our own strength, we can do it through *His* strength, though! All you have to do is allow the peace that comes from Christ to control your thoughts. The more you choose to do this, the more natural it will become to you.

Then there's that pesky little verse 16—the focal passage for our devotion today—where it says you are to *use your wisdom to teach and instruct each other*. Wait, what? You think you can't instruct anyone else when you're still struggling to try to figure it out on a daily basis? He wouldn't ask You in His Word to do something unless He is going to give you what you need to do it.

So, away with the excuses! It's time to march forward, knowing who You are in Christ Jesus, walking and living in the peace that comes from Him and using the wisdom He gives you to instruct others in the same way!

Today's Prayer

Father,

May the message about Christ completely fill each of our lives. May we use our wisdom to teach and instruct each other and to sing psalms, hymns and spiritual songs to You with thankful hearts.

Amen.

Let the message about Christ completely fill your lives, while you use all your wisdom to teach and instruct each other. With thankful hearts, sing psalms, hymns, and spiritual songs to God.

—Colossians 3:16

December 6

Blessings

What do you immediately think about when you see the word *bless-ings*? Does your mind go to material things like your home, your job, your car, your big fancy television or any of the other gadgets you may have? Or does your mind go to the intangible things like your salvation; God's forgiveness, grace and mercy; the love of your family and friends; and other intangibles?

Let's be honest, we all want our blessings, right? We are all more than ready for God to shower us with them, aren't we? When you see someone who is blessed by the Lord in some way, are you happy for them, or do you find yourself asking, "Why can't you bless me like that, God?" without ever stopping to think about what they went through to receive that blessing?

A song came out a few years back that talked about blessings and asked some hard questions about them also. Do you really want to receive the blessing that other person received, when you realize they had to go through a really dark time in their life to get to the place of being able to receive that blessing?

Do you ever thank Him for your blessings—material or intangible? Or do you take them for granted, as if you are *entitled* to them? Remember when Jesus healed the ten lepers, and only one of them returned to thank Him (Luke 17:11–19)? He asked where the other nine were.

Don't be one of the nine—be the one. The one that returns and says, "Thank You, Lord, for my blessing." Whether you have to go through a hard time or whether He just chooses to bless you because He loves you, always remember to thank Him. Will you choose to thank Him today for the blessings you've already received? Will you share His goodness and faithfulness so others can know Him too?

Today's Prayer

Father,

Thank You for every good and perfect gift You send down to us. You are always the same, and You never cast shadows by changing. Thank You for wanting us to be Your own special people. Thank You for the greatest blessing of all—the true message—so we might have new birth.

Amen.

Every good and perfect gift comes down from the Father who created all the lights in the Heavens. He is always the same and never makes dark shadows by changing. He wanted us to be His own special people, so He sent the true message to give us new birth.

—James 1:17–18

December 7

God's Kisses

You know God loves you. You know He sent His Son, Jesus Christ of Nazareth, to die for your sin. But, have you ever thought about God *kissing* you?

Well, I never really had until this morning. As I was writing the scripture assignment for today, the last verse caught my attention. Apparently, when my eyes saw the word *misses*, they moved ahead and thought they saw something about God's *kisses*, when in reality, it was about God's kindness. However, Father used that to set my mind to thinking, "Do we get kisses from God?" So, of course, I went searching to see if Scripture talked about God *kissing* us. I was surprised at what I found!

In the Old Testament, a kiss was a way to show friendship. Even in the New Testament, Paul speaks of kissing. I found two scriptures where Paul says to "greet one another with a holy kiss" (Romans 16:16 and 1 Corinthians 16:20). He is not talking about a romantic type of kiss, but a holy kiss! What better way for God to show us He cares for us than to *kiss* us from time to time?

I found other references to the *breath of God*, but one that really surprised me was one that spoke of God's breath as a kiss —that He *kissed* us into existence! Oh wow! If that doesn't make your heart melt just a little, you might want to check your spiritual pulse!

What might happen if you made sure no one missed out on God's kindness or His *kisses*? Can you imagine the joy you would receive from watching another person get loved on by Him? What if you allowed Him to kiss and love on you for a little while? He longs to do so, you know? He won't force Himself on you, though. He is a gentleman, and He will wait for you to ask Him—but, when you do, get ready for some life-changing spiritual things to happen in your *spirit man*! You will not be able to remain the same once God has kissed you!

Today's Prayer

Father,

Thank You for using a misread of this verse to show us that You do give us kisses from time to time. Help us be sure no one misses out on Your kindness or Your kisses! Help us encourage all we meet so they won't become bitter and cause trouble.

Amen.

Make sure that no one misses out on God's wonderful kindness. Don't let anyone become bitter and cause trouble for the rest of you.

—Hebrews 12:15

December 8

Generation to Generation

How many times have you heard someone say, "I'm not hurting any-one but myself if I choose to do _____ [you fill in the blank], so leave me alone!" Have you ever said something similar yourself? Me? Guilty as charged, but oh do I have some wonderful news for you today!

What you don't realize, when you are living in sin, is how every choice you make has an eternal impact! Not just for you, but for your children, your grandchildren and your great-grandchildren! Whoa! That is some sobering news, isn't it? It is true though. He tells us in His Word, in Exodus 34:7, "I keep My promises to My people forever, but I also punish anyone who sins. When people sin, I punish them and their children and also their grandchildren and great-grandchildren." That grabs your attention real fast, doesn't it?

When Father showed me that verse this morning, I felt Him speak to my spirit, "I want you to share this with them today to *en*courage them, not to *dis*courage them." You may be wondering how that could be encouraging, right?

It's just like He said: every choice you make affects your family line for years to come, and when you are living in sin, those choices are affecting them in a bad way. But, here's the most wonderful news you could ever hear: once you make the decision to accept Christ and all He has done for you, when you turn around from your old ways and come running straight to Him, then you begin to affect those same generations in a most wonderful way!

Once you are His, you begin to make good choices, and He can pour out His blessings—not only on you, but He will pour blessings on your children, your grandchildren and your great-grandchildren!

No, you aren't suddenly perfect; and yes, you will still make wrong choices sometimes, but your heart is in a different place entirely, and God knows your heart!

Today's Prayer

Father,

Thank You for loving us so much that You would call us Your children! Thank You for reminding us our decisions today definitely impact not only any tomorrows You give us, but also the tomorrows of our children, grandchildren and even our great-grandchildren!

Amen.

Behold what manner of love the Father has bestowed on us, that we should be called children of God!

—1 John 3:1a

December 9

Determination

Have you ever been determined to do something only to lose that determination later? Were you determined in your strength or in the Lord's strength? Sometimes, you may think you are determined in the Lord's strength, only to find out, later, you were fooling yourself. How can you tell where your determination comes from? Most likely in the follow-through. Let me share a personal experience with you to explain why this is on my heart.

Last month, a Facebook memory, from five years ago, popped up; and when I read it, I found myself getting a little sad. Here's what I wrote in that post:

> OH! MY! WOW! Have you EVER imagined what it would be like to live as the person God sees when He looks at you instead of living as the person YOU see when you look at yourself???? All I can say is WOW! God has been showing me, over the last few weeks, how HE sees me and I believe it is time for me to start living in the truth of that! Won't necessarily be easy, but He never promised me easy—only to be here right beside me to help me any time I need Him! Watch out world, cause......... IT. IS. ON! 😊

Powerful, right? I was determined! Or so I thought. Did I really begin to live that way? Maybe, for a few days, and then I allowed the enemy to take it away. Why? Because, apparently, my determination did not come from the power He placed inside me.

When you are determined to do something, you can only do it in His strength. Once you learn to be determined in His strength and power, you really don't have to do anything else because He will take over! He has helped me grow a lot in the last five years; and now, for the most part, I do live as the person I believe He sees when He looks at me. But, it didn't happen overnight for me. It took much prayer and surrender. Where does your determination come from? Don't wait five years; grab hold of His power and see what happens today!

Today's Prayer

Father,

Thank You that we are mistaken when we try to do things in our own strength and not Yours. We have Your power inside us, and we ask You to help us learn how to rely on it.

Amen.

Jesus replied, "Your mistake is that you don't know the Scriptures and you don't know the power of God."

—Matthew 22:29 (NLT)

December 10

The Gift of Peace

Before you became a Christian, you probably heard others talk about having a peace they didn't understand and couldn't explain, right? You probably also heard them talk about loving the Lord with all your heart. But, did you ever imagine that one had anything to do with the other? I sure didn't—until I read that verse this morning and this thought went through my head, "How can you have the peace I have given you if you don't love Me with all your heart, soul and mind?"

I was just searching for the scripture He wanted to use to speak to me this morning. Because of something happening in my own life, I felt Him leading me to speak about the peace we can have in Him. So, when I first read these verses (37–38), I dismissed them, thinking they have nothing to do with this peace.

He stopped me before I even got the thought out of my mind and before I turned the page. I felt Him ask, "How do you not see these verses have everything to do with the peace you can only get from Me?" As soon as He asked the question, He gave me the answer only He could give.

Look at the verse found in Philippians 4 that says, "And the peace of God, which surpasses all understanding, will guard your hearts and minds through Christ Jesus" (verse 7, NKJV). But, He is asking you this morning, as He did me, how can you have that peace if you don't first love Him with all your heart, soul and mind?

If you don't love Him with everything in you, how can you trust Him? Without that trust, how can you have the peace only He can give? Do you have that peace when you are facing trying times? If not, ask Him to show you what you are loving more than Him, then make the necessary changes so you can have that peace. There's nothing in the world that can compare to this gift!

Today's Prayer

Father,
Thank You for this new perspective on this commandment. Help us to love You with all our heart, soul and mind so we can have that peace, no matter what our circumstances are.
Amen.

Jesus answered: Love the Lord your God with all your heart, soul and mind. This is the first and most important commandment.

—Matthew 22:37–38

December 11

Peace on Earth?

Yes, we talked about peace yesterday; and this morning, again, He spoke to me in these verses. Maybe it's because of the season we are in right now—the Christmas season. So many people rushing around trying to get so many things done. Everyone trying to find that perfect gift for everyone on their list. I don't know about you, but it seems to me the very thing this season is about has gotten lost in all the hustle and bustle.

Peace on earth? Not much of that to be found in this season anymore, if you look on the surface. But, let's look a little deeper than the surface today. Look deep into your own heart. What do you find there?

Do you find inner turmoil, stress and a longing for peace? Could you take a minute to slow down today and be honest with yourself and the Father? If you aren't finding peace in your heart today, do you know why? Are you hurting? Are you mourning the loss of someone dear to you this year? Are you fighting an illness you never thought you'd have to fight? Are you just feeling angry or bitter, but you don't really know where it's coming from?

Read today's verses again. Do you see what He tells you in verse 19? *No matter where you are*—literally and/or spiritually—means exactly what it says. Whether you are living in a beautiful mansion, a simple home or in your car or on the streets, He will heal you and give you peace. Whether you are living close to Him or have drifted so far away you think you can't get back to Him, He will heal you and give you peace—and you can never get too far away to find your way back. See what He says in verse 18? "But I will heal you, lead you"— see? He will lead you, if you will ask Him. He also says He will give you comfort. Not that He will take away the hurt. He understands you are hurting over your loss or what you are going through, but if you will ask Him, He will comfort you until you can start singing His praises again.

Peace on earth? It starts with you having peace within. Are you ready for it?

Today's Prayer

Father,

Thank You for reminding us, especially in this season we are in, that You will heal us and give us peace no matter where we are.

Amen.

I know what you are like! But I will heal you, lead you and give you comfort, until those who are mourning start singing My praises. No matter where you are, I, the Lord, will heal you and give you peace.

—Isaiah 57:18–19

December 12

Better Than Chocolate

If you are a chocolate lover, as I am, you will understand the cute saying I have over my kitchen door:

Chocolate doesn't ask silly questions,
Chocolate understands.

Fellow chocolate lovers know what that implies—chocolate gives us comfort.

There is only One, though, Who can truly give us comfort. He also doesn't ask silly questions, and He certainly understands way more than chocolate ever could! This One knows the very number of hairs on your head, and He even knows when one little sparrow falls from the sky. Don't you know you are worth way more than a sparrow?

If you are hurting, He not only knows, He knows why. If you are upset, He not only knows, He knows why. No matter what you are going through, He knows, and He, alone, knows why. He doesn't ask you silly questions either.

He simply understands. He gives you comfort. In fact, He loves and cares about you so much, He sent the Comforter to live inside you, the Holy Spirit. While it may be hard for you to understand or comprehend how He could love, understand and comfort you in this way, you can rest in knowing He doesn't expect you to understand or comprehend it. He only wants you to receive it. He wants you to fall into His arms and let Him carry you through the difficult times. This One, His name is Jesus.

The world will tell you to "put on a brave face," "suck it up, buttercup," or "stay strong." But, He wants you to shut out the voices of the world, which is the voice of the enemy. He is there, waiting for you to ask Him to pick you up. When you ask, that gives Him permission to move into action on your behalf. Your simple request is all He needs to take care of you. And, believe it or not, He is way better than any chocolate you'll ever put in your mouth!

Today's Prayer

Father,
   We will never understand how You know the number of hairs on our heads, but we thank You for showing us You care about even the smallest, tiniest details of our lives.
   Amen.

Aren't two sparrows sold for only a penny? But your Father knows when any one of them falls to the ground. Even the hairs on your head are counted. So, don't be afraid! You are worth much more than many sparrows.

—Matthew 10:29–31

December 13

When God Speaks

God speaks in many different ways at many different times. He speaks through His Word, of course. As a Christian, you have at least some of His Word stored away in your heart, correct? When you find yourself searching for His direction, you may think about a scripture you read or heard somewhere, and that could be God speaking to you through His Word.

As you read His Word, you see how God speaks in many different ways. He can speak in a whirlwind, as in Job 38:1, "Then the Lord answered Job out of the whirlwind" (NKJV); or an earthquake, as in Exodus 19:18, "Now Mount Sinai was completely in smoke, because the Lord descended upon it in fire. Its smoke ascended like the smoke of a furnace, and the whole mountain quaked greatly" (NKJV). Several places we read where His voice was as thunder, as in John 12:29, "When the crowd heard the voice, some thought it was thunder, while others declared an angel had spoken to him" (NLT), and in Job 37:2, Psalm 104:7 and 1 Samuel 2:10. Other times, it could be a combination, as in Psalm 77:18 and Revelation 4:5.

In other words, God can speak to you one way today and a different way tomorrow. The question is, are your ears spiritually tuned so you will hear Him in whatever way He chooses to speak to you? One day I hope to be able to hear His voice so clearly that I have no doubt when it is Him. Like in Isaiah 30:21, "Whether you turn to the right or to the left, you will hear a voice saying, 'This is the road! Now follow it.'"

One sure way to get there is to remember Jeremiah 29:13, because when you search for Him with your whole heart, you will find Him, and then you will be able to hear Him when He speaks.

And, when He speaks, He will often use others to confirm His word to you. Are you listening with spiritual ears?

Today's Prayer

Father,

Thank You for speaking to us in many different ways. Help us learn to listen with our spiritual ears and be able to discern Your voice from all the others that clamor for our attention.

Amen.

And after the earthquake a fire, but the Lord was not in the fire; and, after the fire, a still small voice. So it was, when Elijah heard it, that he wrapped his face in his mantle and went out and stood in the entrance of the cave. Suddenly a voice came to him, and said, "What are you doing here, Elijah?"

—1 Kings 19:12–13 (NKJV)

December 14

To Know and Honor

In this digital, social media world we live in, it is quite possible to know more people than you ever imagined. Of all these people you "know," how many of them do you honor? There is a big difference in knowing someone and honoring them.

Merriam-Webster has several definitions for the word *honor*. When used as a verb, one definition given is "to regard or treat (someone) with admiration and respect." Now, with that definition in mind, think about all those *friends* you have on social media. Do you honor any of them, or do you mostly just know them? Then, think about all the real friends you have—those people you actually interact with in real life, possibly on a daily basis. Do you honor any of them?

Lastly, think about the most important relationship you have— the most important one ever: your relationship with the Lord. If you have a relationship with Him, you know Him, correct? But, do you honor Him? Do you truly treat Him with regard or with admiration and respect? Or is He more like a genie in a bottle to you? Do you only go to Him when you want or need something? If that's the case, do you even have a relationship with Him, for real?

Have you ever really given much thought to honoring not only your friends, but the best, most important friend you will ever have? Do you honor the Lord, or do you treat Him more like any other friend you have? Yes, He wants you to think of Him as your friend, and He wants you to feel comfortable to call on Him any time, but He also expects—and deserves—your honor!

Even the enemy, satan, knows Him. But he certainly doesn't honor Him. In fact, just the opposite. The enemy will use every tactic in the book to keep you from honoring the Lord, as well. Make your decision, today, to begin honoring Him, if you haven't already been doing so. Honor Him with the choices you make, and honor Him with the way you live your life. Funny thing is, when you honor Him, you will be amazed at how He honors you in return!

Today's Prayer

Father,

Help us become people who not only know You, but honor You as well. Not just with our words, but with our actions also.

Amen.

Just as water fills the sea, the land will be filled with people who know and honor the Lord.

—Habakkuk 2:14

December 15

Presents versus Presence

It's that time of year when many people are running around trying to find just the right present for someone. Nothing wrong with that, but a friend's Facebook post a few days ago really touched my heart.

It did more than touch my heart, it started me thinking about what she had said. She said (and I'm quoting with permission), "Now that my oldest is old enough to understand presents vs. presence, I tell him, 'I'd much rather spend time with you than spend money on things that you will only appreciate for a little while.'" She said this year, for Christmas, each of her two children were going to receive a calendar filled with different things they plan to enjoy in the coming year. She said making memories has become a family priority.

What better present can you give someone you love, or even a stranger you meet along life's journey, than your presence? God understands how important presence is. Without His presence, we wouldn't even be here! He is always with us (Deuteronomy 31:8). Think about how good it makes you feel knowing He is always with you, always ready to listen, always there for you in whatever way you need Him to be there. It is only His presence in you that enables you to truly be present for the people in your life. He created us to live with each other, to interact with one another, to care about and look out for each other.

Sometimes, the absolute best thing you can do for someone else is just to be there to listen, to be a shoulder to cry on or even to listen to something they've accomplished in their life. Believe it or not, there are some who don't even have anyone to share good things with!

What difference could you make for someone by offering your presence in their life? Be present for them today, and if they don't know the Lord, your presence might be the thing He uses to introduce them to His presence. Are you willing to make the change to be more aware of your presence for others? Whether it be loved ones or someone new you meet along your journey?

Today's Prayer

Father,

Thank You for Your presence with us. Please help us be more present with our loved ones and others.

Amen.

And He said, "My Presence will go with you and I will give you rest."

—Exodus 33:14 (NKJV)

December 16

One Day Closer

Have you ever had anything you looked forward to and found yourself counting down the days until it was time for it to happen? What about when you were a child? Maybe you counted down the days to your birthday or to Christmas or even to the last day of school!

You probably still have things you look forward to—a trip, a vacation, even a day to do absolutely nothing! Every day you find yourself looking at the calendar and counting the days. Oh, the excitement when the day finally arrives, right? You've been anticipating it for a while, possibly even a long while, and you just can't believe it has finally arrived! You are so excited!

Now, think about that person (or people) you've been praying for—for their salvation, their healing, their relationship, whatever the reason is you've been praying for them—and ask yourself this question, "Am I excited to see the answer to this prayer?" Are you counting down the days, realizing that every day you pray means the answer is one day closer?

Earlier this year, our pastor challenged us to choose one person to specifically pray for, and it took me a little while, but I finally knew who I was to pray for and what I was to pray for. Actually, the Lord put two people on my heart, so I am praying for two, and I am praying for their salvation. I began praying for them in April.

Yes, that's a long time to be praying for someone, specifically, every single day; but, the alternative is to not pray, and then they might never come to their day of salvation, and that, my friend, is not an option!

Remember, the Lord doesn't measure time as we do, and everything happens in His time. So, instead of getting tired of praying for something or someone, thinking it will never happen, remember this: every day brings you one day closer to the answer to your prayer! Don't stop now! Keep counting down!

Today's Prayer

Father,

Thank You for reminding us You have a totally different idea of time than we have. Time means nothing to You, actually, for You always have been and always will be! Thank You for the gift of time You give us!

Amen.

Dear friends, don't forget that for the Lord one day is the same as a thousand years and a thousand years is the same as one day.

—2 Peter 3:8

December 17

Wings

One day I was driving down the road and came upon a bird. This bird was just sitting there like it owned the road. As I approached, the bird slowly began walking to the side of the road, and I said, "God gave you wings, use them and go on!"

No sooner had that thought left my head than I heard in my spirit, "I gave *you* wings too. Are you ever going to use them?" Wow! Ouch! "What, Lord? What are You talking about? I don't have wings." To which He replied, "I gave you spiritual wings a long time ago, but you just haven't been using them!"

Have you ever said something and immediately feel like God is speaking to you about the same thing? It can be a little disconcerting, can't it? How like God to point us to our own flaws when we point out someone else's, correct? Maybe He wants us to learn to look in our own eye before we try getting the board out of someone else's eye (Matthew 7:3–5). As for God giving us wings, of course He didn't give us physical wings, but He did give us spiritual wings; and He wants each of us, including you, to learn to use them. How?

He wants you to stop being afraid to move forward in the things He is calling you to do. He wants you to take that step of faith, though it may seem more like a formidable leap to you! Stop walking along at a snail's pace, timidly asking Him if it's the right time for you to do whatever *it* is. He wants you to stop using the phrase, "I'm waiting to hear from the Lord," as an excuse or a crutch. Yes, there is a time to say that—and do it as well; but, after a while, when He hasn't taken away the thought that you should do it, maybe it's because He wants you to move forward in faith, using the wings He gave you. I know what He's been asking me to do, and I'm ready and willing to give these wings a try. What's He been asking you to do? Are you willing to use those spiritual wings and move forward?

Today's Prayer

Father,

Thank You for giving us spiritual wings. May we learn to use them, in Your strength, to complete the tasks You assign each of us and to soar high like the eagles.

Amen.

But those who trust the Lord will find new strength.
They will be strong like eagles soaring upward on wings;
they will walk and run without getting tired.

—Isaiah 40:31

December 18

Where Are Your Eyes Focused?

Keep your eyes on the road! Watch where you're going! These are things we have all heard at one time or another, most likely when we were learning to drive an automobile for the first time.

Even after you've been driving a while, you may hear those words from people riding in the vehicle with you. It is true, if you don't keep your eyes on the road and watch where you're going, you could be in real trouble, real fast!

The same is true in your spiritual walk with the Lord. If you don't keep your eyes on Jesus, you could be in real trouble, real fast! How do you keep your eyes on Jesus? Stay in His Word, listen to His voice and follow His leading. It's not always easy, but He knows your heart, and He knows if you are truly seeking after Him or if you just want to go off in your own direction.

When you are in a worship service, where are your eyes? Are they seeking, looking to see what He has for you in that service? Or are they too busy watching what others are doing and seeing if they can find something to criticize? Are they on the clock, watching to see if the preacher is going to finish by a certain time? Do you realize, if you are watching what others are doing or watching to find something to criticize or even watching the clock, then your eyes are not on Jesus! How can He speak to you if your mind is on these other things?

Wouldn't you rather keep your eyes focused on Jesus and see what He has for you? Listen to what He tells us in Philippians 3:14, "I run toward the goal, so that I can win the prize of being called to Heaven. This is the prize that God offers because of what Christ Jesus has done." Where are your eyes focused?

Today's Prayer

Father,

Help us keep our eyes on Jesus and allow Him to lead us and make our faith complete. Thank You that He was willing to endure the cross for us and that He is now seated at Your right hand! Amen.

We must keep our eyes on Jesus, Who leads us and makes our faith complete. He endured the shame of being nailed to a cross, because He knew that, later on, He would be glad He did. Now He is seated at the right side of God's throne!

—Hebrews 12:2

December 19

No Argument Here

Is anyone on earth perfect? No! Is any marriage perfect? Absolutely not! Is there such a thing as a perfect friendship? Again, the answer is no. But social media is not the place to have your quarrels. Part of your duty, as a spouse or a friend, is to encourage, edify and build up. Does that mean a married couple or friends never argue or disagree? No, but arguments or disagreements should be kept between three—the two people involved and God—certainly not on display on social media.

Should a husband and wife argue or disagree in front of their children? Not talking extremes here, but on a normal level, yes. Children need to know how to have healthy arguments or disagreements. They don't need to grow up thinking Mom and Dad have a perfect marriage, because that is unrealistic. In fact, I chuckled when I read this somewhere:

> Sometimes we think our young children don't understand the ups and downs of our lives. Recently, my wife and I were having a disagreement, when our 7-year old exclaimed, Dad, this is a "For Worse Moment," do you still love her?

That, my friend, is a child who knows his parents are not perfect and doesn't expect them to be. It is also a child who has, obviously, been taught about healthy arguments or disagreements.

Commit to taking all complaints you have about your husband or friends to God alone. Then ask Him to change your heart instead of asking Him to change the other person. You'll be surprised at the difference it makes! It's amazing how you miss the things you once complained about when that person is no longer with you, especially when it's due to death.

Remember, when it comes to social media, post things that some may call bragging about your spouse or even a friend. Do this to encourage, edify and build up! Don't just do it on social media though. Also do it in person, face-to-face and in texts throughout the day. You never know just how much you could be helping the other person! Will you make a positive impact today?

Today's Prayer

Father,

Thank You for reminding us to encourage one another and to build one another up. We never know how much we might help another just by following this simple recipe.

Amen.

So, encourage each other and build each other
up, just as you are already doing.

—1 Thessalonians 5:11 (NLT)

December 20

Which Mirror Are You Using?

How many times a day do you look in a mirror? Probably more than you realize! When you look in a mirror, you see a reflection of yourself, right? Do you ever use anything besides a mirror to look at yourself?

What about other people? Your friends, your family or even people you don't really know, like people on social media. Do you ever play the comparison game? You know, comparing yourself to them to see how you measure up and coming up short or even maybe a little ahead, in your mind?

What about your job, your occupation? Do you find you measure yourself by looking at what you do for a living? Your job isn't who you are, it's just what you do.

The only mirror you need to look in to measure yourself is a book. Not just any book, *the* book—the Bible, God's Word. Reading and studying in His Word is the only way to truly get a good look at yourself. Jesus is the only One you need to be using as a measuring stick.

Will you ever measure up to Him? Of course not, but the great thing is you don't have to! Yes, we need to strive to be as much like Him as we can, but He gave His life as the ultimate sacrifice for us—for you! When you accepted Him as your personal Savior, you were immediately covered by His blood.

When the Father looks at you, He doesn't see you; He sees His Son's blood covering you! The blood is what makes you acceptable in His sight. The blood is what makes you worthy to be in His presence. When you look in the mirror of His Word, He will not only show you the things you need to remove from your life, He will help you remove them. He will work on one thing at a time. He loves you just as you are, but He loves you too much to let you stay that way. So, which mirror will you be using now?

Today's Prayer

Father,

Help us use Your Word as the mirror for our souls and not what others think or how others are living. Thank You for giving us Your Word to help us evaluate our lives and see which areas we need to improve in.

Amen.

If you hear the message and don't obey it, you are like people who stare at themselves in a mirror and forget what they look like as soon as they leave.

—James 1:23–24

December 21

It Ain't Over

When I opened my Bible this morning, I found a note I had stuck in there many years ago. It was the words to a chorus I had forgotten about. As soon as I saw it, I knew what Father wanted to share with us today. We are living in troublesome times right now. We are living in the days when evil is called good and good is called evil, and you can read what His Word says about that in Isaiah 5:20. We wonder how things have gotten so bad, even though He clearly tells us in His Word (2 Timothy 3) it will happen.

You can look around at all the evil and ungodly things going on, and if you aren't careful, you can become very depressed and hopeless. However, you must remember that no matter how bad things seem to be, God is still, always has been and always will be in control!

That battle you are facing, He already has it worked out. That job you didn't get, He has one that is so much better for you! That child who has wandered so far away from God, God will remind that child of their upbringing, and that child will come running back to Him.

I read where Corrie Ten Boom said, "When the train goes through a tunnel and the world gets dark, do you jump out? Of course not. You sit still and trust the engineer to get you through." So it is in life; sometimes, you just have to be still and trust God to get you through.

Remember the words to that chorus I found in my Bible: "It's not over 'til it's over," or as I like to sing it, "It ain't over 'til it's over"! Our fight won't be finished until that final trumpet sound! Look up the song on You Tube and be encouraged today!

Today's Prayer

Father,

Thank You for reminding us You are in control. Not one thing happens without going through You first. Remind us to put our complete trust in You during these difficult times.

Amen.

Jesus said to His followers, "So I tell you, don't worry about the food you need to live. Don't worry about the clothes you need for your body. Life is more important than food. And the body is more important than clothes. Look at the birds. They don't plant or harvest. They don't save food in houses or barns. But God takes care of them. And you are worth much more than birds."

—Luke 12:22–24 (ICB)

December 22

Insignificant?

While looking for something in the dishwasher the other night, I sliced the end of my right thumb on the blender blade that was on the top rack. Later, it reminded me of just how important some things are, though we may regard them as small and insignificant most of the time.

This incident happened just before bedtime, and I still had to get my contacts out. As I tried to remove the first contact from my eye, I realized just how much I needed my right thumb to help with the process. It was of no help to me because it had a bulky bandage on it to stop the cut from bleeding.

The next morning, as I started to write in my prayer journal, another realization hit: it is hard to write with a bulky bandage on my thumb too. And, again later, when I had to wash my hair! However, as usual, God brought something good from the pain and inconvenience. He used these things to remind me of something He wants me to share with you.

You may be going through life thinking you don't matter. You may feel you are insignificant and that you don't contribute anything of importance to anyone. Nothing could be further from the truth! If you read 1 Corinthians 12:12–31, you will be reminded of how important every person is—including you! You touch more people's lives than you could ever imagine! (Just watch *It's a Wonderful Life* to remember that too!)

Others may not always necessarily tell or show you just how important you are to them or just how you have impacted their life, but that doesn't mean God isn't using you to do those things. Sometimes, people may not know how to tell you what you mean to them. It took my thumb being bandaged for me to realize just how much I use it and how I just seem to take it for granted, that it will be there when I need it. If you were insignificant, God wouldn't have put you on this earth! As long as you are here, it means you have a purpose, and He isn't finished with you yet. You are significant, so be you today!

Today's Prayer

Father,

Thank You for reminding us, no matter how small or insignificant we may feel at times, we are part of Your body, and You would not have put us here if we weren't significant. Thank You for giving us purpose!

Amen.

Together you are the body of Christ. Each one of you is part of His body.

—1 Corinthians 12:27

December 23

Gift Giving

It's the time of year when many are buying gifts for the ones they love and, quite possibly, for some they don't even like very much. They do it simply because it's "that time of year." As for us, we haven't bought any gifts at all the last few years.

This year, several people have been asking if we're ready for Christmas. What they are really asking is, have we bought a lot of presents for the grandbaby? The answer is no. We have not bought any gifts for her at all. I've been saying, "We aren't giving her anything. When you don't have the money to spend, you don't spend it." The Lord showed me I've been giving the wrong answer though. I've been saying, "We aren't giving her anything." While it's true we aren't *buying* her anything, we are most definitely giving her something.

There are plenty of gifts to be bought in the store, and there are plenty of gifts you can make with your own hands. Even the gifts you make with your own hands can cost money though. But, did you know the best gifts you can give cost a lot more than money? These gifts are too expensive not to give!

The gift of your time, the gift of unconditional love, the gift of grace and mercy, the gift of wisdom and the list goes on and on. Imagine how special you make someone feel when you are willing to give even a portion of your time to them! Giving your time to someone tells them you truly care. Try giving grace and mercy to that person who just cut you off in traffic and see if it doesn't make you feel better than getting upset with them. Try loving others just because you know God wants you to. Share your wisdom with the younger ones—and sometimes even the older ones!

So, yes, we are giving our granddaughter gifts this year, but not just at Christmas. We will give her the gifts that are too expensive not to give all year long. Will you give the gifts that are too expensive not to give?

Today's Prayer

Father,

Thank You for reminding us to give the gifts that are too expensive not to give! In the name of Jesus Christ of Nazareth, we ask You to, please, show us ways to do this throughout the year.

Amen.

Each of you must make up your own mind about how much to give. But don't feel sorry that you must give and don't feel that you are forced to give. God loves people who love to give.

—2 Corinthians 9:7

December 24

Who, Me?

You can't. You won't. You never have. You never will. You aren't smart enough. You aren't good enough. You're too young. You're too old. Do you feel like you are the only one hearing these lies from the enemy? Be assured, you are not.

Do you ever feel like God is asking you to do something that you don't feel qualified to do? Do you give Him arguments about it, quoting some of the above statements about yourself? Do you feel the Holy Spirit convicting you as you quote those things? You probably do, but what do you do about it?

Do you ignore it and go on about life as usual, or do you take heed to His voice? What might happen if you decided to listen to God's voice instead of listening to the lies of the enemy? How do you stop those lies from coming?

Well, you don't. The enemy is after you, and he will never give up trying to discourage you or keep you from what God has for you. The good news is that you can drown out those lies by choosing to listen to God's voice and the prompting of the Holy Spirit instead! The more you choose to believe what God says about you, the less power the enemy's lies will have over you.

God will never call or ask you to do anything He hasn't already prepared you for. You may not know you are prepared; you may not feel you are ready, but you can be sure of this: If He calls you to do it, He knows you can do it, through His power in you! He may give you just what you need to get started and give you the rest as you need it. One thing you can be certain of: He will give you everything you need exactly when you need it!

Are you ready to trust Him? Are you ready to say, "Here am I, Lord, send me"? even if He sends you somewhere you may not want to go? Are you ready to accept His power and do the miraculous things He wants to use you to do? You may ask, "Who, me?" God answers, "Yes, *you!*"

Today's Prayer

Father,

Thank You for Your power working in us. Help us drown out the enemy's lies by listening only to Your voice telling us what You can and will do through us.

Amen.

With God's power working in us, God can do much,
much more than anything we can ask or think of.

—*Ephesians 3:20 (ICB)*

December 25

The Ultimate Gift

Christmas Day—the day set aside to celebrate the earthly birth of Your Son, Jesus. The day set aside to celebrate the fact that Jesus willingly gave up His throne to be born of the Virgin Mary so He could live and walk on this earth as fully man, yet fully God.

Wise men, a few years after His birth, brought Him gifts. Yes, they brought gifts to the One Who was Himself the ultimate gift! Did they truly understand? Did they realize what they were doing?

Today, we have God's Word, the Holy Bible, to explain it all to us, but how many choose not to even try to understand? Without the Holy Spirit, you cannot even begin to understand any of it. Since we know it was most likely not this time of year when Jesus was born, why was this month and this day chosen for when we celebrate His birth? Does it really matter? The important thing is not when we celebrate it, but that we *do* celebrate it! Not the commercialism of it, but the real reason for it—to celebrate that He *chose* to do this for us—for *you*! He chose to be born as man, face the same challenges we face, yet remain sinless so that He could be our ultimate sacrifice! He was born to *die* for me—for *you*!

He loved you so much, He left His throne to live a life He knew would end the way it did, yet He did it! Yes, He knew He would live again, but He still had to die first and face total separation from God, His Father, before He could live again, and He was still willing to do it!

Some days it's just too hard to try to wrap my mind around that idea! Then again, maybe we aren't supposed to be able to do that. Maybe the point is to allow Him to wrap Himself around our minds—our total beings! He isn't a gift to be wrapped—He wants to wrap me and you in His love! Will you accept His ultimate gift today? Will you let Him wrap you in His love so He can present you to the Father, pure and unblemished, covered by His blood?

Today's Prayer

Father,

Thank You for the ultimate gift of Your One and only Son so that we could live forever with You!

Amen.

For God so loved YOU that He gave His only begotten Son, that WHEN YOU believeth in Him, YOU should not perish, but have everlasting life.

—John 3:16

December 26

The Value

Yesterday was Christmas Day. A day when many gifts are exchanged, including gift cards. Did you receive a gift card? We received a couple of them.

One thing that got my attention about these cards was the value of each one, what each one was worth, as it were. Some cards have the value (or amount) printed right on the card. Others don't have it anywhere, and you have to call a number or go online to find out the value.

That got me to thinking about our salvation and the value of it. You don't have to wonder what the value of your salvation is. You don't have to go searching online or even call a number to find out how much it is worth. How do you know the value?

It's printed right there in your Bible for you to see: your salvation was worth Jesus's blood! It cost Him every drop He had, and He willingly paid it because He loves you so much! Even though He didn't necessarily *want* to do it that way (Matthew 26:39), He was still willing to go through with it and do the will of the Father, Who had sent Him, if there were no other way.

Have you ever really considered what your salvation is worth? Has it ever crossed your mind? I imagine, for most of us, we were probably very aware of the value of our salvation when we first surrendered to His call. Then, somewhere along our journey, we allow life to get in the way, and we forget to remember just how valuable our salvation is. We may even begin to take it for granted! We tend to forget all that Jesus actually went through for us.

How nice to be reminded, this morning, of the value of our salvation. Thank Him for reminding you not only of the value of your salvation, but for reminding you of just how truly valuable He says you are! Do you think He would have allowed His Son to die for you if you weren't priceless to Him?

Today's Prayer

Father,

Thank You for rescuing us by the precious blood of Christ! Thank You for showing us clearly in Your Word the value of our salvation. Help us never forget the cost and always remember how much we are loved by You, the Son and the Holy Spirit!

Amen.

You were rescued by the precious blood of Christ,
that spotless and innocent lamb.

—1 Peter 1:19

December 27

Where's the Evidence?

You must be on guard 24-7 because your adversary, the devil, is like a roaring lion, sneaking around to find someone he can attack (1 Peter 5:8)! We all need reminders now and then—at least I know I do.

He launched a strong attack yesterday morning. Praise the Lord, though, the Holy Spirit helped me! Came to my defense like you wouldn't believe! Helped me stay strong and shout praises to the Father instead of giving in to worry and fear, and Father got the victory for it!

You better believe the enemy didn't give up that easy, though. Since his first attack didn't work, later in the day, he decided to attack on a more personal level. Remember my butterfly story back in July? Yesterday, the enemy began whispering to me, "You're no butterfly! You are still the same way you were before. You haven't changed a bit! Where's the evidence?"

Holy Spirit was on top of it almost before the whispers even reached my ears. In the millisecond it took for me to think, "Yeah, that's right. I am still the same," Holy Spirit was already reminding me that was a lie. True, I haven't had a drastic personality change. He didn't change me into someone who is able to engage in a lot of small talk and keep conversations going on my own. What He changed was my heart! That's where the evidence is! I am now ready and willing to share my story with any and all He asks me to share with. Did I suddenly become an eloquent speaker? No way! I simply know I can trust Him to give me the words He wants me to share.

What changes has He made in you? The evidence will not necessarily be found on the outside, but in your heart, and the heart is where the Father looks anyway (1 Samuel 16:7)!

Today's Prayer

Father,

Thank You for giving us the ability to do any and all things You call us to do. If You ask us to speak, You will supply the words. If You ask us to go, You will supply the resources needed to go. Thank You that all we have to do is trust You.

Amen.

But the Lord answered, "Who makes people able to speak or makes them deaf or unable to speak? Who gives them sight or makes them blind? Don't you know that I am the one who does these things? Now go! When you speak, I will be with you and give you the words to say."

—Exodus 4:11–12

December 28

Marvelous Grace

There's a song that has been stuck in my head for the last few days. Well, one line of a song anyway. It just hasn't gone away, so this morning I knew I needed to look up the lyrics to see if I could figure out why it keeps playing in my head.

As I read the lyrics to the song, I began to realize the line that's been stuck in my head isn't even what the song is really about. It's about forgiveness and God's grace. It even talks about not wanting to abuse God's grace.

Do you ever wonder how you could abuse God's grace? Is it even something you ever thought about? First of all, what is God's grace? I've seen it defined this way: "Grace is getting what you don't deserve and not getting what you do deserve."

Another definition of grace is knowing God will forgive us when we mess up. Does that mean we can keep living in sin and just keep asking forgiveness and all will be well? No!

Grace isn't about being able to do what you want, expecting God to forgive you. Grace is about God loving you and forgiving you no matter how many times you mess up in a single day or a single hour or even in a single minute, though you are trying hard not to. Does that even make sense?

Honestly, I don't believe you can abuse God's grace. I believe you can *think* you must abuse His grace sometimes because of how much you seem to need it. Some days more than others.

But, rest assured, if you have accepted Christ as your personal Savior, truly love the Lord and are staying in His Word and striving to be more like Him, you can't abuse His grace. He gives His grace abundantly because He loves you!

Today's Prayer

Father,

Thank You for Your grace and forgiveness, especially Your forgiveness when we think we are abusing Your grace.

Amen.

So, do you think that we should continue sinning so that God will give us more and more grace? No! We died to our old sinful lives. So how can we continue living with sin?

—Romans 6:1–2 (ICB)

December 29

True Love

Ah, true love! Isn't it marvelous? Isn't it grand? It's flowers and kisses and holding hands and spending every minute possible together. Well, that's how it seems when we're young anyway. But, is it true love?

Then we grow older, and we come to know love is so much more than that. Love is being there when you don't want to be there. Love is choosing to stay when it would be easier to go. Love is commitment. But is it true love?

Would you believe someone loves you if they only came to see you once a week for maybe an hour? Would you consider yourself in a relationship with that person? Would you believe someone loves you if they never spoke to you, except for when they needed something or were in trouble?

Would you be there for someone who was never there for you? If you wrote someone a love letter, and they tossed it aside, would you believe they care for you? Would you care for someone who never showed they cared for you?

Be honest, your answer to all those questions would be a resounding no! Now, let's take a look at those questions as they relate to your relationship with the Lord. How much time do you spend with Him? When do you pray and talk with Him? How often do you make time for Him? No matter what your answers to these questions were, do you know God loves you anyway? Yes, He longs to have a relationship with you, but His love for you isn't based on that. He loved you before you ever came to be!

He willingly gave His only Son to be the sacrifice for you, knowing you would be born a sinner! Knowing you might choose to reject Him. Knowing you might accept Him, but not develop a relationship with Him. That, my friend, is true love. Agape love. A love neither you nor I are capable of, but one we can aspire to. Will you begin today to develop that relationship with Him, if you haven't already? He's ready and waiting anytime! Why not start right now?

Today's Prayer

Father,

Thank You for loving us so much You were willing to give Your Son as a sacrifice for us. If You never did another thing for any of us, that would be more than enough!

Amen.

But God showed His great love for us by sending Christ to die for us while we were still sinners.

—Romans 5:8 (NLT)

December 30

Are You a Carrier?

Oh! I thought I knew where this devotion was going, but God just spoke something to my spirit that I never realized until this very minute! We can be carriers of many things, but we usually think of some kind of disease when we think of being a carrier, right?

Here's the part He just dropped in my spirit: Being a carrier doesn't mean you display symptoms associated with the disease. You can be a carrier and never have any symptoms of the disease yourself, yet you can pass it to someone else; they become infected and begin showing the symptoms of the disease. God's Word is definitely not a disease, but the same idea applies. A person can go to church all their life, know the Bible backward and forward, have a lot of head knowledge and become a carrier of God's Word to others without ever coming to Jesus themselves. That person is a carrier.

But someone who has had a personal experience with Jesus, has asked forgiveness of their sins and strives to be as much like Jesus as possible—that person is an infected carrier! Whether you are a simple carrier or an infected carrier, people can't come to know Christ if they don't hear the message. God will use anyone who is willing to spread His message—even the uninfected carriers.

A few months back, I heard a song, and the Lord brought it to my mind as He was giving me today's devotion. There's a line in it that speaks volumes! In essence, it says the message of Jesus isn't just good news, it's the best news ever! It is the best news ever! Are you willing to share that message with others, no matter where He may send you to share? Will you be an infected carrier?

Today's Prayer

Father,

May we all be infected carriers of Your Word and Your message. Let each of us be willing to go where You send us to tell others about You. May our feet be a beautiful sight to those who are longing, waiting to hear the best news ever!

Amen.

*How can people have faith in the Lord and ask Him to save them,
if they have never heard about Him? And how can they hear,
unless someone tells them? And how can anyone tell them without
being sent by the Lord? The Scriptures say it is a beautiful sight
to see even the feet of someone coming to preach the good news.*

—Romans 10:14–15

December 31

Moving On

It's hard to believe the end of this journey is here, yet here it is. I was looking back at my prayer journal entries from a few days before this time last year, and I was still asking God, "Am I really hearing from You? Is this something You really want me to do?" I couldn't imagine what He had in store!

These devotions, whether ever printed in a book or not, served a much greater purpose than encouraging and challenging others. It was a challenge for me, personally, to get up every morning and seek to hear His voice above all the other chatter in my head (and there's plenty of that all the time!), to search the Scriptures and listen for Him to speak to my spirit what He would like to share. Yet, He was faithful every, single day! He taught me so much more than I could ever truly convey through a short devotion. He took me from a turtle to a butterfly, and He has already been speaking to me about the next journey He has for me.

Why do I share this with you? What kind of devotion is this supposed to be? I share this with you because He wants you to know you can trust Him too! When He asks you to do something that you think is beyond your capability, say yes anyway! As we all know, He doesn't call you for your ability, He calls you for your availability! He will give you everything you need to do anything He asks you to do! I'm not going to say don't be afraid—a certain amount of reverent fear is good for you. It keeps you in His Word and seeking His will and His way.

You are probably thinking of something right now that you've felt called to do before, but you didn't act on it because you didn't think you were good enough or smart enough or whatever enough.

Those doubts are lies the enemy uses to keep you from moving forward. Move forward anyway! What is God asking you to do? Go for it! Jump in! Spread your wings and fly! He is with you. Even if there are bumps along the way, He will keep you safe!

Today's Prayer

Father,
    Thank You for this journey of devotions. While none of us know what You have ahead for us, we know we can trust You to be with us, guide us and show us the way—even in the dark valleys.
    Amen.

I may walk through valleys as dark as death, but I won't be afraid.
You are with me and Your Shepherd's rod makes me feel safe.

—Psalm 23:4

About the Author

Kathryn Gossett is a poet, blogger and author of the new devotional *Challenging Encouragement*. She has been married to Frank Gossett, an ordained minister with the Assemblies of God, for seven wonderful years. Between them, they have two daughters—both named Jessica—and three grandchildren.

Kathryn retired after twenty-five years of working for the State of Alabama and now works part-time in a small, southeastern town in that same state. She is also a part-time consultant for Thirty-One Gifts, LLC. Kathryn has always loved to write in her free time.

Kathryn started writing poetry at a young age, and she has allowed God to grow that love of words into something wonderful for Him. Kathryn devoted the last year to obeying God's call on her life for this particular project. He was calling her to spend time each morning truly listening to what He had for her each day. Now He is calling her to share it with everyone else, and *Challenging Encouragement* is the result of her obedience to Him.

Kathryn completed a creative writing course at Faulkner State Junior College and has been allowing God to be her pilot for many years. She is an ordinary person who has a love for God and words and an extraordinary message of encouragement from a Father who loves us all.

To see how God has taken Kathryn *From Turtle to Butterfly*, head over to www.flashthoughts.wordpress.com and find out how He can do the same for you. She would love to connect with you on a deeper level. While you're there, join fifty others who have subscribed, and enjoy.